PENGUIN BOOKS

LLOYDS TSB SMALL BUSI
1999

Sara Williams is chief executive o₁
the magazine *Small Company Investor* and *The AIM ...*
a weekly columnist for The *Express* and has contributed to The
Sunday Times, *The Times*, and The *Financial Times* and is a frequent guest on *Money Box Live* and other radio and TV programmes. A former investment analyst and lecturer in finance, for a
number of years she wrote for *Which?* and is a co-author of *Lloyds
Bank Tax Guide*. In 1984 she co-founded the company Vamp
Health, supplier of computer systems to the medical profession,
which was sold in 1993 to Reuters.

Sara Williams

 Lloyds TSB

Small Business
Guide 1999 EDITION

PENGUIN BOOKS

PENGUIN BOOKS

Published by the Penguin Group
Penguin Books Ltd, 27 Wrights Lane, London W8 5TZ, England
Penguin Putnam Inc., 375 Hudson Street, New York, New York 10014, USA
Penguin Books Australia Ltd, Ringwood, Victoria, Australia
Penguin Books Canada Ltd, 10 Alcorn Avenue, Toronto, Ontario, Canada M4V 3B2
Penguin Books (NZ) Ltd, Private Bag 102902, NSMC, Auckland, New Zealand

Penguin Books Ltd, Registered Offices: Harmondsworth, Middlesex, England

First published in Penguin Books 1987
Second edition 1988
Third edition 1989
Fourth edition 1990
Fifth edition 1991
Sixth edition 1992
Seventh edition 1993
Eighth edition 1994
Ninth edition 1995
Tenth edition 1996
Eleventh edition 1997
Twelfth edition 1998
10 9 8 7 6 5 4 3 2

Printed and bound in Great Britain by
William Clowes Ltd, Beccles and London

Contents

Acknowledgements vii
Foreword *by David Singleton, Managing Director, Business Banking, Lloyds TSB Group* viii
What is in this guide? ix
Going for growth xiii

section i: Before taking the plunge

1. **You and your ideas** 1
2. **Who will buy?** 13
3. **A spot of coaching** 27
4. **Your business identity** 38
5. **Are you sure?** 53
6. **The business plan** 64
7. **Timing the jump** 71

section ii: Getting a head start

8. **Toe-dipping** 76
9. **Off the peg** 81
10. **Franchises** 101

section iii: How to sell your product

11. **The right name** 120
12. **Beating the pirates** 128
13. **Getting the message across** 137
14. **Selling** 149
15. **How to set a price** 162

section iv: The working environment

16. **Choosing your workplace** 174
17. **Getting equipped** 185

18. **Professional back-up**   192
19. **Getting the right staff**   201
20. **Your rights and duties as an employer**   220
21. **Insurance**   244

section v: Financial preparation and control

22. **Forecasting**   251
23. **Raising the money**   269
24. **Staying afloat**   282
25. **How to increase profits**   300
26. **Not waving but drowning**   308
27. **Keeping the record straight**   313

section vi: Tax

28. **Tax and the sole trader**   325
29. **Tax and the partnership**   346
30. **Tax and the limited company**   349
31. **Tax on spare-time earnings**   356
32. **VAT**   362

section vii: Planning for retirement

33. **Retirement**   375

Reference   382
Index   408

Acknowledgements

The number of people who have helped me produce this comprehensive guide continues to grow. My debt to those who commented and supplied information for the original edition remains enormous; they helped me improve the quality and content of the advice it contains to help you get new enterprises up and running, and keep them that way. For the twelfth edition, some of the checking and up-dating was carried out with remarkable efficiency by Frances Worlock and Paul Taylor carried out the dtp work.

I remain indebted to the Business Banking team of the Lloyds TSB Group for giving me the opportunity to bring my ideas to a very wide audience and their understanding of the need for independence in the content of the book.

note

I have taken every care and effort to check the information and advice in this guide. Nevertheless, with a book as comprehensive as this one, the odd slip may occur. Unfortunately, I regret that I cannot be responsible for any loss that you may suffer as a result of any omission or inaccuracy.

Foreword

*by David Singleton, Managing Director, Business Banking,
Lloyds TSB Group plc*

This edition of the Lloyds TSB Small Business Guide builds upon the tradition of previous years, in continuing to provide an invaluable and essential source of ongoing reference for both new and established business people. Sara Williams' definitive style ensures that the guide is a comprehensive review of the issues, while remaining clear and concise.

I would like to take this opportunity to wish every reader success in their business ventures.

September 1998

What is in this guide?

Lloyds TSB Small Business Guide will help your business get off to a cracking start. It plots the decisions you need to take, whether you are going to be self-employed, in partnership or forming a company. But it will not only help you start your business, the guide will be an invaluable reference once you are up an running. It is packed with ideas for increasing your profits, controlling your cash, improving your image and getting your message across – to name just a few of the topics covered to help you run your business. The guide will stay with you until you are no longer 'small'.

The chapters in outline:

section i: Before Taking the Plunge

1. You and your ideas (p. 1)

You. Your ideas.

2. Who will buy? (p. 13)

Who will buy? Why will they buy? How much will they buy? How to do the research.

3. A spot of coaching (p. 27)

Training courses. Checklist: how to choose a course. Counselling and consultancy. Sharing problems with others. Small business organizations. The media, books and exhibitions. Advice aimed at specific groups.

4. Your business identity (p. 38)

Sole trader v. a partnership v. a limited company. Quiz. How to set up as a sole trader. How to set up as a partnership. How to set up as a company. Forming a cooperative.

5. Are you sure? (p. 53)

Four checklists to help you make your decision: You. Your family. Your skills. Your idea. What next?

6. **The business plan** (p. 64)

The objectives of the plan. How many plans? Who should do the plan? What should be in the plan?

7. **Timing the jump** (p. 71)

Initial preparation. Getting into greater detail. Setting up. Ready to trade.

section ii: Getting a Head Start

8. **Toe-dipping** (p. 76)

Testing the water. Permanent toe-dipping. Toe-dipping: What you need to know.

9. **Off the peg** (p. 81)

Search for a business, a guide. The business profile you want. Finding a business for sale. Investigation. Changing the business. Setting a price. Tips on negotiation. Brief guide to management buy-outs.

10. **Franchises** (p. 101)

A brief guide to franchises. The pluses and minuses. A guide to choosing a franchise. How a franchise works in detail. The contract. Setting up as franchisor.

section iii: How to Sell Your Product

11. **The right name** (p. 120)

Choosing a name. Building your reputation.

12. **Beating the pirates** (p. 128)

What to do with an invention. What to do with a design. What to do with a trade or service mark. Getting help and advice.

13. **Getting the message across** (p. 137)

The message: who, what, how. What can advertising do for you?: Brochures and leaflets. Public relations. Mail shots. Advertisements. Directories. Your own web site. Deciding the advertising strategy.

14. **Selling** (p. 149)

How to increase sales. How do you sell?: You. Sales representative. Agent. Distributor. Mail order. Over-the-counter. Consortium or joint venture. Personal selling skills.

15. **How to set a price** (p. 162)

The price range. The highest price. The lowest price. Setting a price. A guide to setting prices. Price near the top of the range. Price near the bottom of the range. Pricing with more than one product.

section iv: The Working Environment

16. **Choosing your workplace** (p. 174)

Where is your business to be located? What sort of premises? Searching for premises. Investigating and negotiating.

17. **Getting equipped** (p. 185)

Choosing equipment. How to pay for equipment.

18. **Professional back-up** (p. 192)

The advice available, how to choose, cost for these advisers: accountant, bank, solicitor, surveyor/estate agent, designer, corporate finance adviser.

19. **Getting the right staff** (p. 201)

The job that needs doing. The employee you want. Getting the right person to apply. Interviewing. The cost.

20. **Your rights and duties as an employer** (p. 220)

Bird's eye view of your rights and duties. Legal life-cycle of an employee. Taking on an employee. Pay and working hours. Safe and healthy working environment. Discrimination: what to watch out for. Maternity. Saying goodbye to an employee.

21. **Insurance** (p. 244)

Buying the insurance. Insurance you must have. Other insurance you can get. Insurance for you and your family.

section v: Financial Preparation and Control

22. **Forecasting** (p. 251)

Cash flow forecast. Profit and loss forecast. Balance sheet forecast.

23. **Raising the money** (p. 269)

The money. Lenders and investors. The presentation: how to do it.

24. **Staying afloat** (p. 282)

Break-even point. The plan to control the business. Cash. Your customers. How to chase money you are owed. Your suppliers.

25. **How to increase profits** (p. 300)

Cutting costs. Increasing prices. Selling more. Doing all three. Profits through your employees.

26. **Not waving but drowning** (p. 308)

The warning signs of failure. The final process: limited company, sole trader, partnership. What happens afterwards?

27. **Keeping the record straight** (p. 313)

Why you need records. Which records? A very simple system. When the business is more complicated.

section vi: Tax

28. **Tax and the sole trader** (p. 325)

When you pay income tax. Working out your income tax bill. Business expenses. Capital allowances. Losses. National insurance contributions. Capital gains tax. You and your tax inspector.

29. **Tax and the partnership** (p. 346)

How your partnership bill is worked out.

30. **Tax and the limited company** (p. 349)

How taxable profits are worked out. Losses. The tax you pay. Close companies. Paying yourself.

31. **Tax on spare-time earnings** (p. 356)

What you must do. Being self-employed. Casual income. Property income. The black economy.

32. **VAT** (p. 362)

How the VAT system works. Who has to register? What rate of tax? Voluntary registering. How is the tax worked out? The records you need. Paying the tax.

section vii: Planning for Retirement

33. **Retirement** (p. 375)

What you get from the state. If you are self-employed. If you are the director of a company. When you retire or sell.

Reference (p. 382)

A list of useful reading, names and addresses.

Going for growth

Growth businesses are the cream. They make up the top five per cent of small companies – and around 20,000 a year are started. There are several subtle differences between the growth companies and the rest. What marks them out?

The definition of a growth company will usually be based upon one of the following measurements: growth in sales, growth in employees and growth in profits. Fast-growing businesses might be aiming for sales of £500,000 in three years from a scratch start or show sales growing at over 60 per cent a year from a base sales figure of say £100,000 or so.

The motivation of the entrepreneur, the team leader, is what drives the business. If you are looking at your business solely to provide you with an income you're unlikely to have the oomph to push the enterprise into fast-growth. The same consideration applies if you have set up your own business because you prefer the lifestyle with its attendant freedom and options to that of being an employee in someone else's company. To make a success of founding a growth business, a driving force is likely to be that you have the ambition of wealth. You want to make yourself financially independent; you want to give yourself that quantity of 'drop dead' money (that is, to know you're financially so secure that you can tell someone to drop dead if you are so minded!).

Without this extra ingredient, the determination to create wealth, there may not be enough motivation to push the business into the highest level of growth. Fast growth is uncomfortable and painful. It creates pressure points and stresses internally. It often requires an unreasonable owner to dragoon unwilling employees to produce the impossible. If your aspiration is simply to create a good lifestyle for yourself, you're unlikely to have the necessary drive to grow a business quickly.

How do you make your business fast-growing? It's possible to identify a number of key requirements. First, the quality of the management is crucial – and that means you and your team. You need to have the character to lead your team; you need a broad set of business skills, including sales and marketing, often gained through management experience in a large company, and the ambition to grow fast. A good education, often a higher-level qualification, also helps. If you have already run and sold a successful business, this will give you a head start for two reasons: you're more experienced and less likely to make mistakes and you may have finance available to invest in your new enterprise.

Your team needs to be balanced: there needs to be someone who is skilled in finance and accounting, someone in marketing and sales, someone in production and so on. And it makes sense for the team to be offered incentives based on growth, such as share options or the opportunity to invest in the company.

As for the business, it is also possible to identify some factors which contribute to growth. Businesses which select a well-defined market opportunity, frequently a market niche, will find that their sales people are knocking at a door already ajar. Beware the product which is unique, but which as yet has no clear defined customer base. People must want to buy your product.

It is important to develop a culture within your enterprise which focuses on product quality and customer satisfaction. It can make your whole business much more confident to know that you are selling a product which people hold in high regard and that you have a lot of customers who are satisfied. It can be so demoralising for employees who have to deal with a whole stream of dissatisfied customers.

Businesses which are technology based and which are constantly striving to introduce efficiencies through the clever use of technology will also have a head start on the fast-growth route. Innovative businesses, which have a competitive advantage, can also make larger strides than the average company, as long as the product is one the consumer wants to know about. Finally, many fast-growth businesses are also exporters. The UK domestic market is really quite small. So, if you have a product with global demand, the size of the market you can service would imply greater opportunities for growth.

If you want your business to be in the fast-growth track, but you don't match up with the characteristics described above, how can you adapt? You can look at recruitment and training to improve your management style and team. Analyse your products to improve the quality and look carefully at your current market. Investigate the possibility of raising risk finance to allow you to grow faster. Focus on business planning and improve the systems infrastructure of your business.

But do you have the desire? Only you know.

1. You and your ideas

As a way of earning a living, running your own business has two distinctive features. The first is that you do not submit yourself to a selection process; there is not, as there is with a job as an employee, a sifting carried out of possible applicants for a vacancy. There is no personnel manager wielding a battery of psychological tests or cunning interview questions to test your suitability for the job or the level of skills you have acquired.

You are the sole arbiter of your fitness to start and run your own business. This puts a very heavy responsibility on your self-knowledge, because without a doubt not everyone is suited to being an entrepreneur or being self-employed. The only external check, which may be carried out on your fitness to found a business, occurs if you need to raise money; in this case, a bank manager or other lender or investor judges you. But by the time you reach this stage, you may already have committed time and money to your project.

The answer to the dilemma of this self-selection process is self-analysis: know thyself. Additional insight can be provided by the opinion of colleagues, friends or family. But this can be fraught with emotional problems. Those you ask for an opinion may feel under pressure to give a favourable view for fear of offending. If an unbiased view cannot be expected, do not seek an opinion at all. Later in this book (p. 53), there is a checklist which you (and others) can use to carry out an assessment of your character and abilities. This should provide some assistance in answering the question 'Am I the right sort of person to succeed in my own business?'

In this chapter, there is a description of the type of person who makes the break. Some people talk over a number of years of running their own show, but never take the ultimate step. Why do some people break the mould while others only dream of it?

The second unusual characteristic of starting your own business to create your own income is that you decide what type of business it is and what market you will be selling to. While you can select a salaried job in a firm of a particular size or selling to a particular market, you are restricted by the vacancies that are available.

When it comes to establishing a business, in theory, the world is your oyster. A well-run business should succeed in any market. In practice, however, you can make success more likely by choosing your product and market carefully.

What is in this chapter?

The first section **you** focuses on individual characteristics and tries to answer these questions:

❏ Who are you? (see right)

❏ What do you want? (p. 4)

❏ What will it be like? (p. 5)

❏ Why will you succeed? (p. 7)

❏ Why will you fail? (p. 8)

❏ How big a business? (p. 8)

The second section **your ideas** focuses on the business and your choice of business idea. It looks at two ways to select an idea:

❏ What are your skills? (p. 9)

❏ Which is the best market? (p. 10)

And if you have no particular business in mind, there is also help for those tyros who do not know where to begin:

❏ No ideas at all? (p. 11)

Finally, once you have two or three ideas for consideration, read:

❏ Defining your ideas (p. 11).

You

The greatest determinant of the success of your business is you, your character and skills. This you must believe if your business is to have any chance of prospering. The type of person who blames external factors for failure and believes that their own decisions have little impact on the course of future events is not suited to building a business.

Who are you?

How frequently do you overhear, or partake in, conversations which run along the following lines: 'In a couple of years I would like to start off on my own if I can', 'I would love to have my own business but my financial commitments mean that I can't take the risk', or some other variant? Quite a number of people dream of running their own show, but relatively few take the plunge.

In some ways, it is not surprising that so few take the final step. Lying ahead of them, maybe for a number of years, is the unknown: financial insecurity, long working hours, long-term financial obligations and, at the end of it all, possible, or even probable, failure. What is different about those who jump and those who only talk?

The conventional image of an entrepreneur is of a strong-minded, positive risk-taker with a sense of destiny, seizing the ever-present opportunities. Well, this may be a reasonably close approximation of some successful entrepreneurs and you may be that sort of person, but this still does not explain why you are starting your own business and why now. There are many people like this who stay employees for the rest of their lives. No, the most plausible explanation for why some do and some do not is that those who go solo often have received a rude shock to their lives. Their previously cosy existence has been disrupted.

At the extreme, it is noticeable that in the past refugees frequently started their own businesses. But more common examples today are:

❑ being sacked

❑ being made redundant

❑ not achieving the promotion you confidently expect

❑ having your plans/proposals/ideas rejected by your boss

❑ having a new boss foisted upon you

❑ being transferred to a different job or location

❑ finding the business you work for is to be sold

❑ reaching a particular age and feeling no sense of achievement, for example, coming up to forty

❑ seeing a friend, who is in very similar domestic or work circumstances to you, founding a business.

If you have experienced one of these shocks, the comfortable niche in life which you have created for yourself may suddenly feel restrictive and unsatisfactory. Your response may be to try to seize control of your own life by creating your own job.

Obviously, this shock theory does not explain everyone's decision. There are those for whom starting on their own is a positive, not a negative, move. Some have mapped out their lives to include starting their own business. There are others for whom being an entrepreneur seems commonplace, because most of their family are either self-employed or have started a business. But there is no doubt that the proverbial kick up the backside is the starting point for many a new venture.

The conclusions that can be reached from this are that:

❑ not all the people starting a business have the necessary ingredients for success, and

❑ there may be many people who live out their working lives as employees who possess the vital skills and characteristics in full, but fail to take advantage of them.

What do you want?

An important part of your self-analysis should include what it is you hope to achieve by starting a business. Motives may range from achieving monetary gain to enhancing status to establishing a comfortable working environment. You could have a combination of business and personal objectives. It may be a helpful exercise to sit down and note what your objectives are under the following headings which are not exhaustive:

❑ *money:* how much? when? in what form? as much as possible? enough to live on?

❑ *working hours:* number of hours? amount of holiday? flexibility?

❑ *risks:* like a gamble? only low risk acceptable? prefer calculated risks?

❑ *stress:* looking for lower levels of stress? can cope with stress?

❑ *type of work:* want to be able to do the work you like? want to choose which work to do and which work to leave for others? want to concentrate on what you are good at? feel your skills are being wasted? want to achieve your full potential?

❑ *independence:* fed up with being told what to do? no longer wish to explain your actions to your superiors? think you can do better than your boss?

❑ *achievement:* want to have the feeling of satisfaction that building your own business can bring? like to set yourself standards to achieve? to see if you can do it where others fail?

❑ *power:* looking for the sense of power which being the boss can give? want to enhance your reputation or status? want to do better than someone else?

❑ *personal relations:* want to get away from the problems of having to coexist amicably with others? prefer the feeling of isolation? happier on your own, away from irritating workmates?

❑ *any other objectives?*

Once you have drawn up a list of objectives which you hope to achieve from being your own boss, you need to assess how realistic these are. A number you will find fit ideally with the notion of being self-employed; others will be quite contradictory. Part of your self-analysis should be to see how good or how bad a match your objectives are to the reality. In the next section, you can derive some idea of what life on your own may really be like.

What will it be like?

Most probably the answer is much worse than you can imagine. There are a few people who start out and find the whole operation flows smoothly from the beginning; there are others who pretend everything is going well, while the reality is quite different; and there are others who openly admit how hard it is. One of the more dispiriting aspects is that while you may expect hard work for one or two years, it could continue for several.

Statistics about the proportion of businesses which succeed and which fail are hard to come by for the UK. One guesstimate is that a third of new businesses are no longer in business at the end of the third year. Taking advice, such as counselling, and training are both likely to improve your chance of success.

If you manage to survive, life will not always be easy. Your business life may follow this pattern:

❑ *money:* your income can prove to be a problem. At the outset, if not later on, you may find you cannot draw as much income from your business as you would like. Initially, you will need extra funds to fall back on; it can be very helpful if your husband or wife is earning so that your requirement can be fairly low

❑ *working hours:* surveys show that self-employed entrepreneurs and bosses running their own companies, on average, work around 60 hours a week. While, in theory, you can choose your working hours and be flexible, in practice you may find that you work all the hours possible. If your business is not going well, you will need dedication, drive and energy to overcome problems; even if the business starts off well, you may still find you cannot turn your back on it, because you want to make as much money as possible in case things start going wrong! You cannot win. Whichever way it is, until your business is well established you will need to work long hours

❑ *risks:* a gamble is unlikely to form the basis of a successful business; and if you only want to pursue low-risk ventures, you may be short of ideas to follow up. You stand the best chance of success if you are prepared to take calculated risks which allow you to make a sound estimate of the chances of success

❑ *stress:* come what may, running your own business is a very stressful experience. You need to be able to cope with it or to seek advice on ways of overcoming it. Stress is not only caused by business problems, but it may also occur in your domestic life as a result of allowing the business to overwhelm you. Your husband or wife and close members of your family need to be very supportive and to be prepared for what is to come

❑ *type of work:* you need to be a jack of all trades. Unless you are forming a partnership or hope to raise sufficient funds to allow you to employ someone who can complement your own skills, you will find you act as salesman, technical expert, accountant, administrator or whatever. The wider the range of skills you possess, the greater your chance of success. Be honest about what you can do well and what you do badly. If there are gaps, consider being trained in the area of inadequacy (see Chapter 3, 'A spot of coaching' (p. 27)) or try to make sure you can afford expert assistance

❑ *independence:* you remain totally independent in your business decisions only if you never borrow or raise money. Once you have done that, you may find that you have to explain your actions, although not usually on a day-to-day basis

❑ *achievement:* founding and controlling a successful business can yield a tremendous sense of achievement, but what happens if there are failures? What would be your reaction? To be a successful business manager, you need to be able to deal with failure. You must be able to accept failure without finding the effect devastating and yet to draw all the lessons possible from it, so that in future you will not make a similar mistake and your performance will be improved

❏ *power:* power can be a destructive influence in a business. There is no problem if you are a sole trader, but once you begin employing staff, you are trying to operate your business through others. Should the desire for power lead you to try to control employees in a way which is counter-productive to their work performance, your power will be a negative influence on the success of your business. Managing people properly is more important

❏ *personal relations:* one of the advantages of running your own show is that you select the people who work for you and if you do not like them you do not need to employ them. But if you find it difficult to associate in a friendly manner with most people, you are unlikely to be a successful owner-manager. You need to be able to establish good relations with suppliers and customers, as well as with those you employ.

Why will you succeed?

The conventional view is that your business is more likely to be successful if it fulfils three criteria:

❏ the people involved realistically assess their strengths and weaknesses and try to overcome shortcomings. This could apply to you alone if your business is as a sole trader. Or, if it is on a larger scale, it means you as the leading figure plus the rest of your management team should be balanced and with no obvious lack of skills. This is the most important criterion

❏ the idea and the market for it has the necessary growth potential and you have experience in that market

❏ financing is sufficient to cover the shortfall of working capital (p. 271), especially in the early days.

If you cannot fulfil these criteria at the moment, do not accept defeat; you may be able to in the future. Most of the processes can be learned and acquired if your personality allows for realistic self-assessment. At this stage in the chapter, you should already have some self-knowledge about your strengths and weaknesses as an owner-manager. In Chapter 5, 'Are you sure?', the information is drawn together in a checklist (p. 53), which you can use as a quick test of where you stand.

Why will you fail?

You will fail if your operation does not match up well to the three criteria mentioned above. But some more specific problems are:

❑ overestimating sales and underestimating how long to achieve them

❑ underestimating costs

❑ failing to control costs ruthlessly

❑ losing control over cash, that is, carrying too much stock, allowing customers too long to pay, paying suppliers too promptly

❑ failing to identify your market because of inadequate market research

❑ failing to adapt your product to meet customer needs and wants

❑ lacking sufficient skills in one of the following areas – selling and marketing, financial, production, technical

❑ failing to build a team which is compatible and complementary, if your business is on a larger scale

❑ taking unnecessary risks

❑ underpricing.

Many of these causes of failure are a result of lack of skills. Running your own business does not mean you have to be an expert at everything; but you do have to appreciate the importance of all these aspects so that you can control your business properly. Try to acquire an appreciation of the crucial factors to watch out for by seeking training or advice from others in those areas in which you are weak. Use this book as a starting point. If more help is needed, there are training courses to attend and advice agencies to consult (pp. 28, 30).

How big a business?

One factor to consider at an early stage is which track are you in – the fast-growth, medium-growth or slow-growth lane? You may know, from the assessment of your skills and character, that the most you aspire to is being a one-person business, pottering along steadily. Or your analysis may convince you that, with the right funds and the right management team, you have the potential to look for swift growth to a substantial size. Your plans about raising money are determined by this consideration.

Your ideas

Frequently, the reason given for failing to take the step and start on your own is that you lack an idea of what you can produce and sell. This may be because there is a misconception about what is needed for a business to be successful. Your idea does not have to be novel, original or revolutionary. If it is, it may be helpful; but equally, it could be a hindrance. Trying to sell a product or service which has not been available previously can be an uphill struggle. Being first is not always best. The first to offer such a product has to educate a market and possibly establish a distribution structure. The second or third into a market can capitalize on all the effort and investment made by their predecessors. The moral is that you should not veer away from an idea because it is not original.

However, it does not follow that you can offer something identical to another business. If you do, how can the potential customer choose? It could only be on the basis of price (p. 162), which suggests that you will struggle to make a profit, unless, of course, you can sell in volume. The ideal product or service to choose as a basis for your business is one which you can distinguish from the competition by including some additional feature or benefit which is not available in other products.

If you are starting from scratch, how do you come up with a business idea? The first stage is to draw up a shortlist of two, three or four ideas which you can define and research before selecting the one to run with.

There are two possible ways of choosing an idea:

❑ using an established skill, product or knowledge, and, in general, this gives you the greatest chance of success

❑ identifying a market which looks ripe for development by your business and acquiring the necessary technique and knowledge.

In reality, the approaches must be closely interlinked; your business will not succeed if you have the skill or product but not the market, and vice versa.

What are your skills?

The logical business idea for most people is to choose an area in which they already have considerable expertise. Many self-employed people are simply practising their own acquired knowledge, such as engineers, solicitors, design consultants, for example. Your expertise may be acquired as a result of your education or training on the job. If you have been employed as a manager of a supermarket, one obvious idea is to do the same but on your own. Or you may have worked in the computer industry and so possess considerable knowledge about products, the market and distribution.

Many people also opt to begin a business using a skill which they have acquired in their spare time as a hobby. Obvious examples are the craft-type business, such as jewellery-making and pottery. The disadvantage with these is that you have not acquired any of the business knowledge needed to turn hobbies into a living. You will not know the suppliers or the distribution network, for example. However, given determination, this disadvantage should not be insuperable. A more serious problem may emerge later: you may have decided to base your business on a pastime because you found it enjoyable; but a few months of struggling to keep your head above water can soon turn a pleasure into a chore.

Which is the best market?

An alternative to choosing an idea based upon your existing skills and knowledge would be to research some markets in which you believe there are profitable opportunities. The ideal market to base your business in is one which:

❑ is growing or is large

❑ is supplied by businesses which are not efficient or are outdated

❑ has a niche or sector (p. 14) which you can exploit

❑ is not heavily dependent on price to help consumers select one product rather than another

❑ is not already supplied by products which are heavily branded, that is, there is not considerable customer loyalty to products from one or more businesses

❑ is not dominated by two or three very large suppliers, but instead has a number of smaller would-be competitors.

In practice, there is only a remote chance of finding such a market; and if you did, so would many other businesses, which would make it very competitive. But it would be unwise to base your business in a market which does not come up with some of these positive indicators. The moral is, do not be afraid of competitors; they prove that there is business there to get.

It is, of course, difficult to enter a market if you have none of the technical skills or industry knowledge necessary. In particular, if you need to raise money, the decision-makers will want to see some, if not considerable, knowledge and experience in that market. If you do not have it, you have to concentrate instead on demonstrating your all-round business skills and experience, the strength offered by your character and abilities, and the research you have undertaken into your chosen market.

No ideas at all?

If you cannot come up with an idea on your own, do not despair. Try organizing what is called a brainstorming session. Ask two or three colleagues, friends or relations to join a discussion. Hold it as a proper meeting in peace and quiet, with paper and pencil in front of you. Spend a couple of minutes outlining the sort of idea you are after and what you have already considered but dismissed and why. Ask for their reactions and cross your fingers that some ideas will emerge. A brainstorming session need not last a long time. Probably a quarter or half an hour will be sufficient.

Defining your ideas

At this stage, you may not have focused on just one idea, but still be considering two or more. Whether it is only one or several, your next step is to draw up a pen portrait of each idea. Clearly, some of the aspects will be nothing more than wild guesses; you will need to carry out research before encapsulating your final choice in a detailed business plan with realistic forecasts. The brief sketch should define the following points:

❑ a description of the product or service

❑ an indication of why it will sell

❑ a description of the intended market

❑ an indication of whether your idea is for the UK or European market

❑ your estimate of the approximate price

❑ how you think it will be sold, for example, through shops, salespeople, distributors

❑ a first stab at the amount of sales you can make

❑ how it will be made, if it is a product

❑ its approximate cost.

Having drawn up these broad-brush definitions of a couple of the most promising ideas, you will find that during the detailed estimation and calculation stage, one idea will emerge as the favourite. You can concentrate on developing this one into your business plan.

Summary

1. An unusual aspect of starting your own business is that you make the decision yourself that you have the necessary qualities and abilities to make a success of it.

2. Analyse what you expect and hope to achieve from self-employment.

3. Do not underestimate the problems and difficulties which emerge for business owners.

4. Use the checklists in Chapter 5, 'Are you sure?' (pp. 53, 56, 57, 60), to identify your weaknesses and strengths.

5. Try to take advantage of the many training courses and advice agencies available to help improve those weaknesses listed in Chapter 3, 'A spot of coaching' (p. 27).

6. Do not be dissuaded from launching a business because you do not have an original idea. With the right management and a promising marketplace, a well-worn idea can be successful.

7. The market can be crucial in determining success or failure (rated second most important factor after management by providers of finance). Carry out detailed market research following the advice in Chapter 2, 'Who will buy?' (p. 13).

8. Develop brief descriptions of a couple of ideas before researching more thoroughly. Select the favourite and make up a detailed business plan before setting up the business.

Other chapters to read

2. **Who will buy?** (p. 13)
5. **Are you sure?** (p. 53)
7. **Timing the jump** (p. 71)

2. Who will buy?

By now you have probably narrowed down your shortlist of ideas. You may know which market you want to enter; you may have got your eye on a product which you think has potential. What you must do next is to study your prospective marketplace in detail. Researching the marketplace comes before raising money, making profit and cash flow forecasts, finding premises or any of the other steps you have to take to form your business.

This is especially true if you need to raise money for your proposed business and have to produce a business plan. You will not obtain financial backing from anyone unless you can show with confidence that you understand the structure of your market and have a clear idea of where your product will be positioned compared to the competition. The crucial questions are – who will be your customers, why will they buy from you and how much can you sell.

Knowing the number of customers is not the only information yielded by studying the marketplace. More importantly, you should be able to obtain information about what your potential customer needs. This, in turn, should aid you to angle your product or service to satisfy the greatest demand.

It is much easier to persuade people to purchase something they already want; educating a market to buy your product if the market has expressed no great desire for it can be a long haul.

What is in this chapter?

This chapter is about market research and how you can proceed to find out about your particular market. But the first part of the chapter concentrates on what it is you need to know about the market, rather than how to carry out the research.

First, the chapter helps you to define the bit (or segment) of the market you are specifically going for, **who will buy?** (p. 14): which are your customers and what are their common characteristics?

The next section, **why will they buy?** (p. 17), helps you form your sales proposition to your target market. What are the main features and benefits which your potential customers are looking for? Can your product supply them? This process helps you to define your service or product specifically, and in relation to the competition, so that your product is differentiated from the run-of-the-mill.

The third section, **how much will they buy?** (p. 19), leads into how you can utilize the information about market and potential customers to make realistic sales forecasts.

The final section, **how to do the research?** (p. 22), looks at the nitty-gritty of carrying out the market research needed. How is it done? What sources do you use? Are some more important than others?

Who will buy?

Knowing which market and which product is only the start of the work you need to do before you will be able to begin selling. First, you have to research the market. You are not simply looking for lots of statistics to blind potential backers with information. You need the details to help you plan your business strategy.

It would be a mistake to assume that you have an equal chance of selling to every customer in your market. If it is that sort of market, it implies that you are looking for volume sales. In turn, this suggests a market which is very sensitive to price levels and in which it is difficult to sort out one product from another. If this is the sort of business you are planning, think carefully. Few small businesses have the resources to make a success of this.

Basically, you should be looking for a niche in your proposed market which allows you to charge a reasonable price and so maintain reasonable profit margins. To achieve this, your product needs to be clearly distinguishable from the competition (called *product differentiation*).

The purpose of your research at this stage is to look for that niche. This process is called market segmentation. In everyday language, it means looking for a group of customers within your target market which has common characteristics, tastes and features. If you can find such a group, it allows you to tailor your product to meet its particular needs. Your search for a market segment need not be confined to the UK – extend your horizons that little bit further, and see if you can identify a market segment running across different European countries.

Once you have sorted out the groups, you must look at the competitive position. Are there already suppliers to that group of people? The existence of competition does not mean that you should not try to enter the market, but it does mean that you need to be able to offer customers some additional benefit in your service or product, and it must be a benefit they want.

For a small firm, a strong attraction of using this market segment approach to sales is that you may be able to achieve a dominant position in that segment. This could mean becoming the market leader with its attendant advantages of selling more at a higher price (p. 169).

If your business is on a smaller scale (perhaps only yourself or a couple of employees), it still makes sense to look for a niche to exploit, because of the advantages it offers in being able to keep your prices above rock-bottom level.

There are several different ways of grouping people. These include looking at potential customers by examining facts about their life, such as where they live or the kind of work they do. Or a more satisfactory way of grouping could be based on how they behave when they are deciding to buy a product, such as whether price makes a substantial difference to their buying decision. Use the step-by-step analysis (see below) to help you sort out groups or segments.

What makes a useful market grouping?

The fact that you can identify a group of people with similar tastes in your target market does not necessarily mean that you have unlocked a source of sales for your product. To be useful, a market grouping needs to have certain characteristics. In the first place, the segment needs to be big enough to give you the living you require. You must also be able to differentiate it from other groups, so that its size can be measured. Another necessary characteristic is that the segment must be easy to reach. There is no point in selecting a target group which is difficult to reach. If it is, you will experience problems getting your message across or supplying the product because of location. Finally, the group must have common features which actually lead to similar buying decisions.

A step-by-step analysis to identifying market groupings

1. Is your target market a consumer market? Or is it an industrial or professional market? If it is a consumer one, go to 2; if it is industrial or professional, go to 11.

2. Look at family and personal factors. Would age, sex, family size or marital status form the basis of different groups?

3. Is your product the sort which relies on supplying a local area? Location may be an important feature of a group.

4. Look at social class. Could this be important for your product?

5. Can you distinguish groups of potential customers on the basis of how much or how little they use or buy your product? Could your product be tailored to appeal to heavy or light users?

6. Are there psychological or social factors at work? Could the product appeal to those wishing to 'better themselves'? Are lifestyles important? Would prospective customers be likely to 'follow the crowd' or want to be seen as stylish?

7. Could there be snob or prestige appeal? Some customers like to think they are getting the best.

8. Price could be a feature which distinguishes one group from another. Is there an element of value for money in a target group's make-up? Some people go for the cheapest, no matter what. Most customers would say that they want good value for the money they spend.

9. How do the potential customers buy? Local shop, large supermarket or store? Mail order? Can you create a niche out of distribution methods?

10. Now go to 16.

11. What type of industry will you be selling into? You could specialize in one industry or profession (called vertical marketing).

12. How big are the companies or businesses you are likely to sell to? Size can mean different procedures in buying and in frequency of purchasing. Can you create a distinguishing product benefit from the need to satisfy large, medium or small businesses?

13. Will one group of potential customers require quicker or more frequent deliveries than others?

14. Price could well create different market segments in industrial or professional users.

15. Will one group of customers be looking for a higher level of after-sales care or maintenance? Could this be your distinguishing product feature?

16. Consider what other categories might apply to your market. Each market will have its own specialized characteristics apart from the general ones listed above.

17. Now look to see if there is a group with more than one of the characteristics listed above. This could define your target group.

What do you know about your likely customers?

To help you understand your potential customers, and to help you sell to them, you need to know a range of information about them. If it is a business you are selling to, you need to have information on the organization and buying policies. Investigate the other suppliers to your customers and acquire and analyse information on the products bought by them.

Why will they buy?

Before you can answer this question, you have to find out what your customer wants. What are the benefits and features of a service or product which your target group rates most highly? Research is essential (p. 22).

Once you have the framework of your customer needs, you can begin to vary your service or product with the aim of meeting those customer wants and needs more successfully than any other supplier. There are a number of ways in which your sales package (that is, your product/service plus a range of other sales features of your business) can be altered to achieve the desired objective. These include:

❑ *appearance:* what material is the product made of? Does it look stylish? How about the colour? How is it packaged or presented? All these can be changed to match your target customer profile. If appearance is an important feature for your target group, it may be worth using a designer to help you achieve this (p. 198)

❑ *delivery time:* if speed or reliability of delivery is important to your potential customers, concentrate on how you can improve or stabilize your delivery times

❑ *maintenance:* does your target market look for very prompt attention to faults? Or very frequent maintenance visits? Whatever it is, adjust your strategy to allow for this

❑ *performance:* identify the main requirement – for example, it may be speed, reliability or a low level of noise. This sort of consideration should be taken into account when you specify your product. If it is already past the specification stage, can it be altered?

❏ *quality:* this is rather an ethereal topic, as quality can be subjective, existing in the eye of the beholder. Or it can be objective, for example, the evenness of the stitching. You can create an impression of quality by building up the image or reputation of the product to suggest this (p. 120). The appearance of quality tends to depend on all the variables of a product: appearance, service, packaging, reliability, performance and so on.

By adjusting your service/product in this way to meet the wants and needs of your target market, you are trying to establish that you have at least one unique feature which your competitors don't have. You can use this as the basis of your selling message to persuade people to buy. Your target market will purchase the product if you convince them that it meets the need which they have, conscious or unconscious. Of course, if your competitors already meet these needs, it is difficult to see what additional benefit your product can offer, but usually there is something.

It would be a mistake to believe that buyers act in a rational way, comparing products and choosing their purchase on the basis of some organized assessment. Even in an industrial market, buyers are affected by a number of emotional factors, sometimes not openly admitted. These can include wanting to be like someone else, to be considered stylish or a leader, or to be liked. Your potential customers may also want the best, a change, or to improve their personal standing. They may be trying to outdo the competition or to gain revenge on another person or business. So, if you do not believe your product can be differentiated in practical benefits, can it be distinguished in emotional ways?

One possible way you could think about your target market is to consider how they would match up to the range of cars available. The variety of cars available is very wide; each car model has tried to establish its own niche and it is possible to categorize buyers in your target market by the car you imagine they are most likely to buy. For example, if your market is likely to buy a Ford Fiesta, you can picture them as young, wanting something cheap and cheerful and not minding the lack of comfort. If it is a Rolls-Royce segment, your customers are looking for the ultimate in prestige, comfort and specification. A BMW is an executive car, indicating business success and achievement; the car is stylish and luxurious. And so on.

Once you have a mental picture of what your target group is looking for in a car, you might be able to use this picture to adapt your service or product to meet those same needs.

How much will they buy?

This is the third question which market research should help you answer. You cannot plan your business unless you have some estimate of how much you are going to sell and when that is likely to happen. You need this data to help you formulate your sales and cash forecasts.

The level of sales you can make over the years depends on:

❏ the market size

❏ the market structure

❏ the market share you can establish (and the competition you face)

❏ the market trends, that is, whether it is growing, static or declining

❏ the investment in time and money to sell your product. You need to be able to forecast how much you need to put in to get sales established and how long this will take. Many business failures occur because this is under-estimated. And, of course, many businesses would not start at all if the development period was accurately forecast at the outset.

Market size

The first step is knowing the market size. This could be either its monetary value or the number of units sold in the market. Beyond this you need an estimate of the market potential, which is unlikely to be the same figure as market size, because it is unlikely that everyone in the market will buy your, or an equivalent, product. Obviously, if you have the figure for the overall market, but have decided to concentrate your business resources on a particular market segment, your next step is to assess the size of the particular segment you are interested in. Even then, this may not give you your estimated market potential (the amount of sales you stand some chance of being able to make over a period of years).

Market structure

This is the process by which the final product is sold to the end-consumer. In very simple markets, there will be only the business producing the goods and the final consumers buying directly from the manufacturer. But many markets are much more complex and there are several links in the selling chain before the final consumer is reached. As well as businesses selling direct, there could be a network of distributors, and yet another layer of agents or dealers before reaching the retail outlets and the consumers.

You need to know how your particular market works to be able to estimate the value of sales. If you choose the direct route for sales (that is, you are selling to your end-users), once you have fixed the selling price and estimated the number of units you can sell, you know the value of the sales. Your forecast profit will depend obviously on the costs of the direct selling as well as all the other costs and overheads. Because direct selling can be an expensive burden, especially for a small business, many try to sell through other businesses. Or this may be the way that the market is already organized. In this case, your selling price to the distributor or network has to be low enough to allow the distributor to earn the required income and still sell to the consumer at the right price.

Any study of market structure can only apply at the time the study is made, because distribution networks are constantly evolving. The research should help you formulate your own sales plan. If there are many end-users with a ready-established distribution network, you may decide to sell via the distributors or agents and encourage sales to end-users by PR and advertising. However, if you are aiming at a few, large consumers, direct selling may be the answer.

Market share

Unless you are supplying a completely new product or service, you are going to share the market with other businesses. To be in a dominant position (that is, the supplier of 25 per cent or more of the market) would be very rare for a small business.

To be able to forecast your sales you are going to need some idea of what share of the market your competitors have. You also need information about your competitors' business and products to enable you to position and price your own offering. Knowing the market shares gives you a measure of how successful the other businesses have been.

Monopolies are unusual, but there may be a duopoly (two businesses supplying 25 per cent or more of the market each) or an oligopoly (three, four or five businesses dominating it). However, many small businesses are likely to face a fragmented supply position, where there are lots of suppliers and one business is unlikely to achieve more than 5 per cent of the market. This is particularly true if it is a new industry or market.

Measuring market share is one thing, achieving it another. But there are some ways of influencing the share you can seize. On the whole, it is helpful to build a reputation for good, consistent quality. For this to be translated into market share, a second influence is maintaining a reasonable level of marketing activity: PR, advertising and sales activity. A third influence is if your product is recognized as being ahead of the competition in performance, design or whatever.

Look at your competitors in a detailed fashion. Some of the data it would be helpful to have includes:

❏ what are the competitive products and how much do they sell?

❏ how well have they done in the last few years?

❏ how is the company organized?

❏ how is their selling carried out?

❏ if they produce goods, how is it done and what are the facilities?

❏ who are the main customers?

❏ what is the pricing policy and what sort of delivery is offered?

Market trends

Market size, market structure and market shares do not remain the same. What happens today may be totally irrelevant to what is happening in one, two or three years' time. The usual method of deciding what is going to happen in the future is to look at what has happened in the past and project it forwards. This approach is fraught with dangers. At the very least, you need to adjust the figures for changes which may occur or are forecast to occur.

On a general level, anticipated changes in the economy can affect the buying patterns of individual markets. There may be changes forecast in tax or other laws which will influence purchasing decisions. New information or research may emerge on the effect of certain items (for example, health hazards).

On a more specific level, there may be changes caused by government or local authority policy. And so on. You need to look closely at your market to guess what changes will occur which might affect the market trends. In any conversations with people already operating in the market, remember to ask what likely changes they think are on the cards. You may be better able to take advantage of them as a new entrant with no constraints from existing products, methods of operating or overheads.

Investment needed in sales

This is really nothing more than your need to make realistic forecasts of how much you will sell, when you will be able to do it and what you need to spend on selling and promotion to achieve it. Inevitably, if you are starting your own business, you are optimistic, but do not let optimism blind you to the uncertainty of making sales.

If you are in any doubt, a rule of thumb is to double the length of time you expect it will take you to achieve a certain level of sales. In this way, you will organize sufficient funds to keep the business going until you reach break-even. The danger of this rule of thumb is that your business may not seem sufficiently attractive to lenders and investors. Keep a balance.

It might be possible to obtain a more reliable estimate of sales by carrying out test trials (p. 25) on a limited basis, although this is difficult for a small business to do.

How to do the research

There are a number of techniques for researching a market. The ways open to a small business are likely to be fewer than to a larger organization, simply because of money. In most cases, it will be you, the owner, who does the research. The basic research methods for small businesses include:

❏ desk research, studying directories and other literature

❏ interviews with customers, suppliers, competitors, distributors, ex-employees of competitors

❏ test trials.

Desk research

The main sources of information are:

❏ directories

❏ government information

❏ information from within your own business, if already up and running

❏ the internet

❏ trade associations

❏ the trade press and special features in the quality papers

❑ competitors' literature

❑ published statistics and reports

❑ former colleagues.

Your starting point for a lot of information can be your local lending library or the reference library. You will need to organize your research in a systematic way, because the danger is that you may end up with too much information, a lot of it irrelevant, and with no way of being able to gain quick and easy access to the data that matters.

Some of the directories which may be useful include:

Kompass UK	Business Pages
Key British Enterprises	UK Trade Names
Kellys	Municipal Year Book
Directory of British Associations	Thomson Local Directory
BRAD (to find trade magazines)	The Retail Directory
Yellow Pages	

There will also be directories for the particular industry or market you are interested in. You must be wary, with all directories, of claims of comprehensive coverage. Entries often have to be paid for, so you cannot assume that all the information is there.

The government also produce a range of statistics which are easily obtainable. However, they may not be very useful as they tend to be rather generalized. Some of the more readily available government publications include:

Business Monitor	Family Expenditure Survey
Business Briefing	General Household Survey
Economic Trends	Regional Trends
Labour Market Trends	Annual Abstract of Statistics
Social Trends	

If you have a computer and a modem, you have an enormous treasury of information at your fingertips in the Internet. The world wide web lets you tap into computers around the world to gather a diverse range of data and ideas. However, there is so much information out there that it is easy to get bogged down. You need to use a good 'search engine' to help you find your way around. A search engine is a piece of software within the Internet which searches for items on the web by keyword or key phrase. Different search engines are better suited to different tasks, for example:

❏ *AltaVista* is fast and covers a huge part of the Web, but you'll usually come up with a very large number of possible entries to follow up

❏ *infoseek* is a good tool if you are carrying out detailed analysis

❏ *www.yell.co.uk* is the Internet version of Yellow Pages and includes a good A to Z of business web sites.

A lot of useful information from different government departments, such as the Department of Trade and Industry, the Inland Revenue and Customs & Excise, can be found on the government's own web site at http://www.open.gov.uk/.

As well as these published sources of information, you should not neglect the information you have within the business if you are already established. Keep good sales records and encourage your employees to be on the look-out for market information.

There are also the trade sources of information. Find out which are the trade magazines and, if they are not free, take out subscriptions. Organize cuttings files. Contact the relevant trade association and obtain information about its members. Use trade exhibitions as an opportunity to pick up literature about your competitors and talk to potential customers about the market, the suppliers, the products and the gaps.

Interviews

The term 'interview' can cover anything from a chat at an exhibition, to a brief telephone call, to a long face-to-face discussion in private. The main point is that you can pick up a lot of information simply by talking.

Whether you have started your business or not, good sources of information are customers, potential or actual. Perhaps you could carry out a telephone survey, limiting each interview to ten minutes, say. It would help you analyse the information if you had prepared a questionnaire sheet. On the whole, you will find that most customers are usually ready to cooperate, as it may mean you develop a product more suited to their needs. Carry on the number of telephone interviews until you begin to feel that you are learning nothing new, because the same points are being repeated.

If you want detailed information, you will not find that the telephone is the best method of acquiring it. Instead, try to carry out a number of in-depth interviews.

If you are researching a consumer market, you should try to talk to the distributors and retailers as well as to the end-users. Most people are flattered to be asked their 'professional' opinion. Talking to the final consumers can be a bit of a problem because you may not know who these are. Perhaps a retailer will allow you to spend a day in the shop talking to customers? Asking people in the street outside the store is another possibility.

If your product is likely to be exhibited at trade fairs for the consumer, spend some time there asking about the market and product. Use a brief questionnaire to ensure that you ask the same questions so that the information can be analysed.

Interviewing competitors may sound an odd idea, but there is no harm in it and it can help you understand what are common problems. If you come across any ex-employees of competitors, it is always worth a discussion, although you have to bear in mind that their view may not be entirely objective if they did not part on good terms with the business. And the information may be out of date.

Before you start your business, you could carry out some discreet research into how the competition organizes their businesses by pretending to be a prospective customer. In this way you can gain some idea of the literature, prices, the way telephone queries are dealt with, selling methods or even how your potential competitors quote. It may seem unfair, but it is an unrivalled source of information and you may rest assured that once you are in business others will do it to you.

Test trials

It would be a great help to you if you could test market your product, especially if you will be setting up production facilities or ordering very large quantities. If you can try out a few before you make the substantial investment needed, you would be able to refine the product, satisfy yourself that the demand does exist and define the likely sales cycle (the length of time from first contact to purchase). To test this, buyers of the trial product need to be followed up and interviewed.

Summary

1. Market research which is undirected is not very useful; it needs to concentrate on who will buy, why will they buy and how much will they buy.

2. It is much easier to sell a product which meets some already perceived need rather than to try to educate a market to buy a new, perhaps revolutionary, product or service.

3. Look for groups within your target market which you think you can sell to, either because no one is currently selling to them or because you can adapt your product to meet their needs.

4. Use the step-by-step analysis (p. 15) to identify a suitable market group.

5. Rational and emotional factors affect your target group's willingness to buy. Research these and alter your product or sales approach to match.

6. Knowing how much customers will buy is crucial to your business planning. You need to research market size, market structure, market share, the competition and market trends.

7. Try to carry out your research in a systematic way so that it can be properly analysed. Use desk research, interviews and test trials, if possible.

Other chapters to read

11. **The right name** (p. 120)
15. **How to set a price** (p. 162)

3. **A spot of coaching**

'I don't have the time' might be the instant reaction of a budding entrepreneur, if it is suggested that training or asking for advice would be beneficial. At the other end of the spectrum, there may be people who could make a success of self-employment, but 'don't know how to start'.

Training, counselling and seeking advice can all improve your chances of success, so do not dismiss the idea. If you have not yet started on your own, try to fit in some sort of training before you do so. If you are already under way, look around to see what training or help is available to fit in with your schedule – and don't wait until things are going wrong. Give yourself the greatest chance of success and consider it now.

There are an extraordinary number of organizations able to help new or small businesses – the network of Business Links, local enterprise agencies (LEAs), Training and Enterprise Councils (TECs), local Chambers of Commerce, economic development units of local authorities, banks, accountants and local colleges. However, you can tap into the vast majority of sources of help through your local Business Link (Business Shop in Scotland and Business Connect in Wales).

This chapter looks at the various sources of help and advice grouped into six categories. This is slightly artificial as many of the categories overlap; but it should help you to decide which direction to take to find the sort of advice which comes closest to meeting your needs.

The groups are:

❑ training courses

❑ counselling and consultancy

❑ other business people

❑ small business organizations

❑ the media, books and exhibitions

❑ advice aimed at specific groups.

Training courses

Obviously the main purpose of attending a training course is to learn new skills and techniques. But a secondary purpose is that it gives you an opportunity to meet people with similar problems and possibly meet potential partners, suppliers and customers.

The diversity of courses available makes it difficult to describe an average course. On the other hand, this very diversity should ensure that you will find a course run somewhere which meets your needs and suits your personality, although obviously you do not want to travel too far.

How long a course?

The length of courses available varies. There may be a one- or two-day taster, which would allow you to get the feel of whether self-employment is for you. Or there could be a series of short modular courses, attended part-time. Part-time could mean either a series of weekends spent on the course, or it could be evenings, or it could be a period of a few weeks spread over a few months.

What topics are covered?

The content of most of the general self-employment or small business courses leans heavily on the financial side. Topics such as cash flows, business plans and sources of finance, financial control, tax and book-keeping are covered. There should also be a substantial content on selling and marketing. Apart from these key areas, other topics which may be covered include premises, micro-computers, employment law, recruiting, time management, exporting, other legal aspects of business and insurance.

As well as general courses, organizations run more specialized ones, for example, a two-day course concentrating on finance or marketing. If you feel fairly confident in general about your business expertise, this sort of course could help you to brush up your knowledge in your weakest area.

What sort of training?

Inevitably, with a fair number of courses, quite a lot of the information and training is given in a fairly traditional classroom format. However, in all courses there should be an informal atmosphere which allows for discussion and questions. The success of the course can depend as much on the quality and interest of the participants as on the trainers. Before you choose a course it might be worthwhile to try and find out a little bit about the type of participants attending the course to gauge if it is the right level for you.

An increasing number of courses are trying to introduce a 'hands-on' approach. Your business plan will be presented to a trainer and the other course participants for discussion, suggestion and improvement. On a few courses, there may be an opportunity to present your plan to someone from a bank or other source of funds. This could simply be a training exercise. However, if you present your case well, the bank may want to discuss your business idea in more detail.

Who runs the courses?

Courses are run by a wide variety of organizations, including training and enterprise councils, local enterprise agencies or colleges of further education or technology. The ideal trainer for a small business course is someone who has had experience of running a business and is a trained tutor. Before you choose a course, look at the backgrounds of the people running it.

One ingredient for successful business training can be the support which you can get before and after the training course itself. To maximize the benefit from the time you spend, look for an organization running the course that can provide counselling as well as training or has close links with an organization that can provide support.

How to find a course

You can go direct to any of the sources listed below to find out about courses being run in your area. There is now a high degree of partnership between the different outlets, so your Business Link, TEC or Local Enterprise Agency will usually be able to give a good overview of the courses available throughout your district.

❏ *Business Links*. This is a national network of organisations to provide 'one-stop' shops for business support and services. By 1998, there were some 240 Business Links outlets covering the whole of England and Wales and 37 Business Shops in Scotland (try the telephone directory, public library or your local TEC for your nearest outlet)

❏ *Training and Enterprise Councils* (TECs) in England and Wales and LECs in Scotland. Contact your local office (see Reference for addresses)

❏ Local Enterprise Agencies: contact your local one (try the telephone directory or your local library)

❏ local college, polytechnic or university, library.

Checklist: how to choose a course

1. If you don't know whether training will meet your needs, ask for advice from your local Business Links or enterprise agency or TEC.

2. Decide whether you want a general or specialized course.

3. Try to find out about the trainers. Is there a good mix of practical business knowledge and teaching experience?

4. Find out about the kind of participants for whom the course is designed, and, if possible, the individuals who will be on the course with you.

5. Ask if the training is mainly classroom based. Go for courses with practical emphasis on business plans, especially if there can be a mock presentation for raising finance.

6. Look to see if pre- and post-course counselling is provided or can easily be arranged.

7. Check the cost – there may be training allowances available.

8. Check whether you can get tax relief on the cost. If the course is connected to your business and involves updating your skills, you should be able to deduct the cost as an allowable trading expense (see p. 331). This generally does not apply if you're acquiring new skills, but you may be able to get vocational training allowance in which case basic tax relief can be deducted from the price of the course – ask the course provider whether this applies.

9. Check the hours of the course and, if applicable, find out the child-care facilities.

Counselling and consultancy

Help and advice on a one-to-one basis is given by counsellors. You could approach a variety of advice agencies at any stage of starting a business. Initially, counsellors can help by discussing your idea, and its strengths and weaknesses and suggesting ways of carrying out market research.

At a later stage, counsellors can help you to prepare a business plan, including cash flows; you may even find a counsellor prepared to approach a bank manager with you. And counsellors will spend time with you if your business is hitting a sticky patch or if you feel you have a weakness in a particular area of your business and need fresh ideas or guidance.

The background of counsellors can vary a lot. All of them should be able to help in discussing your business idea, finding out about markets, preparing plans and budgets, advising on finance and helping you find your way around the business world. If you need specialist advice or have more detailed problems, your counsellor will either be able to help you or, if not, will know who can. Many of the enterprise agencies have a counsellor seconded from a bank or large company.

Advice agencies very often will also provide an information service. So, if you need to know a particular business fact and do not have the information at your fingertips, try ringing your local advice agency.

For established businesses, there may be a need for consultancy on specific topics: design, marketing, quality systems, manufacturing processes and so on. Agencies can signpost you to consultants and may be able to offer help at a 'fair' rate.

Who provides counselling or consultancy?

There are several sources:

1. *Business Links* in England (Business Shops in Scotland and Business Connects in Wales). This is a government initiative started in 1993 and designed to provide a single source of information and advice for small businesses. They are formed by partnerships between local agencies such as TECs, Local Enterprise Agencies, local authorities and chambers of commerce.

Business Links offer a range of core services on behalf of the Department of Trade and Industry (DTI), together with more specialised services. Although the broad range of support is similar across the country, each Business Links outlet operates at the local level adapting and developing services to meet local demand.

Business Links provide:

❏ information and initial advice for growing businesses, including sources for detailed information, the availability of grants, and so on. These initial services are usually free or available for a minimal charge

❏ training and advice services, which include finance, marketing, business start-up, a diagnostic service and a consultancy service to identify areas critical to future growth and competitiveness which is subsidised by the DTI. An initial business review would typically be free, but there is usually a fee for further services

❑ more specialist services, such as technology, design and intellectual property. There is also an export service aimed particularly at small and medium-sized companies with growth potential

❑ other services. These are constantly being developed either as government initiatives or in response to local needs. They include a 'networking brokerage' which aims to bring together small businesses in joint ventures to tackle larger deals or markets than they normally would alone and a 'business bridge' service whereby large companies provide mentors for small businesses. Different services will be on offer at different outlets.

The main advice services are delivered or co-ordinated by Personal Business Advisers (PBAs) who either give advice themselves or arrange for relevant experts to come to you. All PBAs go through a common training standard and the vast majority (90 per cent) have run their own business and have substantial experience to pass on. Charges for Business Links services are set locally and vary from one outlet to another.

2. *Training and Enterprise Councils* (TECs) try to ensure that good advice, counselling and training is available in their area. The exact details of the service will vary and are decided by each TEC. Many TECs subcontract provision of these services to Local Enterprise Agencies and others. In Scotland, TECs are called Local Enterprise Companies (LECs).

3. *Local Enterprise Agencies*. There is no standard agency; they are dissimilar in name, in size, in how they are funded and in what they can do for you. They are independent, not-for-profit organizations and they all have a common aim. The shared objective of the enterprise agencies is to help and advise small businesses. In Scotland, they are called local enterprise trusts.

As well as local agencies, there are also agencies which provide assistance and help on a regional or national level (see Reference).

4. Other ad hoc agencies providing support for small businesses, such as the Rural Development Commission, Development Board for Rural Wales, Local Enterprise Development Unit (based in Belfast), Welsh Development Agency and so on (turn to the Reference section for addresses). They offer many of the services of enterprise agencies and may also have grants on offer.

5. *Banks*. Many banks offer specialist services for small businesses and have a network of small business centres or advisers. They can direct you to appropriate counselling organizations and information services. In February 1997, five major High Street banks announced that they were expanding a pilot project called Golden Key which offers cheaper loans to businesses whose owners or managers undertake a financial training course. You can find out whether the scheme is available in your area by contacting your local Business Link.

Sharing problems with others

The business problem you are currently struggling with is unlikely to be unique; other businesses may have faced similar dilemmas. Picking someone else's brains can be a useful source of ideas and advice – if you can find the right brains, that is. One way of meeting other business people is to find out if there is a small business club operating in your area. Try asking in your local library or Local Enterprise Agency (some enterprise agencies also run small business clubs).

The aims of a club like this are to promote the growth of small business in the area, to keep small businesses informed of relevant information and legislation, to provide a social situation in which business can be discussed, to act as a voice for small businesses both locally and nationally and possibly, to promote trade between members.

If one of your problems is being too small to undertake effective marketing of your products, you could consider working with other businesses by forming a joint venture or consortium. This is sometimes called a purchasing or marketing cooperative. Contact your local Business Link or TEC to see if they can provide further information and assistance.

Small business organizations

There are many trade associations covering different sectors – and you may gain information or support by joining one of them. There are also three well-known small business organizations (see Reference for addresses) which can lobby at a national level.

1. The federation of small businesses

With over 120,000 members, this is the largest small business support package and lobby group. Members receive free legal advice and have access to a free package of expenses to meet many legal fees they face in running their business. There is also a free business information service, insurance package, and two bi-monthly magazines. The yearly membership is £60 for a sole trader and £70 for businesses with one to four employees, increasing after that on a sliding scale according to the number of employees. There is a £20 registration fee in the first year.

2. The forum of private business

This is an independent, non-profit-seeking organization which offers its 24,000 members a voice on issues affecting their profitability, a telephone information service and profit advantage through utility discounts and other money-saving products. Members make voluntary contributions (on average £110).

3. The small business bureau

This is a group that lobbies parliament on behalf of small and medium sized companies. It produces a quarterly newspaper, as well as providing an advisory service to members. The yearly subscription is £115. The subscription is reduced to £58.75 if you pay by standing order.

The media, books and exhibitions

Some of the national newspapers devote a page each week to the small business sector. The *Financial Times*, *The Express*, the *Guardian*, and *The Times*, for example, have pages which include business-to-business ads for businesses offering or wanting services, products or money, or businesses to buy and sell or franchises available – but see p. 82 for how to find a business to buy. The pages also have some editorial. There may be an article on the experience of one small business, but there are also usually up-to-date bits of information, for example about training courses, exhibitions, books and new finance packages.

There are quite a number of books written for small businesses. Some of them aim to be comprehensive, such as this one; others are more selective in particular areas. You could contact your local library, whose staff can be very helpful on suggesting sources of information. The Internet contains numerous sites offering general business advice. Use the search engines (see p. 23) to track down areas in which you are particularly interested.

At an early stage of your business planning, wandering around business exhibitions can give you some ideas and useful literature. These are also an opportunity to speak to some potential customers and competitors. Ask your Local Enterprise Agency if there is soon to be a local exhibition.

Advice aimed at specific groups

If you are under twenty-six and thinking of starting a business, or if you are unemployed with little prospect of obtaining employment, or a woman or from an ethnic minority, you are often able to choose more specialized counselling or advice.

If you are from an ethnic minority, you may find that there is a local agency in your area specially to help members of ethnic minorities who start small businesses. Many other agencies now recognize that you may prefer to see a counsellor from an ethnic minority.

An increasing number of local agencies now understand that some women prefer to attend women-only training courses or see a woman counsellor. There are also some specialized agencies which have been set up to encourage women to become self-employed or start a business. They look to boost women's confidence in their ability to run businesses by publicizing women's successes, establishing a women's business network and providing training or counselling.

Here is some information on three specialist national organizations:

1. Instant Muscle

Instant Muscle is a national charity which helps unemployed people who are disadvantaged or discriminated against in the jobs market. There is no age criteria but participants generally need to be over 18 – there is no upper age limit. Instant Muscle specialises in one-to-one enterprise counselling and training to help people set up their own small businesses.

Instant Muscle helps people to think about and plan a viable business. Clients are encouraged to identify their own skills and to look at the commercial possibilities of being self-employed. Training is geared towards producing a quality business plan. Advisers can also help you to approach bodies which may have funds available for financing the business, and will help you find the facilities you will need to get started.

There is also a 24-month after-care service available to people who have started their businesses via Instant Muscle, which provides on-going support and advice during the first two critical years of trading.

If, after preparing the business plan, self-employment does not look like the right option after all, Instant Muscle can often provide professional job search guidance as an alternative.

2. LiveWIRE

LiveWIRE is a UK-wide community investment programme funded by Shell to stimulate young people aged 16–30 to explore the option of starting or developing their own business.

LiveWIRE runs several schemes. The OUTREACH Programmes provide information to young people wanting to start up their own businesses and a link to free local advice and support. Each enquirer receives a booklet and factsheet on their business idea (if one is available) which help them to understand what is involved and the first steps to take. *SHELL-LiveWIRE* Business Planning encourages sound business planning and continual monitoring of the business. The *LiveWIRE* Business Start Up Awards provide over £200,000 of cash and in-kind support to young owner-managers in their first year of trading.

LiveWIRE operates through a UK–wide network of over 100 local co–ordinators all of whom have been identified as a focal point for youth enterprise development. Contact the address in the Reference section for more information.

3. The Prince's Youth Business Trust

The Prince's Youth Business Trust helps eighteen to thirty year olds to set up and run their own business, providing loans of up to £5,000 (average £2,500), bursaries of up to £1,500, test marketing grants of up to £250, business advice and marketing opportunities. To qualify for the help the young person must have a viable business idea and be unable to raise all or any of the necessary finance elsewhere. The Trust is particularly concerned to help the unemployed, those from ethnic minorities, disabled applicants and ex-offenders.

Each business starting up has its own volunteer business mentors – someone with suitable business experience – who keeps a friendly eye on the business for a couple of years or more.

The work of the Trust is carried on through 52 area offices. Each office has its own board made up of volunteers from the business community who ultimately decide who shall receive funding. A huge range of businesses are supported by The Trust – everything from hairdressers to farmers, computer experts to fashion-designers.

Summary

1. There is a great deal of help and assistance available to businesses in the UK, much of it free. Please make use of it, as it can help you avoid mistakes.

2. Business Link provides a centralised source of information about what help is available. It is often your best starting point.

3. Choose your training course carefully. Check that it is a practical course with emphasis on your own business plans.

4. Counselling can be a useful source of advice, not just when you start, but when you have been in business for some time.

5. Other business people can provide help and contacts – see if there is a small business club in your area.

6. You may be able to find special counselling help if you are young, from an ethnic minority or female.

4. **Your business identity**

An important decision to make early on is to decide what legal form your business will take. Whatever you decide is not irrevocable, but it will take time and money to undo mistakes. You can choose between:

❑ sole trader

❑ partnership

❑ limited company

❑ cooperative.

If you want to work on your own, your choice is either sole trader or limited company. If you want to work with others, your choice is between partnership, limited company or cooperative (or you could be a sole trader if you intend to employ others, rather than work with them).

The form you choose can hinge on emotional factors, as well as objective ones. If you choose a cooperative as your form, this may be because of political, social or ethical reasons. If you choose a partnership, this may be because you have a close colleague with whom you work well. However, the choice between a sole trader or limited company will probably be made because of monetary reasons.

What is in this chapter?

This chapter compares the pros and cons of becoming a sole trader, a partnership or a limited company. And on p. 44, there is a quiz, to help you make your decision. Next, the chapter shows you how to set up each of these legal forms. Finally, it looks briefly at forming a cooperative.

Sole trader v. partnership v. limited company

There are twelve elements you have to look at so that you can weigh up the pros and cons of each legal form.

1. The credibility of the business

There is probably very little to choose betwen a sole trader and a partnership when it comes to credibility. On the whole, it is thought that a limited company may give your business more credibility than a partnership or sole trader; but this may not work if a customer researches your company and finds, for example, that it has a paid-up capital of £100, which is the typical situation of a very small business.

Summary

On balance, if you are going to be selling to large companies, becoming a limited company will probably have the edge on credibility.

2. What happens with money you owe

If you are a sole trader, you are liable for all the money your business owes (your liability is unlimited). Your own personal assets, such as your house, furniture and car, can be seized to pay your business debts; in the final breakdown, you can be made bankrupt.

This unlimited liability also applies to a partnership, with a further drawback: you are liable for your partner's share of the debts.

By contrast, the concept of limited liability appears very attractive. Shareholders' liability for debt is, in most cases, limited to the amount they paid for their shares in the first place. The personal assets of directors can only be touched if that company has been trading fraudulently. But this protection for your personal assets may be illusory. When you are starting in business and still operating on a fairly small scale, it is common for you as a director to be asked for personal guarantees for a bank overdraft, leasing agreements, rent or credit from suppliers. However, once you have become established you may be able to shed your personal guarantees; a sole trader or partner cannot shed unlimited liability.

Summary

If yours is the sort of business which buys materials or services from other businesses, needs a small overdraft or has to operate from rented premises, forming yourself as a limited company has the edge. You may be able to get away without guaranteeing all of these debts; it is certainly worth negotiating to avoid doing so.

3. What you do to start up

It is very easy to start up as a sole trader. Simply tell your tax inspector or your local Contribution Agency. They operate a joint registration scheme, so that you need give details only to one office – they will pass the details to the other and also notify Customs & Excise which will then send you the form you need if you decide to register for VAT (see Chapter 32).

In theory, it is equally simple to start a partnership, as you do not have to get a written partnership agreement. But, this would not be a sensible or businesslike approach. Partners argue, including members of the same family; you should accept that this may be so, no matter how unlikely it appears when you start your business. You must get a solicitor to draw up a written agreement which covers things like profits split, work split, tax split and partner changes. See p. 48 for more on what should be in the partnership agreement.

You can start a limited company from scratch. Alternatively you can buy one 'off-the-peg', which costs around £100 (plus agent's fees, if used) and for a further £10, you can change its name. You have to register the company with the Companies Registration Office, which involves a number of formalities and costs £20. There is also a special fast-track registration service which enables you to register a company within one day and this costs £100. You could get a solicitor and/or accountant to help with starting your business as a limited company.

You must also meet the disclosure requirements set out in the Companies Acts if you form a limited company. This includes sending in an annual return, accounts and changes in the company's directors and secretary plus other information. A leaflet is available from Companies House – Disclosure Requirements.

Summary
Setting up as a sole trader involves the least work and fewest formalities.

4. Your accounts

As a sole trader and a partner, your accounts need to show a true and fair picture. But the exact form of the accounts is not laid down by law. In practice, this means you do not have to produce a balance sheet. It would, however, be advisable to do so to impress your tax inspector or bank manager (see p. 262 for what a balance sheet is). Some self-employed people now have to supply only 3-line accounts to the tax inspector (see p. 343). The new self-assessment tax returns provide a format for your accounts.

In contrast, the form of accounts for a limited company is laid down by law. The accounts have to be filed at the Companies Registration Office: any member of the public can inspect them there. A small company can file a shortened balance sheet and special auditors report if it chooses. The definition of 'small' is having two of the following: sales of £2.8 million or less, balance sheet total of £1.4 million or less, fifty or fewer employees on average.

There are penalties if you file your accounts late, even one day late. For private companies, the potential fine ranges from £100 to £1,000.

Summary

The rules about your accounts are more onerous if you set up as a limited company.

5. Getting your accounts audited

As a sole trader or partnership, you do not have to get your accounts audited, if you do not want to. You may want to consider doing so, if the cost would not be too exorbitant, as it can help in dealings with your Tax Inspector. It may also help you if you need confirmation of income from your business – for example, to get a mortgage to buy a house.

If your business form is a limited company, you may have to get your accounts audited by an accountant. If your company has sales of less than £350,000, you will not need to do so.

Summary

Small companies are very similar in audit requirements to sole traders, otherwise the rules for a limited company are more onerous.

6. Paying national insurance

If you are a sole trader or a partner, you pay national insurance in two ways. If your earnings are above a certain amount, you pay what are known as Class 2 contributions. These are weekly flat-rate payments of £5.35 for 1998–99. You may also have to pay Class 4 contributions, which is worked out as a percentage of your taxable profits. You may be able to claim incapacity benefit, basic maternity allowance, and basic retirement pension, and if you are a married man your Class 2 contributions would entitle your wife to the basic widow's benefits in the event of your death. Class 2 contributions don't entitle you to jobseeker's allowance but in certain very limited circumstances you may be able to claim it (see leaflet FB30, Self-employed?, available from the Contributions Agencies and Benefits Agencies). Nor do Class 2 contributions entitle you to disablement benefit or additional earnings-related pension or widow's benefits.

If the earnings from your business are small, you may well be within the small earnings limit and need not pay Class 2 contributions, but you do have to apply for exemption.

If you form a limited company, you will usually become a director and so, for legal purposes, an employee of the company. You will have to pay Class 1 national insurance contributions as an employee and your company will have to pay contributions as your employer. These rates are much higher than those for a sole trader or partner. For example, for 1998–99, if you are not contracted out of the state pension scheme, for a salary of £25,000 the rate is £1,905 as an employee plus employer's contribution of £1,797, but only £1,391 if that were the level of profits for a sole trader.

Summary

National insurance contributions will cost you more as a limited company, although you are entitled to more benefits.

7. The rates of tax on your profits

If you operate as a sole trader, you will pay normal rates of income tax on your profits (including any salary you pay yourself) – either at the lower rate (20 per cent), basic rate (23 per cent) or the higher rate (40 per cent).

For partnerships each partner is taxed on their share of the profits as if they were operating as a sole trader.

As a director of a limited company, you will pay tax on your salary at the normal rates of income tax – up to 40 per cent. You pay corporation tax on the profits which you leave in the business. If your profits are £300,000 or less, you will pay the small companies' rate of 21 per cent in 1998-99 (20 per cent from 1 April 1999).

Summary

You could pay less tax if you form a limited company.

8. When you pay tax

If you are in business as a sole trader or a partner, you will pay tax on your profits for any year in up to three instalments: interim payments on 31 January and 31 July and final payment (or repayment) on 31 January the following year.

With a limited company, on your salary you pay tax each month under the PAYE system. On the profits of the company, you pay tax nine months after the end of the accounting year.

Summary

There is little to choose between business forms.

9. What you can do with losses

If you are a sole trader or in a partnership, you can deduct losses from:

❏ future profits of the same trade

❏ other income or capital gains either in the year of the loss and the year before OR in the year of the loss and the year after, depending on when you started in business. This includes any personal income you may have

❏ other income in the previous three years if the losses occur in the first four years of the business.

If you form a limited company, the relief is not so generous. You can deduct losses from:

❏ company profits of the previous year

❏ future profits of the company

❏ any capital gains the company makes.

Summary

If you are likely to make losses in the first year or so, you would be better organizing your business as a sole trader or partnership, if you have another source of income.

10. Providing yourself with a pension

The amount of contributions a company can make to a pension scheme free of tax is broadly limitless. In some cases, contributions could even exceed current salary. As well as the contributions your company can make on your behalf, you can also invest up to 15 per cent of your salary as a director and employee, and get tax relief on the full amount at your highest rate of tax.

In contrast, if you are a sole trader or in a partnership, the maximum contributions on which you can get tax relief is between $17^1/_2$ and 40 per cent of your taxable profits (strictly, net relevant earnings) with a ceiling of £87,600 of your profits for 1998–99 (see p. 412).

Summary

The advantages are weighted towards a limited company.

11. Raising money

If you need money for your business, the form of your business can dictate your choice.

As a sole trader, your options are fairly limited and basically depend upon your bank manager and getting an overdraft or bank loan. As an outside possibility, you may find an individual who could lend you the money.

In a partnership, you may be able to find a new partner to bring in some extra capital.

But, if you form a limited company, the choice is wider. You may be able to raise venture capital from a fund or a venture capital trust. Or you may be able to raise funds under the Enterprise Investment scheme. You may also be able to raise money from your bank secured with what is known as a floating charge on your assets. For more about these methods of raising money, see pp. 274–280.

Summary

Your choices for raising money are wider if you form a limited company.

12. Selling part of your business

This can be slightly tricky if you are a sole trader or in a partnership. One way of solving this could be to take on a partner (or a further partner), but this obviously means you must have trust in the person. If part of your business is easily separated, you might be able to sell it as a going concern on its own.

It should be somewhat easier to sell part of your business if it is in the form of a limited company. You could sell some of your shares. This may not be so easy if the company is unquoted; but it should be less of a problem if the company is quoted.

Summary

Selling part of your business is easier if it is a limited company.

Quiz

Use this quiz only as a rule of thumb. It is essential to read the detailed comparisons on pp. 39–44. In this quiz, the scoring of each factor is equally weighted, that is, assumed to be of equal importance to you. You should put in your own weighting. For example, if raising money is crucial to your business, multiply the score by a number, such as 3, to give this sufficient weight in your decision.

Set up a piece of paper with three column headings: sole trader, partner, limited company. Answer each question and tot up the scores for each form of business – the higher the score, the more suitable the business type.

	sole trader	partner	limited company
1. Are you selling to large businesses?			
If YES, score and go to 2	0	0	2
If NO, go to 2			
2. Are you likely to be buying substantial supplies from other businesses on credit?			
If YES, score and go to 3	0	0	2
If NO, go to 3			
3. Do you have another person you want to start the business with?			
If YES, score and go to 4	0	1	1
If NO, go to 5			
4. Can you trust that person completely to make decisions on your behalf, to pay the tax bill and debts?			
If YES, go to 5			
If NO, score and go to 5	0	0	1
5. Are you willing to meet the more onerous reporting requirements for a company?			
If YES, go to 6			
If NO, score and go to 6	1	1	0
6. For the effect of national insurance contributions			
Score and go to 7	2	2	0
7. Do you expect to pay higher rate tax on your profits (that is, taxable profits of £27,100 for 1998–99)?			
If YES, score and go to 8	0	0	2
If NO, go to 8			
8. Want to pay as much as possible into a personal pension scheme – for example, if you are forty or over, say?			
If YES, score and go to 9	0	0	1
If NO, go to 9			

	sole trader	partner	limited company
9. Is raising money, other than by overdraft, an important consideration? If YES, score and go to 11	0	0	2
10. Might you want to sell part of your business at a later stage? *If YES, score*	0	0	1

Example

Peter Jones is thirty and wants to start a business selling frozen Chinese food with his wife Laura.

	sole trader	partner	limited company
1. He will be trying to sell to large retail chains	0	0	2
2. He is likely to be getting supplies from other businesses on credit	0	0	2
3. He is going into business with his wife	0	1	1
4. He trusts her absolutely	–	–	–
5. Neither finds book-keeping easy	1	1	0
6. National insurance contributions	2	2	0
7. Peter's business plan shows taxable profits of over £50,000 after three years	0	0	2
8. Peter and Laura are not yet bothered about pensions (both aged thirty)	–	–	–
9. Any money will be raised as an overdraft	–	–	–
10. They don't think they want to sell part of the business later	–	–	–
TOTAL	3	4	7

Peter and Laura should choose to form a limited company

How to set up as a sole trader

It is really very easy and straightforward. You need to:

❏ tell your local tax inspector and Contributions Agency. You can do this by filling in a single form CWF1 which is included in a joint Inland Revenue/Contributions Agency leaflet CWL1 Starting your own business. You can get a copy from any tax office, Contributions Agency or VAT office (see telephone book for your local offices)

❏ check with the Planning Officer that your place of work will be suitable (p. 182)

❏ if you decide to trade under a name different from your own, you must put your own name on your headed paper (p. 125)

❏ consider whether you have to, or whether you should ask to, register for VAT (pp. 364, 367).

How to set up as a partnership

The fundamental drawback of a partnership is that each partner is jointly liable with the other partners for all the debts and obligations that each partner incurs. This financial responsibility can include all your own personal assets, which could be seized to pay partnership debts (which might have happened as a result not of your actions but of your partner's).

You must be able to trust your partners. Do not drift into an informal partnership. Make sure you and your partners have discussed difficult problems right at the start and come to some clear agreement.

Types of partners

There are several different sorts of partners; but only two are suitable for consideration in a business partnership:

❏ a full partner who will share in the profits and losses in an agreed proportion and will be part of the management

❏ a sleeping partner who will have no part in the management of the business, but will still be held responsible for the debts.

The partnership agreement

This is a job for a solicitor (and find out about the Lawyers for Your Business Scheme, on p. 196). Briefly, an agreement should include among other points:

❑ the names of the partners, the name of the business and its activity

❑ the date the partnership starts and how long it will last

❑ the capital and the interest on it

❑ the profits split

❑ management and control of the business

❑ holidays

❑ what happens on retirement, on death and if one of the partners wants to leave.

How to set up as a company

This is also a job for a solicitor or an accountant, but you can get a 'starter pack' from Companies House (see Reference). If you form a company from scratch it can take several weeks, although there is now a fast-track one-day registration service. You could form a public company – this would mean you must put PLC after its name. It must have an authorized share capital of at least £50,000 and at least one-quarter must be paid on each share, plus any premium. This means you need at least £12,500 to form it. Or you can form a private company (which is any company which is not a public company). A public company must have two directors and a private company one. Every company must have a secretary and a sole director cannot act as a secretary.

You need to register the company with the Registrar of Companies. You need to send in:

❑ Memorandum of Association. Among other requirements, this should state the name of the company (this will need to be approved by the Registrar), the intended location of the registered office and the objects of the company.

❑ Articles of Association. This should have the detailed rules about internal management of the company. If you don't draw up your own Articles, the standard format set out in the Companies Act will be adopted. You can also buy a Memorandum and Articles of Association from law stationers

❏ Form 10 – notification of the first directors and secretary and the intended situation of the Registered Office. You should also send in details of any director's business occupation, nationality and other directorships held within the last five years

❏ Form 12 – Declaration of Compliance

❏ Form 117 – which you have to send in before the company starts trading

❏ registration fee of £20 (£100 if you are using the same-day service), made payable to 'Companies House'.

Instead of forming a company from scratch, you can buy a ready-made one. This is a quicker process, but it may take three or more weeks to change its name to whatever you want to call your business, but if there is no problem with the name it could be five working days. To change a company's name you need to convene an annual general meeting or extraordinary general meeting and pass a special resolution. A signed copy of the resolution should be sent to the Registrar of Companies with a registration fee of £10.

There are certain rules about displaying information. For example, the Certificate of Incorporation and the registration date need to be displayed publicly. On your letterheads and other stationery, for example, you need to show:

❏ the full registered name of your company

❏ either all or none of the names of the directors

❏ the place of registration (for example, Registered in England and Wales)

❏ the registration number

❏ the registered office address (marked as such) as well as the trading address of the company.

You must put the company name outside your office premises.

There are rules on what name you can give your company – see Chapter 11, 'The right name', on p. 120.

What directors must do

In practice, a director's general obligations are not much worse than those for a sole trader or partner, and indeed they can be better. This is because by forming a company you can separate your own assets from the business assets (in theory at any rate). But this separation is conditional upon what could be called, in layman's terms, responsible business behaviour.

However, a director also has to cope with some technical, more detailed requirements, for example sending in your accounts, which aren't there to trip up a sole trader.

Some of a director's duties, responsibilities and potential liabilities are:

❑ to act in good faith in the interests of the company. This includes carrying out duties diligently and honestly

❑ not to carry on the business of the company with intent to defraud creditors or for any fraudulent purpose

❑ not knowingly to allow the company to trade while insolvent ('wrongful trading'). Directors who do so may have to pay for the debts incurred by the company while insolvent

❑ not to deceive shareholders

❑ to have a regard for the interests of employees in general

❑ to comply with the requirements of the Companies Acts, such as providing what is needed in accounting records or filing accounts.

If a company is insolvent, and the directors have failed in their duties and obligations, they could be declared 'unfit' and disqualified from being a director of any other company for up to fifteen years.

Most of the big firms of accountants and the Institute of Directors have booklets explaining what a director's responsibilities are (see Reference). You can also get insurance to protect yourself, Directors' and Officers' Liability. Ask your insurance broker, see p. 244.

Forming a cooperative

What is a cooperative all about?

There are four basic points:

1. The management, objectives and use of the assets of a cooperative must be controlled by its workforce. If the assets are not all owned by the workforce at the outset, it must be an aim of the cooperative to own them eventually.

2. You need to organize a voting system. An example would be one vote for each worker. Decisions would be made on a simple majority.

3. The only payment for providing money for a cooperative can be interest on a loan. Any profits should be shared among the workforce.

4. You should agree at the outset that the cooperative can be disbanded only if its members agree. With some cooperatives the proceeds from selling the assets will not be distributed to the members.

Choosing a legal form

You will need to get legal registration or incorporation for the cooperative. There are four possible legal forms.

First, you could form a partnership. The disadvantage with this is that there is no limited liability. And the business could be sold for the benefit of its members; this is not in keeping with a fundamental principle of a cooperative. On the other hand, you can form a partnership with only two people, whereas to form a cooperative society (see below), you need seven.

Second, you could form a limited company; but the aims of a company run counter to some of the basic principles of a cooperative, so it would be difficult to organize.

Third, you could seek registration as a cooperative society under the Industrial and Provident Societies (I & PS) Acts 1965–75. You will need seven founder members. You will find registration will be quicker if you apply through a 'promoting body', such as the Cooperative Union or the Industrial Common Ownership Movement. ICOM or other Model Rules can be used to form it.

Finally, you could organize the cooperative as a company limited by guarantee. This needs only two people to form it.

Types of cooperative

There are different types of cooperative structures, and depending on the objectives of your enterprise you should discuss with your sponsoring body which types of structure will suit your requirements the best. The main ones are:

❑ worker cooperative

❑ marketing or service cooperative

❑ neighbourhood cooperative

❑ community cooperative

❑ equity participation cooperative.

Summary

1. A limited company has several advantages: limited liability, greater credibility, lower tax, better pension rules, more avenues for raising finance and easier disposal of part of your business.

2. Sole trader and partnership have less onerous rules about accounts, lower national insurance payments and better tax treatment of losses.

3. If you are forming a partnership, get a solicitor's help to draw up a written partnership agreement.

4. The simplest way of all to start a business is to begin as a sole trader.

Other chapters to read

11. **The right name** (p. 120)
23. **Raising the money** (p. 269)
27. **Keeping the record straight** (p. 313)
28. **Tax and the sole trader** (p. 325)
29. **Tax and the partnership** (p. 346)
30. **Tax and the limited company** (p. 349)

5. **Are you sure?**

Every would-be entrepreneur should take stock before undertaking the final commitment; reassessments are a vital part of the decision process. Are you the right person? Have you got the necessary skills? Will you be able to earn enough to live on? Is your idea the best one? All of these aspects are crucial and deserve to be analysed and considered more than once.

What is in this chapter?

This chapter draws together all the key points made in the previous four chapters, presenting them in a series of four checklists. This should allow you to reconsider previous decisions to confirm that you are on the right road. The checklists are:

❑ You (see below)

❑ Your family (p. 56)

❑ Your skills (p. 57)

❑ Your idea (p. 60).

Checklist: you

Underline the word in one of the four right-hand columns which best describes how you fit each question.

You can also ask friends, colleagues or relatives to fill in the checklist about you, so that you can obtain an external view of your character and fitness for self-employment. Make sure they respond truthfully.

	1	2	3	4
1. Can you work long hours?	*always*	*sometimes*	*occasionally*	*never*
2. Do you have persistence and stamina?	*always*	*most of the time*	*occasionally*	*rarely*

	1	2	3	4
3. Is this business more important than leisure or family, for example?	*completely*	*much more*	*as important*	*less important*
4. If the business struggled for five years, would you keep going?	*yes, easily*	*yes, fairly easily*	*yes, with difficulty*	*no*
5. Is financial success your main guide to what you have achieved?	*completely*	*mainly*	*partially*	*not at all*
6. Are you thought of as a survivor?	*always*	*usually*	*occasionally*	*never*
7. If you were in a tight corner, would you be able to come up with an original way out?	*frequently*	*sometimes*	*rarely*	*never*
8. Do you keep going until a task is complete?	*always*	*usually*	*sometimes*	*occasionally*
9. Are problems a challenge?	*always*	*usually*	*sometimes*	*never*
10. Can you live with insecurity about job and income?	*yes, easily*	*yes, fairly easily*	*yes, with difficulty*	*no*
11. Are you self-confident?	*yes, always*	*yes, usually*	*sometimes lack confidence*	*no*
12. How do you view failure?	*opportunity to learn*	*a disappointment*	*a setback*	*disaster*
13. Can you take criticism?	*always listen; may reject*	*always accept*	*don't like it*	*always reject*

	1	2	3	4
14. Do you ask for comments on your performance so that you can do something better the next time?	*always*	*usually*	*sometimes*	*rarely*
15. Do you believe your success will be dependent on outside factors?	*strongly disagree*	*disagree*	*agree sometimes*	*agree always*
16. Do you like being the leader in situations where you can be assessed?	*very much*	*quite a lot*	*not really*	*not at all*
17. Are you good at finding the right person or source to help you achieve what you want?	*very good*	*quite good*	*not very good*	*poor*
18. Do you recognize when you need help?	*always*	*usually*	*sometimes*	*no*
19. Do you set your own high standards to compete against?	*always*	*usually*	*sometimes*	*rarely*
20. In the past, which sort of risks have you preferred taking?	*calculated*	*high risks*	*low risks*	*seldom take risks*
21. Can you identify which decisions are important and which not?	*yes, always*	*yes, usually*	*yes, sometimes*	*no*
22. Can you delegate to others?	*yes, when appropriate*	*yes, sometimes*	*with difficulty*	*no*
23. How is your health?	*very good*	*good*	*quite good*	*poor*

When you have completed the checklist, look at the pattern of underlined words. The more underlined in columns 1 and 2, the greater your probable success as a business owner.

Checklist: your family

If you are single, you may not need to consider this section. But if you have a husband or wife and children, involving them in the decision to go it alone is important. Starting a business is an all-embracing existence and your family life is unlikely to remain the same after taking the plunge. They will need to understand that the home atmosphere should be very supportive, particularly during the early business problems.

Your family may also turn out to be an important business resource. They can provide extra input in all you do: clerical, manual, problem solving, for example. With a family, deciding to found an enterprise is likely to be more successful as a family decision. Having said that, many succeed without the support of their families; but, in this case, the strain on domestic relations can be severe. In the extreme, the choice may be business or marriage.

Cross out whichever is inapplicable:

1. Have you discussed your thoughts about starting a business with
your family? *yes no*

2. Are they willing to help out if necessary? *yes no*

3. Will they be able to live easily with job or financial insecurity? *yes no*

4. Have they accepted that there may be a permanent drop in living
standards? *yes no*

5. If you need to raise money using your home as security, do they
understand the full implications? *yes no*

6. Is your family self-sufficient, that is, can they manage without
you to do the shopping, keep the garden tidy, do the decorating? *yes no*

7. Does one of the members of the family earn a living in another
way, which can be used to tide the whole family over? *yes no*

8. Have you worked out a family budget to see how you will cope? *yes no*

If you have not, this pro forma cash flow may help you. Remember to use conservative estimates of your likely income and allow for all the costs.

Month:	1	2	–	11	12
Balance at bank at start of month	...	...	–	...	...
Income					
Estimated from business	...	...	–	...	...
Other family	...	...	–	...	...
Total income	...	...	–	...	...
Expenses					
Mortgage/rent	...	...	–	...	...
Loan interest	...	...	–	...	...
Council tax	...	...	–	...	...
Pension	...	...	–	...	...
Life insurance	...	...	–	...	...
Tax on business income	...	...	–	...	...
Electricity/gas/phone/fuel	...	...	–	...	...
Travel/car	...	...	–	...	...
House: insurance/repairs	...	...	–	...	...
Food	...	...	–	...	...
Clothes	...	...	–	...	...
Subscriptions/newspapers/ magazines	...	...	–	...	...
Other:					
....	...	...	–	...	...
....	...	...	–	...	...
....	...	...	–	...	...
Total expenses	...	...	–	...	...
Balance at bank at end of month	...	...	–	...	...

9. Have you talked to your bank manager about your intended
business and shown him your cash flow to demonstrate how you
hope to cope in domestic finance?   *yes   no*

When you have completed your family checklist, the more times you have
answered 'yes' the better prepared you are for starting your business.

Checklist: your skills

This checklist should help you to look honestly at what you can do well and
what you do badly. If there are skills you lack, this does not mean that you
cannot go ahead. But you need to compensate:

❑ be trained or seek advice from an enterprise agency or other advice body

❑ fund the business so you can employ those skills which are lacking

❑ use professional advisers, if appropriate.

As you answer each question, underline the appropriate word or words:

Financial

1. Have you kept accounting books, for example, sales and purchases daybooks, cash books (see p. 315)?	*many times* *on a few occasions* *not at all*
2. Have you had to chase debts owed by your customers (p. 294)?	*yes, frequently* *yes, sometimes* *no, not at all*
3. Have you ever installed a system of credit control (p. 291)?	*yes no*
4. Have you ever negotiated credit terms with a supplier (p. 297)?	*yes no*
5. What is your experience of drawing up cash flows (p. 252)?	*extensive* *a little* *none at all*
6. Do you understand the importance of controlling cash (p. 288)?	*yes no*
7. What is your experience of drawing up budgets (p. 287)?	*extensive* *a little* *none at all*
8. Is break-even analysis a technique you have used before (p. 283)?	*yes, frequently* *yes, sometimes* *no, not at all*
9. Do you know when and how you would use: ❑ an overdraft (p. 272) ❑ leasing (p. 190) ❑ factoring (p. 296)?	 *yes no* *yes no* *yes no*
10. What is your experience of estimating and raising long-term financial needs (p. 270)?	*extensive* *a little* *none at all*

11. Do you know what are the sources of long-term funds, for example, venture capital (p. 278)?

yes   no

12. What is your experience of drawing up business plans (p. 64)?

extensive
a little
none at all

13. What is your experience of presenting your plan to financiers (p. 280)?

extensive
a little
none at all

Marketing

14. Do you understand the different ways you can establish prices (p. 162)?

yes   no

15. What is your selling experience (p. 156)?

extensive
a little
none at all

16. Do you know how to analyse market sectors (p. 14)?

yes   no

17. What is your experience of identifying product benefits (p. 17)?

extensive
a little
none at all

18. What is your experience of:
❑ advertising (p. 139)

extensive
a little
none at all

❑ public relations (p. 140)

extensive
a little
none at all

❑ product distribution (pp. 19, 152)?

extensive
a little
none at all

19. Have you drawn up terms and conditions of sale on previous occasions?

yes   no

Operational

20. Do you know how to introduce a stock control system?

yes   no

21. Do you understand all the ins and outs of your product; that is, how it works, what it does?

yes, very well
yes, somewhat
no, not very well

22. Do you understand the effect that control of costs can have on profits (p. 301)?

yes, very well
yes, somewhat
no, not really

23. Do you understand the manufacturing process of your product (if applicable)?

yes, very well
yes, somewhat
no, not really

General management

24. What is your experience of staff recruitment (p. 201)?

extensive
a little
none at all

25. What is your understanding of employment law (p. 220)?

extensive
a little
none at all

26. Do you know how to set goals and objectives for employees?

yes   no

27. Have you introduced reporting systems for staff on a previous occasion?

yes   no

28. What is your experience of project management?

extensive
a little
none at all

Once you have finished assessing your skills and abilities, you will have some indication of what improvements you should make. A first step is reading the relevant chapters of this book.

Checklist: your idea

This is an opportunity to have a final check on your idea before you start becoming involved in the actual formalities and expense of forming your business. Note that where the word 'product' is used, this could also be 'service' or 'skill'.

	yes	no	does not apply
1. Have you defined your product ideas?	...	...	...
2. Have you carried out market research into your idea?	...	...	...
3. Have you discerned a market sector or niche which you will sell to?	...	...	...
4. Is that segment big enough for you to build a business on it?	...	...	...
5. Have you researched the characteristics of your likely customers?	...	...	...
6. Have you identified what are the benefits and advantages not yet available to that segment?	...	...	...
7. Will you be able to supply a product which meets those needs?	...	...	...
8. Do you know how your product will be different from the competitors'?	...	...	...
9. Have you estimated how much your likely customers will buy and when that will be?	...	...	...
10. Have you found out how the product will be sold, for example, direct selling, retail, distributors, etc.?	...	...	...
11. Have you made a realistic forecast of the market share you can attain?	...	...	...
12. Is the market likely to grow in the next few years?	...	...	...
13. Have you talked to potential customers and do they like your product?	...	...	...
14. Have you carried out any test selling and has it confirmed your estimates of sales?	...	...	...

	yes	no	does not apply
15. Will the product live up to the reputation you intend to project?	...	...	...
16. Have you estimated a price you can sell for?	...	...	...
17. Do you know how the product will be made?	...	...	...
18. Can you work out an approximate cost?	...	...	...
19. Do you have an initial idea of overheads for the business, for example, rent, telephone, heating and lighting, etc.?	...	...	...
20. Have you made an approximate guess at the profits and when they will be earned?	...	...	...
21. Will this give you an income you can live on?	...	...	...
22. Will you need to raise money and is this a realistic amount?	...	...	...
23. Have you thought carefully about what the principal risks are to your business?	...	...	...
24. Can you put an estimate on the likelihood of these risks occurring?	...	...	...

Now you have completed this checklist; the more times you answered 'yes', the better prepared you are and the greater the chance of success.

What next?

If you have worked carefully through these four checklists, you are now faced with one of three options:

❑ give up because you are not the right person to be self-employed or start a business or the idea is not suitable

❑ carry out further research or training or seek a better idea

❑ proceed.

To proceed, you need to make several decisions and carry out actions. These include choosing advisers, formulating a detailed business plan, deciding the form of your business, working on what your business or product will be called. Chapter 7, 'Timing the jump' (p. 71), should guide you through the maze.

Other chapters to read

1. **You and your ideas** (p. 1)
2. **Who will buy?** (p. 13)
6. **The business plan** (p. 64)

6. **The business plan**

Life can be very chaotic when you are starting or running a small business. The telephone calls to make, the letters to write, the decisions to take – all the day-to-day emergencies can push aside the long-term strategic planning which is essential to keep your enterprise on the right track. Do not let short-term problems divert you from your longer-term objectives.

Writing a business plan is merely encapsulating your longer-term objectives, estimates and forecasts on paper. Once you have put down your plan, do not necessarily accept that it is set in concrete. Forecasts and objectives change as new bits of information and your better experience emerge. The important point is to incorporate your best estimate, given your current state of information. There is nothing like writing something down to help clarify your mind and reveal your uncertainties and weaknesses.

What is in this chapter?

❏ The objectives of the plan (see below)

❏ How many plans? (see right)

❏ Who should do the plan? (p. 66)

❏ What should be in the plan? (p. 66)

The objectives of the plan

The two most important reasons for producing a written plan are:

❏ to show to outsiders to help raise money

❏ to use within the business to keep yourself on your planned course or to alert you to things which are not going according to your strategy. This use is discussed in more detail in Chapter 24, 'Staying afloat' (p. 282).

To persuade someone to lend or invest enough money in your business enabling you to achieve your strategy, you will need to:

❑ show that the lender or investor stands a good chance of being paid back or getting a good return on the investment

❑ instil confidence about your abilities to manage the business and, if applicable, show that you already have the beginnings of an experienced management team

❑ demonstrate that there is a good market for your product or service.

To achieve these objectives you must bring out what is exciting about the prospects of your business, combined with a thoroughly prepared presentation of the back-up figures and research.

Beware of filling your plan with nothing but a turgid series of facts and figures; you must allow the reader of your plan to be able to identify instantly what is so interesting about your business. You need to do this to persuade your reader that it is worthwhile studying the detailed forecasts, which can be very time-consuming. Lenders and investors can be presented with so many plans for consideration that unless yours grabs the reader's attention it could be consigned to the bin before your carefully prepared figures are looked at.

How many plans?

As there are two reasons for having a written plan, will one plan suffice? The answer to this depends on who is advising you. A bank manager, or other person who may be providing finance, may say there should be only one plan, as they would like to know the absolute truth about what is happening in your business. But some small businesses adopt a different strategy and have two plans. One plan is for outsiders; this plan must be one which will not fail and so it will be fairly conservative about projected sales and costs. The reason for adopting a conservative approach with outsiders is that you must not be seen to fail as this can erode confidence in you and your judgement. This could make it difficult to keep the support of your bank manager when you need it later. Of course, if your plan is being used to raise money, your figures must achieve a balance between optimism and realism if you are to persuade banks and others that your business will be successful and so worthy of a loan or an investment. You must always remain confident that the figures are really achievable; if you are misleading the lenders and investors, you are also misleading yourself.

The second plan is for your own use and will set higher targets, although you must believe you can do that level of business. If you pitch the figures too low, you might not achieve as much as is possible. The well-known fleas-in-the-box analogy applies to your plan; if you put a lid on the box, the fleas learn to jump to that height only, but, if there is no lid, they jump as high as they are capable of doing. Your plan should set that lid higher.

Who should do the plan?

It is your job. You will know the product and the market better than anyone else. You have to be prepared to present the plan to banks or other sources of finance, so you need to be fully confident about all the statements and forecasts. You will have that confidence if you have provided the data.

However, as it is so important for your plan to look professional, consider seeking advice and help on its production. This is available from:

❑ Business Links and training courses. Many of the counsellors will be prepared to help you put your plan together (see Chapter 3, 'A spot of coaching' (p. 27)). This help is often free

❑ accountants can help you prepare the figures. Some of the bigger firms of accountants will have specialist departments to do just this (see Chapter 18, 'Professional back-up' (p. 192), for more on this)

❑ corporate finance specialists. These people are mainly interested in helping you raise substantial sums of money from venture capital sources (see Chapter 18, 'Professional back-up' (p. 192)).

If your forecasts are likely to be fairly complicated and to need changing, you might consider using a computer program designed to enable you to produce forecasts and to examine the effect changes will have on the results. Computerized spreadsheets can make short work of a lengthy task and allow you freedom to investigate lots of different scenarios.

What should be in the plan?

Suggested length

1. summary of your plan (highlighting the
    attractions of your business)

  a) what is the business?   one or two pages
  b) what is the market?

c) potential for business
d) forecast profit figures
e) how much money is needed?
f) prospects for the investor/lender

2. the past

a) when business started   one page plus
b) brief summary of past performance (put   Appendix
   accounts for last three years in an Appendix)
c) indication of how relevant or not past
   performance is to future progress

3. management (this is a crucial section)

a) your past employment and business   as many pages as
   record – identify achievements, not just a   needed
   chronological statement
b) the record of other people working with you
c) if there are obvious weaknesses in your
   management, how you propose to deal with them

4. the product or service

a) a simple description of what it does   two pages plus
   (avoid technical words). If essential, technical   Appendix
   descriptions can go in an Appendix
b) why the product is unique or distinct
c) brief survey of competition
d) how the products will be developed, what
   new products are being considered, when
   replacement will be needed for existing product
   range, what competitive products may emerge
e) any patents applied for

5. marketing (also crucial)

The market: three or four
a) its size, its past and future growth   pages (detailed
b) analysis of market into sectors; identification   market statistics
   of sector your business is aimed at   in Appendix)
c) likely customers: who are they, type (that is,
   industrial or consumer), size, how they buy

    d) your competitors: who are they, their size,
       their position in market, likely response to
       your challenge

Selling:
    a) promotion, advertising (if any)
    b) who will sell
    c) some idea of your sales pitch (for example,
       the benefits of your product)
    d) how you will price

6. operational details

a) where you will be based – location, premises	length depends
b) suppliers	on nature of
c) manufacturing facilities	business
d) equipment needed	

7. financial analysis

a) summary of the forecasts	two or three
b) monthly profit and loss forecast for two years	pages plus figures
c) profit forecast for further three years	in Appendix
d) monthly cash flow forecast for two years	(optional)
e) cash flow forecast for further three years (optional)	
f) forecast balance sheet for two years	
g) audited accounts for last three years (if available)	
h) the assumptions behind your forecasts	
i) what are the principal risks which could affect figures?	

8. the prospects

a) your objectives – short-term, long-term	one or two pages
b) the finance needed and what it is needed for	
c) shareholdings suggested (if appropriate)	
d) prospects for the investor or lender (if appropriate, including possible value of business if floated on the stockmarket or sold, so investors will be able to cash in their investment)	

The length of the plan

In the outline above, suggested maximum lengths for each section are given. If your need for finance is small (£5,000, say) and your business simple, these would be too long. Probably all you will need for your bank manager is two or three pages plus the financial forecasts – a bit more if it is not your own bank manager. However, if you need a large sum of money, you may need to put rather more in than the above suggestions. But keep at the forefront of your mind that you need to get across to your reader what is interesting about your business.

One possible way around the conundrum of giving all the necessary information without boring a potential investor would be to include a note of what other figures and data are available, if requested.

Presenting your plan

Financiers will assume that if your presentation to them is unsatisfactory, your presentation to customers is equally unsatisfactory. So while it may seem obvious, your plan will look better if it is neatly typed and presented in a smart folder. The information will also be more understandable if you do not try to cram too much on one page. How you should present your plan and who you should approach for money is covered in Chapter 23, 'Raising the money' (p. 269).

Summary

1. If you want to raise money for your business you will need to have a well-presented, carefully researched business plan to support your request.

2. Producing a business plan also helps you to keep control of your business by allowing you to look at how your actual performance differs from your forecast performance – and forcing you to explain the differences.

3. Preparing the plan can help you clarify your thoughts about the success or failure of your business venture. It can also help highlight in your mind the important steps which need to be taken.

4. Consider whether one plan will suffice for outsiders and inside use, or if two plans will be more helpful to you.

5. Your plan must get across to readers what is interesting about your business. Stress your management ability and demonstrate carefully the market for your product.

6. An ideal format for your plan for outside use is to have between three and ten pages of text which draw out the important points, plus a series of financial figures. Excessive detail should be confined to Appendices.

7. You can get help to produce the plan from an advice agency, an accountant or a corporate finance specialist. It is crucial to try out your plan on someone independent before you try it out on the financiers.

8. Use the checklist on p. 66 to help you decide what should be in your business plan.

9. Your plan should be typed and neatly presented in a folder.

10. Include cash flow forecasts, profit forecasts, and possibly a balance sheet forecast. The more money you wish to raise the more detail your forecasts need to have and the greater period they should cover.

Other chapters to read

22. **Forecasting** (p. 251)
23. **Raising the money** (p. 269)

7. **Timing the jump**

Starting a business can be a confusing operation: so many decisions to take, so many actions to carry out. It can be important to keep to the right path. If you fail to take one step when it is necessary, this can delay your start.

What is in this chapter?

This chapter should help you keep to the critical path. It is based on fifty-seven steps which need to be taken. Not all of them will apply to every business; you should judge which are crucial for your business and which you will not need to do. Nor is the order sacrosanct in every case. You may find it more convenient to combine two steps and carry them out at the same time, even though one of them does not need critically to be carried out until later. However, the steps should be taken in the approximate order given.

The step-by-step guide has four sections:

❑ Initial preparation (see below)

❑ Getting into greater detail (p. 72)

❑ Setting up (p. 74)

❑ Ready to trade (p. 75).

Initial preparation

1. Carry on in your job, if you are in paid employment; carry on drawing Jobseeker's allowance or income support, if unemployed. You can under-take the initial preparation and research while still doing this.

2. Analyse your character and abilities. Are you the right person to start on your own (p. 53)?

3. Discuss with your family the possibility of starting a business. Are they aware of what it will mean to family life? Will they be committed (p. 56)?

4. Come up with a shortlist of ideas for a business. Do you have the necessary skills? Does the market look promising, at least initially (p. 61)?

5. Briefly define product ideas (p. 11).

6. Brush up inadequate skills. Apart from reading the relevant sections of this book, consider training courses and counselling (pp. 28, 30).

7. Consider whether you should start the business with someone who has complementary skills, that is, who is strong in those skills in which you are weak. Negotiate who gets what share.

8. Decide how big a business you want. Will it be large- or small-scale? How much growth potential do your business ideas have? Do you have the essential management skills to opt for a fast-growth route?

9. Did your self-analysis suggest that you needed on-going help? Or have you been unable to come up with a sound business idea? Examine the possibility of buying a franchise. This is only realistic if you have at least one-third of the purchase price (p. 110).

10. Investigate the possibilities of buying a business if you have the necessary funds (p. 81).

11. Carry out detailed market research into a shortlist of ideas (p. 14). Do this whether you are starting from scratch, buying a franchise or buying a business.

12. Identify a market sector (p. 15). Establish what will be different about your product (p. 17). Estimate all of these: market size, market share, market structure, market trends (p. 19). Investigate competition and their products (p. 21). Forecast amount of sales and timing of sales (p. 22).

13. During steps 11 and 12, narrow down possible business ideas to leading prospect.

14. Review yourself, your skills, your family, your idea (p. 53). Take decision to proceed, do further work or abandon. It is better to drop the idea now than carry on with doubts.

Getting into greater detail

15. Draw up an initial business plan. Forecast sales, costs, cash flows. At this stage, figures will be very approximate (p. 251).

16. Make a preliminary decision about your need to raise money. Roughly, how much will you need? Who is the likeliest lender (p. 274)?

17. Discuss with your family what you will be able to invest. Consider what security you can offer (pp. 56, 274).

18. Seek out and employ the professional advisers you need. This could include solicitor, accountant, bank, design consultant, corporate finance adviser (p. 192).

19. Decide how much you will spend setting up, but remember to keep a margin of safety. Tailor the amount to how much you are willing to risk yourself, as the funds you can raise will be a multiple of what you can invest.

20. If you are currently employed, are you able to give the necessary effort to get the business going? Or do you need the extra income? Consider giving up work.

21. Test your product to confirm its performance. Test market your product or service, if possible (p. 25).

22. Apply for a patent to protect the product or register the design or trade mark, if applicable (p. 128).

23. What form will your business take: sole trader, partnership, cooperative or limited company (p. 38)? If you choose a limited company, decide whether to buy a ready-made company or to form one from scratch.

24. Name your product and business (p. 120). Keep in mind what sector of the market you are selling to and what the benefits of the product are. The name is part of your selling effort.

25. Register the company name, or change the name of the ready-made company you are buying (p. 40). First, research that there is no other company with that name. Sole traders and partnerships need take no action.

26. Draw up a partnership agreement, if applicable (p. 48).

27. Come up with some initial ideas about letterheads or consider those put forward by a designer (p. 198).

28. Develop ideas about how to sell your product or service. Identify the product benefits and advantages. What means will you use to get your message across: leaflets, brochures, etc (p. 140)?

29. Identify possible suppliers. Begin your negotiations.

30. Develop a pricing strategy (p. 162).

31. Refine a business plan (p. 64). Be pessimistic about sales and costs.

32. Ask an adviser or colleague to go through the plan with you, challenging all the assumptions and figures. Are you confident you have identified the principal risks?

33. Review the plan yet again. Does the business look viable? Will you go ahead, research further or abandon? Never be afraid of appearing weak by deciding not to go ahead. All the momentum is to push forward because of all the work and commitment put in so far. But, if the idea does not hold water, the right decision is not to proceed but to research something else.

Setting up

34. It is now that you need to consider what equipment your business will need. Investigate how to pay for it: cash, hire purchase or leasing (p. 190).

35. Establish guidelines on what credit to offer, what credit to take from suppliers, how you will control cash (pp. 288–298).

36. Find out what insurance you will need for your business (p. 245).

37. Estimate the amount of initial stock and the amount of production run (if applicable).

38. Make first approaches about raising money.

39. Decide if you will start trading before you raise the money or if you will wait until you have finalized. Remember with complicated finance, it can take several months.

40. Register for VAT if you are forced to and, if not, consider whether it would be beneficial (p. 364, 367).

41. Set up a simple accounting record system (p. 315).

42. Work out what your accounting period should be, given that there is some advantage in having your accounting year end near the beginning of the tax year, 6 April if your profits are rising (p. 328).

43. Start the search for premises, if you are not trading from home.

44. Finalize your decision about letterheads and order stationery, once you have completed your search for premises and know your business address.

45. If you will need staff when you start trading, start the search now.

46. Carry on developing your ideas about image (p. 122), how to sell (p. 152) and how to get your message across (p. 137).

47. Draw up terms and conditions of sale, if applicable. Set up the sales records (p. 154).

48. If you will be selling direct yourself, develop a sales dialogue. Carry out training sessions in the form of a role-play with your husband or wife or a colleague (p. 157).

49. Set up a financial control system, that is, how you will compare actual performance with budgeted performance as drawn from business plan.

50. Finalize your decisions about brochures or literature.

51. Draw up contracts of employment for any staff.

Ready to trade

52. Finalize premises, fitting out, employing staff, sales methods.

53. If you are still employed, hand in your notice. If you are unemployed, contact your local TEC or Business Link to find out whether you will be able to obtain any financial assistance from the start of trading.

54. Inform the Inland Revenue if you are going to be a sole trader or partner (p. 47).

55. If you are forming a company, ask the Inland Revenue for information on how to operate the PAYE tax system (p. 230).

56. Set up a reporting system for your staff.

57. Plan the opening.

Summary

1. Use this step-by-step guide to help you start your business in the right way.

2. The guide is in approximate order; in particular, actions may vary depending on whether you decide to postpone trading until you have raised the money you need.

8. **Toe-dipping**

Toe-dipping might apply to two sorts of people. First, you might have some sort of business idea but be uncertain whether you want to give up your present paid employment to commit yourself to surviving on your idea. It may strike you as a good idea to test the water a little bit in your spare time or to find out more about the idea before you commit yourself further (see below, **testing the water**). The second sort of person who could be interested in toe-dipping might be someone who has to stay at home, for example to look after dependants, children or elderly parents (see right, **permanent toe-dipping**). If this is the case, the amount of time you can devote to your enterprise could be fairly limited. So, you need to be realistic and select a suitable type of business.

Testing the water

There are quite a few drawbacks to trying out your business idea without devoting all your time to developing it. If you are in full-time employment, you will be trying to carry out your business in the evenings or weekends, when you are tired. You will need an awful lot of energy to keep going. The result may be that you give up simply because you are too weary.

The second drawback is closely linked. Because you do not have the time your business idea needs, you will not carry it out successfully; you will assess it a failure because it has not achieved what you hoped. The real reason may be that you have not stoked the fire enough.

The third drawback is that there are not very many businesses which you can start only in the evenings and weekends, because they are not natural business hours for anyone else. Telephone answering machines, call diversion and mobile phones do not always provide the solution.

The big advantage of toe-dipping is that you carry on earning money from your job while you are starting up. This may be essential if you have no other income coming in, as your business is unlikely to provide you with an income for some time.

The model way of testing the water is not necessarily to start full trading while still employed elsewhere, but to use your spare time to carry out all your market research and prepare your business plan during this period. When the initial preparation is completed, you should be able to assess whether your business idea will work and have some idea of when you should be generating an income to live on. Now would be the time to cease full-time employment. One possibility at that point is to try to raise some money to fund the business, but obviously this is not a step to be taken lightly.

Permanent toe-dipping

Your motivation may be quite different; you may not be attempting to start a full-time business at all. You may simply want to earn more money on the side. You may be in full-time employment or you may have domestic responsibilities. In either case the number of hours available for business is limited. And that is the way it is going to stay, at least in the foreseeable future.

You will need a very special sort of business idea. The ideal trade should allow you to fit the work into odd or irregular hours and should not need a permanent presence. Some suitable ideas include:

❏ *fashion, health and beauty:* hairdressing, beauty therapy, dressmaking, fashion design, knitting, invisible mending and alterations, massage, aromatherapy, physiotherapy, chiropody, acupuncture, reflexology, personal fitness training

❏ *office services:* book-keeping, typing, word processing and desk-top publishing, duplicating, addressing and stuffing envelopes, data preparation, printing

❏ *writing:* books and articles, translating, copy-editing, proof-reading, indexing

❏ *arts and crafts:* drawing, illustrating, photography, picture framing, candlemaking, glass engraving, jewellery, pottery, soft toys and dolls, design work

❏ *home-based activities:* catering and cooking, upholstery, childminding, curtain making, garden produce, taking lodgers, rearing animals (goats, poultry, bees, rabbits), boarding animals

❏ *assembly work:* toys, lampshades, clothes, Christmas crackers, fire extinguishers, watch straps, jewellery and so on

❏ *miscellaneous:* teaching (music, exam coaching), repairing (bicycles, china, clocks), agents (mail order, party plan organizer, telephone selling), dealing, building, decorating, electrical repairs, car maintenance, light removals, odd jobs.

Toe-dipping: what you need to know

Starting up

You have to follow exactly the same steps as you would if you were starting in business in a big way. Read Chapter 7, 'Timing the jump' (p. 71). The key steps are:

Establishing your market: your customers and competitors (Chapter 2, p. 13)
Defining what you are selling (Chapter 2, p. 13)
Sorting out your suppliers (Chapter 24, p. 282)
Deciding whether your business will be a company, sole trader or partnership (Chapter 4, p. 38)
Planning where to work (Chapter 16, p. 174)
Organizing your records (Chapter 27, p. 313)
Preparing your business plan (Chapter 6, p. 64)
Sorting out finance (Chapter 23, p. 269).

Tax

Tax on spare-time earnings is covered in Chapter 31 (p. 356).

One particular problem which is faced by people earning money at home is the peril of working for only one business. This may be the case with out-workers or homeworkers assembling things, or doing typing or knitting and so on. If you work mainly for one company, you may be classified as an employee and your tax treatment will be less favourable. On pp. 344, 357, there is a list of the sort of things your tax inspector will look for in deciding whether you are employed or self-employed.

Organizing your workplace

Most toe-dippers work from home. This has several advantages:

❏ it is free

❏ it involves no travelling

❏ the work can be combined with any domestic tasks to be done

❏ there are no fares or lunches to be bought

❏ you can wear what you like

❏ it protects your house from burglars.

However, working from home involves an extraordinary amount of self-discipline. It is all too easy to find some domestic job that needs doing. It can also be frustrating to have your work interrupted by callers or other members of the family. And your work never goes away; you cannot leave it behind when you walk out of the office door. This can lead to extra worry. Ultimately, you may also find it lonely and you may find the lack of stimulation from fellow workers and colleagues very dispiriting.

Good organization is the key to being able to work successfully at home. Your work space needs to be separate from the rest of the house; a room is ideal, but a corner set aside for work is better than nothing.

You should also try to be strict about the time set aside for work. Try to start at a definite time each day, even if it means leaving the washing-up until later. Persuade friends that you are serious about your work and you will be hard at it between certain times, so that they restrict social calls to outside those hours. To solve the problems of loneliness and loss of stimulation, try to build a network of others working from home with whom you can cooperate on facilities and business advice.

Working from a home which you own may mean that some capital gains tax will be due, when you sell it. But you should be able to organize things so that this does not happen (p. 340). You will also need to consider insurance for an office you run from home. A few insurers will let you cover business equipment as an extension to your normal house contents insurance. But more usually, you need to take out separate insurance which might, in any case, give you useful additional cover, for example, for business interruption (see Reference).

Family support

It will be difficult to succeed in your business if you do not have the support of your household: your husband or wife and your children. Before you start, get their cooperation and help.

Summary

1. Trying to start a business while still in a job can lead to failure. Instead, use the time while you are employed to do the basic research about the market and your likely sales and costs. After this, decide whether to take the plunge or not.

2. If you know that you only want spare-time earnings, not a full-time business, choose your business idea carefully to allow you to fit it in with other commitments.

3. Follow Chapter 7, 'Timing the jump' (p. 71), to set up, even if it is to be only a spare-time business.

4. Working at home needs careful organization of your work space and working hours.

Other chapters to read

16. **Choosing your workplace** (p. 174)
31. **Tax on spare-time earnings** (p. 356)

9. **Off the peg**

At some stage in thinking about your business ideas, it probably flickers across your mind that it would all be much simpler if you could buy a ready-made business. Your reasoning might be that this would get you off to a flying start and cut down the period of hard work needed to establish a business from scratch.

But would it? The truth is that there is no easy way to having your own business. Either you must accept that there is a hard slog ahead of you, building up your own business, or, if you decide to buy an established business, you must expect to pay for someone else's work in having built it up successfully. What is more, if you decide to buy, you might end up paying too much for a business which still needs you to work very long hours. If you want to buy a ready-made business because you think it will be easier, you should seriously examine your motives in wanting to take on the responsibility of your own business.

The real temptation to buy a business from someone else is that you might buy a bargain, perhaps because the owner is desperate to sell, or because the business has been run badly and you can see a few easily applied steps which could transform its profitability.

There are three main ways you can get yourself off to a flying start. You can do this by buying:

❑ a franchise (p. 101)

❑ into a partnership (p. 87)

❑ an established business.

This chapter looks closely at buying an established business or buying into a partnership. Franchises are dealt with separately in the next chapter.

You might be able to raise money from a venture capital organisation to back what is known as a management buy-in. This is where a manager or a team from outside the company buys it and becomes its new management.

What is in this chapter?

❏ Search for a business, a guide (see below)

❏ The business profile you want (see below)

❏ Finding a business for sale (see right)

❏ Investigation (pp. 85–99)

❏ Changing the business? (p. 93)

❏ Setting a price (p. 94)

❏ Tips on negotiation (p. 97)

❏ Brief guide to management buy-outs (p. 99).

Search for a business, a guide

1. If you are already in business, pinpoint your overall objectives, the missing factors in your present business and what is holding back growth.

2. Develop a profile of the sort of business you are interested in acquiring – either all of it or a stake (see below).

3. Carry out the same market research as you would do if starting a business from scratch (p. 13).

4. Research the businesses available for sale and produce a shortlist of the likely contenders (see right).

5. Investigate the shortlist of businesses carefully (p. 85).

6. Consider what effect your purchase would have on the business (p. 93).

7. Establish a price for the business; or, better still, a price to open the negotiation and a maximum price you would consider paying (p. 94).

8. Plan the negotiation carefully (p. 97).

The business profile you want

You should try to avoid the random search for a business to buy or a good deal to make. If you were starting your own business, you would set out your thoughts and ideas. This is exactly what you should do when considering which sort of business you could run successfully if you were to buy one already set up.

To help clarify your thoughts, it is a good idea to write down in specific terms a profile of the ideal business. This should include the following, among other points:

❑ the ideal market (or even more specifically, the segment). This choice should follow from a review of your own skills (p. 57), coupled with some market research which should enable you to pinpoint a market providing you with the opportunities any successful business needs. See Chapter 2, 'Who will buy?' (p. 13)

❑ the products or services which fulfil this marketing strategy

❑ your view of the main factors in a business which could enable you to be successful

❑ the price of the business, the maximum you could pay and how that would be financed

❑ the ideal size of the business you are looking for

❑ where it would best be located (for business and personal reasons)

❑ whether the business needs to be successful already or whether you are looking for a company which your extra management skills could render profitable

❑ the minimum level of profitability you could accept and the minimum level of income you require from the business.

Once you have drawn up this profile, you should use it to judge the suitability and likelihood of success of all the prospective businesses you could buy.

On the whole, do not be tempted to abandon the principles enshrined in your profile, because you see what you think will be a bargain. It is safer to adhere to the outline you elucidated in a calm, rational manner when you were not under any pressure to do a deal.

Finding a business for sale

There are two basic approaches which you can adopt; these are not mutually exclusive. You can:

❑ look at businesses which the owner is advertising for sale

❑ search out suitable businesses which the owner may not have decided to sell, but which fit your profile.

The advantage of the second method is that you may be more likely to find the business you want; the disadvantage is that you may not be able to persuade the owner to sell, certainly at a realistic price. If you carry out this research, be prepared for several false starts.

Where are businesses advertised for sale?

There are several sources:

❑ newspapers and magazines. The Small Business pages of the *Financial Times, The Times, The Sunday Times Classified* and the *Guardian* include many businesses for sale. If you are looking locally, your local newspaper may have a section for this. Other possible sources include *Dalton's Weekly* and *Exchange and Mart.*

The details given in the advertisements will be very brief; it may only include the market, the general location and some indication of the income from a business. Note that a number of the advertisers may be the receivers of the business, trying to sell it as a going concern. If the advertisement is by a liquidator, the aim will be to sell off the assets or bits of the business, as it will not be possible to sell it as a going concern because there is no goodwill

❑ business transfer agents and estate agents will carry details of small businesses for sale; estate agents will be mainly concerned with retail businesses. You can find the names and addresses of agents in the area you are interested in by looking in *Yellow Pages.* These agents are not independent advisers but are acting on behalf of the business being sold

❑ asking around in the area you want. Try accountants, solicitors and banks. These sometimes maintain a register of businesses for sale. You can also try someone already in the industry for ideas of what might be for sale. Advertise in the local newspaper or trade magazine for a business you want.

Conducting a search for a business

Apart from following up all the sources listed above, is it possible to identify other possible businesses not yet put up for sale? Yes, by studying the market segment you want to enter. Carry out market research into that sector, identify the competitors and investigate the backgrounds. You may well find that the businesses already for sale are the worst buys. On the whole, go for what you want and not for what is available. There are also a number of organizations specializing in helping you find acquisitions. This includes some of the big firms of accountants.

Some useful sources of information include:

❑ the membership lists of relevant trade associations

❑ *Yellow Pages* and *Business Pages*

❑ *Extel* cards for unlisted companies

❑ trade exhibitions

❑ trade journals for articles on new products and services.

Investigation

Once you have a shortlist of two or three businesses you could be interested in, the next step is to investigate thoroughly and then to investigate all over again. It is crucial to be absolutely confident that you know all the pitfalls, as well as the good points of the business you are buying. Do not be hurried into an acquisition for fear of losing that so-called bargain.

Investigation is largely a question of using your common sense and being very distrustful about what you are buying. Guidance in this section is very much of the 'Don't forget to do this or that' or 'Look out for', but it cannot be an exhaustive list of what you must do. There are also specific investigations which need to be made for each business you look at; some of these will be exclusive to that business.

What help can you get with an investigation?

It would be wise to employ an independent adviser to help you analyse a potential purchase. The most likely candidate for the role of adviser will be an accountant, as a considerable part of the investigation will be analysing existing accounts and assessing asset values.

However, accountants may be expert at the quantitative aspects of a business but miss the qualitative aspects, such as how crucial present employees are to the business. Help and advice from someone in the industry can be invaluable.

Why is the business being sold?

This can be difficult to establish satisfactorily. For example, if it is being sold because the present owner doubts that it will prove to be profitable in the future, you are not likely to be told this. Your investigation of the business prospects must try to identify this sort of reason.

The most likely cause of a sale is that the owner wishes to retire. If this is the case, you need to keep your eyes open for signs that the business is running out of steam as the owner's retirement nears. It is also possible that the business and its equipment are now out of date.

Sometimes you may come across small businesses which are being sold by larger companies. The reason given may be that it does not fit with the strategy or pattern of the larger business. The real reason may be because the large company cannot make it profitable, so you need to look for the warning signs. Look carefully at the past history and what accounting policies have been used.

If the business is in the hands of a receiver, it will be advertised for sale as a going concern. You cannot take for granted that this is so. Investigation needs to pinpoint whether the assets are actually owned by the owner, whether any genuine goodwill exists and, obviously, the reasons for the financial difficulties.

A sale for any of these reasons may present opportunities for the right business person. The ability to turn round a run-down or unprofitable business is a management and business skill, which you may possess. The important point in acquisition is to know the real reason for the sale before you negotiate to buy. Then you can price the business correctly and assess the impact you could make, post-purchase.

What is being sold?

What you are buying depends on the legal form of the business. If you want to buy a business operated by a sole trader or partnership, you are strictly buying its assets, excluding what the previous owner owed and was owed. You could buy all or only some of the assets. If the business has traded under a different name, not the owner's personal name, you might consider buying the right to carry on using this. This is a wise decision only if there is some goodwill attached to the business name. Your agreement should be very specific about the assets you buy and the price you pay.

On the other hand, if the business is a limited company it has a life of its own, separate from the shareholders. In this case, you could be buying only assets or you could be buying the company itself. If it is the latter, as the new owner, you will acquire a business which has obligations and liabilities, such as contracts and debts, as well as assets.

Partnerships

An added ingredient if you are buying a share in a partnership is the necessity to investigate the prospective partner (or partners). All the other business aspects – for example, track record, business prospects, assets – need careful study, but it is also essential to find out what you can about the partners. This is for two reasons.

First, as a partner you are jointly and severally liable for the debts of the partnership. In practice, what this means is that if there are bills to be paid and your partners do not pay up their share, either because they do not have the assets to cover the debts or because they refuse, you can be made to pay for the whole debt, not just your share of it. You must satisfy yourself that the new partners hold some assets which would cover the likely value of their share of any debts and find out their track record of paying bills. A history of unpaid bills or lack of assets of any value (for example, a house) might raise question marks in your mind about their suitability as partners.

Second, the ability to coexist amicably in a partnership is crucial. Personality conflicts can be crippling and may mean, whatever the economic sense of the proposed partnership, that the future of the business would be in jeopardy.

If you are buying a share in a partnership in which there are already two or more partners, be prepared for the negotiation to take a long time. Two or more people have to agree; it is not just one person deciding, as would be the case if you were buying from a sole trader.

Use a solicitor to help you draw up a written partnership agreement or to vet the one offered to you by the partnership (see p. 48 for an idea of what needs to be covered). It might be wise to attach a note to the partnership agreement which would cover areas such as how the business is to be run, who has responsibility for what, what is the extent of the decision-making for each partner and so on. These are not strictly part of a written formal agreement, but it is crucial that each of you has a clear understanding of how the business will be run.

The accounts

The past accounts of the business are written evidence of what has happened in the last few years. But how good is the evidence? The minimum you should insist on seeing is the accounts for the last three years; these should be handed over to your accountant for stringent analysis. However, there are some points you should bear in mind. If the business is a sole trader, partnership or small company (see p. 41), accounts do not have to be audited. Indeed, the only reason that accounts need to be prepared is for tax purposes, and the accounts need only be a statement of sales and expenses; a balance sheet is not necessarily required. The evidence about the track record could be decidedly patchy and even inaccurate.

The fact that the accounts are prepared for tax purposes may suggest that the sales are understated; indeed, vendors may claim just that. But you should be wary of accepting that profits are really higher than stated in the accounts.

Once your accountant has examined the accounts thoroughly, you should begin questioning whether there are any specific reasons why, for example, the profits were high during the period reviewed. Was there no competition? If so, is there now? If the business is retail, has the pattern of shopping facilities altered to make the location less attractive now than formerly? Will there be a rent review, with a likely increase in rent, which will make a dent in future profits? And so on. Query anything which you think might have affected the results of the present owner, favourably or unfavourably.

Land and buildings

With land and buildings you need to consider the following points:

❑ *position:* this is particularly important for shops. You need to study a shop's location very carefully. What are the other shops in the immediate area selling? Direct competition need not be a disadvantage, as customers sometimes like to have a choice and will go to a location with two or more shops selling similar products. The population of the shop's immediate catchment area could be crucial to the success of the business; you should not assume that you can persuade people to travel far to your particular store. What sort of population lives near by? Is there high unemployment? Are inhabitants likely to have high purchasing power?

The future plans for the area, if any, need to be discovered. Are there any redevelopments planned? Any road changes mooted? The effect of these needs to be considered.

An important consideration for many types of retail business is how many potential customers will pass the shop each day, for example, on the way to work, to do other shopping. Test this out for yourself by standing outside the shop on days which are likely to be busy for the business and on days likely to be quiet

❑ *tenure:* if the property is not freehold, what are the terms of the lease? For how much longer does the present lease run? When is the next rent review due and is there any indication of the likely increase? Who has the responsibility for maintaining the exterior of the building? Check that the seller has the right to transfer the lease. Would you be able to sell or sublet at some future date?

❑ *condition:* pay for a survey to be carried out to establish the extent of your likely bills for the property. Run your eye over the decoration and shop or office fittings. Are there any improvements you could make which would improve the potential of the property and what would these cost?

❑ *space:* what is the useful selling space? Is this sufficient to stock the quantity and range of goods you intend to carry? Will there be any surplus space? Could this be used profitably – by you or some other business?

❑ *insurance:* what insurance currently covers the property? Is this relatively expensive or cheap?

❑ *valuation:* take expert advice on the value of the property. You should also ask your solicitor to check the title, any covenants which apply and the likelihood of planning changes.

Plant and equipment

With plant and equipment you need to cover the following points at least:

❑ *condition:* is the plant and equipment old or badly maintained? Is the technology outdated? What volume of business or production levels could the equipment deal with? Can it cope with periods of maximum demand?

❑ *value:* this can be a problem to establish to both vendor's and buyer's satisfaction. The vendor may well seek to be paid a value based on the cost of the equipment. As a potential buyer, you need to look closely at the market value, as this may well be less than cost. Indeed, if the equipment can be used in that business only, the market value may be very low, although the value to this business may well be higher than that. You will have to negotiate a price

❑ *future commitments:* if you are buying a company, you should investigate what capital expenditure has been contracted for which you would be responsible. This may also apply to any advertising expenditure to which the company is committed.

Stock

Stock is likely to be the major area of disappointment after a purchase. Opt for ruthless reductions in the value in the accounts or make an agreement to buy, subject to certain conditions being met, if you can. Check the following points at least:

❑ *how much:* first of all, establish that the amount of stock in the business agrees with the figure in the accounts (particularly if you are buying the business, not just selected assets). Once you have established how much stock there is, you need to analyse whether this is the right amount and the right sort for that business. Get guidance on the mix of stock from an expert in the industry.

Be wary of buying too much stock, even at apparent bargain prices. Keep an eye out for any outdated or damaged stock as well.

You should also check if the business has had a proper stock control system. If it has not, this should raise questions about quoted amounts. It can also be worthwhile to find out whether it is possible to return any stock items to suppliers

❑ *value:* as with plant and equipment, it is likely that the seller will hope to be paid the higher of cost or market value for the business stock. You, on the other hand, may only be willing to settle for the lower of cost or market value (and that may be a very low figure indeed). You should not deviate far from your value of the stock.

Debtors: the customers who owe you money

Your investigation should cover:

❑ *how old?* your main query about debtors must be: 'Will they pay and when?' Ask the seller for what is known as an age analysis of debts. This should show how much is owed and how long it has been owing. Very old bills may suggest that they will not be paid; or may simply suggest that the owner is very dilatory about collecting money. Whichever it is, you need to know

❑ *credit rating:* the analysis of debtors should pinpoint which customers owe the larger sums. Assuming that you were to keep these customers if you purchased the business, it is worth checking the credit backgrounds of those businesses (p. 291). You do not want to buy a business which relies heavily on a few customers who are bad payers

❏ *credit collection:* investigate how the existing owner collected debts. An improvement in this could enhance the profitability of the business

❏ *value:* once you have made a careful analysis of unlikely payers and allowed for the cost of collecting the debts, you should be able to arrive at an estimate of the value of the debtors.

Other assets

There are a range of other assets which the business may hold:

❏ *cash:* confirm the level with the bank or wherever the cash is held

❏ *patents, trade marks, etc.:* investigate their status, for example, is the trade mark registered? You should find out what would happen to these 'intangible assets' if the business should fail. They may prove to be unrealizable assets if the rights revert to their original owner, for example

❏ *investments:* if the business holds investments, perhaps in other companies, your accountant should ensure that an appropriate value is placed on them

❏ *goodwill:* the price you will eventually fix is unlikely to be the sum of the values you set on the individual assets. Negotiation may result in a price above the asset value. The surplus is known as goodwill.

Goodwill can also be described as the reputation of the business and what you are paying to acquire that reputation. Valuing goodwill is a very uncertain process. Will the goodwill disappear once the present owner is no longer part of the business? Will customers and suppliers stay with the business on the same terms, assuming those to be satisfactory?

Liabilities: what the business owes

The main liabilities to be investigated are:

❏ *loans, debentures and overdrafts:* establish the amount, the conditions, the period of the loans and the interest rate. This should be fairly easy to sort out

❏ *creditors:* an examination of an age analysis of creditors should give you some idea of the sort of credit periods suppliers have been extending to the business in the past. If the business has paid very slowly, it may suggest that its reputation with suppliers is fairly low.

Sales

To achieve an estimate of the potential of the business, you will need to look carefully at the sales figures. Carry out a product or service analysis. Does one product account for the vast bulk of the sales? What is the profit margin on this product? Does your analysis suggest scope for streamlining the product list?

Your study of the debtors will also have thrown up information about the customer structure. Does the business rely on one or a few customers? Do those customers account for the major portion of the profits as well as the sales? An over-reliance on a few can mean the business may be fairly risky and prone to sudden downturns should a customer cease using the product.

Crucial information about sales potential can be ascertained by talks with the major customers. These may throw light on the quality and reputation of the business and product. Further evidence can be obtained by a study of the level and nature of credit notes and a study of the percentage of sub-standard goods produced.

Look for any special relationships which exist with major customers, such as an extended credit or returns arrangement.

Other aspects of the sales figures you should study include:

❑ the element of windfall sales, which are unlikely to be repeated

❑ the sales by territory or area

❑ the pricing and discount structure

❑ the distribution of the product

❑ competition

❑ the seasonality

❑ the existence of fixed price or fixed volume contracts, particularly if buying a company.

The products

If the business is the manufacture or distribution of a product, you will need to find out more about it. The areas you should concentrate on are:

❑ *cost:* ask yourself if there are any reasons why the costs should rise or fall in the near future. Have there been any changes in the prices of raw materials and are there seasonal variations? Is there a shortage of skilled labour to make the product? Are any changes likely among the suppliers? Are there any key supplies which need careful management?

❑ *profit margin:* an examination should also be made of the cost of each individual product compared to its price. Do all the products cover direct costs and make a contribution to overheads? Which gives the highest contribution and which the lowest? What is the pricing policy? Have discounts been offered? Turn to Chapter 25, 'How to increase profits' (p. 300), for information about profit margins, contribution and overheads and Chapter 15, 'How to set a price' (p. 152), for pricing

❑ *orders:* if it is a company, what is the amount of advance orders? Will these all be retained if ownership of the company changes hands?

Employees

If the present owner has staff, you will have to find out what your obligations will be to them if you buy the business. If the owner is a sole trader and you are buying some of the assets, there will probably be no legal obligation to offer continued employment; but there may be if you are carrying on the business. If the business is a company, you will most likely have legal obligations to the employees. This is particularly important if it is your intention to replace the staff or make them redundant on change of ownership. You will need to ask your solicitor for advice.

Even more crucial than the legal responsibilities for employees can be the extent to which the business relies on key personnel. You need to understand their calibre, attitudes and responsibilities – before the deal. It is vital to sustain their enthusiasm and commitment through the period of ownership change.

Changing the business

Finding out what has happened in the business in the last few years and what changes are likely to occur as a result of external factors does not give you a complete picture. It ignores the fact that you intend buying the business and have some ideas of how it could be improved. You need to consider what changes you would like to impose on the business, what they might cost and what improvement in profits you estimate they would make.

Realistically, you should also recognize that a change in ownership may mean lower profits rather than higher. This might occur if the business is heavily dependent on personal contacts. The previous owner may have established an extensive network of relationships which means that, in a shop, for example, a substantial proportion of the customers come because of the owner's personality rather than because of its location, its prices or its range of goods. No matter how confident you are that you will handle customers courteously and cheerfully, you may not have that magic ingredient your predecessor possessed. Some customers may drift elsewhere, certainly initially at least.

On the other hand, you may estimate that, in a business where personality is important, the previous owner has not been ideally suited to the nature of the work and that you will be able to bring a change for the better because of your own character.

Other changes you may introduce are more tangible and you will be able to estimate the effect and cost of their introduction. The three main ways you can increase profits are by:

❑ cutting costs

❑ increasing prices

❑ selling more.

See Chapter 25, 'How to increase profits' (p. 300), for some ideas.

Some changes may involve you in spending money, for example, redecorating or refitting a shop, reorganizing the production facilities, buying new equipment, restocking. Include the cost of these intended improvements in the initial cost of acquiring the business. This allows you to set a realistic price which you can pay for the business.

Setting a price

The right price for any business does not exist as a theoretical calculation. The only price which is 'right' is the price which both the buyer will pay and the seller will accept. It is all down to negotiation. This may bear no relation to the prices calculated as a result of the value of the assets or the earnings potential which the business gives you. The first step is to jettison all notions about real value. The second step is to throw out of the window all notions that the price given in the agent's details, for example, is the price you will have to pay. Negotiation is everything.

However, you should enter any negotiation with two prices in mind. If you are the buyer, the lower price will be the price you use to open the negotiation; the higher price is the maximum you will be willing to pay. You should not start negotiating unless you have a clear idea of this maximum price. If you are the seller, the lower price is the minimum you will accept for the business and the higher price, the one you adopt initially.

Nevertheless, it is vital to have used a number of methods of arriving at a price. These can give you a benchmark for establishing lower and upper prices. You must have a base point to work from. The accountant who is advising you should carry out these calculations for you, but you should know the basis for the figures. You can set a value by:

❑ asset value

❑ earnings multiple

❑ return on capital employed.

Asset value

Your investigation will have helped you set values for individual assets. If you are buying the whole business or it is a company, the figure you are interested in is the net asset value, that is, value of the assets less the value of the liabilities. There is no rule on whether you should use the cost of the asset or its market value as a basis for your price estimate, although you will be wise to choose the lower of the two.

The final value agreed upon is unlikely to be a simple sum of the individual assets; any additional value is called goodwill (p. 91).

If property forms a major part of the business, you may automatically think that the price you pay is asset value. However, it is very important to look at what sort of profits those assets will be able to earn for you. See Example 1 in the box overleaf.

Earnings multiple

A second way of valuing a business is to apply some multiple to the earnings from the business, perhaps two or three times. Clearly, you will not take the present owner's figures for earnings at face value; apart from investigating whether they are a fair reflection of what has happened, you also need to take into account in your calculations what interest charges you would be paying after the purchase of the business. This should include loans for any improvements you intend making. See Example 2 in the box on p. 97.

Example 1

George Gabriel is interested in buying a health food store.
The details he has been given are:

Price for the freehold of the shop and flat	£125,000
Price for the stock	£9,500
Goodwill	£6,000
In total, he is being asked to pay	£140,500

George needs to carry out his own investigation. First, he looks at the shop. The size is reasonable (500 sq. ft) for a specialized business and the location is excellent. However, the shop has been fitted in an idiosyncratic way, not especially suitable for the type of business. Although the condition of the fittings is good, George would want to replace them; in particular, he would like to include facilities for serving take-away food, including hot food, which the shop does not have at present. He estimates that the cost of these alterations will be about £36,000, of which £18,000 is for the additional food facilities.

When it comes to the living accommodation, this seems in reasonable condition. He asks a valuer to give some idea of what an alternative 3-bedroom flat would cost in the area and is given an estimate of £70,000 to £75,000.

A close examination of the stock reveals that some of it is damaged but, most importantly, there are very big stocks of a few slow-moving items. George would place a value of only £4,000 on the stock acceptable to him. Nor is he convinced that there is that much goodwill associated with the business; the present owner's odd personality has militated against this.

George's value for the business based on asset values would be £125,000 less £18,000 fittings which need replacing plus £4,000 for the stock. This makes £111,000 for the business, rather than the £140,500 asked.

Return on capital employed

To assess value on this basis you need to decide in advance on a rate of return which you require on the money you invest. This should certainly be more than the rate of interest you could get from leaving your money in a building society account. Once you have decided, you work out what the income before interest and tax is as a percentage of the capital invested. If the figure you get as a result of this calculation is less than your required rate, you would decide not to buy or to lower the figure you were prepared to pay until the return equals your required return.

Example 2

George Gabriel (see Example 1) now works out a value for the business based on an earnings multiple. He has been told that the present owner derived an income of £30,000 from the business. George estimates that, with the improvements he intends, he can increase this figure to £35,000 in the first year; he hopes to push it up to £40,000 subsequently.

George has £100,000 of his own; he intends to spend £5,000 on extra stock plus £36,000 on improvements. This leaves £59,000 towards the purchase of the business. He'll have to borrow the rest of the purchase price – an additional £52,000 if he buys the business for the valuation above. At an interest rate of 0.7 per cent a month, this means interest charges of, say, £4,500 a year (exact amount depends on amount borrowed which will vary with the purchase price).

So George's approximate earnings figure for the last year would be:

£30,000 – £4,500 = £25,500

And for the current year:

£35,000 – £4,500 = £30,500

And once the shop has reached its full potential:

£40,000 – £4,500 = £35,500

These figures give the following values of the business:

2 times multiple: £51,000, £61,000, £71,000

3 times multiple: £76,500, £91,500, £106,500

For negotiation, George should refer to the past year's earnings figure only and go for the two times multiple. This gives a much lower figure for valuation than the asset value basis does. In fact, the range of values he obtains suggests that, on the whole, the asset value basis will result in a figure which is too high for him to get the return he needs on his investment. From these figures, his negotiation should start at £51,000 and go up to £76,500, say.

There are a couple of other factors which might influence his decision; one increases the value he would be willing to pay, the other lowers it. These are:

❏ the savings he will obtain from living above the shop, for example, rent or mortgage payments
❏ the loss of interest his £100,000 was earning.

Tips on negotiation

The negotiation is the key to future prosperity. This may well be the only time you are involved in negotiating to buy a business, so there is no opportunity to practise negotiating skills. But negotiation must be done if you are to buy the business at the right price for you. Follow these tips:

1. An obvious point, but do not agree to the price first quoted.

2. Open the negotiation at the lowest price you can. This price must be one which you can back up with credible reasons, so a good deal of planning is needed before negotiation begins. A shock opening bid can lower the seller's expectations and undermine resolve.

3. Look carefully at apparent bargains. If the seller accepts your first low bid, perhaps given the seller's better knowledge, your opening price was too high. Think again.

4. During the negotiation you can undermine the opposition's confidence by asking a lot of 'what if' questions. For example, 'What if the government changes?' 'What if your major customer goes bankrupt?'

5. Do not fall into the trap of making a concession for the sake of the good-will of the negotiation. The opposition will most likely strengthen his or her resolve to hold out for the highest price possible.

6. Do not answer questions of how much you can afford to pay, at least until you wish to use it as a negotiating tactic at an appropriate time. Answering the question at the timing of the sellers choice may lead you into discussion of helping you foot the bill by loans or easy instalments. Later you can use what you can afford as a limit on price.

7. Sometimes, you will find that if you start out as a tough negotiator, the reaction from the other side is a soft response. A tough reply to a tough opener is more unusual.

8. Never be offensive and over-critical; it draws a defensive response.

9. Keep your reactions very low-key; never indicate whether the news is good or bad. Keep calm.

10. If the other side makes a concession, do not feel you must respond in kind. Stay tough. There is no law that if you make an agreement with the seller, the agreement should be mid-way between the two initial positions. On the contrary, the purpose of negotiation is to try and make sure the pendulum swings your way.

11. If you are probing for solutions which will allow you and the seller to agree, always begin your possible concessions with 'If'.

12. Planning your arguments and rehearsing them before the negotiation will give you confidence in the strength of your bargaining power.

13. Try role-playing before the negotiation occurs with a colleague or wife acting as an objectionable seller.

14. Whatever the treatment meted out by the seller, do not let it get to you and your confidence in your own bargaining position. Do not be affected by the other's apparent wealth, status, success or attitude.

15. The best way to counter any threat is to indicate that you are indifferent to its being carried out. Making threats yourself can be unproductive.

16. If it is possible to produce some outside authority who limits your bargaining position, do so. This could be your wife, your partner or the person lending you money.

17. Keep in mind whether the goodwill of the previous owner is needed after the change of ownership.

18. It is often useful to link part of the price to future performance. This reduces the risk of failure against forecast.

Brief guide to management buy-outs

In recent years, there has been a growing number of management teams buying out and running the business in which they were previously employed. There are three main occasions when this occurs.

First, a large organization decides to sell or close down a subsidiary. This could be because:

❑ the business does not fit the strategy of the organization

❑ the business does not give the rate of return required by the organization, or it could even be unprofitable

❑ the parent company does not have the resources to provide the funds needed by the business or it simply needs to raise cash.

Second, a private company may want to sell out in toto. This may be for personal reasons, such as the family not wanting to run the business any longer or the need for cash.

Third, the company may have gone into receivership. There may be a part of the business which could be profitable if separated.

Raising money is likely to be the major problem for a management buy-out, as the management team may not be able to finance more than 10–20 per cent of the business. There is also a need to raise the money quickly before the opportunity slips. Lenders and investors will want to go through the same process as with any investment or lending decision (see Chapter 23, 'Raising the money' (p. 269)). A large proportion of the money put up to buy the business will be interest-bearing loans. In times of high interest rates, it can be very difficult for a business to make the interest payments.

Summary

1. Do not be tempted into paying too much to buy a ready-made business because you want your business life to get off to a flying start.

2. Clarify your thoughts about the market you want to enter, the size of business you want to run, the type of product or service you want to offer and how much you want to pay before you start searching for a business to buy. Summarize it in a business profile.

3. Consider seeking out a business which fits your profile as well as investigating all those currently advertised for sale.

4. Use advisers to help you investigate a partnership or business.

5. Adopt a sceptical approach to investigation; query and question everything about the business.

6. Be realistic about the effect of a change in ownership; there could be changes for the worse as well as the better.

7. Set two prices before you go into negotiation; the lower one with which you start the bidding, a higher price beyond which you will not go.

8. Negotiation is everything. There are no rules; there is no right price for any business. It is up to you to summon your facts and marshal your arguments to keep the price as low as possible.

9. Use the negotiation tips listed on p. 97.

Other chapters to read

1. **You and your ideas** (p. 1)
2. **Who will buy?** (p. 13)
10. **Franchises** (p. 101)
23. **Raising the money** (p. 269)

10. **Franchises**

It would be lovely if there were a way you could start your own business with a much greater chance of survival than most people. And this is just what is claimed by the franchising industry. The statistics seem to back this up, although they are rather patchy. What information is available suggests that a franchised business has a much greater chance of surviving the first three years (the danger years) than other new businesses.

Clearly you don't get something for nothing. The price of choosing the franchised route can be high. It is up to you to weigh up the costs of buying a franchise and the risks of starting from scratch.

Some of the costs are obvious; you may have to pay a lump sum at the outset as well as paying an amount each year to the person selling the franchise. Less obvious is the cost if you buy a franchise in which you have to buy products from the sellers company at a price determined by it; in this way, you cannot benefit from shopping around to buy your supplies at the cheapest possible price.

One of the economic theories behind the success of franchising is that the franchised business can earn for the product as a whole, higher-than-normal profits. The intention of the seller of the franchise is to cream off the above-normal bit of the profits, for example, by charging a percentage of sales each year, leaving only the normal bit of the profit for the person who buys the franchise. These higher-than-normal profits can build up a brand image for the product or business by carefully positioning the product in the market and using advertising and PR to promote it. In this way, the end-user of the product, the consumer, will pay higher prices than for an equivalent product.

If you think you can create the right image for your own business, franchising could be expensive for you. You might do better trying to go it alone and not seeking the apparent safety net of a franchise.

What is in this chapter?

This chapter looks mainly at what happens if you buy a franchise (become a franchisee) and only briefly touches on how to form a franchise to sell to others (become a franchisor). It concentrates on what is called *business format franchising*. This sort of franchising is where you buy a complete business system or way of trading. All the franchisees trade under a common name, appearing to be branches of one large firm, rather than a whole series of independent businesses.

The chapter includes:

❑ A brief guide to franchises (see below)

❑ The pluses and minuses (see right)

❑ A guide to choosing a franchise (p. 105)

❑ How a franchise works in detail (p. 107)

❑ The contract (p. 115)

❑ Setting up as a franchisor (p. 118).

A brief guide to franchises

This brief guide to a typical franchise describes what happens in the different stages of a well-organized and properly developed franchise; occasionally, there may be a franchise which is not developed in a model fashion and you should beware of buying one of these. Use the guide on p. 105 to sort out the wheat from the chaff.

In the first step, a business is developed or set up. It could be based on a novel or revolutionary product, a comprehensive and well-organized business method, particular marketing style and so on. The business (or pilot) will have run for a couple of years, so that all initial problems have been sorted out. Preferably there should be more than one pilot, which demonstrates that the business idea can be repeated.

Next, the owner of the business (the franchisor) decides to expand, not necessarily by creating more branches but by selling franchises to the business format already developed in the pilot operation. Note that the two forms of expansion, selling franchises and opening branches, can be carried on at the same time. The franchisor develops the franchise operation which should be a mirror of the successful pilot. The franchisor should produce an operating manual, to show how each franchise should be set up and run.

Once the format has been developed, the franchisor will try to find suitable people to buy the franchise (a franchisee) for a particular territory. There will be careful investigation by the franchisor to make sure that the franchise is sold to a suitable person who will develop the particular territory successfully. A prospective buyer should investigate the franchise, the pilot operation, the contract, operations manual and so on to ensure that the franchise will be worth buying. Mutual suspicion should rule.

When the franchise is bought, the contract (p. 115) will be signed and the buyer will usually pay an initial fee to the franchisor. The initial fee will probably include a straight fee to the franchisor, as well as the money needed to set up the business, for example, premises, initial stock and so on. For this fee, the franchisor helps the franchisee set up the business: helps with finding premises, fitting them out, stocking the business, training, finance, the opening.

After the opening, the franchisor should continue to provide advice and should carry on advertising and marketing the product name. The franchisee will normally pay a fee each month, perhaps based on a percentage of sales or profits. The product will normally be purchased from the franchisor, which may be another way that the franchisor makes his or her profit instead of the percentage on sales. The franchisor has the right to make visits to the franchisee's business to examine the accounting records. At the end of the contract, which lasts five or ten years or more, the franchisee can usually renew, subject to the franchisor being satisfied with performance.

The pluses and minuses

Your main consideration before buying any particular franchise is whether it will work as a business for you and provide you with the sort of living you require. Assuming that you have found such a franchise, there are advantages and disadvantages of which you should be aware.

The pluses

1. It is your own business.

2. If the business format has been well worked out and tested in the pilot operation, many of the problems experienced in setting up a business can be side-stepped. This reduces your risk.

3. You receive on-going advice and support. This can be particularly important for someone who has had little business experience.

4. You hope you are buying a product with a recognized brand name. To create a brand image all by yourself can involve considerable resources. But in the case of a franchise, the franchisor should carry on promoting it, using the management service fee (or royalties) or possibly an advertising levy (p. 109) which all the franchisees will pay. So the brand name of your business will be getting a bigger selling push than could be achieved by each franchisee's individual contribution.

5. In the case of many franchises, you need no knowledge of the industry before you start your business. The training given by the franchisor should be sufficient to overcome any ignorance.

6. Franchisors, because of size, have greater negotiating power with suppliers than you do on your own, although not all of them pass this benefit on to the franchisees.

The minuses

1. While it is your own business, you are expected to act in the best interests of other franchisees and the franchisor. You could find this irritating and restrictive.

2. As well as the initial fee, part of your profits will have to go each year in a payment to the franchisor. You might find this galling.

3. Often the continuing fee to the franchisor is based on your sales rather than profits. This could lead to problems if you are struggling to make profits, perhaps because the costs are too high. This will not be reflected in the level of the fee.

4. The franchisor has the right to demand that you send in sales statistics and other documents promptly, plus the right to come to your business premises and inspect your records. Again this might strike you as a loss of independence.

5. You have to adhere to the methods laid down in the franchisor's operating manual. This could be restrictive and allow little room for you to exercise your own initiative and enterprise.

6. You may have to purchase all your stocks from the franchisor. This allows little room for you to seek competitive alternatives. Again, you could find this stifling, if you want to run your own business.

7. Should the franchisor, despite all your preliminary research and investigations, fail to maintain the brand name by promotion or fail to meet commitments about training and the search for better products, frankly there is little you can do about it. If this is all buttoned down in the contract, however, you may be able to get somewhere.

8. If you want to sell the franchise before the end of your contract, the franchisor has to agree.

9. The franchise runs for a certain number of years. Normally, if your performance is satisfactory (whatever that means, see p. 116), you will be able to renew for another period; but you may have to commit to spending more money on refurbishment and more modern equipment. What happens about further renewals is not always clear. You should assess the return on the money you invest over the first period of the franchise only. If, for some reason, you are not able to renew, you may have little to sell, because you cannot sell the name or the goodwill.

A guide to choosing a franchise

1. Keep a healthy dose of scepticism about franchises, franchisors and franchise specialists.

2. Make your own choice of advisers, do not use those suggested by the franchisor. The most unbiased advisers are likely to be a clearing bank – all of which have specialized franchise units giving independent advice – and the solicitor and accountant you employ to advise you.

3. Get your accountant to examine the forecasts given to you by the franchisor and to advise you on how realistic they are.

4. Ask your solicitor to go through any contract carefully to bring out clearly the restrictions and also the ways in which the franchisor will be making money. A legal affiliate to the British Franchise Association will have specialist experience.

5. Find out how many franchises have already been sold and how long they have been going.

6. Find out, visit and talk to existing franchisees. Do not allow yourself to be restricted only to the franchisor's choice of references.

7. Be particularly careful if the franchise you are interested in is one of the first to be sold. You will need to study the pilot operation with a fine-tooth comb. Does it mirror your likely business? Does the manager of the pilot have the same sort of knowledge and skill as you? Are the premises and their location much the same? Is the stock identical?

8. Watch out if the initial fee is relatively large and the continuing fee relatively small. It is essential for the franchisor that the business continue to be promoted and properly managed. The success of your business depends on how effective the franchisor is in marketing and purchasing.

9. Look carefully at the arrangements for purchasing equipment and stock. You do not want to be forced to buy new equipment if it is unnecessary, nor do you want an arrangement in which the franchisor can increase the mark-up on products sold to you. Is it possible to purchase supplies from alternative sources?

10. Investigate the franchisor. The continued existence of the franchisor's business is important to you, because it carries out the marketing, purchasing and other centrally organized functions. Get references and credit ratings. Ask the franchisor to give you a copy of the latest accounts and ask your accountant to study them.

11. Be careful about buying a franchise from a franchisor who is not a member of the British Franchise Association (see Reference for address). Membership does not guarantee the success of your business or the franchisor's business. And a number of quite reputable franchisors do not belong to the association. However, members agree to abide by a code of ethics. Ask a franchisor why it is not a member, if it is not.

12. Check that your territory is properly marked out (and you receive a clearly defined map of it). What market research has been done to ensure the territory is promising enough to provide the estimated sales? Do your own analysis – don't rely on the franchisor.

13. Examine what will happen if you die, want to sell your franchise, disagree with your franchisor or want to renew at the end of the term of the franchise (see p. 116).

14. What sort of product is it? It must have a useful life of at least the length of the franchise which you are purchasing. There is very little point in buying a five-year franchise for a product with a life of only three years.

15. Carry out market research in exactly the same way as if you were setting up the business on your own. Chapter 2, 'Who will buy?' (p. 13), should help you to do this. Do not rely on market statistics or views passed on by the franchisor.

16. Check that the product has been patented or the name registered as a trade mark, otherwise the franchise you buy could be worthless.

17. How will the advertising levels be maintained? Does the franchisor make a firm commitment in the contract to spend certain amounts on promoting the brand name?

18. What is the quality of the field force run by the franchisor? How often will they visit? Are they competent to give sound business advice? What will happen if your business runs into difficulties?

19. The relationship between franchisee and franchisor may, in a few cases, prove difficult to maintain at a harmonious level. What are the lines of communication? Do you think that you will be able to build a good relationship with this particular franchisor?

20. If it is a good franchise, you will face competition from other would-be franchisees. So you should expect a grilling. And if you are not subjected to close investigation, this may indicate that the franchisor is short of buyers.

21. Many points on which you need information before you tie up an agreement with a franchisor are listed in this chapter. Make sure you cover them in your discussions, and check the franchisor's response.

How a franchise works in detail

In this section, the following topics are examined:

❏ Cost (see overleaf)

❏ Finance (p. 110)

❏ Territory (p. 110)

❏ Premises (p. 111)

❏ Operations manual (p. 111)

❏ Training (p. 111)

❏ Opening (p. 112)

❏ On-going support and supervision (p. 112)

❏ Franchising and pyramid selling (p. 113)

❏ Finding and buying a franchise (p. 114).

Cost

The cost to you could be made up of one or more of the following charges. There will be the initial cost of a franchise, which includes the initial fee, and most likely there will be a continuing fee (also called royalty or service fee). There may also be an advertising levy, a mark-up paid on goods or equipment supplied by the franchisor and a mark-up if you lease premises from the franchisor.

You also need to look out for any hidden costs of financing, which may occur if the franchisor obtains a commission on introducing you to a business providing finance or to a leasing company, if you lease equipment. It is only a cost to you, of course, if you could have arranged cheaper finance elsewhere.

❑ *initial cost:* the range of prices for all franchises is wide; it could be as little as £5,000, for example, or as much as £5 million, but typically £200,000. Usually, the initial fee which goes to the franchisor is between 5 and 10 per cent of the total investment but can be as much as 40 or 50 per cent.

There is no typical start-up package, but below is an example of the sort of items which could be included in the initial cost:

Shopfitting	£13,000
Equipment	15,000
Initial stock	8,000
Initial franchise fee	4,000
TOTAL	£40,000

The initial franchise fee is what you are paying to be given the right to use the brand name within a certain territory and to be trained and provided with advice

❑ *service fee:* the service fee payable can also vary quite a lot, from nil up to 20 per cent of sales, but is probably on average around 7–8 per cent. The service fee could be paid weekly or monthly. The fact that the service fee is nil does not necessarily mean that all you are paying will be the initial start-up cost. Franchisors can also be paid by using mark-ups on products and equipment.

A low service fee is not necessarily an advantage for you. It is crucial that the franchisor retains an on-going interest in promotion and improvement of the business format, and that will only be achieved by the reliance on some sort of continuing payment from the franchisee.

The franchisor prefers to base the service fee on sales rather than profits. This is because monitoring the franchisee accounts to ensure that the franchisor is receiving the proper amount can be time-consuming and expensive. If the fee is based on profits rather than sales, the monitoring has to apply to costs as well as sales, doubling the difficulty of the task.

However, a fee based on sales can be disadvantageous to the franchisee. If the costs of the enterprise prove to be higher than forecast, paying the service fee could be an onerous burden for the franchisee.

You should not underestimate the size of the service fee, because it is based on sales not profits. If, for example, your costs are 60 per cent of your sales value, a service fee of 10 per cent of sales translates into a service fee of a quarter of the profits you make. Work out the figures before you sign.

One point to watch out for is what happens at the end of the original franchise contract if you want to renew. Does the contract allow the franchisor to increase the size of the service fee? Try to negotiate on this, as you do not want a bigger percentage of your hard work to be passed over to the franchisor

❑ *advertising levy:* a number of franchise packages charge an advertising levy as well as the service fee. This is usually calculated as a percentage of sales and paid at the same time as the service fee. The existence of an advertising levy could be regarded as an advantage for a franchise if promotion of the brand name is a very important part of the franchise success. If an advertising levy is made, look to see if this will be audited separately in the franchisor's accounts so that you can see that it has indeed been used for that purpose and that alone, not just disappeared into the franchisor's pocket.

If there is no separate advertising levy, the franchisor may undertake to spend a certain proportion of the service fee each year. The other common alternative for advertising is that the franchisor will undertake to advertise as and when needed. With some franchises, the franchisee is expected to advertise as well as, or even instead of, the franchisor. This could lead to promotions which are at odds with each other – and may mean that the prestige of the franchise name deteriorates

❑ *mark-ups:* one apparent advantage of grouping together can be that buying in greater bulk can mean bigger discounts and cheaper supplies. This should also apply to franchises, where supplies are often an important part of the cost of the enterprise. However, some franchisors put on mark-ups which deprive the franchisees of any benefit from bulk purchase

❑ *hidden costs of financing:* it is not unusual for companies to pay commission to someone who introduces a new customer to them. This does not necessarily mean that you will get a bad deal if your franchisor helps you to arrange finance. But it does mean that you should shop around to satisfy yourself that you cannot organize a more attractive deal elsewhere. In practice, you may find it difficult to arrange finance except through the franchisor, but you should examine the possibility.

Finance

Raising money to finance the purchase of a franchise is treated in the same way as raising money to start any new business. All the clearing banks have specialist franchise units and, on the whole, they appear to look more favourably upon the average franchise application than on the average start-up. This is because a franchise is believed to offer a lower risk to a lender.

However, any bank will require that a prospective franchisee contributes a proportion of the start-up capital, around forty per cent. The remaining sixty per cent could be financed by the bank. Of course, don't forget that the lower the level of your borrowing the greater the chance of your business surviving.

Any loan will need to be repaid by the end of the franchise term; however, there may be some leeway on the initial repayments of capital. For example, a repayment holiday could be arranged until the business is showing a profit.

If the bank requires security this could be provided by a charge on the business assets, such as premises or equipment, but only if you run the franchise as a limited company. If you remain a sole trader, a mortgage on your house may be acceptable.

Territory

The interests of the franchisor and franchisee may clash when it comes to the allocation of territory. The franchisor would like the option to introduce another franchisee to the area to maximize sales and profits. The franchisee, on the other hand, does not want to be competing with another business on the same patch, selling identical goods.

Whatever is granted in terms of rights, it is important to have clear identification of the territory. Check that it is clearly specified in the contract. The delineation of the territory should also be relevant to the particular trade. If it is a shop, perhaps a certain number of miles from the site would be relevant. If it is a service franchise, perhaps a Yellow Pages division of territories would be more suitable.

It is also important to ensure that the territory is large enough to support a business of the type proposed. If you have any doubts, do not buy.

Premises

There is no set practice on whether the premises are owned or leased by the franchisor and sublet to the franchisee or the premises are owned and leased by the franchisee. It varies from franchise to franchise. Controlling the premises has advantages either way. If the franchisor owns the site, and if the franchise is not renewed, a valuable, well-placed site is not lost, as far as the franchisor is concerned. Conversely, if you are the franchisee and the premises are in your name, when it comes to renewal, you can use the site for another business if you would prefer.

Whatever the position about tenure, the location of a site, especially if it is for a shop, needs to be examined carefully, in exactly the same way as for any other business (p. 174). Do not take the franchisor's word for it.

Operations manual

This is where the franchisor puts all the know-how of the business; it should incorporate the essence of the business format you are buying. One of the terms in the contract will be that you must adhere to the manual.

It will include details on everything: accounting systems, recruitment, how to carry out the actual process of the business (for example, grill a hamburger, print a leaflet or unblock a drain), reporting systems and so on. You should see a copy of the manual before you buy. Make sure you understand what is in there; it is how you will have to behave in your business while you own the franchise.

An indicator of the on-going interest of the franchisor can be how frequently the manual is updated. Ask how often this has been done.

Training

Training is an important part of what a franchisor is offering. Before you sign the contract, you need a clear idea of how much training there will be and how long it will take. You should expect training in all the basic business skills you will need to run a business. This includes financial methods, stock levels, operating the equipment, carrying out the process of the business, working out accounts and PAYE, employment law, VAT and so on *ad infinitum*.

Opening

The franchisor should help you to start your business. If it is a retail business, once the premises have been found, the franchisor will help organize the shopfitting. Indeed, it may be part of the agreement, as it may be that the shopfitting has to conform to the brand image: the colours, style of counter, type of shelves and so on.

Additionally, there will be advice available (it may even be a requirement to follow it) on the equipment and amount and mix of opening stock you should have. Find out before you sign what the franchisor's policy is on this and satisfy yourself that you are not being cornered into a policy of over-equipping and over-stocking.

To have a successful opening day, you will need publicity and perhaps an opening ceremony; you should get help and advice on how to advertise and arrange media coverage. Find out the franchisor's level of commitment on this.

On-going support and supervision

This could consist of six elements:

❏ refresher training (p.111)

❏ product research and development (see below)

❏ troubleshooters and supervisors who give regular visits (see opposite)

❏ updated operations manual (p. 111)

❏ advertising the brand as a whole (p. 109)

❏ advice on an individual level about promotion (see opposite).

Products do not last for ever. So for any business there needs to be continuous assessment of the product to see how well it meets its customers' needs, not just in the past, but now and in the future. Any market trends need to be taken into account and the product may need altering over the years to meet the new criteria. Or, a completely new product may need to be evolved. For a franchise to be successful, the franchisor should devote some energy to this. Check what your franchisor's policy will be on this before buying.

The downside to this is that any innovations or alterations could end up being costly for the franchisee. Try to establish what the future plans of the franchisor will be and check what the agreement says about implementation of any new developments.

Another element of support and supervision by the franchisor is the help available if you or the business are in difficulties, for example, are there troubleshooters to provide guidance? The sort of questions you want the franchisor to answer include:

❑ how often will support visits be made and what is the calibre of the support staff?

❑ if the business is struggling to break even, does the franchisor have special troubleshooters? If not, what sort of help will be available?

❑ what happens if the equipment does not work properly? Are there maintenance facilities and what is the response time?

❑ if you are ill, is there an emergency staff team available to take over?

As well as the positive side of providing support, you must recognize that the supervisory team also fulfil the role of monitor for the franchisor. You will have to accept that they will want to examine your records and books on a regular basis, check that you are not understating sales (or whatever it is that the service fee is based on) and ensure that the service fee is paid on time.

A final element of support which you need to investigate before you buy is the advice available on promotion of your business. While it is a better arrangement for the franchisor to carry out the advertising and promotion of the product name on a national basis, you may feel that there are opportunities which allow you to boost your business by advertising and promoting locally. The franchisor may be able to advise on this. In fact, the franchisor may insist as part of the agreement that you promote locally. For example, is the amount of expenditure specified and will it prove onerous?

Franchising and pyramid selling

As a result of problems with pyramid selling schemes (where people join a scheme on the promise of making a gain through recruiting further members), the Trading Schemes Act came into effect from 6 February 1997 onwards. The Act was not intended to cover bona fide businesses which actually have goods or services to sell. However, pyramid schemes come in many guises, so the Act has been designed to apply to all trading schemes unless an exemption applies. This means that the Act, which imposes strict rules on how schemes may be advertised and run, could affect many franchises. The two main caveats which would exclude a franchise from the terms of the Act are:

❑ if all the franchisees are registered for VAT, or

❑ the franchise operates through a single tier only. For example, if there is a single franchisor for the UK and all franchisees are recruited by that single master franchisor, the scheme could be exempt. But if there is a layer of several different franchisors for different regions of the UK who each recruit franchisees, the scheme would be caught by the Act. Similarly, if the franchisees themselves recruit further franchisees or even if they contract self-employed people to carry out their work, the scheme would be caught by the Act.

Finding and buying a franchise

There are several hundred different franchises. There are 66 full members of the British Franchise Association and 34 registered associates. Associate members have begun franchising but do not yet have a track record; full members are longer established franchisors. In addition, there is a provisional listing for companies which are developing a franchise concept along the lines recommended by the British Franchise Association but who do not yet have any franchisees in place.

To start your search for a franchise you could write to the Association. It has a Franchisee Guide which provides advice on how to evaluate a franchise, together with a list of franchisor members and affiliated professional advisers. The Guide costs £25 including postage and packing. The details are given in Reference.

There are a number of organizations operating as franchise consultants who say they will give advice on finding a franchise. Before you use one, be absolutely certain that it is not an organization concerned solely, or even mainly, with finding franchisees for one or two franchise companies. If this were the case, the impartiality of the advice can be discounted. There are a couple of directories which may give you a head start (see Reference).

Work out some rough guidelines for the sort of business you would be happy to be in and the sorts of areas of the country you would be prepared to move to. Estimate the sort of price you could pay, bearing in mind that you should be able to invest at least one-third, while borrowing the remaining two-thirds is a possibility.

Write to a shortlist of five or six franchise companies, asking them to send you the details you need. This should include projections of the likely level of business and a draft contract, as well as the areas where the company currently has a franchisee vacancy.

Once you have received the information, the hard work begins. Consult your solicitor and accountant. Carry out your own very thorough research investigating among other aspects, marketing, advertising, product lines, financial aspects, supervision. Use the guide on p. 105 to assess each franchise.

It is important to remember that if the franchise is a good one, the franchisor will be able to pick and choose from applicants. Treat the negotiation with the franchisor from two points of view:

❑ the need to investigate and assess the worth of the franchise

❑ the need to sell yourself as an ideal applicant to the franchisor.

For a good franchise, you will need to provide references along with much more information about your suitability as a franchisee.

While you are negotiating, you may be able to reserve a particular territory by placing a deposit. The amount of the deposit and whether it is partially refundable or not varies from franchise to franchise. Sometimes the deposit is set against the initial fee on signing. Check the terms and the franchisor's references before you pay it.

The contract

This is the kernel of all franchises. Once you have signed it, it will rule your life. Do not skimp on independent legal advice, although it is unlikely to be negotiable as the franchisor will want to ensure that the same conditions apply to all franchisees.

The contract will attempt to ensure that you run the business along the lines specified by the franchisor. The contract should cover these areas:

❑ the type of business, its name and the use to which it can be put

❑ the territory where the franchisee has the right to use the name

❑ how long the franchise will run

❑ what the franchisee will have to pay (the initial fee and service fee)

❑ if the franchisee wants to sell

❑ if either the franchisee or franchisor wants to end the agreement

❑ what both the franchisor and franchisee have agreed to do.

The type of business, its name

This part of the contract will describe the franchise. It will indicate that the franchisor has registered any relevant trade mark or patented any invention. The franchisee will probably have to agree not to handle any trade mark, product or service belonging to a competitor of the franchisor.

The territory

The contract may specify a protected or privileged right to carry out your business in a particular area, defined by a map or postal code, for example. Unfortunately, it is very difficult to stop another franchisor, or indeed any competitor, encroaching upon your particular area.

How long the franchise will run

The typical length of a franchise could be five years or could be ten. But it could be as short as three or as long as twenty. Normally, you can renew the franchise at the end of the original agreed period, but this may be subject to satisfactory performance. You should certainly want an option to renew and you should try to ensure that the legal wording about what constitutes a 'satisfactory performance' is clear to you, fair to you and can be enforced by you. This is essential, because unless you have the lease on the premises, you would have very little to show for your work at the end of the initial franchise period. You would not be able to sell the business as a going concern, because you would no longer have the rights to the name or to use the business format, and without these there is little goodwill to be attached to the business.

Some contracts specify that if you do not wish to renew, the franchisor will buy the business from you, including a value for goodwill. The value put on the business will be set by an independent accountant.

If you have an option to renew, the contract may specify that certain sums of money are spent to update the premises and smarten the business. The details of this commitment need to be buttoned down in the contract. In any case, the option to renew may well be to renew on the terms currently on offer to franchisees; these may be less favourable to a franchisee than the terms on which you originally signed.

If you have decided not to look for another agreement with the franchisor, the contract may restrict your activities. It may specify that you cannot carry on a similar or competing business for a certain length of time.

What the franchisee will have to pay

The contract will specify the amount and the nature of the fees which will be paid, that is, the initial fee, the service fee (or royalty) and, if applicable, the advertising levy.

If the franchisee wants to sell

Most agreements include some arrangement whereby the franchisee can sell their business during the course of the term. The contract may specify that the franchisor will be entitled to first refusal. Additionally, one of the conditions will be that the franchisor has to agree that your buyer is properly qualified to run it. Your buyer will have to receive training and probably have to be prepared to sign a new agreement. However, in reality, it will be difficult to give the same sort of rigorous vetting that the franchisor can do for the initial holder.

Watch out for the sort of agreement which allows the franchisor to charge high transfer (or other) fees on a sale. This sort of condition could effectively block any sale you might make, except to the franchisor on poor terms.

A contract should also include the terms and conditions which apply if you die during the agreed period of the franchise.

If franchisee or franchisor wants to end the agreement

It is possible that you want to end the agreement, if you find that the business is hard going, for example. In those circumstances, it may be difficult to find a buyer. On the other hand, it is not especially in the franchisor's interests to insist on keeping you to the agreement if you are not making a success of it. The contract should deal with what can be done in these circumstances. You need to satisfy yourself that the contract would treat you fairly.

The contract will also specify the conditions under which the franchisor can end the agreement. This could occur if you break the agreement which you sign and fail to meet your obligations under it.

A few of the more stringent conditions may be:

❑ minimum performance target

❑ agreement to purchase minimum amounts of goods and merchandise

❑ the requirement to bring your unit up to standard, if necessary.

Experience is now indicating that, with a good franchisor, renewals are made and some are now on their third or fourth term.

What franchisee and franchisor have agreed to do

The contract will stipulate what both of you must do to keep your side of the bargain. For example, for the franchisor the rules about training, supervision, advertising, support and maintenance and management services etc. should be specified.

The franchisee will have to operate according to the manual and allow the franchisor's staff to monitor the business activities. There will be a requirement not to handle the trade marks, products and services belonging to any competing business of the franchisor's or possibly to trade in any other area allocated to another franchisee.

Setting up as a franchisor

This aspect of franchising is beyond the scope of the guide, although your interests can be interpreted from what is said about the franchisee's interests. Here are a few brief guidelines:

❏ you need to have proved in practice that the business format works. This is done by establishing a pilot operation which should be run exactly along the same lines as the proposed franchise. All the systems and products should be tried out here and all the wrinkles ironed out before selling any franchises. Ideally, the pilot should have run for two years. It goes almost without saying that the pilot has to be successful, otherwise you will not be able to sell any franchises

❏ the business format needs to be distinctive in its image and/ or its way of operating

❏ it must be possible to pass on the format successfully to others

❏ the format needs to be capable of earning high enough profits to give both the franchisee and franchisor an adequate living.

The British Franchise Association (see Reference) has a Franchisor's Guide, which costs £44 (including postage and packing) and provides advice on franchising an existing business.

Summary

1. The main advantage of starting a business by buying a franchise is that a lot of the initial start-up problems have already been sorted out; this means there should be a greater chance of survival than starting a business from scratch yourself.

2. The main disadvantages are that there is a loss of independence because of your commitments to a franchisor; you also lose the possibility of earning exceptionally high profits, because the profits are divided between the two of you.

3. Use the guide to choosing a franchise on p. 105 to help you sort out the good from the bad.

4. The franchisor should provide support and development throughout the franchise.

5. Because of uncertainty about what will happen at the end of the initial agreed period of the franchise, your decision to buy or not should be based on the initial period only.

6. Use your own advisers, for example, bank, solicitor and accountant, and carry out your own research into finance, the market, the product, the franchisor, the location and the detailed terms of the franchise. Do not rely on the word of the franchisor.

Other chapters to read

2. **Who will buy?** (p. 13)
5. **Are you sure?** (p. 53)
23. **Raising the money** (p. 269)

11. **The right name**

At an early stage in your planning, the question will come up: 'What am I going to call my business?' or 'What am I going to call my product?' You may be tempted to spend a couple of minutes and then plump for your own name or your initials, and move on to other more important planning tasks. But this would be a mistake.

Choosing a name is a long-term decision, which is all wrapped up with working out what you are trying to sell and identifying why customers will buy from you rather than your competitors. Your company or product name should encapsulate a message to potential or existing customers. This will not happen overnight; it takes many years to build up a name to carry the message you want. But one thing is for sure, you cannot change horses mid-stream. The name you plump for now should be the name you still have in five, ten years' time.

Choosing a name

Before you start the search for a name, there is quite a lot of background thinking you need to do about your marketplace, your competitors and your product.

Why do people buy from you?

If you analyse why people buy a particular product or service, the list might include things like:

❑ it is cheaper

❑ the product has a special feature which others do not have

❑ the service is near by and is very convenient

❑ its running costs or maintenance are less

❑ there is 24-hour-guaranteed service.

These are all rational reasons, capable of proof. If your product or service has one feature, or more, which are like this you have a primary benefit. You may be able to achieve your sales on this alone.

The list of reasons why people buy a product might also include:

- ❑ it is better

- ❑ it looks good

- ❑ the quality of the service is high

- ❑ it is believed to be very reliable

- ❑ it is better value for money

- ❑ the design is excellent.

These are all emotional reasons, which may be real or imagined. But they reflect how customers feel about a product.

A combination of the emotional and the rational reasons gives a product its reputation (or brand image).

How does your product rate?

Your product may have some unique element; if so, you are probably unusual. The chances are that there is nothing that much different or better about what you are going to do than your competitors. But that does not mean you will not be more profitable, make more sales and get a bigger share of the market than someone with a product which does have unique features.

Creating a 'good feeling' among buyers about your product can give you a better general reputation, can make you better thought of and more widely known. Giving your business an identity can make you successful.

However, creating an image of quality and reliability for a utilitarian product can lead to a downfall if your product or service does not live up to it. The product must be good, if it is not the best; the service must be reliable, if not the most reliable.

Where does name come in?

You want to get the name of your business or product into the position that it summarizes all the emotional and rational feelings about the product. So, if a potential customer hears the name, it instantly gives a good connotation. On day one of your business, this will not happen. You must plan carefully to achieve it over a number of years.

Your first step is to select a name which does not, by itself, cause any feeling of antipathy. Ideally, the name on its own should give a clue to your image, but this is a counsel of perfection. You should at least aim for the name to generate neutral feelings in the early stages, until you have built the image from scratch.

One name or two?

Should your business and product share the same name? There is no clear-cut answer to this one, and for a small business it may not be very important. You will not have the resources to create two brand images, one for the product and one for your business. In any case, it could be confusing. So, even with separate names, you will be promoting only one.

If I'm selling to industry, do I bother with image?

Yes. You may be selling to a buyer from an industrial firm but, with the other hat on, the buyer is also a normal human being. This means that he or she will probably have the same amount of prejudices as a member of the general public buying soap. It is as important to create a good feeling about your product with an industrial customer as with a domestic one.

If my product has a unique feature, do I have to bother with image?

Yes. You may have some original feature, but once you have launched it on the market, your competitors will be beavering away to make sure that it does not stay unique for very long. And, on the whole, you cannot patent an idea, only a mechanism, so you may not be able to rely on protection (p. 128). If you do not concentrate on the image of your product, and your competitive advantage is subsequently eroded because other products are improved, the future of your business may not look so rosy. Building an image for your product is a low-risk safety route.

What image do you want to create?

This is all linked up with the market research you will have done (p. 13), a crucial stage of your planning. You will have found that there are sectors within the market. For example, if you were considering opening a picture framing business, you might find the following sectors:

❑ do-it-yourself

❑ speedy service

❑ mail order

❑ high-quality frames

❑ a service with advice from a designer or artist.

Your research will identify the size and growth of each sector, where the competition lies, and what are the prime demands by customers in each sector. In turn, your decisions will be to go for one or more sectors, to look at your service compared to the competitors and to focus on what your customer wants. This will give you guidance on what sort of image to build for your business.

Logo – a no-go?

A logo or logotype may be nothing more than a word, the name of your company or product, always shown in the same typeface or in the same colour, or, perhaps, within a simple shape. It could also include an unusual or memorable shape; one which people will recognize quickly, and eventually come to associate with all their perceptions of your product.

Using a logo can emphasize your name and get greater customer awareness. If you can afford to do it, do it. But, do not rely on your printer. Paying an adviser, such as a designer, may be worthwhile (p. 198). In your dealings with an adviser, specify that the logo must be cheap to reproduce, as once you have got it, you will use it on everything you can. So you do not want to end up with a beautiful logo which costs you an arm and a leg every time you want new quantities of stationery.

Do not make snap decisions on logos; if you can, try a little bit of market research on potential buyers to assess their reaction or possibly ask colleagues, family or friends.

Tips on choosing a name

1. Made-up words can make good product or business names. They may not arouse any positive feelings about your business, but they are also unlikely to create negative ones. If you are going to register that name as a trade mark, you will stand a greater chance of success in doing so, if it is a made-up word (p. 134).

2. If you are going to use an existing word, if possible try it out on potential buyers to check that you will not create a bad impression simply because of the name.

3. Use brainstorming sessions with family and friends as well as colleagues to produce a list of names for consideration.

4. Check that the name you prefer is not used by another product or business in the same or similar market.

5. Avoid initials: it is difficult in the short term to create a comfortable feeling about a business or product with initials.

6. If you think that some of your business will come through Yellow Pages or other alphabetic listings, choose names beginning with A.

7. Check that the name you choose does not mean anything nasty in a foreign language (for example, look it up in dictionaries in the library). If you are interested in selling throughout Europe, consider whether your proposed name is suitable.

8. Very complicated words need careful consideration. If a customer has to ask you to spell the word when it is first mentioned, this can be a positive reinforcement for recognition in future. But, if it is just too difficult, it may be a disadvantage.

9. A name which uses all capital letters, for example, FLAG, can stand out in a chunk of written text, giving the name prominence.

10. Finally, ask yourself if the name seems right for the image you want to project.

What the law says about names

With a limited company, you will not be allowed to register names:

❑ which are considered the same as that of an existing company. You can check this by looking at the Index in the Public Search Rooms at Cardiff, Edinburgh or London or by phone to Companies House

❑ contains 'limited' or its equivalent anywhere else in your company name but at the end

❑ could be considered offensive or illegal.

And you're unlikely to be able to register a name which could give the impression of a connection with the government or local authority. There is also a range of words that require the agreement of the Secretary of State or various other bodies before you can use them. Examples are Abortion, British, Building Society, Royal, Windsor, National and English. There are around eighty of these words altogether. There are other rules about company names, so advice from your solicitor would be helpful.

If you are a sole trader and want to use a business name other than your own surname, there are certain rules you have to observe. However, you are not required to register your business name anywhere, but you must disclose your own name in various ways. You must put your own name and address legibly on all business letters, on written orders for goods and services, on invoices and on written demands for payments of debts. You must display your name and address prominently at your business premises or at any place to which your customers and suppliers have access. And if anyone with whom you are discussing business asks you to disclose your own name and address, you must do so immediately in writing.

Companies and sole traders can get free advice on business names from Companies House in Cardiff (see the Reference section).

Building your reputation

Once you have selected your business or product name, your next strategy is to devise means of getting your name noticed by as many of your target customers as you can. Obviously, you do not want your name to be associated with any bad news, so you may find that you do not want to take up every opportunity to publicize your business name. What you should aim for is that your business or product name comes instantly to mind in your potential buyers, but with a favourable impression.

Letterheads

This is the single most important way for most of the self-employed and small businesses to create some sort of image about themselves. Poor quality paper suggests cheap, poor quality service. Spend more on the paper to create that good impression.

It is tempting, especially if you know little about marketing or design, to play safe and choose white paper with black type for your letterheads. But consider experimenting with some draft versions before making your choice; it may cost a little extra, but if it helps create the image you are seeking you should do it. Your local instant print or photocopying shop can be very helpful, either printing small-run samples of different types or positions, or at least letting you re-arrange elements (name, logo, address) and photocopying the permutations.

Consider:

- ❏ different colour paper
- ❏ different colour type
- ❏ try positioning your business name in the centre or to the right
- ❏ different typefaces for name and address
- ❏ try big-sized and small-sized typefaces
- ❏ adding a line to give a more finished appearance

Once you have settled on your letterhead, look carefully at your other stationery needs. If your work is the type where you send out few invoices for large sums of money, you may not need separate invoices, but can use ordinary stationery. Will you need compliments slips, or will business cards suffice if you will only need them for a few occasions? Whatever stationery you do require, the colour and typeface should be uniform throughout the range. If you have a logo, it should be included in all your stationery.

If you are in retailing, you may decide that letterheads are not an important tool for you in creating an image. While this may be so with customers, letterheads are still needed to create that right image with suppliers, on whom you rely for credit.

Labels and stickers

If you can see any opportunity for using labels and stickers on your products, seize it. These can also carry the message you want. There must be continuity with your chosen letterheads: colour, style, typeface and logo – if you have one – all identical to your stationery. In a shop, you might consider having price stickers. On garments or other material items like rugs, tablewear and so on, labels should be sewn in.

Packaging

The package says lots about the goods, so take the opportunity to reinforce the message you are sending to customers. The style of the packaging should be consistent with all the other items for promoting your image, and with your chosen image itself. Packaging is an extension or even an integral part of your products.

Other ideas

These can all help build your reputation:

❑ advertising

❑ public relations

❑ appearance of salespeople

❑ how you answer the telephone

❑ vehicles: their cleanliness and livery, that is, the colour or markings on them.

Summary

1. People buy particular products for rational and emotional reasons.

2. You should aim to create a 'good feeling', a brand image, a reputation, about your product among customers. Make sure that your product can live up to this.

3. Industrial or unique products still need brand images.

4. Analyse your market and customer requirements to decide on image.

5. A business or product name will be built up over the years to summarize what your image is all about.

6. If you can afford it, have a logo designed for you.

7. Try to encapsulate as many pleasant (or positive) associations in your name as you can.

8. Letterheads are a most important way of projecting messages about your business. Keep the style consistent with labels, stickers and packaging.

Other chapters to read

2. **Who will buy?** (p. 13)
4. **Your business identity** (p. 38)
13. **Getting the message across** (p. 137)
14. **Selling** (p. 149)

12. **Beating the pirates**

Successful small businesses do not need to be founded on an invention or an original design. The Eureka syndrome can play a very small part in the success of a business. A much more important factor is that there is a market there which wants to buy your product. The ultimate in good indicators for success would be a strong market and an original product. But often there is not a ready-built marketplace waiting for inventions. You may need to educate customers. This can be expensive as well as time-consuming.

However, if you have thought of an invention, a trade mark or an original design which could form the kernel of a successful small business, is it worth trying to protect it with the law? Almost certainly, yes is the answer. If the idea, for example, can be turned into profits, someone else may try to copy it and you should obtain the best protection you can, so that you make the profits, not the imitator.

The law cannot protect alone. First, you have to be vigilant in watching out for infringements. Second, and more importantly, the best protection of all is guaranteed by carrying out effective marketing: this can turn a product based on an invention, for example, into the leading product and establish your business as the market leader (p. 169).

What is in this chapter?

❑ What to do with an invention (below)

❑ What to do with a design (p. 131)

❑ What to do with a trade or service mark (p. 133)

❑ Getting help and advice (p. 135).

What to do with an invention

What is an invention which can be patented?

There are four requirements for something to be regarded as an invention for patent purposes. These are that it must:

❑ *be new:* it must not have been published or made known anywhere in the world previously

❑ *involve an inventive step:* by and large this means that it must not be obvious to another person with knowledge of that particular subject

❑ *be capable of industrial application:* an idea which cannot be made or used will not be counted as an invention

❑ *not be excluded:* there are various categories which are excluded by law. These include something which is a discovery (that is, you found out about it, but did not invent it), scientific theory or mathematical method, mental process, literary, artistic or aesthetic creation, playing a game, presentation of information or a computer program.

Other ideas which are excluded are anything which would be regarded as encouraging offensive, immoral or anti-social behaviour, a new animal or plant variety or a method of diagnosis or surgery for animals or humans.

What is a patent?

A patent of invention is granted by a government body. It gives the owner of an invention the right to take legal action against others who may be trying to take commercial advantage of the invention without getting the owner's permission. This right is granted in return for complete disclosure by the owner of his invention.

The body which grants the UK patent is the Patent Office (see Reference for address). A UK patent can last up to twenty years from the date on which you first hand over documents to the Patent Office. After the first four years you have to pay a yearly fee to keep it in force. Note that the four years start from the date you first applied for the patent. A national patent only gives protection for the country in which it is granted.

If your invention is of a type that you believe you may want to exploit throughout Europe, not just in the UK, it could be cheaper to take advantage of the European Patent Convention. This allows you to obtain patent rights in a number of European countries. You need to make only one patent application, whereas if you applied for a UK patent first, you would then need to apply for patents in each of the individual countries which you thought important.

To file a European patent application, if you live in the UK, you apply at the Patent Office in Newport, Gwent (see Reference for address).

Can you get a patent?

The main criterion for granting a patent is whether or not the invention meets the four guidelines about what an invention is (see p. 129).

One area you have to be particularly careful about is that you should not tell anyone (apart from in confidence to a patent agent, which would be a good idea) or publish information about your invention before you file your application at the Patent Office. If your invention is not kept secret, it may mean that, even if no one else has thought of your idea, you will not be able to get a patent.

Occasionally, even if you have been granted a patent, you may find that someone challenges it. This could be on the grounds that someone else had already thought of the invention and had made details of it public before you filed your application for your patent. The other person may have decided not to bother to apply for a patent. Making details of it public would include describing it in a trade journal or exhibiting it or selling it.

What does it cost?

When you first file your application, you have to enclose a fee of £25. Within a year, you will have to pay a fee of £130 for a preliminary search and examination. If you still decide to go ahead with your patent application there is another fee of £70. To keep the patent in force for the maximum twenty years, there is a yearly renewal fee, which increases each year. For the fourth year of the patent it starts at £110 and rises to £450 for the final year.

However, many inventors use a patent agent (p. 135) to help with the application, as it can truly be a complicated and very lengthy task. You would have to check the fees before employing one. The cost (in official fees up to grant of the patent) for a European patent is more – in total around £1,750 if you want the patent for five countries, for example, compared with the UK patent of around £225. After the patent is granted, renewal fees are payable to each of the designated countries.

A guide to obtaining a UK patent

1. Keep mum about your invention, unless to a patent agent (p. 135).

2. Complete and file patents form 1/77 in the Patent Office, together with the necessary fee. With the form should be sent a description of the invention. This description must be drafted in accordance with the rules laid down by the Patent Office which specify the exact format it should take. It must describe the invention fully and clearly enough so that a competent person could follow the description and build it or carry out the process. Enclose two copies, preferably typed and on A4 size paper.

3. You will receive a receipt with the date of filing and a number. This gives you your priority date which gives you precedence over the same invention being filed later. But this is no guarantee that the same invention has not already been publicized elsewhere by another person (see left).

4. During the next year, examine the commercial possibilities of your invention and decide whether to press on with your application or let it lapse.

5. If you make an improvement to your invention, you cannot add it to your first application but would have to file a new one. However, as long as you do this within a year of the priority date, that date will apply to whatever is in the new application which was also in the first application. The first application can now be allowed to lapse.

6. Within a year of the priority date you need to file a request for a preliminary search and examination on patents form 9/77, together with the required fee. If you do not do this, your application lapses. You will also need to file the patent 'claims' which define in words the monopoly sought and an 'abstract', a short summary of the invention.

7. Once the search has been carried out by a Patent Office Examiner, a search report will be issued. This is a list of relevant documents so you can compare your invention with others and decide whether your application is likely to be successful.

8. If you do not withdraw your application at this stage, your application will be published by the Patent Office without any changes.

9. Within six months of publication of the application, you have to file the next form (Form 10/77), plus the required fee. There is now a much more detailed examination of your invention.

10. As a result of this substantive examination, amendments may be required by the Examiner. If these are carried out satisfactorily and within the required time, the patent will be granted.

What to do with a design

Sometimes the success or failure of a product depends not only on how it works, but on what it looks like. The outward shape or decorative appearance of a product can also be protected, either by:

❏ relying on the automatic protection of design right (a bit like copyright), or by

❏ registering the design, by applying to the Patent Office. This gives stronger protection but not all designs can be registered – and it takes time and money to register.

What protection does design right give you?

Design right means someone else cannot copy the shape or configuration of an article if it is an original, non-commonplace design. Design right does not apply, for example, to items like wallpapers or textiles (but these may still be protected by copyright and you may be able to register them).

Design right protection lasts for the shorter of:

❏ ten years from the end of the year in which you first start selling articles made to the design, or

❏ fifteen years from the end of the year in which you created the design.

You have an exclusive right for the first five years after you start selling the articles, and in the remaining five years others can obtain a licence to the design – but you don't have to hand over drawings or know-how.

The limits to design right are that:

❏ something you design to fit or match an article designed by someone else won't get protection

❏ design right protection applies in the UK only.

What is a registered design?

Registering a design gives you a monopoly right for the 'look' of an article or set of articles manufactured from the design. The protection lasts for twenty-five years, but you must renew it every five years.

You can't register a design either if the outward appearance of the article is not important or if the shape of the article is determined by the shape of another item. And the design must be 'new', otherwise registration won't be granted. For this reason, it is important to keep the details of the design secret before you register; if you have not done so, it will not count as new.

Registration gives protection in the UK; some countries accept registration as equivalent to an independent registration in their country. In other countries, UK registration will be accepted as establishing a 'priority' date for a local application.

What does it cost?

If you are registering the pattern of an article made substantially of lace or a textile design which consists of checks and stripes, the fee is £45. For all other single items, the fee is £60. You can register the design of a set of items for £90. To count as a set, each item must basically be a variant of the other – for example, a three piece suite would usually count as a set; a teaset could count as a set if you wanted just to register the pattern used on all the items, but if you wanted to register the shape of the items too, you would need to register separately the cup, the teapot, the creamer and the jug.

A guide to registration of a design

1. Keep mum about your design, except in confidence to a patent agent.

2. Tell the Designs Registry what the design is and what is going to be made from it. You must do this with a copy of the design, for example, a drawing or a photograph, in accordance with the rules laid down by the Designs Registry. Remember to send the required fee.

3. The Registry carries out searches and assesses whether the design is original and new. If it is, registration is granted.

What to do with a trade or service mark

What is a trade mark?

A trade mark is something which identifies a product in the eyes of the consumer. The consumer will know who has manufactured the goods or who is selling them. A service mark is something which identifies a service. Trade and service marks are closely linked with the idea of building loyalty among customers, so that they will choose your product or service over another similar one.

A trade or service mark can be a word or a symbol, such as a logo. Since 1994, distinctive smells and three dimensional shapes can also be registered as trade marks. Obviously, what you use as your trade mark should be carefully considered, as it needs to fit in with the image of your product and business which you are trying to put across.

How can you protect it?

You can register a trade or service mark with the Trade Marks Registry (part of the Patent Office). To be eligible for registration, the mark must be distinctive. A made-up word or a new symbol would be considered distinctive. Ordinary words would not; although after a number of years, with the advertising you put behind such a trade mark and the reputation for the product and business which you build up, the mark can acquire distinctiveness. Consumers will now recognize what was formerly an everyday word or name as identifying your product.

Registration entitles you, and only you, to use the mark. It gives you the right to take action against someone else to prevent them using it.

Since April 1996, it has been possible to obtain an EU-wide trademark which is effective in all the member states of the EU by making a single application to the Community Trade Marks Office.

As well as legal protection, there are also some simple steps you can take to help protect the mark yourself. For example, put TM beside the mark when you use it in advertisements or sales literature. It can also help to include a sentence like 'Microtops is the trade mark of Matthews Computer Stores'.

What does registration cost?

The cost will be £225, but could be more if anyone challenges the mark. However, this would only be for one class of goods, and there are forty-two altogether. If you intend to use your mark on more than one product, you may need to apply for registration in more than one class.

A guide to registering a mark

1. Consider whether the mark will distinguish your product from another. Is it similar to another mark? Could it confuse consumers about the nature of the product or service? Even if the mark is an ordinary word or name, do you believe that your reputation has built it up into a distinguishing feature for your product or service?

2. Apply to have the mark filed at the Registry. Include the required fee and a description of the goods on which your mark will be used. This must be done in accordance with the rules laid down by the Registry.

3. The Registry considers the application; if there are any objections you will be told, so that you can decide if the situation can be redeemed or if you should choose another mark and start again.

4. After about fifteen months from the application, the Registry will advertise the mark in the Trade Marks Journal. If there is no opposition, the trade or service mark is registered.

Getting help and advice

There are a number of organizations and associations which inventors and designers can join. These provide publications and hold meetings. To get help with the actual process of patenting an invention or registering a design or trade mark, you can approach a patent agent or trade mark agent, who should be a member of the Chartered Institute of Patent Agents or the Institute of Trade Mark Agents (see Reference for addresses).

Help and advice may also be available from local innovation centres. Ask at your local Business Link. The Patent Office can also give limited help.

Inventors should beware of organizations which demand a sum of money before any help is given.

Summary

1. The strongest way of protecting an invention, design, service or trade mark is to use effective marketing (Chapters 2, 11 and 13) to build up a reputation among customers for your product.

2. Patents and registration provide protection; but the law cannot achieve this alone. You need to follow up infringements of your rights.

3. With inventions and designs the crucial factor to remember is to keep quiet about them before you apply for a patent or design registration. If you have not, the invention or design is no longer new and you will achieve no protection.

Other chapters to read

2. **Who will buy?** (p. 13)
11. **The right name** (p. 120)
13. **Getting the message across** (p. 137)

Useful publications

What is intellectual property?
Patent Protection

How to prepare a UK Patent Application
Basic Facts: Copyright
Basic Facts: Registered Trade and Service Marks
Basic Facts: Designs
All available from the Patent Office

13. **Getting the message across**

Do you know what message you want to say about yourself, your product, your business? If you do not, how can your customers know? But knowing the message is not the end of the story. You have to decide who to send it to and how you are going to do it. If your message is not received loud and clear, your customers will not understand why they should buy from you or what it is they are getting. If they do not know the reason for buying, there will be no sales; if they have the wrong reason for buying, there will be dissatisfaction.

If you do not manage to communicate effectively the benefits of your product or service, your business will fail. The message, and getting it across, is crucial. But think carefully; the obvious solution is advertising, but advertising can swallow up a lot of money. There are other techniques that may work as well, and be cheaper.

What is in this chapter?

This chapter concentrates on written communication about your product to your potential market.

First, it helps you define your message. Second, the chapter looks at what your advertising should aim to achieve. And it explains the main types of promotion which could be useful for a small business or the self-employed. These include:

❏ Brochures and leaflets (p. 140)

❏ Public relations (p. 140)

❏ Mail shots (p. 141)

❏ Advertisements (p. 144)

❏ Directories (p. 146)

❏ Web sites (internet) (p. 147).

Finally, it gives brief hints on how you make your promotional choice.

The message: who, what, how?

Who is the message to?

If you do not know what your target market is, you really do not deserve to succeed. You need this information at your fingertips from a very early stage of planning your business, see Chapter 2, 'Who will buy?' (p. 13). Defining the target market necessitates sorting out its characteristics: the number, the location, the spending power, the class structure (if consumer).

Knowledge of the target market is needed to help refine the message and to select the most useful way of communicating the message to that particular group.

What is your message?

You need to work out what message you want to send to customers. The two main constituents of your message are:

1. *the long-term reputation* you want to build for your product or business. This can be things like good quality, good service, reliability, quick service, good value and so on. There is more about the reputation you want in Chapter 11, 'The right name' (p. 120).

2. *the specific message* you want to get across now. Of course, this may simply be part of building your reputation, as above. Or it could be that you want to describe your product, giving customers the information they need to make a buying decision. Or it could be some specific offer you have available. Or it could be an item of good news about your business. The potential list is endless, but you must know the specific objective you want each communication to achieve.

How to send the message

There are numerous ways of trying to get across your message to your target market. The trick is to select the most cost-effective way of reaching your group. The cost of communication should be measured by what you have to spend to reach each potential customer or, if possible, by the number of sales leads each pound spent generates. Obviously, any cost-conscious small business has to look at the total figure, too. But it would not make good sense to plump for a way of sending the message on the grounds that the overall cost is least, if few customers are reached. What matters is how many possible buyers receive the message compared to the total expense. Very broadly, you can communicate with your customers by:

❏ *speaking the message:* this includes direct selling to customers, carrying out demonstrations, and attending exhibitions (see Chapter 14).

❏ *writing the message:* this includes advertisements, brochures, mail shots and using the internet.

❏ *implying the message:* this does not give any specific details, but gives an impression about your business or product. For example, the quality and design of your letterhead, a business gift or van sign send an implied message to anyone who sees them. You should recognize that all ways of communicating the message, such as selling and advertising, also include an element of this. An advertisement does not simply have a picture and some words describing a benefit; the whole adds up to more than this, or it should. It should build up the general impression you want.

What can advertising do for you?

Sell more. Unfortunately, it does not seem to work quite like this. The direct link between spending money on advertising and generating more sales is sometimes difficult to establish; the linkage is there, but measurement can be fraught with problems. Direct mail or advertising with coupons can be measured much more accurately. General advertising is an investment decision, as are all the other ways of trying to get your message across. Spend money now in the hope of more sales later; but the outcome and the return are not certain.

Your advertising strategy should aim to move the potential customer from ignorance about your product to purchasing it. It should:

❏ get attention for your product

❏ help them understand the product or service

❏ get them to believe in the benefits

❏ establish a desire for the product

❏ generate action

❏ improve the reputation and general impression of the product.

You should not expect one particular form of advertising carried out at one particular time to achieve all this. To expect it might be counter- productive, if it leads you to cram too many objectives into one small piece of advertising. Your strategy should be to use a mix of different forms to achieve these aims over a long period of time.

And if you can sell as much as you want by personal contact, do not waste your money on advertisements, PR or literature. With large-value items sold to a few buyers, spending more on direct selling might be a better use of your money.

Apart from the obvious form of advertising – advertisements in newspapers and magazines – there are other forms which small businesses will probably find more useful.

Brochures and leaflets

Brochures and leaflets can be used to send out in response to sales queries or as mailings to generate interest. They can be given out by salespeople to reinforce the sales message and shown to suppliers to give credibility about your business. They are relatively cheap, although it is important that they should look consistent with the image you are trying to build. So they should not look tatty and the style should follow on from letterheads.

A brochure can be used to describe your product as well as drawing attention to the benefits. Beware of filling a brochure with a mass of technical details; if the only recipients are going to be highly technical people, consider cheaper forms of advertising, such as leaflets. If necessary, keep the brochure jargon-free and tuck a one-page technical sheet in the back.

Leaflets are cheaper still, as they may be only one or two pages or a foldover. But again, the style should be consistent and the leaflet should not look low-quality. A leaflet can be used more widely than brochures, given out at exhibitions, sent out in mail shots or dropped through letterboxes. As with brochures, a leaflet should not be crammed with technical detail, unless it is specifically for technical people; instead, it should try to attract attention and increase awareness of your name and product. What is likely to catch a target reader's eye will be the benefit which can be obtained from using your service or product.

Public relations

This can be a low-cost method of getting across a message to the marketplace, although it can be time-consuming. The basic aim is to get information or news about your business in magazines or newspapers, in the form of an article or news item. If you can achieve this, such items are seen as very credible and 'true', in a way that advertising is not, because readers place greater trust in the objectivity of journalists. Sometimes the newspaper or magazine will only accept editorial material if it is accompanied by an advertisement, which obviously you have to pay for.

The main ways of achieving this use of the press are to:

❑ *issue press releases* when there is a news item. You will have to write this yourself, or pay someone else to do it. If you do the latter, you are losing one of the benefits of public relations, which is its low cost.

To write a press release yourself, keep to the facts, brief and salient. The length of the press release should be as short as possible and summarize all that you want to say in the first paragraph, as this may be all there is room for in the journal. Somewhere on the press release, put your name and telephone number, where editors and journalists can speak to you.

If there is a good quote which you can include from yourself or the person in your business responsible for this item, this can be an excellent way of lightening the copy and making it more readable. If there is any other personal or human angle, which might appeal to the public, do not forget to introduce that. Do not be too optimistic about the chances of getting your press release in – hundreds will be sent each week.

Press releases stand a better chance of publication if there is a photograph attached. It can be a good investment to have some interesting photos of you and the business, which can be appended to the release

❑ *get to know the editor or journalist.* In this way, if you have a story, you could ring your contact before issuing a press release, to see if they would be interested because it is 'exclusive'. This may well be a more successful way of publicizing your story than issuing press releases

❑ *try writing suitable small articles,* for example, for trade or technical papers, and sending them in.

Mail shots

There are many ways of trying to ensure that your communication reaches your target market in the most efficient manner possible. These are:

1. Using a mailing list and sending leaflets or a letter through the post.

2. Putting an insert in a trade or regional magazine.

3. Delivering by door-to-door distribution agencies, such as postmen, free newspapers. Look in *Yellow Pages* under *Circular and Sample Distributors*

to find the names of agencies. Alternatively, you could see if teenagers or retired people might be interested in the work.

4. Sending direct mail shots with other companies. This would work if you are doing a joint promotion, or, if you are not competing with the other company but are aiming at the same target market.

5. Leaving your leaflets or whatever at a sale outlet, for example, a shop, to be picked up by customers.

6. Delivering your communication by a salesperson. This is very expensive.

The most personalized method in the list above, apart from delivering by sales staff, is sending your message through the post using a mailing list. The other methods might work best for fairly general notices to raise awareness of the existence of the business or product.

The success of a mail shot depends on:

❑ the accuracy, recency and relevance of the mailing list

❑ the impact of what you have written.

To have a successful mail shot by sending to customers through the post, the accuracy of the mailing list is paramount. Why waste the postage and cost of printing letters or leaflets to send to customers who have died, moved away or gone out of business?

Here are some steps to help you organize a mail shot:

1. Build up your mailing list from all past, present and potential customers. You can get names from personal contacts, through existing customers, following up requests for information, from exhibitions and so on.

2. Add to your mailing list by checking trade directories, members of trade associations, in fact, any likely place for finding potential members of your target market.

3. Consider renting or exchanging mailing lists with other organizations. If you can buy a list it means you can use it as often as you like, but few organizations sell them. If you are going to rent or exchange, the other organization may insist on using a specialist mailing service, so you cannot copy the list. The organization may also want to see what you are going to send out, so that they can approve what is going to their customers. If necessary ask a list broker to help find suitable lists for a fee. Always test a list first. If the test works, on the second occasion you use the list, don't use more than three times the size of the initial test.

4. Weed out all 'gone aways', 'cannot be founds' and 'died' from your mailing list. To achieve this you need to keep working on your mailing list on a regular basis and feeding in any information which comes in. But keep a separate note of old sales leads that appear to have gone away, in case they resurface.

5. Find out the name of the most suitable individual to receive your message. If you are sending to businesses, do not simply send to a company or to a position, for example, the chief accountant. Finding out names may mean telephoning the company first.

6. Always include a letter addressed to the individual and, if possible, signed personally by yourself or someone in your business, not pp'd (that is, signed by someone else on your behalf).

7. Remember what image you are trying to build. Choose good quality literature, paper and envelopes.

8. Look carefully at what you are sending. If it is a letter, do not make it too long; probably one or two pages is the maximum. Nor should it be too cluttered with jargon. Try to grab your reader's attention in the opening sentence or headline. Make sure that the letter ties up with any other material, such as leaflets, catalogues. If you are making some special offer, make sure it is understandable.

9. Consider how you can increase the response. Would reply cards or coupons be a good idea? Could you use Freepost for replies? The charge for the standard Freepost service is $\frac{1}{2}$p on top of normal postage for the replies you receive, plus a yearly licence fee of £57. The Royal Mail asks for a £100 deposit. There is also a bar-coded service under which you are given a bar-code version of your postcode.

10. Test your mailer first, if you think it necessary. Learn from your mistakes and improve your full mail shot.

11. Work out the cost. Try to assess your likely response rate. Only one or two per cent is considered to be a good response. A poor mailing list could mean even fewer inquiries. Calculate the cost for each response by dividing total expenses by number of likely inquiries or follow-ups. Is this a cost-effective way of reaching potential customers?

If the mail shot is expected to achieve awareness rather than instant sales, this could only be checked for cost effectiveness by researching afterwards. This could be done by contacting a sample of the mailing list to see if the mail shot was received and to get a reaction.

12. Do not forget to find out about any cheap rates on offer to new businesses and for large postings from the Post Office.

Advertisements

You can advertise in:

- ❑ local newspapers and directories
- ❑ technical or special interest magazines
- ❑ local radio, cinema or TV
- ❑ local shops, pubs and so on
- ❑ national newspapers and magazines
- ❑ reference handbooks and trade directories.

TV advertising will be too expensive for most small businesses and would be appropriate only if you are looking for volume sales nationwide. You can often target a national audience more effectively and more cheaply if you pick a specialist publication aimed at your target audience. If you run a locally based business, local advertising is clearly most appropriate and there may be numerous opportunities – for example, sponsoring the printing of raffle tickets for a local school or charity in return for your ad on the back of all tickets, ads on boxes used by a local video library, special features in your local newspapers, and so on. Clearly, which form of advertising suits you will depend crucially on the nature and scale of your business.

Before embarking on an advertisement, every small business has to decide six things:

1. Which newspaper or magazine?

2. What size and position of advertisement?

3. What goes in the advertisement?

4. When do you advertise?

5. How often do you run this, or any other, ad?

6. Whether to use an agency or not?

1. Which newspaper or magazine?

Choosing the right place to put your advertisement is crucial. To be cost-effective, the ad must be placed where it reaches the biggest possible section of your potential customers. The journal or paper must be read by the people or businesses you want to talk to and by people at the right level in the organizations or in the right class grouping in the population.

Two important statistics you need to find are the number of copies sold and what is the readership. Larger magazines have their circulation figures independently audited by the Audit Bureau of Circulations (ABC), although it may be necessary to rely on publishers' claims for smaller magazines. Rates charged for space usually bear some sort of relationship to circulation. Do not assume that the cheapest or the most expensive will be the best bet. Try to estimate the cost per reader for any ad you want to put in.

A listing of magazines and journals accepting advertising, together with the prices charged for space can be found in British Rate and Data (BRAD). Look in your local reference library.

2. What size and position of ad?

Clearly the cost of your ad is affected by its size and its position; the bigger the ad and the better the position, the more expensive it will be. For example, an ad on the front page will be seen by more readers and an ad which does not have to compete with others on the same page will be more easily seen, too. There is no clear-cut advice which can be given about whether to go for bigger and better.

In a trade magazine, a good rule of thumb is:

❑ in the first third of the magazine

❑ on a news or editorial page

❑ on a right-hand page, and

❑ one-third the size of the page.

3. What goes in the ad?

Here are some general guidelines, none of which is sacrosanct:

❑ have a clear, straightforward message

❑ do not be afraid of white space in an ad

❑ use as few words as you can to get your message across

❑ steer clear of humour; readers may not share your sense of what is, or is not, funny

❑ do not copy other people's ideas

❑ remember you are speaking to your customers, and no-one else

❑ the reader is more interested in the message than in your name, so do not put your name at the top of the ad

❑ an ad is easier to read if the words go from left to right and from top to bottom.

4. When do you put the ad in?

There may be seasonal fluctuations in your business and an advertising strategy may need to take this into account, using ads at the start of the summer for summer goods and at the start of the winter for winter ones.

5. How often do you run this, or any other, ad?

One isolated ad on its own may, frankly, achieve little. If that is all you can afford, you may be better concentrating on the other ways of getting your message across. To achieve objectives such as increasing awareness, generating further action or reminding existing buyers, an ad may need to be repeated several times. A different ad may be required to follow the first one to consolidate the improvement in awareness, and, ultimately, in sales.

6. Whether to use an agency or not?

You might want to consider using either an advertising agency or a media buying agency. A media buyer is likely to be able to buy ad space much more cheaply than you can by going direct. The agency's fee is paid by the publication. If you want help producing the ad (the copy, design and layout) you may want to use an advertising agency. There are lots of small agencies willing to work for small businesses. An ad agency will also place the ad in publications and very often, what you pay is based on a percentage of the advertising space you take in newspapers and magazines. But the agency may require a minimum fee. There may also be a percentage charged on the cost of items like brochures and leaflets if the agency is involved in helping you design those.

Directories

It may be important in your type of business to pay for entries in various directories, the commonest of which is *Yellow Pages*. Before you commit yourself to paying for an entry, investigate how many copies of the directory are sold and to whom. The longer-established directories may be the ones with the biggest usage by potential customers. If you expect to find most of your customers locally, there might be a town directory (check with the library or chamber of commerce) which would be suitable – often a simple listing is free and charges for display ads may be modest. Directories tend to be published once a year and entries need planning a long time in advance.

Your own web site

Web sites need not cost a fortune to set up – you can rent space cheaply from an internet service provider. However, there is the cost involved in designing the site and the time and commitment needed to keep the site fresh and interesting. Finally, you have to consider how potential customers will know your site exists. Pushing your site across the internet needs you to understand how to market products on the web which is rather a specialist topic. Your own web site may simply prove to be a burden you can do without unless your product and strategy is based all around the web.

Deciding the advertising strategy

For most small businesses, the single most important determinant of what advertising is done is the cost. If you cannot afford much, there is one area which should not be skimped on: good letterheads, good quality paper, labels, product packaging and, possibly, this should be extended to include a professionally designed logo.

Once you have established this as a priority, what advertising forms part of your strategy will vary depending on the nature of your business. However, it would be a mistake to think of each type in isolation from the other.

A successful strategy will include a mix of advertising. Each form of communicating your message will support the other forms, and will be consistent with the image of your product or of your business which you hope to sustain. A strategy should also be considered as extending over a long period of time, rather than isolated actions.

Summary

1. To communicate your message about your product's benefits, you need to know who you want to talk to, what your message is and the best way of getting your message across.

2. Advertising can create attention, inform, remind, prompt sales and improve the image of your product. But the return from advertising is uncertain. It costs more and takes longer than you think.

3. Advertising which is most suitable for small businesses includes brochures and leaflets, public relations, mail shots, advertisements in technical magazines and entries in directories.

4. Do not rely on one form of advertising to achieve your objectives. If you can afford it, use a mixture and try to organize a spread of advertising over a period of time (unless you have specific timing to consider for your product).

5. The advertising must be consistent with the impressions of your product and business which you are endeavouring to foster among potential buyers.

Other chapters to read

2. **Who will buy?** (p. 13)
11. **The right name** (p. 120)

14. Selling

The simple truth is that if you do not make any sales, you do not have a business. This chapter looks mainly at direct selling: the face-to-face encounter, the telephone conversation or the demonstration.

However, one important rule for you to remember is that every part of your business will be involved in selling, in the search for more sales. This extends from answering the telephone, to your notepaper and literature, to any person or activity in your business which may one day come into contact with an existing or potential customer. Train everyone who answers the telephone in the correct way to do it; they must be prompt, polite, friendly and helpful. If necessary, provide them with a script to follow. But also read Chapter 11, 'The right name' (p. 120), which gives lots of useful tips on building your reputation: from choosing the right name, to the right notepaper. Chapter 13, 'Getting the message across' (p. 137), gives some simple and cheap ways of getting your company or product message across to potential buyers. You should not think of selling as confined to your sales representative or whoever does the direct selling.

The first step in gaining sales is to plan and organize. You will need to keep records of your present customers, as well as keeping track of your negotiations with potential ones. If you do not record what has happened, possible sales can drop through the cracks, for example, if you fail to follow up an initial contact or forget to provide something which is promised.

Sales records are needed for another reason: to help in business planning. For example, you will need to know week by week what are the likely sales so that you can forecast what working capital you will need.

The second step for effective selling is to brush up personal selling skills. If you are going to do the selling, and it has not been your job previously, it is vital to have well-thought-out dialogues and presentations. It could well be worthwhile to spend some time acquiring some training in selling skills by attending a specialized training course.

What is in this chapter?

How to increase sales

❑ Existing customers (see below)

❑ New customers (see right).

How do you sell?

❑ You (p. 153)

❑ Sales representative (p. 153)

❑ Agent (p. 155)

❑ Distributor (p. 155)

❑ Mail order (p. 155)

❑ Over-the-counter (p. 156)

❑ Consortium or joint venture (p. 156).

Personal selling skills

❑ Developing your own sales approach (p. 157)

❑ The stages of a sale (p. 157)

How to increase sales

Probably the quickest and easiest way to increase sales is to persuade existing customers to buy more of your product, more frequently. You may even be able to convince them to buy other products you offer. But a business will not prosper on current customers alone; you must be able to broaden your base and sell to new businesses or buyers.

Existing customers

When a new customer signs an order, this is not the end of the selling story. You should aim to build up a long-term relationship, because, in most businesses, you will be hoping for repeat orders or for additions to the original order. These will not come to fruition if you do not follow up orders, see they are delivered on time, or, if they are going to be late, warn your customer in advance. You need to give prompt attention to any problems or criticisms.

If your business depends on a few sizeable customers, it will be important for you to establish a network of contacts in the customer's business, not just the buyer.

Another important reason for building up a good working relationship with your present customers is that they can often be the source of your new business, too. They may be able to suggest others in the same line of business who may be considering buying a similar product to yours. They may even be willing for you to use their name as an introduction. If the customer is very satisfied with your service or product, they may be willing to act as a reference for you, although obviously you must ask first. A reference means that you can give their name to potential customers and they will be prepared to discuss your business with them.

At some stage, preferably before your business has really got going, you should plan a way of recording information about your present customers. The record will need to be tailored to your individual business or product, but more than likely should include:

❏ name, address and telephone number of business

❏ customer's type of business

❏ what the customer has bought from you, how frequently and in what amounts

❏ the name of the decision-taker, plus his position and the names and positions of other contacts within the firm

❏ the customer's credit-rating or information about paying

❏ a record of visits

❏ any complaints and how they were resolved.

New customers

The first stage in acquiring new customers is to work out a possible list by market research and other methods. You may, for example, start with the raw list which you use for doing mailings (Chapter 13). But you could not possibly follow up and sell direct to everyone on this list; your efforts would not be effective because you would not be pinpointing those most likely to buy. So the list needs narrowing.

This is done in many ways:

❑ *following leads:* leads are those people who have approached you, either as a result of your advertising or mailers or having seen your business at an exhibition. They may have asked for your literature or for a demonstration or simply expressed interest

❑ *using referrals:* ask your existing customers if they know of other businesses who might be interested in your product or service. On the whole, referrals are more likely to lead to a successful sale than a lead, because you have several advantages. You already have an introduction, you know something about the person you are trying to sell to and your existing customer may have already expressed satisfaction with your business

❑ *by qualifying potential customers:* when you are first starting up your business, you may not have any referrals or leads to follow. All you may have is a list you have built up from market research. To reduce the list to the best prospect for you, you need to qualify. Find out the name and position of the decision-taker. Look for information about the potential customer's business. Work out what are likely to be the main factors which mean a business is likely to buy your product or service. This could be volume of sales, numbers of employees, location. You also need to know if the potential customer is considering buying a product like yours or has recently bought one. Your market research will identify what the key factors are for your product or service.

Two important aspects of sales organization are:

1. recording the information you have about each potential customer

2. devising a strategy for following up at regular intervals those potential customers who are not interested in buying just now, but may do so in the future. Keeping in touch is important.

How do you sell?

There are seven possibilities:

❑ You, directly as a salesperson

❑ Sales representative

❑ Agent

❑ Distributor

❑ Mail order

❏ Over-the-counter

❏ Consortium or joint venture.

You

When you are first starting your business, or if it is a very small one, it is more than likely that you will be selling yourself. If you have not previously worked on this role, the prospect may be fairly daunting. But you are likely to start with one major advantage – complete product knowledge – which is very important for selling. It is possible to acquire and develop many of the personal selling skills which you need. There are many courses available which can help you do this. If you are doing the selling, it would be a mistake to think that you do not need to organize and plan because you have stored it all in your head. You need the same information, sales systems and records as any sales rep.

Sales representative

At some stage you may decide to employ someone else to carry out or help with the selling. To enable a sales rep to work effectively, you need to make several decisions:

❏ how will the rep be paid?

❏ how much training is needed?

❏ what sort of back-up organization and systems will be needed?

❏ how to control the rep's activities.

Pay

Most salespeople will have an element of business-related remuneration. The purpose is twofold. First, commission or bonuses can be a motivator for salespeople to achieve greater sales. Secondly, it allows you to keep your overheads lower by not having to pay a greater fixed salary.

Three of the possible combinations of salary and commission are:

❏ basic salary, plus commission on all the sales the rep makes. The rate of commission could vary depending on the volume of business already achieved, that is, the more sold the greater the rate. Commission could be based on value of sales, or if there is some discretion on pricing, possibly the amount of gross profit (p. 284) achieved by each sale

❑ basic salary, plus commission on sales once a certain level (or quota) has been achieved

❑ commission only, that is, no basic salary and every sale made triggering commission payments.

Training

Unless you yourself as the business owner are a sales specialist, it would be unusual for a small business to take on someone who needs basic training in selling skills. If you do employ a trainee, you need to be prepared to wait for a long period before the person is achieving a good level of sales.

However, even if you employ experienced salespeople only, you may find it difficult to employ someone who knows your particular market and product in great detail. You must be prepared to provide good product training, plus detailed analysis of the strengths and weaknesses of competitive products. If you fail to do this, your sales are likely to be disappointing.

Back-up organization

There needs to be a number of systems and records in place to enable the sales effort to work effectively.

1. Sales staff spend a lot of time out of the office. This is incompatible with the need for existing and potential customers, as well as new leads, to be in contact. You should have a well-organized way of recording phone calls, for example, name, position and company of caller; date and time call received; brief message about purpose of call and what response was promised at your end. It goes without saying that any good sales rep will keep in touch with your office to ask what calls have been received and to follow those up.

2. Every sales rep needs a comprehensive and up-to-date price list, plus copies of any literature, press releases and publicity material.

3. If yours is the sort of business which has to issue quotes to customers, try to standardize these as much as possible. This cuts down the amount of time the rep has to spend on paperwork. This also applies to any other sales job which can be standardized. Sales letters, follow-ups to those not currently buying, and terms and conditions of the sale can be standardized. Terms and conditions can be printed on the back of the order form.

Control

You need to exercise effective control over your sales staff. This can be difficult if they spend most of the time out of the office. You must insist on a weekly sales meeting with prepared information, such as number of phone calls or sales visits made, demonstrations carried out, quotes issued and orders received. The sales rep should be able to give you an estimate of the probability of receiving an order from each potential customer and when it is likely to be received.

The information provided by salespeople is crucial in helping you to plan your business. You may be able to produce 'conversion ratios' to help you predict your likely level of sales. This would be something like:

❑ a percentage of initial phone calls which become a sales visit

❑ a percentage of sales visits which move to the quote stage

❑ a percentage of quotes which turn into orders.

Agent

Agents are not employees. They are in business on their own. They are likely to be agents for several products, but you should insist that they are not agents for any competing products. They work for commission on each sale, often between $7\frac{1}{2}$ and 15 per cent. The agent does not buy the product from you; instead, you invoice the customer direct.

The advantage of an agent is that you do not have to fund the overheads: no salary, car, office space and so on. The disadvantage is that you may find it difficult to control the agent's activities and the effort put in to sell your product. If you have a continuing responsibility for your product or service, you need to be particularly careful that the agent does not sell to unsuitable customers.

To mitigate the disadvantages, you need a written agreement which you should enforce carefully. The agreement should include the details on territory, products the agent will sell, the type of customer the agent can sell to, the rate of commission and the duration of the agreement.

Distributor

Wholesalers and distributors are not the same as agents. They are your customers. They buy direct from you. When they sell on to their customers, they expect to be able to put on a mark-up of at least 30 per cent, if not more. If you choose this route for your business it cuts out most of the costs of direct selling, as you will probably deal with only a few distributors. However, you have no control over their selling effort.

Mail order

You can sell your product direct to the end-user, cutting out the middlemen, by selling through mail order. This can be done either by advertising a particular product in a magazine or newspaper and asking customers to buy the product direct, by direct mail or by producing a catalogue which consumers use to make their choice. If you are selling a product direct, make sure you meet the requirements of the Newspaper Publishers' Association's Mail Order Protection Scheme and your advertisement should also conform to the Advertising Standard Authority's code.

Selling by mail order can work well if you are selling to a specialist niche and can use the appropriate magazine for your advertisement. The product should also be relatively small and relatively high-priced, otherwise the cost of postage and packing makes the whole thing unattractive for the consumer. However, response can be unpredictable, with consequent problems for you in deciding the right level of stock.

Over-the-counter

If your product is a specialist item, for example, a craft item, you can sell direct to shops, who in turn sell to consumers. To persuade the retailer to stock your product you need to be able to convince him or her that it will sell to that shop's customers.

On the other hand, if you are the retailer the sales process is quite different from some of the others discussed in this chapter. You cannot approach a potential customer in the same way as a salesperson selling direct. Instead, you have to tempt them into the shop before the sales process can begin.

Consortium or joint venture

You could form a marketing cooperative with other businesses in your industry. And for selling in Europe you could seek a partner, for example through the Business Cooperation Network (BC-Net) (see Reference for addresses).

Personal selling skills

Many people regard salespeople as liars, cheats and commercial vultures. Some salespeople may be like this; while others can be more successful by being honest and responsible, but by paying attention to every small detail and developing their own selling style to match the product, as well as their own character.

What you need to do to improve your selling skills is develop a sales strategy, which can be simple but which should be applied to every sale. One approach is to produce a series of lists. These should include:

❏ main features of your product

❏ major benefits it offers

❏ most likely objections and your planned response

❏ advantages and weaknesses of competitive products

❏ the key characteristics of your potential customer

❏ in what ways your product meets the customer's needs or wants.

There are also simple rules you can follow which will vastly improve your selling ability:

❏ know your product

❏ listen to your buyer

❏ relate what you are selling to your customer's needs and wants

❏ plan your sales strategy for each prospective customer, so that you know what you want to achieve at each stage of the negotiation

❏ have clear and well-worked-out sales presentations, demonstrations or even telephone calls

❏ make sure at all times that you know who the decision-maker is in your prospective client's business.

Developing your own sales approach

The first time you try out your selling approach should not be in a potential customer's office. It is important to feel confident in your dialogue and handling of the client. This means practice. Ask a relative or a colleague to take part in a role-playing session. The best practice for you will be obtained if the customer is played by your relative or colleague as hostile, vindictive and uncooperative. Try to carry out role-playing sessions many times before you come face-to-face with a genuine customer so that you can develop confidence in your style.

The stages of a sale

There are three stages to making the sale:

❑ opening stage (often a telephone call making an appointment to visit)

❑ building the sale (including sales presentations, demonstrations and dealing with objections)

❑ closing the sale (recognizing buying signals and asking for the order).

Opening stage

Your objective at this stage will usually be to make an appointment to visit a prospective buyer of your product and commence the negotiation. Obviously, you do not want to spend the time doing this unless you have already qualified this potential customer and satisfied yourself that there is a chance of selling your product.

The most efficient way of arranging appointments is to do so by telephone. The first hurdle may be to get past the buyer's secretary. Do not allow your name and phone number to be taken with a promise of ringing back. Instead, ask when your prospect will be free to take a telephone call.

The purpose of the phone call is to make the appointment, not sell your product at this stage. Try to keep it fairly brief and plan ahead what you are going to say. It may run along these lines:

❑ an opening statement

❑ any qualifying questions you would like to put (such as 'Are you likely to buy this product in the next three months if it meets your requirements?' or 'What is your budget?')

❑ why your prospective customer should arrange a meeting to see you and your product

❑ be prepared with a list of answers to the possible objections your prospect might throw out

❑ offer alternative times for the appointment

❑ finish the phone call.

Jot down the important parts of the conversation while you are speaking on the phone or straight afterwards.

Building the sale

You must plan in advance any sales call, presentation or demonstration.

Carefully analyse your potential customer's needs and requirements and decide the relevance of your product or service to these.

The opening phase is important. First impressions are important so make sure that your appearance fits in with your customer's, as well as being neat and clean. Do not waste too long on social trivialities but establish why you are there and awaken your listener's interest in your product. Before making your detailed sales pitch, ask about the customer's needs, so you can sell to these.

Important points you want to communicate to your listener are:

❑ the good reputation of your business, product and yourself

❑ the benefit your potential buyer will gain if your product or service is purchased.

This suggests that you are talking while your possible buyer is listening. But this is unlikely to achieve your sale. Salespeople have a tendency to talk too much. Instead, you should spend over half the sales call listening to your prospective customer. If you do not do this, you cannot judge the chance of making the sale and you cannot relate your product to the customer's needs. You must be able to see yourself, your product and your company through your prospective customer's eyes. This involves listening.

It also implies that your prospective customer will talk. Some try not to, which can be disconcerting. Prepare a number of open questions which you can put during the sales call. An open question is one which cannot be answered by 'yes' or 'no'.

References to other customers who are already dealing with you can be very powerful, as long as your buyer sees the reference as relevant. So the reference must be a comparable business and use.

At some stage, the subject of your competitors may be raised by your buyer. The traditional stand-by advice is 'Don't knock the competition!' On the whole, the advice is sound; criticizing the competition may have an adverse effect on your listener, because it tends to make you sound rather weak. However, do emphasize any benefits which you know your competitors do not have, as long as they are important to your buyer.

Demonstrations can be an effective selling device. You must take great care in preparing the demo. Make sure everything works before you leave your office for the appointment. Handle the equipment carefully during the demo and if it is possible involve the buyer in using and handling it during the demo.

With some products or services, quite a lot of investigation needs to be done by you before you can suggest a solution and give a quote. If yours is this sort of complicated sale, before you make a proposal you should carry out the following steps:

❑ make sure you are investigating the right problem

❑ ensure you have assembled all the facts you need by speaking to everyone involved

❑ keep an open mind about the solution you will propose

❑ keep in touch with the decision-maker and talk through your proposed solution before committing yourself to paper.

The sales proposal should simply be a restatement of what has already been said.

Little has been said so far of your potential client's reactions. If there is to be any chance of making a sale, at some stage objections will be raised. Do not view these negatively as a nuisance. An objection displays that your listener is interested in the negotiation process. An objection should be treated as a request for more information. It would be a mistake to respond to sales resistance by becoming too persistent or pressurizing too much.

There are some general guidelines to follow:

❑ do not contradict or argue and remain calm at all times

❑ do not allow the objection to become too important by spending too long replying to it or making several attempts to reply

❑ if possible, anticipate the objections and prepare a response

❑ the best way of dealing with an objection appears to be either to turn the objection into a sales benefit or to agree with the prospect, but counter with a benefit.

Closing the sale

It is important to ask for the order at the right psychological moment. This could be after overcoming an objection or if your potential buyer is showing buying signals. These might include asking about delivery terms or financial terms, arguing about price or asking about extras available.

If your prospective customer is hesitating, extra pressure is unlikely to be effective. Instead try to create a relaxed atmosphere to have a discussion and assume the decision will go your way. Talk about what will happen in the future and assume that there will be a continuing relationship between the two businesses.

Once you have got the order verbally, do not relax – you can still lose it. Do not count it as an order until you have received written confirmation; in particular, do not order materials until you have the order in writing. If it is a new customer, it is financially prudent to take up references or find out credit ratings before you accept the order. The last thing you want is to do all the work and find that you will not be paid.

Summary

1. Do not neglect your existing customers as a way of increasing sales. You will need to achieve a good long-term relationship to exploit their full potential.

2. Existing customers can be a useful source of new leads and you can use them as references in your negotiations with prospects.

3. Qualify all potential customers to avoid wasting time and effort. Narrow down your list to those most likely to buy from you.

4. If you employ salespeople, you will need some back-up organization and system. You need to be able to record information about customers to help with negotiations and to help you plan, control and forecast your business.

5. If you are doing the selling, try to develop personal selling skills. There are some hints about starting sales negotiations, developing them and closing the sales on pp. 157–60.

Other chapters to read

2. **Who will buy?** (p. 13)
11. **The right name** (p. 120)
13. **Getting the message across** (p. 137)

15. **How to set a price**

There are four ways you can increase your profits. You can cut your costs, you can sell more, you can change your product mix or you can increase your prices. Clearly your aim should be to set your prices initially at the level which gives you your highest profits possible. Needless to say, as with everything else to do with your business it is easier said than done. There is no clear-cut or agreed method of establishing a price for your product.

Some people use the level of costs as a way of fixing price. This may seem a straightforward calculation, but it has drawbacks. For example, if your costs are very low, does it automatically mean that your prices should be low too? And even working out the cost can be fraught with possible errors.

Other people argue that the price should be set by what the market can bear. But there are no quick and simple calculations which can tell you what this should be. Instead, you have to establish the price by looking at the market you are in and the particular part of it your product appeals to. How does your product rate against others competing in the same marketplace? There are also different strategies you can adopt depending on whether your product is a new or old one. Often over-riding all your plans can be the effect which your competitors' pricing policy has on yours.

It is probably more realistic to think in terms of a range of prices. The lowest price you should consider setting will be fixed by the cost. You should not go below this price; if you have to, it would be better not to be in business at all. There are a couple of exceptions, of course, where temporarily it may make sense (p. 165). The highest price will be the highest the market can bear without sales disappearing altogether. Between the two will be the price which will give the highest possible profits.

What is in this chapter?

❑ The price range (see right)

❑ The highest price (see right)

❑ The lowest price (p. 164)

❑ Setting a price (p. 166)

❑ Price near the top of the range (p. 169)

❑ Price near the bottom of the range (p. 170)

❑ Pricing with more than one product (p. 172).

The price range

There is a range of prices open to you to charge for your product or service. Your aim should be to get as near as possible to the price which is going to give you the highest profit. But this is a long-term strategy; there may be short-term considerations which imply that another price could be more appropriate at that time.

The highest price

This strategy means you have decided to go for the cream at the top of the market. In marketing jargon, it is called price skimming or prestige pricing. You are pricing your product to appeal to those of your potential customers with the highest incomes or those seeking the snob value of buying a very high-priced item. You can also carry out this price-skimming policy if you have a product with a genuine technical advantage or if it has novelty value.

Adopting a price-skimming policy implies usually that you are accepting that you could make bigger profits if you lowered the price, because you would sell correspondingly more. Nevertheless, this sort of strategy can be very appealing to small businesses. To sell more you may need to invest in bigger production facilities, or employ more staff if you are offering a service. This could involve raising funds to be able to do so. And you may find that this bigger business is harder for you to control. Creating a specialist niche could be ideal for the self-employed and small business owner. While it may not give the highest possible profits, it could make you a very acceptable living.

A pitfall to watch out for is that high prices attract competitors. Your profitable niche may soon be invaded by those offering lower prices or a better service or product. You need to allow for this competition in a price-skimming strategy. This particularly applies if you are adopting a price-skimming policy because your product is new with a technical innovation. It is unlikely to remain unique for long. Your strategy needs to involve either reducing prices in the longer term or concentrating on other advantages or benefits, so that your product establishes its own image. This allows it to carry on commanding a higher price even when the technical advantage no longer exists.

The lowest price

The lowest price you should consider accepting for your product is the one which covers your direct costs and contributes something to the cost of your overheads. But this must be regarded as a last resort and not to be accepted if you can obtain business at a higher price.

How is it worked out?

You need to find the direct costs of your product or service. Direct costs are the costs which you would not have if you were not producing that particular item. Your business will also have other costs, indirect costs or overheads. You will still have to pay for these whether you produce the item or not.

Example

Sidney Smith knows that the cost of producing his stationery pads is as follows:
Direct materials (paper, glue)	10 pence
Direct labour	5 pence
Total direct costs	15 pence

Lowest price Sidney should consider accepting for his stationery pads is 15 pence plus something towards the cost of his overheads, for example, 16 pence a pad.

Note that the terms direct costs, indirect costs and contribution to overheads are explained in much more detail in the section **break-even point** on p. 203.

When should you use this price?

As little as possible, must be the answer. You would need to sell very large volumes of your product to have enough contribution to cover the cost of your overheads, never mind make a profit.

The main circumstance in which you can justify selling as cheaply as this is if you have spare capacity in your business, with very little prospect of using it for product or services selling at a higher price. If this is the case anything you sell which helps to contribute to the cost of your overheads should be considered.

However, making this decision can have longer-term effects which must be considered. If you are operating in a market which is very competitive or in one in which your customers tend to be in contact, you may find that you are being forced to sell all your products or services at this very low price. If your customers talk to each other, it will soon become an established fact that you can be forced to sell at this low price. Raising or maintaining your prices can be very difficult in these circumstances.

Selling your product at the lowest price, even on a one-off basis, can have an even worse effect on your business if it triggers off price-cutting by your competitors. This could well occur if customers use your low price to force the competition to lower their prices.

The moral is only sell something at this contribution price if it is a one-off product, perhaps not part of your normal range of goods, and if you are very confident that it will not lead to secondary effects on your other products or the competition. You must only consider this price if you have spare capacity. If you do not have any spare capacity, choose the price which gives you the biggest contribution.

Can you go lower than this price?

Only in exceptional cases, such as if you need to clear excess stocks or low-selling lines. If this is the case, try to clear these outside your main selling channels, so it can have no counter-effect on your normal selling activity.

Why you should not use cost as a basis for establishing your normal price

Many businesses work out their prices by calculating what it costs to make the product or service and adding on what they consider a suitable profit margin. But this approach is not satisfactory for two reasons:

❏ it is surprisingly difficult to work out what it costs to produce an item

❏ the cost of an item tells you nothing about whether customers will buy it at that price at all or whether they would have paid much more.

There are various different ways of working out the cost of something. But very often businesses use some variation of a standard costing system. Typically, it looks something like this:

Direct materials	£100.00
Direct labour	75.00
Indirect materials (50 per cent of direct materials, say)	50.00
Indirect labour (30 per cent of direct labour, say)	22.50
General overhead (40 per cent of direct labour, say)	30.00
Total cost	£277.50
Profit margin (add 20 per cent)	55.50
Price	£333.00

Of course, there may be various discounts offered on this price.

The problem with this system is the difficulty of working out how much of the indirect costs and overheads should be added to each product to work out the cost. To be able to attribute a certain percentage to the product, you need to have:

❑ some idea or forecast of the total amount of overheads and indirect costs for the year, and

❑ some idea of the total amount of your product you will sell during the year.

In other words, a pricing system based on cost is based on your best forecasts. Obviously, forecasts can be wrong. You may find that you have not sold at a price high enough to cover the cost of overheads, because either your sales are lower or your overhead costs higher than your forecast.

The problem is multiplied if you have more than one product or service. How do you decide how much of the indirect costs and overheads should be apportioned to each product? There is no clear-cut answer.

Setting a price

There are several influences which will determine how near the top or how near the bottom end of the price range your product should be placed. These are:

❑ how your product compares to competitive products

❑ the life-cycle of the product, that is, how new or mature

❑ how price sensitive are your customers

❑ what price conveys to your customers

❑ what position your product has in the market.

How your product compares to competitive products

Assuming that you face competition in your chosen market, it is realistic to assume that the price you can place on your product will, to a certain extent, depend on the competition. This does not mean that if your competitors price very low, you have to follow suit. But it does mean that you should analyse your product carefully in relation to the others. The sort of characteristics you should look at include:

❑ what your product looks like and how it compares to the others

❑ how it is packaged and presented

❑ what is the availability?

❑ is your delivery and after-sales service better or worse than competitors?

❑ how do customers pay?

❑ has your product a better image or reputation?

If your product compares favourably with the others, you may be able to justify a higher price than the competition, even if you are relatively new into the market. Do not be afraid of putting a higher price than the competition. If your product does really have benefits, such as better delivery and service, or a better image, the marketplace may well accept that your price should be higher.

What stage in its life-cycle?

If it is a new product, one not before produced, as CD players were a few years ago, there are two possible strategies to adopt. One possibility is a price-skimming policy (p. 163), which goes for an initial high price. The other possibility is to try to secure a very large share of the market for your product before the competition appears on the scene. This would be achieved by setting a low price, known as penetration policy (p. 171).

How price sensitive are your customers?

If you put up your prices, do you have any idea how many of your existing customers would switch to another supplier? Or if you dropped your prices how many new customers would you acquire? How great an effect change in prices has on the amount you sell is called price sensitivity (or elasticity of demand). If customer response to price changes in your product is not that great, you can push nearer the upper end of the price range.

Broadly speaking, if your product is not bought that frequently, that is, one purchase will last quite a long time, the sales of it will not be so sensitive to price changes. On the other hand, if it is bought at regular intervals, sales may react much more strongly.

If it is difficult to differentiate one product from another in your market, this also implies that it will react much more strongly to price changes. If, on the other hand, your product can be differentiated from others by perceived benefits such as image, delivery and so on, sales will be more resistant to price changes.

What price conveys to your customers?

Price alone can conjure up ideas about your product in your potential customers' minds. The consumer often associates higher quality with a higher price; paradoxically, a high price can help the image or reputation of your product. If this applies to your market, a lower price will not generate more sales.

In general terms, a product which has the greatest market share is unlikely to be the cheapest. These products may generate high sales, because despite their high price they are thought by consumers to offer the best package of benefits (or best value for money).

What position in the market?

Often, your ability to set prices may be limited by the market in which you operate. There may be a going rate established in the market, and unless your product becomes the market leader (see right) or is definitely a better product, it may be difficult to establish any other price.

The price of your product needs to fit the market position planned for it. This is the place that the product occupies, compared to competitive products, in the eyes of your existing or potential customers.

A guide to setting prices

1. Analyse the position your product holds in the market. Are your target customers those who are looking for reliability? Has your product already achieved an established image in the eyes of the market? Do buyers view it as good quality, prompt service, stylish, say?

2. Analyse your product. Are you planning modifications or alterations which could alter its reputation or relative position in the marketplace?

3. Analyse the competition. How do their products rate against yours? What is the relative price structure in the market?

4. Decide your pricing strategy. Where in the price range are you going to pitch your price? Is it going to be average for the market, 5 per cent less than the average, 5 per cent above the average or a premium price, 25 per cent above the average?

5. Choose some specific prices. Estimate volume of sales, profit margin and costs to forecast the level of profits for each price.

6. Choose your price.

7. Would you be able to test market the price in a small area of your market? This would allow you to gauge customer reactions.

Price near the top of the range

There are two possible reasons why you may be able to justify a price near the top end of the range:

❑ the product is market leader

❑ the product is set apart from the competition by non-price benefits.

Market leader

The market leader will be the biggest selling product in the market. There are several advantages to being the market leader, and so it is a position worth aspiring to. The advantages include being able to charge a higher price than the average, making greater sales, having more power over your suppliers and competitors, and being less risky in poor economic conditions.

There is, of course, no easy way to become the market leader. Some of the guidelines to achieve the premier position include:

❑ try to be one of the first into the market

❑ develop, by careful marketing, selling and advertising, what is different about your product or business

❑ be ruthless about efficiency and costs

❏ be sensitive to changes in the market

❏ compete intensively on all sales

❏ look for profits over a long period, not the short-term fast buck – so lengthen your horizon.

Non-price benefits

The price you put on the product tells prospective customers something about it. On the whole, a higher price implies high quality, a lower price low quality. You are unlikely to build a business offering a low-quality product at a high price; on the other hand, you are throwing away profits if you offer high quality at a low price. You have to decide where your product is placed in the market compared to competitors and price accordingly.

You will be able to justify a higher price, near the top end of the range, if you decide to offer a high-quality product. You must not be frightened into thinking that the only thing that matters to buyers is price; they are interested in other aspects of your product, too.

In your marketing and selling, build an image or reputation for quality, efficient service, reliability, prompt delivery, effective sales and technical literature. This will allow you to raise prices and generate higher profits.

Price near the bottom of the range

There are three main reasons why your pricing policy might be near the bottom end of the range:

❏ fear (because you mistakenly believe that the main factor in buying is price – but see above)

❏ a strategy of grabbing market share

❏ severe price competition.

Market share

A legitimate strategy for a business is to sacrifice the level of profits in return for an increased market share. To achieve this, you would pitch the price near the low end of the possible price range (in marketing jargon, a penetration price) in return for selling more of the product. The intention in the strategy is to increase your market share, to consolidate your position, to

increase your prices gradually while retaining the share you have established. Essentially, the aim is eventually to become the market leader with
higher unit sales at a higher price.

There are a number of dangers inherent in this strategy:

❑ you may find it exceptionally difficult to raise your prices, without
demonstrating an improvement in the product in compensation

❑ you may find that your new customers do not remain faithful to your
product when you move the price upwards; instead they return to their original supplier

❑ you may trigger off a price war with your competitors.

The likeliest use of the strategy occurs when you are introducing a new
product to the market, and the competition is weak. In this case, you can
establish a large market share without attracting strong competition
because of the large profits to be made.

Few small firms will have the financial and managerial resources available to achieve this strategy of establishing a large market share successfully; it is really too risky to be considered. Instead, they should look more
closely at devoting the available resources to promotion or advertising.

Facing severe price competition

Low prices or a price-cutting war is an advantage to very few people: you
do not want it, other small competing firms do not want it; in the long run,
customers do not want it, if it means a reduced number of suppliers and less
choice. It may only be in the long-term interest of a large company, if that
is your main competitor. So whatever you do, try to avoid triggering it off.

If one of your competitors cuts prices, what should you do? Try to avoid
the instant reaction of following prices downwards. Instead try to concentrate your customers' minds on the non-price benefits (see left) of doing
business with you. If you have carried out some market research you will
know which are the non-price factors which buyers rate most highly, and
these can be emphasized.

However, if you operate in a market which is very price sensitive and
does not differentiate between products, there is little choice but to match
the price cuts. In this case, your survival will depend on savage reduction in
your costs.

Pricing with more than one product

If you have more than one product, the sales could be interlinked if they are:

❑ competing with each other, or

❑ complementary to each other.

You need to ensure that your pricing policy is consistent across the range of your products. With competing products, the prices need to make sense. There needs to be a recognizable gap in the prices, if one is a high-quality product while the other is lower quality.

The pricing considerations are different if your products are complementary, that is, if you sell one, you are likely to sell the other. Once your customer is hooked, there will be lots of scope for charging high prices on a complementary item, as long as it is not so blatant that it puts off buyers from the starting product.

Summary

1. There is a range of prices which you can charge.

2. The lowest price is set by the contribution to overheads that it makes. Never go below this price. Only accept this price if you have spare capacity and there is no prospect of selling your product or time at a higher rate. If you have little or no spare capacity, choose the sale which gives you the biggest contribution.

3. Do not use costs as the basis of setting your prices, at least not without trying to price the product according to what customers will pay.

4. If you go for the highest price possible in the market, you will restrict the amount you can sell. It will not give you the maximum possible level of profits. However, a specialist niche of this type can be attractive to a small business.

5. When it comes to setting a price you have to compare your product with others, establish how responsive sales are to a change in prices, work out your strategy if it is a new product or coming to the end of its life, analyse what price conveys to your customers and decide what position your product is aiming for in the market. Use the guide on p. 168.

6. The market leader has several advantages; the main ones are that it means you can achieve more sales at a higher price than the competition.

7. Justify a higher price by stressing non-price benefits, such as quality, reliability, delivery and so on.

8. Avoid pitching your price too low through fear or misunderstanding what buyers are interested in.

9. A strategy of increasing market share through low prices is dangerous for a small business.

10. If you are facing severe price competition, try to distract attention from price by emphasizing the product benefits.

Other chapters to read

2. **Who will buy?** (p. 13)
24. **Staying afloat** (p. 282)

16. Choosing your workplace

One of the jokes that can be made about people starting small businesses is that the first thing they want to do is search for premises. It is an understandable desire, as premises are tangible proof of the creation of an enterprise. However, if the business is to stand any chance of success, it is not the first step. There is a whole host of other jobs to be done first – researching the market, positioning the product, drawing up the business plan.

Nevertheless, finding a workplace is a very important step to take. It can also prove to be extraordinarily difficult to find the right premises at just the right location for just the right price. It is a problem which is particularly acute for those starting in the UK, especially in the South-east. If your business were transported to the US, the problem would seem much less immense. But the UK is densely populated and land values and hence property values are proportionately high.

The problem looms ever larger for those businesses where premises are critical to success or failure, such as a retail business. If you are planning to start a shop, a large part of the setting-up process will be devoted to a search for a good location. And you cannot afford to compromise and take premises which with a bit of luck will be OK. You have to be satisfied that they meet all your criteria; if they do not, carry on the search until they do.

What is in this chapter?

❑ Where is your business to be located? (see below)

❑ What sort of premises do you need? (p. 178)

❑ Searching for premises (p. 180)

❑ Investigating and negotiating (p. 182).

Where is your business to be located?

An important first exercise would be to start with a blank piece of paper and think about location from first principles. What is the ideal location for the type of business you have in mind? At a later stage, you can introduce the constraints placed on location, such as home and family. You should know the ideal location so you can estimate the effect of concessions you are making to these outside non-business constraints. There may be further business constraints, such as the lack of finance, which may cause you to compromise and choose a less than perfect location.

Communications

How dependent is the success of your business on communications: road, rail, air, bus? This could be important if your business falls into one of the following categories:

❑ you deliver your product

❑ your business is service-based to particular areas of population

❑ you sell your product direct, using salespeople

❑ your business is dependent on import and export.

In these, and other categories of business, an ideal location would allow easy access to the relevant parts of the country. For example, if import/export is your trade, a location within reach of a major airport could be an advantage. Or, if you direct sell to the whole country, you need to be on the motorway system.

Labour

If your business is dependent on the use of certain skills, you may find that one part of the country is more abundantly endowed with potential employees who have already acquired those skills than other parts. On the other hand, skills may be irrelevant; what you may need is a ready pool of unskilled labour, in which case some areas have higher unemployment than others.

Centres of population

Your business may need to be located near particular centres of population. If you are trying to sell your product in large volume, being in a large centre of population may be an advantage. Or you may want to choose an area with a specific structure of population if your product or service is sold only to particular sectors. For example, if you plan to open a bookshop, you need a town or population area of a certain size. You also need a population well endowed with the particular characteristics of those who buy books. Your market research will help you identify what those characteristics are.

Suppliers

Your business may depend on supplies of a particular raw material or some other product. Costs would be lessened if your business was located near the source of supply. This could either be the main distributor of the item or it could be where the item is grown or produced.

Government and local authority assistance

Your business may be location-independent. Thus you can look at some of the deals which the government and local authorities produce to stimulate the founding of new businesses in particular areas, in the hope of increasing employment.

Best known of these initiatives are enterprise zones. The government set up a number of these zones to last ten years. Many have now ended and there are currently seven in existence, the last of which is due to end in 2006. The size of the current zones range from around 150 acres to over 500 acres, but they all contain land suitable for development. The present zones include areas in:

England

Sunderland, East Midlands, Dearne Valley in South Yorkshire, East Durham, Tyne Riverside

Scotland

Inverclyde, Lanarkshire

Benefits last for the lifetime of the enterprise zone and include no national non domestic rates on industrial and commercial property (but water and other service charges have to be paid), capital allowances of 100 per cent in the first year and a greatly simplified and speedy planning regime.

Other initiatives exist to encourage the growth of new businesses and jobs in certain locations. The government has designated certain areas as Assisted Areas and many government assistance programmes were brought together under the umbrella of the Single Regeneration Budget (which includes the Challenge funds and Inner City Task Forces). However, this approach is now under review. There could be grants available which might induce you to locate in an inner city or one of the poorer regions of the country. Such grants may make your business idea more viable and are worth investigating. For example, an area which has been designated as having Assisted Area status offers the following:

❑ regional selective assistance, which provides grants of up to 15 per cent of the costs of a project. Eligible costs include plant and machinery, some associated costs such as patent rights and land costs such as site preparation and buildings

❑ possibly, a diverse range of other types of help provided at the local level, such as training for small business managers in, say marketing, start-up grants, rate relief during the start-up period. It is an increasingly prominent feature of government funded assistance that local areas (represented by the local authority, chamber of commerce, TEC and so on) have to bid competitively for funds, presenting a strategic plan for regenerating the area and showing that partnership funding (eg from local businesses or direct from local authority budgets) is committed to the plan. If successful in the bid, the local area then directs how the funds will be used – that is, what projects will be eligible, what form assistance will take. The aim is to focus help more directly at local needs.

Even outside Assisted Areas, some special help is available to certain types of business in rural areas. Village post offices and village shops qualify automatically for 50 per cent relief against business rates – at the discretion of the local authority, this can be increased to 100 per cent relief. Certain other village businesses can also get help with rates at the discretion of the local authority. In this context, a village means a community with a population of 3,000 or less.

There is a list of Development Areas and Intermediate Areas (both known as Assisted Areas) in the Reference section. Contact your local government office (see Reference) or Business Link for more information on what help is available. This includes information on what EU grants may be available – don't use a firm specialising in telling you about grants (some of them are cowboys).

The final choice of location

It would be unrealistic to assume that domestic constraints are not important in locating a business. The extra benefits gained from moving to another area may simply not outweigh the domestic upheaval and cost of moving house when you want to start your business.

If you decide not to move your home, it makes sense for your offices to be close to your home, as long as other business considerations do not apply. If it would not adversely affect your business to be near your home, it can be an advantage as it cuts down on your wasted travelling time from home to office when you probably need all the time you can get to solve initial business problems.

What sort of premises?

After settling on a location, your search can home in on the premises you need. There are two aspects. First, you need a tighter specification of location, for example, town, district, neighbourhood or even street. This very tight specification mainly applies to retail business. Most of the considerations you need to take into account are explained on p.88. The second aspect is the type of premises.

The factors which influence your choice of premises include:

❑ appearance. If customers and suppliers are likely to come to your offices, the appearance of your premises can affect your credibility and your image

❑ parking or public transport. If you have staff or visiting customers and suppliers, you'll want either good transport or parking. The planning authority (see p. 183) will also need to be satisfied that you have adequate parking facilities

❑ cost. You obviously want to keep your costs as low as you can, consistent, that is, with achieving your business objectives. Keep an eye on business rates

❑ size and layout. Your business activity may impose constraints on the amount and exact physical layout needed

❑ physical environment needed for maximum work efficiency. Cold, noise, dirt, dark can all mean people do not operate at their best.

The type of business may well dictate your choice of premises among office, factory, workshop or warehouse, for example. But there are a number of specialized options open to small businesses.

Home

Many small businesses will start off in the back bedroom. Some, especially if they are part-time businesses, may stay there permanently. The big advantages are cost and convenience. But there are a number of disadvantages or even obstacles. Introducing a business into the home can disrupt family life; it may also mean that it is difficult to leave your work cares and worries behind at the end of the working day. Another disadvantage of using your home as working premises is the poor impression it could create on customers if they need to visit you.

The obstacles which could exist include the possible need to get planning permission. This may occur if your business breaks town planning regulations because you have made a 'material change in the use of land'. Unless your business is very noisy, annoys your neighbours or means that there is a large increase in the number of visitors coming to your house, you may find that planning permission is not necessary. The moral is: keep a low profile.

Other possible obstacles include:

❏ the existence of restrictive covenants on the land (ask your solicitor)

❏ the existence of a mortgage (check with building society or bank)

❏ restrictions on insurance (check with insurance broker or company)

❏ problems with the health and safety inspectorate if your business is food production, for example

❏ the possibility that some capital gains tax may become due on the sale of your home (check with accountant and see p. 332).

Managed workshops and small business centres

In many places, there are centres designed especially for small businesses. These provide small offices, workshops or factory space. There may well be an element of joint services thrown in, for example, telephone answering service, secretarial facilities. There could even be the existence of an advisory team to help you with initial management problems.

Sharing accommodation in this way with other small businesses has its attractions; there can be mutual support and business introductions, for example. You may also be able to run a more efficient business because of the shared facilities than from an office on your own.

Science parks

Finding premises in a science park has its attractions for high-tech businesses. Most science parks are attached to universities or polytechnics. The theory is that by grouping innovative businesses together and in close proximity with the research facilities of the university or polytechnic, this will provide a breeding-ground for new ideas. Whether this happens or not, your business may be able to project a high-tech image as a result of being located in a park.

Searching for premises

There are two aspects to searching for premises. First, you have to find out about premises which are vacant. Second, you have to decide whether any of the premises you see meet your needs.

There are several places to look to find vacant premises:

❑ local newspapers

❑ estate agents. You will find that not all estate agents handle commercial property. The estate agent dealing with a particular property may not be local at all, but could be based many miles away. Nevertheless, find out which of the local agents do deal in commercial property and ask for a list

❑ contact the local authority. Many of them keep lists or registers of vacant industrial or commercial property within their boundaries. Some have disused public buildings for sale. Indeed, it can be worthwhile having a discussion with the local authority, for example, the industrial development officer, as there may be special schemes to help you within certain areas of the authority

❑ local Business Link, enterprise agency or TEC (see Reference section for addresses)

❑ a number of national agencies or organizations who provide premises, especially in areas of high unemployment (see Reference section).

Once you have gathered together information about premises for renting or buying in the area, the next step (before you go to see any of them) is to draw up a checklist of the priority points your premises need:

1. Space (How many sq. ft do you need? For offices, allow roughly 100 sq. ft per employee.)

    Office ....

    Storage ....

    Factory ....

    Retail ....

2. Working environment What is the importance of these factors:

Appearance for customers and suppliers ....

Light ....

Noise ....

Cleanliness ....

Smells ....

Fire hazards ....

Neighbours (type of work) ....

3. Ease of access Do the premises need:

Good access for pedestrians ....

To be near to bus stop or railway ....

Good parking facilities ....

Delivery facilities ....

4. Services and facilities

Would you like already-installed:

Partitions/fittings ....

Telephone/ISDN line ....

Burglar alarms ....

Central heating ....

Lighting/electricity points ....

Air conditioning/ventilation ....

Cooking/refrigeration ....

Computer network ....

5. What about cost?

Rent per sq. ft ....

Rates per sq. ft ....

Maintenance ....

Running costs ....

Rent reviews ....

Premium for getting in ....

Rent-free period ....

Decoration ....

Fittings needed ....

Phones, electricity, security, etc. ....

Length of lease ....

When you have worked out a shortlist of properties which you want to see, it can be useful to draw a quick sketch-plan of the premises. At your leisure, you can mark where the various parts of the business will be put and get some idea of how comfortably your particular business fits into those premises.

Investigating and negotiating

Before you sign anything, there are several steps to take to investigate the premises further. These steps are:

❑ to estimate costs

❑ to check structure of property (if it is freehold or a repairing lease)

❑ to investigate the legal side of things, and

❑ to look at local authority requirements.

To estimate costs

There are a few things to investigate before estimating costs. First, do not rely on the measurements given by the estate agent or landlord. Measure the premises yourself. There is a chance that the area is less than said which could mean lower rent for you, if you have been quoted a rent per sq. ft.

Second, it would be a good idea to look at the premises a number of times on different days and at different times of the day. This should allow you to get a better idea of decoration, heating, lighting or noise insulation needed.

Third, make sure you estimate or allow for all the running costs as well as alterations and improvements you would need to make.

It is always worthwhile trying to negotiate a lower rent and, in particular, asking for a rent-free period of three, six or twelve months if there is a lot of vacant property around, as for example in a recession.

To check structure of property

Many leases make the tenant responsible for the repairs and maintenance of the premises. It would be advisable to ask for a survey from a member of the Royal Institution of Chartered Surveyors (see Reference). You can also use a survey to negotiate that the landlord pays for certain improvements before you take the premises.

To investigate the legal side of things

Your solicitor should be asked to undertake a perusal of the lease. The sort of points to look out for are:

❏ can the premises be used for the type of business you have in mind?

❏ how long is the lease? Commonly, it is between three and 20 years

❏ will you have the right to get a new lease when this one runs out?

❏ are the premises listed? This can restrict the way you adapt and extend them to suit your business needs

❏ are there rent reviews and when are they?

❏ can you sublet part or all of the premises?

❏ who is responsible for the repairs and the insurance?

❏ is the lease actually owned by the person trying to sell it?

❏ are the premises likely to be affected by any road or town improvements or alterations?

❏ who is paying for the landlord's legal costs? It is general practice for you to pay them, but it is always subject to negotiation. At any rate, agree beforehand that you will only pay a reasonable amount

❏ is it possible to rent the premises on a weekly agreement, rather than sign a long lease? This gives you flexibility, but you lose security. An informal arrangement like this may be possible at times when there is a glut of vacant property

❏ does the landlord want you to give a personal guarantee? Your solicitor should spell out to you the implications of doing so and help you to negotiate to try to avoid this.

To look at local authority requirements

A simple step you can make for yourself is to call the planning and building control officer to find out what is the current approved use for the premises. If your intended use is the same, you may need to do nothing more. If a change of use is required, your solicitor should be able to help. The planning officer can also advise you, if your premises have listed building status.

Depending on the nature of your business, you may need to consult:

- ❑ town planning and building control officers
- ❑ environmental health officer
- ❑ fire officer
- ❑ health and safety executive.

Summary

1. Look at location with an open mind. Would your business be off to a better start moving to a different part of the country? Enterprise zones and locations with development area or assisted area status can offer considerable benefits.

2. As well as conventional premises, small businesses can also look at shared workshops and offices, use of home as a place of work and setting up in a science park.

3. Before you inspect any premises, draw up a list of what you think are your business needs.

Other chapter to read

17. **Getting equipped** (p. 185)

17. **Getting equipped**

One area which is infrequently covered by books and training courses is how you get your business equipped. Equipment is a very loose term to cover the infrastructure of your business. Obviously, with a manufacturing business, the equipment is very specific to the type of business. This may also apply to the equipment you need for an office.

The infrastructure of your business ranges from cars to phone systems, from office furniture to computer systems. One part of setting up your working environment is to select what you need, at what level of sophistication and for what price.

What is in this chapter?

The topics covered in this chapter include:

❑ What to consider when choosing equipment (see below)

❑ How to pay for equipment (p. 190).

Choosing equipment

There is some equipment which it is very important to choose correctly as it can make a tremendous difference to your business efficiency, including:

❑ the right communications equipment

❑ the right computer system.

You are also likely to devote some time to choosing:

❑ the right furniture

❑ the right car.

The right communications equipment

Installing a telephone which is suitable for your business is a high-priority task. Of course, if it is a one-person business, you may need nothing more sophisticated than a telephone with features like call diversion and call waiting and a very efficient telephone answering machine to cover when you are out. However, you must realize that using a machine is making it clear to all callers that you are a one-person outfit, which may lower credibility.

There are many other ways of improving communication with potential customers. These include fax machines (now regarded as indispensable by many business owners), mobile telephones (very useful for people who are frequently out of the office) and pagers. On your telephone, you can now use a number of services, such as diverting calls to any telephone number, even your mobile phone. All these – and more – can dramatically improve the manner and efficiency with which you can communicate with others outside your business.

Once your business is growing beyond the one-person stage, spend some time researching to find a telephone system which meets your requirements. Failing to find one that is adequate can lead to inefficient working.

The right computer system

The first question you need to ask is what you want a computer to do in your business. The sort of tasks which can be carried out are:

❑ *word processing:* a computer can be invaluable if in your business you send out a lot of routine letters, such as sales letters, quotes, mailing shots. A computer with a word-processing program can be time-saving and produce a high-quality service

❑ *accounts:* there are a number of computerized accounting packages. But you might find it worthwhile to consider these only when the number of transactions has grown

❑ *financial control and planning:* the programs range from cash management to sophisticated systems for working out forecasts and updating them at regular intervals. Again the importance of these depends on the size and complexity of your business. Ask your accountant for guidance. But a software program can considerably simplify the task of forming and updating cash-flow and profit-and-loss forecasts. Some of the banks now give business planning software away free as part of an introductory package

❑ *database-type work:* if you have a large list of potential customers and send out mail shots or want to record information about them, using database software can improve your efficiency dramatically

❑ *stock control:* this can be important for retail outfits. Some computer systems link up to the cash till, so that levels of stock and need for re-ordering are worked out automatically.

A computer system is made up of:

❑ the hardware, that is, the computer and peripherals such as printer, modem, scanner. These are now mass-market products and you can easily shop around to get the cheapest deal. If you have more than one computer you will probably want to network them to improve efficiency and allow you to swap information from one to the other and share printers

❑ the software, that is, what makes the computer carry out various tasks.

There are two sorts of software: the operating software which makes the computer go and the application software which does the specific job, for example, cash management, word processing, e-mail. This software can come as a 'package' and be sold along with your hardware. You may find that software, ready packaged for personal users, may meet 98 per cent of your needs – and it is significantly cheaper than software sold for business users. Don't even consider having software written specially for you, apart from simple adaptations to the packaged software.

Both aspects of a computer system are important, although with the development of cheaper and better hardware, choosing the software becomes the prime task. You can buy computer systems from:

❑ high-street stores

❑ computer dealers who specialize in business computers and software, but may be dealers for a limited range

❑ mail order.

A modem – either installed internally within your computer or attached externally – lets you communicate with others direct from your computer screen using your phone line. You can send and receive e-mail and faxes, which can be read on screen, printed out, saved wherever you choose on your system and even dropped into other files you are working on, such as a database or a word-processed report. E-mail, in particular, is very flexible, allowing you to send and receive whole files, not just simple messages. A modem can also open up the world of the Internet to you, giving you the ability to explore external databases, gather information from governments, libraries, universities, companies and others. It is now possible to get on to the Internet for the cost of a local call from virtually anywhere in the UK, so 'surfing the Net' need not be costly.

If you have a computer system, you must comply with the requirements of the Data Protection Act. If you require a computer on which you intend to hold computerized personal data, you will need to register at once as a 'data user' with the Data Protection Registrar (see Reference for address).

Tips on choosing

1. Decide what you want the computer and the software to do, before you ask anyone for advice. But remember that a computer will not solve management problems caused by flawed systems. It is not a super-hero.

2. Contact your local Business Link (see p. 31) to find out what help is now available with consultancy to advise on the appropriate computer system for your business.

3. Ask the suppliers to come in, and set out for them what you want to do, and ask for detailed proposals and installation plans.

4. Do not be overwhelmed by jargon or be drawn into discussions about the number of bytes or the operating systems. Insist that the suppliers explain what the computer system will do for your business.

5. Ask the suppliers for a full customer list, so you can take up references. Be suspicious of anyone who will only tell you the names of two or three customers. Take up the references fully and carefully.

6. Ask the supplier these questions: 'How many systems identical to this one have you installed?', 'Are the businesses similar in operation and size?'

7. Ask to see everything and anything you need working. If there are any excuses, however plausible, do not commit yourself to any order. You must see it all working and doing what you want.

8. Always buy software packages; never agree to have anything which will need to be designed from scratch.

9. If an important part of what you need is not ready yet and 'is coming in a couple of months', delay buying until it has come and been fully demonstrated to you. Do not be the 'first' buyer of any computer system. You have your own business to run without pioneering for the computer industry.

10. Be prepared to spend more now to install the right-sized system with the right back-up. If you choose the smallest version, you may well find that you upgrade the system within a short space of time and the cost could be much higher than doing it right in the first place.

11. Remember the binary law of computing; it will do half as much, cost twice as much, take twice as long, as the salesman says or you think.

The right furniture

Choosing the right furniture for your business depends essentially on the type of business. Cheap, second-hand desks and chairs may not be good business sense. If you think it possible that customers or suppliers will visit your premises at regular intervals, it is crucial to select furniture which projects the image (p. 121) you have planned for your business. People are very affected by appearances, even other business people. Choosing good-quality furniture can suggest to customers that your business is good quality, too. And if exports are likely to play a big part in your business, smart offices are crucial.

Suppliers, too, can be affected by appearances. Well-planned and smart offices suggest that this is how you run the business and can help in your negotiations on credit terms and prices. In the case of furniture, cheap may mean expensive in the long run. However, what you choose is obviously determined by what you can afford. But don't forget that tidiness and cleanliness play an important role in appearances.

The right car

A car can arouse great emotions. It is one of those peculiar purchases where it can be difficult to disentangle desires from needs. The car you drive somehow projects something about your own personality; it is often regarded as an extension of it. Nevertheless, caution is needed before personal desires get confused with business needs.

It is often argued by business owners that a prestige car is needed to project an image of credibility, for exactly the same reasons outlined above for furniture. But a cool, hard look is needed at that claim. Will customers and suppliers really see you driving into their car parks? To project the image that is needed, is the souped-up version essential? Will not the same effect be created by the slightly cheaper version? The argument that one car will only cost £50 more a month to lease than another is weak. You need to look at the cost over a longer period of time, say two years, or however long you intend to keep the vehicle. It would, of course, be a mistake to swing too far in the opposite direction and choose a second-hand car which is rusting or requires excessive maintenance.

How to pay for equipment

There are four main ways you can pay for equipment. Two of them involve buying the equipment, so you become the owner; the others do not, the ownership being retained elsewhere. The ways are:

❑ buying outright

❑ hire purchase

❑ leasing

❑ contract hire.

Buying outright

This does not necessarily mean buying it with your own money; you could use a bank loan or overdraft to finance the purchase of the equipment. The advantage of buying outright is that you own the asset, which will be entered in your balance sheet. This will make your balance sheet stronger. The disadvantage is that it uses up large lumps of cash, maybe at a time when you are short of funds.

Hire purchase (or credit sale)

Ultimately, you will own the asset outright at the end of the hire period. This means that hire purchase confers some of the same advantages of buying outright. As with outright purchase, you can claim a capital allowance from the time you start using the equipment, and you will be able to take the equipment into your balance sheet as an asset, with what you owe as a liability on the other side.

Using hire purchase also means that you are not laying out such a large sum initially, compared with buying outright, which can be helpful for cash flow. However, the payments you make will consist of capital, as well as interest. You only get tax relief on the interest part of the payments. Hire purchase deals used to fall within the scope of the Consumer Credit Act 1974, but have recently been taken out of the Act where the deal is with a sole trader or partnership. This means that hire purchase agreements can now be more flexible.

Leasing

If you lease equipment, you are not the owner of it, although you may be able to buy it at the end of the lease. The company who organizes the lease is the initial owner. The main advantage of leasing is that there is no capital outlay, so it can be a big help to cash flow.

You do not claim the capital allowance for the equipment; the company organizing it claims the allowance, although you should get some benefit such as reduced rental. However, all the payment you make is treated as an expense and so you get full tax relief on it.

There are different sorts of leases. If the lease is a closed-ended one, it means there will be a fixed period of one to five years. At the end of the agreed period, there may be an option to take on a further lease for a nominal rent. Or you may be able to buy the equipment. An open-ended one means you can end it when you like after the expiry of an agreed minimum period. Yet another type of lease is a balloon lease, which allows you to make part of the capital payment at the end of the lease.

Contract hire

This is a form of leasing, mostly used for financing a fleet of vehicles. In this case, what is in the contract is not a specific vehicle or vehicles, but the use of an agreed number of the specified type. The length of the agreement is usually shorter than the estimated life of the equipment. Use of the vehicles can be provided with or without the maintenance. You may be able to arrange to buy the car at the end of the agreement.

Summary

1. Choosing the right communications equipment can be important for the efficiency of your business.

2. The furniture and fitting out of your premises can have an impact on your credibility with customers and suppliers.

3. Your car may affect the image of your business less than you believe.

4. There are four main ways of paying for equipment: buying outright, hire purchase, leasing and contract hire.

Other chapter to read

16. **Choosing your workplace** (p. 174)

18. **Professional back-up**

Luck can make a lot of difference to the success or failure of an enterprise; but you cannot sit around waiting for luck to land on your doorstep. You must take all the steps you can to ensure success. Weaknesses in specific skills must be covered; you may be able to obtain advice and guidance from your local Business Link, an enterprise agency or TEC. But there may still be some skills for which you must seek outside professional help.

The time to seek out and engage professional advisers will be fairly early in the planning stage. Thus their expert advice can be taken before your plans are firmly formulated. If the adviser is good, this should help you avoid making the sort of expensive errors and misjudgements which could mean your business begins with a permanent disadvantage.

The sort of advisers who could be helpful to you include:

❑ Accountant

❑ Bank

❑ Solicitor

❑ Surveyor/estate agent

❑ Designer

❑ Corporate finance adviser.

Accountant

The advice available

The advice accountants may be able to give ranges from the basic services, such as book-keeping, to the more sophisticated, such as tax planning or raising funds. Not every accountant will offer every sort of advice. For example, a big firm of accountants is unlikely to undertake weekly book-keeping functions; a sole practitioner may not have the expertise for help with raising funds.

Some of the areas of advice include:

❏ *accounts:* doing the book-keeping, setting up accounting systems, advising on computerized accounting packages, auditing for a limited company

❏ *finance:* managing cash, helping to raise finance and to negotiate with the bank manager, raising venture capital

❏ *business purchase:* investigating possible acquisitions, analysing franchise opportunities, negotiating purchase prices

❏ *tax:* preparing income tax and VAT returns, carrying out PAYE and national insurance requirements for employees, personal and business tax planning

❏ *general business advice:* preparing business plans, budgets, forecasts and advising on the form of your business, that is, whether you should be a sole trader, in partnership or form a limited company.

Quite a lot of accountants, particularly the large firms, also have management consultancy divisions, which can advise on the setting up of internal systems, computerization and so on.

How to choose

The term 'accountant' does not necessarily mean that the person so described has any formal accountancy qualification. If you want to employ someone who is a member of a recognized body, you should look out to see if there are letters after the name. The main organizations which will be of interest to you as a small business are:

❏ The Institute of Chartered Accountants in England and Wales and The Institute of Chartered Accountants in Ireland, whose members put ACA or FCA after their name, and The Institute of Chartered Accountants of Scotland, whose members put CA after their names (see Reference)

❏ Association of Chartered Certified Accountants (see Reference), whose members put ACCA or FCCA after their name.

❏ Association of Authorised Public Accountants, (see Reference),whose members put AAPA or FAPA after their name.

What you gain by using a member of one of these bodies is the knowledge that a required course of training has been followed and certain exams passed. In addition, if you want to appoint an auditor, you must appoint someone who is a member of one of these bodies, which have been recognized by the Department of Trade as auditing bodies.

If you need to find someone who will help with your book-keeping and preparation of your tax returns, and your business is fairly small-scale, employing fully qualified accountants may be the equivalent of cracking a nut with a sledgehammer. You may be able to find someone else quite competent to carry out the limited range of jobs you have in mind, but obviously at a much cheaper rate.

The only satisfactory way of choosing an accountant is by recommendation and taking up references. Ask your bank manager. Colleagues and friends who use the services of accountants are also possible sources of recommendation. References should always be taken up.

There is a case to be made for opting for one of the big firms of accountants, which have specialist small firms divisions, if you want to raise money from the venture capital industry. Venture capitalists may look with more confidence if your financial advisers are well known, rather than from a small firm of accountants however good at their job.

As with any business negotiation there should be a discussion about the scope of the work to be done and clear agreement on what this is and what it will cost. Really you must satisfy yourself, before any work is begun, that the accountant knows what you want and is capable of doing it.

If it is management consultancy that you are interested in, find out if the consultancy is a member of the Institute of Management Consultants or the Institute of Business Advisers (see Reference for address). An important point to check is that the consultant has experience of the problems of small businesses.

Cost

What an accountant costs can be difficult to establish. The answer is it usually depends on the type and the amount of work involved. But the range can be wide, depending on whether you are using a large London firm, a smaller provincial one or a book-keeper.

Before you decide to use someone, you must have a clear statement on costs, otherwise they will come as a shock to you.

With some types of work, raising venture capital for example, you may not have to pay the fee if you do not succeed in raising the money.

Bank

The advice available

Banks obviously offer a great range of financial facilities, such as current accounts, provision of overdrafts, longer-term loans, leasing and factoring, import and export assistance. There is more detail about the provision of finance in Chapter 23, `Raising the money' (p. 269). Most of the banks also have specialist services for small businesses and networks of small business centres or advisers which can give general business advice. Some of the banks offer free banking for the first year or longer if you open a business account with them.

The role of adviser sits rather uneasily with the provision of finance. Some small businesses may hesitate about discussing business problems completely frankly in case it should affect the bank's judgement about extending an overdraft, for example. However, this worry may be illusory, as most bank managers or advisers should be competent enough to spot problems from the figures presented.

A group of High Street banks made a study of failed businesses and discovered that nearly three-quarters suffered from a serious lack of financial management skills. As a result, they have established a project called 'Golden Key' which offers cheaper loans to businesses whose owners or managers have completed a recommended training course. The scheme is gradually being extended to more areas of the UK and is run in conjunction with Business Links.

How to choose

The bank which holds your personal account may not be the automatic answer. There can be a strong case made for separating your business and personal affairs so that one cannot influence the other.

If your business is planned to be on a large scale, if, for example, you are raising substantial funds and are looking for very fast growth – such as profits of £200,000 to £300,000 within five years – it may make sense to put your account with one of the larger branches. This is particularly so if you can build up a relationship with the bank manager. The manager of a large branch will have more discretionary power; this means that fewer decisions will need to be referred upwards to regional decision-makers within the bank, thus losing the personal touch.

There is probably no advantage in opting for a larger branch if you are likely to be working on your own or on a small scale. Convenience will be more important.

Cost

You should definitely shop around to find out what it will cost you for the finance you need. Cost does not only include the interest rate, but also the terms surrounding any loan or overdraft. However, there may be other reasons apart from cost which govern your choice, for example, any 'special relationship' you have established with a manager.

Solicitor

The advice available

Solicitors can be particularly useful during the formation of your business. Some of the specialist advice they can give includes:

❑ *business advice:* on the legal form of your business (that is, sole trader, partner, limited company), on personal guarantees, steering you through the maze of employment law, helping with debt collection by advising on writs and winding-up orders

❑ *contracts:* conditions and terms of sale of your product, leases, franchise contracts, for example

❑ *legal entity:* forming companies and drawing up partnership agreements

❑ *product protection:* helping to obtain a patent or register a trade or service mark or an industrial design.

Many solicitors belong to the Lawyers for Your Business scheme, see Reference. This offers a free initial consultation for those running young or growing businesses, plus a clear indication of the cost of further advice.

How to choose

Very similar considerations apply to the choice of solicitor as to that of your accountant. Solicitors specialize in different branches of the law, so you should ensure that the firm can give you the advice you need on specialized topics. If the specific partner you deal with cannot do this another partner in the same firm may be able to do so, but it is your responsibility to question abilities closely to satisfy yourself that the advice will be soundly based. A wise precaution can be to take up references.

As with accountants, some businesses would be advised to choose a large firm because of the credibility the name would add to your quest for raising large sums of money.

Cost

For whatever you want doing, ask for an estimate of costs; if the answer is that it is not possible because the solicitor does not know how long the work will take, ask for the daily rate. But a solicitor who cannot give you an estimate is not impressive. Many solicitors offer a package price for jobs like forming a company.

The law requires solicitors' fees to be 'fair and reasonable'. When you receive the bill, if you do not understand how it is made up, your solicitor will have to get a certificate from the Law Society declaring the bill fair and reasonable if you demand it.

Surveyor/estate agent

The advice available

You may at some stage want the help and advice of a surveyor or estate agent in your search for suitable premises. This may include:

❑ structural surveys. This could be important if you are considering buying a freehold or signing a lease which includes the condition that you carry out repairs and maintenance

❑ funding and assessing of suitable premises and negotiation with the landlords or vendors

❑ advice on whether planning permission or the landlord's consent for change of use is required and helping to make the application for you.

How to choose

For advice on structure, repairs and maintenance use a qualified surveyor, that is, a member of the Royal Institution of Chartered Surveyors. If it is a question of valuation and negotiation, (consider using the Incorporated Society of Valuers and Auctioneers – see Reference).

Cost

The answer is much the same as with other advisers: agree with your chosen adviser the scope of the work to be done before any of it is carried out and ask for a quote.

Designer

The advice available

Design can be a crucial element in the success of a business. It may not appear as obvious as the need for accounting or legal expertise, and yet it is. Designers can give help and advice on the visual elements of your business and product. There are specialists in:

❑ setting the image of your business or corporate identity (p. 121)

❑ fitting out premises, where this is important for customers or suppliers (p. 185)

❑ designing what your product looks like or product positioning (p. 17)

❑ selecting what your employees wear and what your vans look like (livery specialists)

❑ using letterheads, logos, brochures and leaflets (pp. 125, 123, 140)

❑ packaging.

Using a design shop can be a more cost-effective alternative than an advertising agency for a small business, especially as you are likely to adopt other means of getting your message across than straight advertisements.

You may find that some printers have designers working with them, and this could be the most cost-effective of all. However, cheapness is not the best option, if you fail to achieve your objectives because of the poor quality of advice. You must still assess how good the advice is.

Before you approach a designer you should have a clear idea of what you want, although be prepared to listen to suggestions. You should ask the designer to show you a wide range of ideas in what is called 'scamp' form, which is a very cheap way of letting you see what sort of impression the idea will give. Settle on two or three ideas that you think are consistent with your product or business and ask the designer to work in more detail on these.

How to choose

The best way of finding a designer whose advice you value is to ask friends and colleagues for recommendations. Another approach is to keep an eye open for work you admire which other businesses have, for example, a logo you think good, an effective premise fitting and so on. Most businesses will be flattered if you ask who helped design it. Whichever way you choose of finding some names of designers, ask for references and see examples of the work done.

Cost

There are two elements of cost: the idea, and carrying out the idea into production. A designer should be able to give you a quote.

Corporate finance adviser

As well as advising on the financing of businesses, these advisers can act as an intermediary between those wanting funds and those with money to invest, such as venture capital funds or business angels (private individuals with the funds and the willingness to invest in private companies). They are likely to be interested in advising those who wish to raise substantial funds.

They may also be able to give advice on raising money and floating on the Alternative Investment market or AIM (the Stock Exchange's junior market for young and small companies). Finally, there is also a trading facility called OFEX which your advisor might be able to introduce you to. To get information on AIM and OFEX see Reference.

The advice available

Corporate finance advisers will look into a business plan and proposal, and their sponsorship of it should carry some weight with investors, but this only applies if their reputation is sound. Many of the large firms of accountants have specialist corporate finance sections. There are four ways they may be able to help you:

❏ advice on the marketing strategy

❏ advice on the organizational structure, in particular whether there are gaps in the top management and how the structure can be strengthened

❑ a check on your projections

❑ advice on the amount of money and how to raise it.

How to choose

There are those who are very good and those who are awful, but, unfortunately there is no clear-cut way of finding the name of a good adviser. Probably the best way is to ask other people how they raised funds and if they would recommend the person who helped. Magazines which are aimed at those running small businesses may have articles about who has raised money and how much. Contact the managing director of the firm who raised the funds and ask for a recommendation. However you get the name, always ask for references.

Cost

A corporate finance adviser may charge a flat fee or a fee dependent upon the sum raised, say, between 2½ and 4 per cent of the money raised. But there may also be demands for shares or options on shares and directorships.

Summary

1. You can improve your chances of success by using professional advisers with their expert knowledge. Select your advisers at an early stage in your business planning.

2. Agree with your advisers at the outset what work they will do for you. Make sure you both understand and agree the scope of the work.

3. Take up references and ask for estimates of costs before the work begins.

Other chapters to read

3. **A spot of coaching** (p. 27)
21. **Insurance** (p. 244)

19. **Getting the right staff**

Deciding when to take on an employee is a delicate balancing act. On the one hand, if you increase your manpower, you might not be able to cover increased costs straightaway. On the other hand, extra manpower could free you to spend more time on other activities, such as marketing or planning, which should, in the end, mean increased profits.

A useful rule of thumb for choosing the best time to increase your manpower is to ask yourself if you can generate enough extra sales to cover the cost of taking on that extra employee. If you will not be able to increase your sales straightaway, you could still employ someone; but, in this case, you will need to be able to keep your business going until you have been able to build your sales up to the new level you need. It all sounds straightforward, but in practice it is very tricky. It is like being on a seesaw. One step in the wrong direction can tip the balance against you.

If you are clever enough, or lucky enough, to get your timing right, you will not want to throw away your advantage by employing the wrong person. The whole process can take several months; so finding you have made a mistake and having to recruit again can throw your business off its planned course. Nor should you underestimate the emotional problems of getting rid of an unsuitable employee, which can unnerve the toughest of businessmen or businesswomen and unsettle other employees.

What is in this chapter?

This chapter looks at how to recruit. It should help you to answer three questions:

❑ Do I know what I'm looking for?

❑ Will I recognize it when I see it?

❑ Can I make sure that, if I offer the job, it will be accepted?

There are sections on the job that needs doing (p. 202), the employee you want (p. 204), getting the right person to apply (p. 206) and interviewing (p. 211). The cost of employing staff is covered on p. 215.

The job that needs doing

Before you plunge into adding that extra employee, look carefully at the work to be done. It is very important to sort out in your own mind what the job entails. Once you have done this you can define the person you need. If you fail to do this preparatory work, you might find yourself employing someone who is not capable of doing the work. This list of topics might help you to organize your thoughts about the job:

❑ *level of skill:* when you decided you needed an extra pair of hands, was it because you needed work done which you did not feel competent to carry out yourself? Does the work require a special skill?

❑ *training:* if you have the skill to do the job, but not the time, would it take a lot of training to employ someone without that particular skill and teach them on the job? Would you have the time to carry out that training?

❑ *length of time:* do you estimate that this extra work will need doing for a long period of time? Or is it a temporary bulge? Watch out for mistaking a backlog of work which can be cleared up quickly for a permanent increase in activity

❑ *how much extra work:* can you quantify how much time will need to be spent by someone to carry out the work? Is it a full working week? Do not assume that if you find work difficult and time-consuming, because it is outside your range of skills, a skilled employee will take as long as you to complete the work

❑ *experience:* do you think the job requires a lot of experience? Would the employee need to be able to make independent judgements? Or is it intended that the work will be closely directed by yourself or another?

❑ *responsibility:* how much responsibility will the employee have? Will the employee be required to man the office alone? If the job is selling, will the person be required to go out selling unsupervised? Will the employee handle money? Or be responsible for other staff? To whom will the employee be responsible – yourself or some other member of your business?

❑ *tasks:* list the things that need to be done by your new employee. Work out for whom the tasks will be done and the importance of the tasks

❑ *authority:* work out what your new employee can do without asking you or someone else for permission – for example, making appointments, spending money up to a certain limit

❏ *contacts:* will your new employee need to deal directly with the general public or your customers? Will the contact be face-to-face, on the telephone or by letter?

❏ *special circumstances:* does the job involve working during unsocial hours? Will your new member of staff need to do much travelling away from home? Will the working conditions be unpleasant or dangerous?

❏ *future developments:* consider how the job might develop and expand in the future. You need to assess a job hunter for this potential, too.

Setting out your thoughts in this way may seem like overkill, if the job is relatively simple. But hiring and firing a succession of unsatisfactory people will be more time-consuming and disruptive to your business than spending an hour or so defining the job; and marshalling your thoughts in this way will also help you to decide whether there really is a job that needs doing.

Another way of examining your needs would be to fill out a job description form. Try using the simple one below:

Example: job description

Job title: ....

Purpose of job: ....

Whom the employee works for: ....

Who works for the employee:..

Main tasks:..

1. ....

2. ....

3. (and so on) ....

What authority the employee has: ....

1. ....

2. ....

3. (and so on) ....

Duties: ....

1. ....

2. ....

3. (and so on) ....

Contacts: ....

Internal: ....

External: ....

Possible development of the job: ....

The employee you want

Your next task is to match the employee to the job. Decide if you need some-one full-time or part-time. Think about what experience and qualifications the employee will need and specify clearly what personal abilities are need-ed to do the job.

Full-time employees?

Conventionally, most employees are permanent, full-time and salaried, but this may not suit your business. Do not ignore other ways of getting the job done. Look closely at the following:

❑ help from your family

❑ contract or temporary staff

❑ part-time staff

❑ commission-only salespeople or agents.

Your family

Do not overlook the possibility of your wife or husband or other relative helping out. Employing your family may not be the permanent solution you seek, but it may help to tide you over until you are confident that taking on an extra employee is justified.

Freelance staff

For quite a number of jobs it is possible to get people who are happy to work on a freelance basis. This means you will pay an agreed fee, but have no responsibility for national insurance contributions, sickness payments or holiday pay. And if the extra work comes to an end, you need feel no responsibility towards finding more work for a contractor, as long as you made it clear that the work was temporary or was a contract for a particu-lar piece of work or period of time, but less than a year.

A further advantage of using freelance staff is that it can be a good opportunity for you and the person to size each other up and see if you could work together, before you offer a permanent job.

There are two main disadvantages of solving your extra workload in this way. First, it can cost you more than taking on permanent staff to get the particular piece of work done. If the job involves a skill which is widely demanded and in short supply, a self-employed contractor's rate is likely to be correspondingly high. And if you are using a temp, you will have to pay a fee if an employment agency introduces the temp. Second, while some contractors or temps may be keen and enthusiastic, others may be less so.

Your legal obligations to temporary freelance workers or to people who contract out their services is rather hazy. You may also find that someone you regard as a freelance is considered an employee by the Inland Revenue and DSS. You could also consider whether you may be able to receive some temporary help by using one of the government's schemes, such as the New Deal. This will give you extra help towards the cost of taking on a new employee – a subsidy of up to £60 a week for six months per employee and up to £750 towards training them.

Part-time staff

If the work you want doing does not add up to a full working week, consider getting someone in on a part-time basis. Your duties to a part-time employee vary according to the number of hours worked – see Chapter 20, 'Your rights and duties as an employer' (p. 220).

Commission-only salespeople or agents

Do not automatically think in terms of a salaried employee if you are looking to boost your selling effort. You may be able to find someone competent who would prefer to be paid by getting a commission on each item sold. Again this will cut your risks – no sales means no pay. However, the commission you will pay will be greater per item than to a salaried employee who also gets commission on sales.

Who is right for the job?

Try to develop an idea of the sort of person who will perform well in the job and in your business. Use the groups of characteristics listed below to help you sort out what is important for the job and what is not. You can use this to help you specify the person you need for the job, and use it to help you collect your thoughts while interviewing.

Here are some useful ways of grouping characteristics:

❑ *physical make-up:* this covers the employee's health, physique, appearance, manner, age and speech

❑ *achievements:* what education, qualifications and experience do you expect?

❑ *general intelligence:* this is rather difficult to judge if you are not a psychologist, but what sort of reasoning ability should the person have? How quickly do they understand what you are saying?

❑ *special aptitudes:* what particular skills do you need, for example, mechanical, verbal, numerical or manual skills?

❑ *interests:* what are the person's hobbies and leisure activities? Are there any particular hobbies which would be more or less suitable for the person who is needed to do this job? Check how much time is spent on interests. Is this likely to conflict with the job?

❑ *circumstances:* include only those factors which are essential to the job

❑ *personal characteristics:* this covers the slightly tricky area of whether the person has the right personality to cope with that particular type of job. Try to avoid focussing on characteristics which can be met only by certain sections of the population.

For more details on the above, see Reference.

It would be a good idea to pick out of the list those characteristics which you think are very important and those which would be an advantage but are not crucial for this particular job. It is always tempting to demand very high qualifications, experience and so on, but it is wiser to be fairly flexible in your requirements and not overstate what is needed to carry out the job satisfactorily. In any case you should always remember that employing someone who is over-qualified for a job may lead to a rapid staff turnover, as the employee may soon get bored.

As well as picking out those characteristics which you need or hope to find, it is equally important to sort out those which would be a definite disadvantage to someone carrying out the job.

Getting the right person to apply

Once you have completed the essential preparation and so got a clear idea of what job you need doing and what sort of person you would like to fill the job, your problem now becomes: how can I find the person I want?

The main ways you can tell job hunters about the job on offer are:

❑ by advertising direct

❑ through recruitment agencies and consultants

❑ through friends, existing employees and business contacts

❑ by recruiting direct from colleges.

Use more than one method to fill a job as it will widen the field.

Advertising direct

You can get in touch with the local Jobcentre, if the vacancy is suitable. Failing this, you can advertise direct in the appropriate newspapers or magazines. This could be tricky if writing is not your strong suit. However, there are certain guidelines you can follow to help you.

Remember that the purpose of the ad is to attract someone who will be able to do the job very well and who will settle down happily in your business. You have to tell job hunters enough about the job to stimulate their interest and make them feel it is worth having a closer look; equally, you want to use the ad as a starting point of the selection process. So you want to make it clear to those applicants who would be suitable that they should apply and to those applicants who would not be suitable that they should not. Finally, the ad should be interesting enough to attract attention compared with what else is on offer in that newspaper or magazine the same day.

From research which has been done on what attracts people to join a company, some of the more important points are listed below in order of priority:

❑ the prospects for interesting and creative work

❑ the prospects for promotion and pay

❑ the quality and reputation of the company's products or services

❑ the opportunity to use 'brains'

❑ the security of the job

❑ the company's past financial record

❑ congenial working environment.

How does your business and the job you are offering rate against these points? In your ad, you need to draw attention to your strong points. Most small and new businesses would score high on giving lots of scope for interesting and creative work and the opportunity to use 'brains'. In particular, an employee would be given the opportunity to be part of the whole business and not just in one department. However, if it is a new business, there may be little reputation built up for its products and its financial record may be short.

When it comes to writing the ad, the style could be important in attracting job hunters' interest. Be informal and friendly – but not too friendly. Use 'you' and 'your' when you are speaking about the person needed and 'we' and 'our' when talking about your business, but avoid over-chatty comments and stick to the facts.

Checklist: what should be in the ad?

❏ *company name:* put in the name and logo, if you have one

❏ *job title:* use a title or description which will mean something to a stranger

❏ *pay:* state what salary can be expected. Job hunters interpret phrases like 'salary negotiable' as meaning a low salary

❏ *place:* state where the job is. If you are not offering moving expenses, this is very important. In any case, people like to know what the environment of the job is

❏ *the work:* describe the work to be done and say what authority the job has

❏ *the company:* state what your company does and what size it is. Avoid clichés about dynamism, fast-growing and so on; all companies use them

❏ *the person:* state your requirements, such as experience needed, qualifications, age and other personal qualities

❏ *how to apply:* name the person to write to, not just the job title. Tell the job hunter how you want them to give details of experience and qualifications – for example, send in brief CV, apply for application form and so on

❏ *when to apply:* give a closing date for applications, if possible allowing two to three weeks from the appearance of the ad

❏ *the law:* check your ad is not breaking sex or race discrimination law (see Chapter 20, 'Your rights and duties as an employer' (p. 220)). And make sure the information is accurate, as the ad may form part of the contract between you and your new employee.

How to apply

Asking for too much information from job hunters can deter people from applying, and you should remember that your business is competing with all others for the best talents. Keep your demands to a minimum. Asking applicants to write in has the advantage of letting you see what their written work is like – important, if that is an element of the job. It will also be less time-consuming for you at this stage. If you do give a telephone number that job applicants can ring, make sure it is always manned – and by someone who knows what they are talking about. You can use the telephone to sift out people, as well as to give them information. This can be done by preparing a shortlist of key questions, which you can ask over the phone.

An application form has the advantage of allowing you to compare information presented in an identical format. On the other hand, drawing one up would take you some time and may not be worthwhile, unless you are considering employing many people.

Where to put the ad

It depends on the job. Different newspapers and magazines will give you the response you need for different jobs. There are trade magazines which may have cornered the market for job ads in a particular specialization, for example, computing. For jobs which are not so specialized, local newspapers may provide a good response, for example, for clerical staff. A magazine called British Rate and Data lists newspapers and magazines and gives details of the cost of advertising and a profile of the readership for each of them. Your local library should be able to tell you where to see a copy.

The best market research about where job hunters look for jobs may be to ask people who work in that field where they would look if they wanted a new job.

The cost of advertising

The bigger the circulation of the newspaper or magazine, the more they charge for advertising. You have to weigh up the cost against the benefit of getting the size of response you need. Sometimes if the response is too high, it can overwhelm you.

Recruitment agencies and consultants

If you do not have the time to handle the advertising and to sift through all the applications, you can use an agency. Obviously, you have to pay for this, so you must be sure it is worth the extra cost; and do not forget that you will have to spend time in selecting the right agency, so the time-saving may not be as great as you think. Nor can you afford to skip any of the preparatory stages; you will still have to decide what the job is and what sort of person you want, so that the agency can do their job.

There are several different types of agencies:

❑ Jobcentres

❑ private employment bureaux (Alfred Marks or Brook Street, for example)

❑ selection consultants

❑ search consultants (or headhunters).

Using a Jobcentre is free and can be a useful source of applicants for manual and clerical jobs, but do not expect too much from the screening process. The private employment agencies charge varying amounts ranging from 6 to 20 per cent of first year's earnings, depending on the agency and type of job to be filled.

You can get a list of members of the Federation of Recruitment and Employment Services to help you pick out an agency (see Reference for the address and telephone number).

Friends, existing employees and business contacts

If you do get a strong recommendation from someone, do not rely totally on the friend's advice. Ask your prospective employee for a curriculum vitae (CV) and give them a copy of the job description (p. 203) and the advertisement you would have used. Observe all the necessary precautions by conducting a full and careful interview (see more about all this below).

This method of finding your new employee is not to be ignored, as it has several advantages. First, it is cheap. Second, if it is through a friend, you will start off knowing something about the abilities of the new person. Third, a new employee recruited in this way may find it easier to settle down in your organization.

The main disadvantage arises if the appointment proves unsuccessful; this can prove embarrassing if the contact was made through a friend and disruptive to a previously harmonious working relationship if the recommendation came from an existing employee. You also need to be careful that you do not miss out on possible good applicants because they are not known to you.

Recruiting direct

If you are looking for someone who does not need experience in your particular field or skill, you could try colleges and other organizations direct.

The sorts of skills you might be able to recruit direct in this way include secretarial, hotel and catering, retail management and so on.

If the type of job you have in mind could be done by a young school-leaver to whom you could give on-the-job training, it could be worthwhile finding out about the government's employment schemes for youngsters. Your local Jobcentre or Training and Enterprise Council (see Reference) can give you information. The government will pay you a grant towards the cost of employing and training each young person.

Interviewing

An interview has two purposes:

❏ it helps you choose your new employee

❏ it helps your new employee choose you.

It is important to remember that you should structure the interview process to enable you to find out what the applicant is really like and to allow the job hunter to find out about you and your company and decide that this is the job he or she wants.

Before you get to the interview stage you will have to sift the applications and decide who to select for a closer look.

Who should you see?

If your ad was successful, the sifting process will not be a case of eliminating totally unsuitable candidates; rather it will be to rank the applications according to how closely they match your ideal. If you are tempted to see someone who does not fit the bill but looks interesting, think twice. It means either that the requirements you set for the job were not the right ones or that you will be wasting your time on an unnecessary interview.

Once you have ranked them, choose to see the top five, say. If you do not find anyone in that group, you could try the next five. After that second-ranking group, if you still have not found the ideal person you may have to accept that your ad has been unsuccessful. You will need to reconsider how to find the person you want.

Getting ready for the interview

There are two stages. First, you must gather together the essential information you will need to give the job applicant. This can be conveyed in written form or orally, in which case you need the facts at your fingertips if you are to sound organized and efficient to the job hunter.

The questions you might be asked could be about:

❏ holidays. You need to be able to say how many weeks, when they can be taken and any restrictions you intend to impose

❏ illness. Explain what will happen if your employee is away from work because of illness

❏ starting date of the job, if this has been decided

❏ hours of work

❏ salary matters, such as when they are paid, any rules on overtime, bonuses or commission, if applicable.

The second stage of preparation is to work out what key questions you want to ask. One type of question would give you comparable information about the people you see. This could be a test question, such as describing a typical event in your business and asking what each person would do in those circumstances.

The second type of question is to help you pinpoint each candidate's strengths and weaknesses. The only way this can be done is by good preparation, reading the candidate's CV or whatever. There is no short cut. What you should look for is anything which seems odd or is not a smooth progression. Watch out for any unexplained gaps in the person's story; this may give you hints about poor health, unsatisfactory jobs or character. Notice very frequent job changes as this could raise questions in your mind about job success, as could a failure to match in employment the level of achievement suggested by educational qualifications.

Useful interview questions

1. What is the best part and worst part of your present job?

2. What bit of your work do you find difficult and what bit the easiest?

3. How do you rate your present boss?

4. Describe your ideal boss.

5. What do you consider to be your greatest success and why?

6. What do you consider to be your greatest failure and why?

7. When were you last angry at work? What caused the anger? What form did your anger take?

8. What is most important to you about the job you are looking for?

9. What will your family and friends think of your new job?

10. What are your greatest strengths?

11. What are your weaknesses?

12. What worries you most about the job?

13. What excites you most about the job?

These are all examples of the kind of open question which should prompt the candidates to reveal a bit more about themselves; use whichever seems most appropriate. As well as these questions, there are more straightforward ones about the present job, the career, education and so on which need to be asked.

Testing an applicant's skills and abilities can be very revealing and give you a lot of information to discuss in an interview. Try to devise some simple but relevant test.

Holding the interview

Some thought needs to be given beforehand to where the interview should be held and who should be present. The person you are interviewing will feel more relaxed if the interview is private and uninterrupted, so try to find somewhere where the interview will not be overlooked or overheard. If you are not going to be the new employee's boss, perhaps the person who is should sit in on the interview. If this is not possible, arrange for the new person's superior to see the candidate separately, if necessary on another day, before deciding to offer the job.

What should happen in the interview?

Roughly a useful interview could run along the following lines.

1. Spend a few minutes putting the applicant at ease, for example, talking about his or her interests

2. Ask open questions which the person you are interviewing will have to answer with more than a yes or no. The questions you ask should allow you to get some idea of whether the person could do the job well

3. Also ask closed questions designed to test a candidate's knowledge and skill, specific questions such as 'On what date ...?' and hypothetical questions, 'If you were ...'

4. Try using silence sometimes as a way of getting the person to expand. For example, once the person has finished explaining something, do not always leap in with another question but remain silent. Sometimes, the person being interviewed will be prompted to be more revealing

5. Keep in control of the interview while doing little talking, perhaps less than a third of the total time

6. Concentrate on listening and observing your applicant. This helps you to judge the replies and to pinpoint areas where you need to probe more. You should also reflect on what the person has said and feed it back to them

7. Be flexible; do not stick rigidly to a planned script. Try to develop what your interviewee has said

8. Take notes. They do not need to be very comprehensive, but sufficient to jog your memory when assessing the interview afterwards

9. Give a little detail about the job and how it fits in your business. You can miss out this and the next stage, if you have already concluded that the person is not suitable and thus save wasting time. It is important not to do this stage before asking the questions. If you do, you may have fed the person with sufficient information, so that he or she knows how to answer your questions

10. Ask the job applicant if there are any questions, or if he or she wishes to tell you anything else about suitability for the job, which has not been brought out by the questions

11. If the person seems promising, spend some time making sure that the job would be accepted if it was offered. After all, the person is selecting a new job in the hope that it will last for a while and will want to be confident that your job is really the best choice.

After the interview

You should summarize the interview straight afterwards while your memory is fresh. The aim of the summary will be to allow you to look back when you are choosing between the candidates, and to judge how closely each person matched up to the job you want done. In particular, you will want to remember later the person's strengths and weaknesses.

There are some other important actions to be taken before someone joins your staff. First, always take up references. It can be much better to speak to a referee direct on the phone than to interpret what the written word may be hiding; people can be much more unguarded 'off the record'. Always ask the direct question, 'Would you re-employ this person?' Second, if the job is an important one, consider having a medical done. It might throw up a problem which you would want to know about before hiring. Third, if the job involves driving, always ask to see the driving licence; do not be fobbed off by excuses.

Making the offer

Always make sure your written offer letter is conditional upon satisfactory references and medical, if applicable. Remember that this letter (and the ad) forms part of an employee's contract of employment (p. 225).

When the new employee joins

A new employee will feel more positive when starting a new job if presented with a planned induction and training period. It is well worth the extra effort on your part to prepare this in advance.

If it all goes wrong

Sometimes you can make mistakes. If it is a really bad one, you will need to know how to deal with it. In Chapter 20, 'Your rights and duties as an employer' (p. 220), there are details about the law on dismissing staff.

It could be worthwhile to interview a job leaver to see why it did not work out from the employee's viewpoint. You can learn from your mistakes and make a better choice next time.

The cost

The costs can be divided into two groups:

❑ one-off costs of employment, such as advertising costs and increased use of telephone. As well as these costs, there is also the time you spend interviewing or sifting through applications and the time and possible expenditure spent on training a new employee

❑ continuing costs of employment, such as salary, employer's national insurance contributions, fringe benefits you offer and extra office equipment. There will also be the extra costs created by the person carrying out the job; these may include more stationery, petrol, telephone or whatever.

What is your break-even point?

Your break-even point is the point at which your business is making the right amount of sales to give you enough profit to cover your overheads, which include rent and rates, heating and lighting. Sometimes employee costs are overheads and sometimes they are not. It all depends on what they do. If what the employee does is related to the level of sales, their costs will be called direct and are not part of overheads. Examples would include staff whose time is paid for by customers, or employees who are directly involved in making a product. But if the employee's job is something like accounting, marketing or general clerical duties, their costs will be included in overheads. In your business there may be a grey area in which it is difficult to decide whether the employee's costs are direct or not.

The purpose of finding your new break-even point is to work out how many extra sales you need to make to cover the cost of your new employee. You can see how to work out the break-even point in more detail in Chapter 24, 'Staying afloat' (p. 282).

Break-even point

First, you have to find what your gross profit margin is. This is your gross profit as a percentage of sales. You work out gross profit by deducting the amount of your direct costs from the value of your sales. Direct costs will be the purchases you need to make to supply your service or product and the costs of any labour directly associated with your sales.

Once you have worked out your gross profit margin, your second step is to work out the amount of your overheads (for example, rent, rates, heating, lighting, telephone costs, professional fees or labour costs, such as secretarial or book-keeping).

To find your break-even point, your third step is to divide the amount of your overheads by the gross profit margin. This will give the level of sales you need to make to cover your overheads.

Checklist: work out the extra cost of employment

	this year £	full year £
Salary or wages	...	...
Employer's NI contributions	...	...
Estimated commission, bonuses, overtime payments	...	...
Other possible costs or benefits:		
❏ employer's pension contributions	...	...
❏ use of car	...	...
❏ payment of subscriptions to professional societies	...	...
❏ cost of sick pay insurance	...	...
❏ others	...	...
....	...	...
....	...	...
....	...	...
Additional office space required	...	...
Additional equipment needed	...	...
Extra use of telephone, stationery, heating, lighting and so on	...	...
Total	...	...

Notes

1. Most small businesses will not be providing many fringe benefits, but you may need to consider doing so if you want to employ an experienced and skilled member of staff, for example, an accountant or salesman.
2. You will need to break down these costs into monthly expenditure (p. 251).
3. This breakdown of costs assumes that you rent, lease or hire any additional equipment, rather than buying it outright. For help in deciding which is the right way for you, see p. 190.

Example: Jeremy Jones works out his new break-even point

Jeremy Jones needs someone to act as a secretary and book-keeper. He used the checklist on p. 217 to work out the extra cost involved. The calculation is quite simple and looks like this for the full year:

Salary	£12,000
Employer's NI contributions	597
Extra use of telephone etc.	350
Total	£12,947

Jeremy now works out how it will change his break-even point:
He has estimated sales of £40,000 for this year with direct costs of £20,000. This gives a gross profit of:

$$£40,000 - 20,000 = £20,000$$

And his gross profit margin is:

$$\frac{£20,000}{£40,000} \times 100 = 50\%$$

His overheads, without taking on an assistant, come to an estimated £5,000 and after would come to £17,947 (£5,000 + £12,947).

Jeremy finds his break-even point before he employs someone. This he gets from the following sum:

$$\frac{\text{overheads}}{\text{gross profit margin}} \times 100 = \frac{£5,000}{50} \times 100 = £10,000$$

of sales to cover his overheads. If he employed an assistant, the break-even point would become:

$$\frac{£17,947}{50} \times 100 = £35,894 \text{ of sales}$$

Jeremy needs to increase his sales by £35,894 – £10,000 = £25,894 to cover the extra overhead created by employing his new assistant. As he has estimated his sales at £40,000 (compared with the £35,894 he needs), he goes ahead with employing an assistant.

Summary

1. Work out the costs of employing an extra person and watch the effect on your break-even point.

2. Make sure there is a job to be done.

3. Look to see if the work can be carried out in a non-permanent way, for example, temporary staff, contract or freelance worker.

4. Draw up a job description, no matter how simple or low-level the job seems.

5. Get a mental picture of the person for the job. Do not overstate your requirements. Pick out the characteristics which would be a dis- advantage in doing the job well.

6. You can save money by drafting your own ad. Use our checklist to make sure you include the necessary information.

7. Prepare thoroughly for interviews.

8. Ask open questions to get the job applicant to talk.

9. Don't forget to insist on a medical, if necessary; check all references and see the driving licence, if driving is part of the work.

10. Work out an induction and training programme. Do not put all the effort into finding the right person for the job and then, by not training them properly, end up with employees unable to function effectively and productively in your business.

Other chapters to read

20. **Your rights and duties as an employer** (p. 220)
24. **Staying afloat** (p. 282)

20. **Your rights and duties as an employer**

The idea of employment law can conjure up images of the Gorgon. You, as an employer, turned to stone when faced with the legal pitfalls of employment. There is further uncertainty over how a minimum national wage and the adoption of the European Social Chapter might affect flexibility and costs for employers. The myth remains that you cannot sack anyone. Well, it is not true.

By and large, you can employ whoever you want. You can set up your own criteria about who you want to employ but there should be good reasons for it – not solely because of sex, race, marital status and so on. There are some rules imposed, including what you can say; for example, you cannot put in an ad 'no blacks' or 'no whites', 'no women' or 'no men'.

You can normally dismiss unsatisfactory employees. But the law sets out that it should be done fairly. Even if you fall foul of the law, you can usually still sack someone, if you are prepared to pay some money in compensation. However, this may turn out to be a risky, time-consuming and very expensive course of action, so why not brush up on your employment law knowledge and follow the rules on what you should do?

This chapter should give you some guidelines about how:

❑ to take on an employee (p. 223)

❑ to pay staff (p. 226)

❑ to provide a safe and healthy working environment (p. 232)

❑ to avoid discrimination (p. 235)

❑ to treat an employee if pregnant (maternity) (p. 238)

❑ to dismiss them if unsatisfactory (saying goodbye) (p. 240)

If you need more advice and guidance, contact Advisory, Conciliation and Arbitration Service (ACAS, see Reference). If your worry is sex discrimination, the Equal Opportunities Commission would be able to help, and the Commission for Racial Equality can give guidance on racial discrimination (see Reference for addresses).

Employment law is very complex. This chapter can do no more than give general guidelines, and the coverage cannot be considered comprehensive.

Bird's eye view of your rights and duties

In general terms, apart from what is in the employment contract, what can you expect from your employees and what can they expect from you?

Your rights

1. Your employees should be honest and obedient and not act against your interests.

2. They should not disclose confidential information about your business to others.

3. They should take care of your property.

4. Any patents, discoveries or inventions made during working hours belong to you.

5. Your employees should be competent, work carefully and industriously.

Your duties

1. You should behave reasonably in employment matters.

2. You should practise good industrial relations, such as clear disciplinary procedures and grievance procedures.

3. You should pay your employees when you agreed to do so.

4. You should take reasonable care to ensure the safety and health of your employees.

As well as these general rights and duties, your employees acquire certain rights by law. Some of the rights in the legal life-cycle of an employee (see overleaf) used to apply only to full-time workers and part-timers had to work five years to qualify for them. However, from 6 February 1995, UK law has changed to bring it into line with European legislation. Now part-time workers have the same rights as full-time employees.

If your business employs more than five employees

There is an additional requirement. An employee may have the right to return to work after pregnancy, and this applies if she has been employed by you for two years or more (p. 239). And if your business has 20 or more employees, disabled employees have the right not to be discriminated against either in the recruitment procedures you use or during the course of their employment (for example, they must be treated equally when it comes to opportunities, training, promotion, and so on). As an employer, you will be under a duty to take reasonable steps to remove physical barriers and to adjust your working practices, so that any disabled employees can exercise these rights.

What is in the rest of this chapter?

The rest of this chapter fills out the details. But it cannot cover every single employment possibility. The Employment Department produces very useful booklets to give guidance on employment matters. The appropriate booklets are listed throughout this chapter. You can get the booklets from local offices of the Employment Service, for example Jobcentres.

Legal life-cycle of an employee

How long employed	What you must do
new starter	**1**. Do not discriminate on racial grounds (p. 236)
	2. Do not discriminate on grounds of sex (p. 235) or against married people
	3. Pay equal pay to men and women (p. 230)
	4. Do not discriminate because of trade union membership (p. 236)
	5. Since 2 December 1996, do not discriminate against disabled people (p. 237)
	6. Give an itemized statement with pay (p. 227)
	7. Give paid time off for ante-natal care
	8. Consult recognized trade union about redundancy (p. 242)

9. Do not dismiss unfairly because of pregnancy (p. 238)

10. Give written reason if dismissing because of pregnancy

11. From 1 October 1998, do not insist an employee works more than 48 hours a week and give 20 minutes rest break after six hours of work (p. 232)

one month or more

12. Give the minimum notice periods required by law (p. 242)

13. Pay guaranteed pay if you have no work (p. 230)

within two months

14. Give a written statement of the main terms and conditions of employment (p. 225)

within three months

15. From 1 October 1998, give three weeks paid holiday (p. 232)

six months or more

16. Pay Statutory Maternity Pay (p. 239)

two years or more

17. Give written reasons for dismissal (other than pregnancy), if requested.

18. Do not dismiss unfairly (p. 240)

19. Do not dismiss due to pregnancy (p. 238)

20. Pay redundancy money (p. 242)

21. Give paid time off work to look for work in redundancy

22. Give job to employee back from maternity leave, unless original/alternative unavailable

Taking on an employee

The most important part of employing someone is to select the right person for the right job in the first place. The techniques of job description, advertising the job, selecting for interview and interviewing are covered in

Chapter 19, 'Getting the right staff' (p. 201). However, there are certain legal points to look out for to ensure that you and your employee get off to a happy start.

What you must do

Broadly:

1. Do not discriminate because of sex, marital status or race in ads, interview and job descriptions. Under the Disability Discrimination Act 1995, you must not disciminate against disabled people, for example, by setting different selection arrangements or offering different terms of employment. This, does not apply if you have fewer than twenty employees

2. Tell your tax office when you take on an employee

3. Give your employee a written statement within two months of starting work.

Starter rules

You should be careful that sex, racial or other sorts of discrimination do not creep into ads or interviews. Avoid using job titles which imply one sex or the other – foreman, for example. If you use this sort of job title, include in the ad a note that you welcome applications from both sexes. Avoid using 'he' or 'she' to describe a job applicant in an ad as it suggests you want applications from men only, if you use 'he', or women only, if you use 'she'. And be careful that illustrations don't give the impression that the job is a man's or woman's job. In an interview avoid asking women about their husband, their marriage or family responsibilities.

The job should be described accurately in the ad and in the letter offering the job. These two can form part of the contract of employment. When you do take on an employee, you should tell your tax office. Remember to get your new employee's P45; if your employee does not have one, fill out P46. When your employee has been with you for two months, you must have given your new employee a written statement of the conditions and terms of the job (see right).

It would be wise to take note of the actual day on which your employee starts. The date can determine whether you may be able to dismiss your employee fairly or not, if things do not work out. Remember that dismissal because of sex, marital status or race will be unfair from day one. And in a recent case, employees made redundant because of their age were said to be unfairly dismissed.

What is the contract of employment?

The words 'contract of employment' conjure up thoughts of a written document. But the terms of your employee's contract of employment can be made up of anything you write or say. It can include what you say in the ad, in the interview, in the offer letter, when your employee starts work and any subsequent chat you have about the terms and conditions of the job.

The basic contract is offer of employment, acceptance of employment and agreed amount of payment; these can be oral or written. Anything else makes up the terms.

What you have to put in the written statement

The statement should include your name and your employee's name. You have to say when your employee's present job began and when your employee's period of continuous employment began.

You also have to give information on various terms and conditions. The terms and conditions are:

❑ the scale or rate of pay, including how it is worked out

❑ at what intervals payments will be made (weekly, monthly, etc.)

❑ hours of work, including normal working hours

❑ holidays, including public holidays, and holiday pay, including how it is worked out

❑ place of work

❑ your employee's job title or a brief outline of the work.

As well as the statement, you must give further information on:

❑ sickness or injury and sick pay

❑ pensions and pension scheme

❑ length of notice to be given by you and your employee

❑ if the contract is "temporary", an indication of the expected duration

❑ details of any collective agreement affecting the job.

There has to be a written note giving information about disciplinary rules but only if you and any associated business have twenty or more employees. And you have to give the name of a person to whom the employee can apply if dissatisfied with any disciplinary decision or if the employee wants to raise a grievance. Finally, you also have to state whether a contracting-out certificate under the Social Security Pensions Act 1975 is in force which applies to your employee.

Who gets a written statement?

Most employees do unless:

❑ you have already given your employee a written contract of employment which includes all the above items

❑ the employment is for less than a month

❑ your employee will be working mainly outside Great Britain.

Booklets

Inland Revenue (IR), *Employer's Guide to PAYE* CWG1
IR, *Thinking of Taking Someone On?* CWL3
Equal Opportunities Commission (EOC), *Code of Practice*
Commission for Racial Equality (CRE), *Code of Practice*
Department of Trade and Industry (DTI), *Written statement of employment particulars* URN96/752
DTI, *Example form of a written statement of employment particulars* PL700A
Advisory, Conciliation and Arbitration Service (ACAS), *Employing People; a handbook for small firms*
ACAS, *Recruitment and induction*

Pay and working hours

There are quite a lot of rules about how you can pay, how much you have to pay and what you have to give with pay.

What you must do

Broadly:

1. Act as collector of income tax and national insurance contributions for the government

2. In most cases, do not deduct anything from your employees' pay unless they ask you to do so in writing or if it is in the contract of employment

3. Pay Statutory Sick Pay and Statutory Maternity Pay if due

4. Give equal pay to employees carrying out broadly similar work or work of equal value.

How much do you have to pay?

In many cases, deciding how much and how often you pay your employee will be negotiated between you and your employee. Whatever is decided will be part of your employee's contract of employment. You can also negotiate the question of bonuses, commission, overtime, holiday pay and sick pay.

If your business was formerly covered by a Wages Council (now abolished), any employees previously covered by a Wages Order, will still retain those rights. You will have to vary their contracts to change this, and this can be a tricky procedure, so take advice.

A statutory minimum hourly rate will be introduced from 1 April 1999. It is proposed that you must pay employees at least £3.60 an hour (£3.00 an hour if aged 20 or less).

What you can, or have to, deduct from pay

You cannot deduct anything from your employee's pay unless it has been laid down by law or unless it has the written agreement of your employee.

By law, you have to act as a tax collector. This means you have to deduct tax and national insurance contributions from your employee's pay (p. 230). And on the rare occasion it happens, you may also have to act to enforce a court order, by deducting sums from an employee's earnings under what is called an attachment of earnings. This may occur, for example, for paying maintenance under a Child Support Agency ruling or for paying a fine.

You can, however, make some deductions, if your employee has agreed in writing. For example, you can deduct a sum of money and hand it over to someone else, such as dues to a union or donations to a charity under a payroll giving scheme.

What you have to give your employee with the pay

You must give your employees a detailed written pay statement when or before they are paid.

What must be written in the statement is laid down by law. It must include:

❑ the amount of your employee's salary before any deductions are made

❑ if you deduct any sums of money, which can vary from pay day to pay day, you must say what the amount of each deduction is and what it is for

❑ if you deduct any sums of money which remain the same on each pay day, you can do one of two things. Either, you can say how much each deduction is and what it is for on each pay slip. Or, on the pay slip, you can say what the total of these fixed deductions is and separately from the pay slip give a statement of what the sums of money are used for.

This separate written statement must be handed out at twelve-monthly intervals. It must say how much, when and why any deductions are made and you must hand it to your employee before or when they are made. If these fixed deductions are changed you have to give your employee written notice or an amended written statement

❑ the amount of your employee's pay after all deductions.

If your employee is paid by more than one method, your pay slip should show how much is paid in each way, half in cash and half by bank transfer, for example.

Do you have to give holiday pay?

From 1 October 1998, all employees are entitled to three weeks paid holiday leave. From 23 November 1999 it is proposed to increase this to four weeks.

Do you have to give sick pay?

Yes and no. If you have agreed to give your employee pay while ill, you must do so as it is part of the employment contract. How much pay and for how long should be set out by you in the written statement of employment, which you have to give your employee within two months of starting the job (p. 225).

For most of your other employees you will have to give Statutory Sick Pay. Employers are required by law to pay SSP to their employees during sickness if the qualifying conditions are met. The weekly rate for 1998–99 is £57.70 for employees with average weekly earnings of £64 or more. All employers are eligible to reclaim the SSP paid out in any month where it comes to more than 13 per cent of the total National Insurance contributions (both employer and employee) paid. This new relief is called the 'percentage threshold scheme' and is designed to protect employers from the heavy cost they would otherwise face if there were an epidemic.

Employees will qualify for SSP if they are aged 16 and over and are sick for at least four days in a row. This is known as a Period of Incapacity for Work (PIW). All days count towards sickness, including weekends and public holidays, but you only pay SSP for qualifying days. These are normally the days your employee works. No SSP is payable for the first three days of sickness in a PIW – these are known as waiting days.

For absences of four to seven days it is usual to ask your employee to sign a self-certificate form (your own or form SC1 or SC2, available free from Social Security offices). For absences of more than seven days it is usual to ask for a medical certificate. You cannot insist on a medical certificate for absences of less than seven days.

Your employee is not entitled to SSP if, for example:

❑ your employee's average weekly earnings before sickness were less than the lower earnings limit for national insurance contributions (£64 from 6 April 1998), or

❑ your employee was 65 or over on the first day of sickness.

For more information about the SSP scheme, see Contributions Agency leaflet CA30 Statutory Sick Pay – Manual for employers.

If you have no work for an employee, do you have to pay?

Generally speaking, pay is negotiated between you and your employees, without any government intervention. Whether employees are paid when there is no work or they are unable to work will be decided by negotiation. However, in most cases you will pay your employees' salary or wages regardless of how much work you have and regardless of whether something happens, such as a power strike, which means your employee cannot do the work required.

But if your employee is paid by the hour or on piece rate, you do not have to pay:

❑ unless you have agreed to do so in the contract of employment, or

❑ unless you have to make what is known as a guarantee payment.

You may have to make this payment, once your employee has worked for you continuously for a month, for any days when he or she is not provided with work throughout a day during which there would normally be work. Guarantee payments can apply to all workers, not just hourly and piece-rate workers. You have to pay for a workless day whichever is the less:

£15.35 a day unless they earn less than that a day.

This payment may be made up to five times in a three-month period. The limit on the guarantee payment is reviewed, but not necessarily changed, each year.

Equal pay

You cannot pay one employee more than another because one is a man and the other a woman. For example, simply to say that a man is stronger is no defence to justify higher wages. If your employees are doing the same or broadly similar work or work of equal value, you should pay the same rate to each and give each the same terms of employment. 'Broadly similar' means that the differences between the two jobs are not of practical importance.

You can pay one employee more than another if there is a genuine non-sex-based reason for it. An example would be if one of your employees had been with you for many years and you had a scheme to pay employees a higher rate after a number of years.

How to operate the PAYE system

You have to act as a tax collector for the government. On each pay day you have to deduct the correct amount of tax and national insurance contributions from your employee's pay and you have to send it to the tax collector. Here are the steps to take when you employ someone:

1. Tell your tax office. If it is your first employee, tell your own tax inspector. You will be told which is your PAYE tax office as an employer, which could be different from the office which handles your tax affairs as an individual.

2. Work out the tax and national insurance contributions you have to deduct each pay day. Your PAYE tax office will send you the tax and NI tables you need to calculate this.

3. Fill in the Deductions Working Sheet you have been sent by the tax office. Do this for each pay day.

4. Within fourteen days of the end of each month send the tax and NI contributions to the accounts office. You will have been given pay slips to send in with the money.

5. At the end of each tax year (5 April), you will receive a return form from the Inland Revenue asking for details of the pay and benefits of each employee. You must send in these details by the date on the form – if you don't, you'll be fined. You can use your Deductions Working Sheet to complete the return. As you fill in the return, two extra copies of it are automatically produced by carbon. You give one of those copies to your employee as form P60 no later than 31 May. The other two copies you send to the tax office, together with a statement summarizing the returns for all your employees.

You will not have to do this if your employee earns less than a certain amount – in the 1998–99 tax year, the PAYE threshold is £81 a week or £350 a month for tax; the lower-earnings limit is £64 a week, £278 a month for NI contributions. But even if your employee earns less than the limits, you still have to tell your tax office.

Your employee should give you a P45 on the first day of the job; if not, you should fill in P46. You should fill in P45 when an employee leaves. You send the top part of it to your tax office and give the rest (Parts 2 and 3) to your employee.

Fringe benefits as pay

Fringe benefits, such as a company car or cheap meals, can often be worth more to an employee than a salary rise, even though the tax treatment changed from April 1994 to make this more expensive for the employer. Also you have now to pay National Insurance on your car benefit. How much of your employee's pay package is made up of salary and how much of fringe benefits is a matter of negotiation.

You have to send in a form P11D each year to the Inland Revenue by the date on the notice requesting information, which gives information about fringe benefits and expenses. The form needs to be filled in for:

❑ employees earning at the rate of £8,500 a year or over, including the taxable value of fringe benefits and expenses. So you might have to fill in a form for employees whose salary is much less than £8,500, if they also have a lot of perks, and

❑ any directors, unless the director earns less than £8,500, including perks, works full-time for you and has 5 per cent or less of the shares, including what his or her family and friends own.

Working hours

From 1 October 1998, the following rules apply:

❑ for most employees, working hours must be limited to an average of no more than 48 hours a week. The average would be worked out over a period of 17 weeks. An employee can agree to work longer than this but it must be in writing and the employee must be able to withdraw agreement.

❑ employees are entitled to one uninterrupted rest day in every seven

❑ a working day should be no longer than 13 hours

❑ after three months' employment all employees are entitled to three weeks paid holiday a year (four weeks from 23 November 1999).

Booklets

IR, *Employer's Further Guide to PAYE* CWG2
CA, *Employer's manual on statutory sick pay* CA30
CA, *Quick Reference Cards* CA27
EOC, *Code of Practice*
DfEE, *Itemized pay statement* PL704
DfEE, *Guarantee payments* PL724
DfEE, *Rules governing continuous employment and a week's pay* PL711
DfEE, *Sex Discrimination and Equal pay* URN98/576
DfEE, *Redundancy payments* PL808
ACAS, *Employing People: a handbook for small firms*
ACAS, *Introduction to payment systems*

Safe and healthy working environment

You have to provide a reasonable standard of health and safety not only for your employees but also for visiting workers, other visitors and members of the general public who may be affected by what you do. This applies to the safety of the premises as well as to any risks arising from the work itself.

Note that an Inspector has the right to enter your workplace to examine it and enforce legal requirements.

What you must do

Once you have employees there are additional rules. Broadly:

1. Tell whichever organisation is responsible for health and safety at work for your business what your business name and address are. If you have an office, shop, warehouse, restaurant or funeral parlour, for example, your local authority (usually the Environmental Health Department) will be responsible. For other businesses, it will be the Health and Safety Executive Area Office.

2. Get employer's liability insurance and display the certificate at each place of work.

3. Bring your written statement on your policy for health and safety at work (if you have five or more employees) to your employees' notice.

4. Display the Health and Safety Law Poster or hand out the equivalent leaflet.

5. Make an assessment of the fire risks of your workplace – and keep a written record if you have five or more employees.

Insurance

You must have employer's liability insurance to cover you for any physical injury or disease your employees get as a result of their work (p. 245). The latest certificate must be displayed.

Safe working environment

You must see that the place where your employees work, and the entrance and exit to it, are reasonably safe. Making a safe place of work includes things like fire exits and extinguishers, electrical fittings, storing material, machinery, hygiene, first aid; the list is very wide and covers all aspects of work.

You also have to take steps to provide a system of working for your employees which will give adequate safety. This includes making sure your employees are given adequate information and are trained well enough to carry out the work safely. And you also need to check that the system of working is actually being carried out.

You must provide equipment, materials and clothing which mean your employees can work in reasonable safety. You could be held responsible if there is a defect in the things you give to your employee which causes an accident.

If there is a risk of injury from criminals or others, you must take steps to protect your employees.

Competent workers

If you know one of your employees is incompetent, and if one of your other employees is injured as a result of that incompetence, you could be held liable. And even if you do not believe your employee to be inefficient, but your employee behaves negligently while carrying out your work, and another employee or a member of the general public is injured, you can be held liable.

If one of your employees breaks a safety rule which you have publicized, you can fairly sack your employee. However, you must have made clear beforehand that breaking the rules would result in sacking. The reverse side of the coin is that if you do not take reasonable steps for the safety of your employees, an employee could resign and claim constructive dismissal (p. 242).

Paperwork

If you have five or more employees, you must have a written statement on your policy for health and safety at work and how that policy is to be carried out. This statement should be displayed so that employees can see it.

Regardless of the number of employees, you must also either display the Health and Safety Law Poster at work or hand out the appropriate leaflet. You can get these from your local HSE office.

If you have ten or more employees, you must keep an accident book to record work accidents. If you have a 'factory', you have to keep a book like this, regardless of the number of employees. And for all businesses certain accidents must be notified to the authority which regulates your business for health and safety.

You must make an assessment of the risks relating to your work premises and identify any safety measures you need to take. If you have five or more employees, you need to keep a written record of this.

Booklets

HSE, *Everyone's Guide to Riddor* HSE31
HSE, *Five Steps to Risk Assessment*
HSC, *Writing and safety policy* HSC6
ACAS, *Health and employment*

Discrimination: what to watch out for

In general, you cannot discriminate on grounds of sex or race, and in employment, you cannot discriminate against married people or those with union membership. Whether you can impose age limits (for example, thirty or under to be considered for a job) is debatable because these may be more difficult for women to meet than for men (because they have had time off work to have children). This would be indirect sex discrimination. And a recent case established that while age discrimination is not illegal, it can be unfair dismissal if there are no good grounds for dismissal.

What you must do

Broadly:

1. Do not discriminate on grounds of sex or race or marriage

2. Do not refuse to allow your employees to join a trade union or dismiss them for trade union activity.

Sex and marriage

Discrimination means less favourable treatment of a man or woman on the grounds of sex or because they are married. It covers pay and conditions of the job, as well as opportunities for promotion, for example. You cannot discriminate:

- ❏ in advertising or interviews for the job

- ❏ in the terms in which the job is offered

- ❏ in deciding who is offered the job

- ❏ in opportunities for promotion, transfer or training

- ❏ in benefits to employees

- ❏ in dismissals.

You need to be particularly careful that you do not introduce requirements for a job or promotion which are likely to be met by one sex more than the other. For example, if you insist that the person for the job needs to be six feet tall, you will be discriminating against women. The same could apply if you insist on some technical qualification more likely to be held by men than women. But you can insist on height, technical or other qualifications, if you can show that these are genuinely necessary for the job.

Race

Racial discrimination means treating one person less favourably than another on racial grounds, which includes colour, race, nationality or ethnic or national origins. As with sex discrimination, racial discrimination also applies if you make a requirement for a job which one racial group would find more difficult to meet than another group. This is known as indirect discrimination and is unlawful. An example of this would be to insist on certain clothing being worn or to ask for a high standard of English when it is not necessary to do the job. And you cannot discriminate against a black employee because of how customers might react (for example, someone working in a pub).

You cannot discriminate:

❑ in advertising or interviews for the job

❑ in the terms in which the job is offered

❑ in deciding who is offered the job

❑ in opportunities for promotion, transfer or training

❑ in benefits to employees

❑ in dismissals.

If one of your employees takes you to an employment tribunal claiming racial discrimination, it is unlawful for you to victimize the employee. It is also unlawful to instruct or put pressure on others to discriminate on racial grounds.

The Commission for Racial Equality has produced a code of conduct to help you eliminate racial discrimination.

Trade unions

An employment tribunal will find the dismissal unfair if you sack an employee for:

❑ belonging to an independent trade union (that is, a union which is not controlled by an employer) or for not being a member of a trade union

❑ taking part in trade union activities (for example, meetings) at the appropriate time, which is normally outside working hours or inside working hours with the agreement of the management. Industrial action does not count as a union activity.

Employees can also complain to an employment tribunal if you penalize them, but do not dismiss, or if you make them redundant for any of the above actions.

Criminal offences

In some cases, people who have been convicted of an offence do not have to tell you about it. If you ask, they can lie about it quite legally. The people who can do this are usually those who have had sentences of thirty months or less. They can keep quiet about their convictions after a specified time, which varies, but is not more than ten years and not less than six months, but it also depends on the type of conviction.

If you employ someone who is entitled to keep quiet about their convictions and you subsequently discover their past, you cannot fairly dismiss the employee.

Health and disablement

You can refuse to employ someone if you are unhappy about their state of health. And if one of your employees has absences from work which are interfering seriously with the running of your business, the chances are that you can fairly dismiss the employee. With the employee's consent, it would be wise to get a doctor to give the employee a complete medical before doing so and to give an adequate warning.

If you employ twenty or more people, it is illegal to treat someone less favourably than other employees because they are disabled – for example, by offering them lesser benefits or fewer opportunities for promotion or training.

Booklets

EOC, *Code of Practice*
CRE, *Racial Discrimination and Grievance Procedures*
CRE, *Code of Practice: for the elimination of racial discrimination and the promotion of equality of opportunity in employment*
DTI, *Union membership and non-membership rights* PL871
DTI, *Maternity rights – a guide for employers and employees* PL958

Maternity

Pregnant employees, married or unmarried, have several rights, such as the right not to be dismissed unfairly, the right to maternity leave and the right to return to work – but there are many conditions and exceptions which can only be glossed over in this section.

What you must do

Broadly:

1. Give reasonable paid time off work so that your employee can have ante-natal care

2. Do not dismiss your employee because she is pregnant

3. Give your employee Statutory Maternity Pay – SMP (see right)

4. Give your employee her job back – but see right.

Dismissing while pregnant

A woman will automatically be held to be unfairly dismissed if (among others) the reason for dismissal is that she is pregnant or for any reason connected with her pregnancy.

An Employment Appeal Tribunal has also found that it can be sex discrimination to dismiss a woman because of pregnancy if you would not dismiss a man who would need similar time off for an operation.

You can fairly dismiss an employee because of pregnancy if:

❑ her condition makes it impossible for her to do her job properly, or

❑ it would be illegal for her to do that particular job while pregnant.

If either of these applies, you must offer your employee a suitable alternative vacancy if there is one available – and it makes sense to do this in writing. If you do not have one, your employee is still entitled to SMP and has the right to return to work, provided she otherwise qualifies.

Maternity leave

If your employee has worked for you continuously for two years or more, she has the right to take maternity leave up until the 29th week following the birth of her child. During this time her pension and other employment rights must be protected and she has the right to return to work at the end of the leave (see below).

Following changes to bring UK law into line with European legislation, if your employee has worked for you for less than two years, she is still entitled to up to 14 weeks statutory maternity leave, during which her employment rights must be protected. Once again, she has the right to return to work. In addition, the employee is not allowed – and you cannot require her – to work during the two weeks immediately following the birth of her child. If you breach this ban, you can be fined.

Maternity pay

You will normally have to pay Statutory Maternity Pay (SMP) to a pregnant employee even if she is not going to return to work for you after the birth of her child. It is payable for a maximum period of eighteen weeks. You pay SMP if your employee:

❑ has stopped working for you

❑ is still pregnant at the eleventh week before her baby is expected

❑ has average weekly earnings of at least £64 a week for 1998-99

❑ has been continuously employed by you for six months or more when the baby is due.

The amount of SMP is 90 per cent of average earnings for six weeks followed by twelve weeks at the rate set by the government – £57.70 a week in 1998. For more information obtain *Statutory Maternity Pay – Manual for employers* (CA29) from your local Contributions Agency.

Generally, only 92 per cent of SMP is reimbursed to employers – maybe 100 per cent if you come within 'small employers' relief'. This will apply if the National Insurance contributions you pay each year come to no more than £20,000. You get the relief by deducting it from the National Insurance Contributions you hand over to the Inland Revenue each month.

Right to return to work

If you had five or fewer employees at the time your employee's maternity absence began *and* it is not reasonably practical to take her back in her old job or to offer another suitable vacancy, your employee is unlikely to be able to claim unfair dismissal.

If you have more than five employees, your employee has the right to return to work if she has worked for you continuously for two years at the beginning of the eleventh week before the baby is due. Your employee may lose the right to return to work if:

❏ her job no longer exists because of redundancy and there is no suitable alternative job (in which case redundancy pay may be due)

❏ it is not practicable for her to return to her job and you have offered suitable alternative work, which she refuses

❏ if your employee fails to meet some rules about written notification.

Booklets

DE, *Maternity rights* URN97/909
CA 29, *Statutory Maternity Pay – Manual for employers*

Saying goodbye to an employee

In most circumstances, you have got two years to assess employees, and during that time you can dismiss them without any fear of being taken to an employment tribunal and accused of unfair dismissal. The only exceptions to this are if you dismiss someone because of sex, race, pregnancy or trade union activity; you would be guilty of unfair dismissal right from the start of the employment period. And if you dismiss an employee who would qualify for paid suspension on medical grounds, you could be guilty of unfair dismissal if the employee had been with you for a month or more.

However, be careful in how you dismiss an employee who has been with you for less than two years, in case he or she can claim breach of contract.

What you must do

Broadly:

1. Behave in a reasonable way when dismissing an employee

2. Give your employee the right notice.

How you can sack an employee

After the initial period is up, it is still not too much of a problem to dismiss someone. There are five reasons which may mean a dismissal is fair, although you will also have to demonstrate that you have been reasonable in the circumstances. The reasons are:

❏ being incapable of doing the job. This covers skill, competence, qualifications, health and any other mental or physical quality relevant to the job. Note that you do not have to prove to an employment tribunal that an employee is incompetent, merely that you believed it to be so and that you have acted reasonably. But you must make sure that your employee is aware of the requirements of the job and why and how they are not being met

❏ misconduct, for example, theft, insolence, horseplay, persistent bad time-keeping, laziness

❏ redundancy (see p. 242)

❏ illegality, if it would be illegal to continue employing the employee

❏ some other substantial reason, for example, if it is in the best interest of the firm to sack an employee.

As you can see it is possible to dismiss an employee if you are dissatisfied. But it is very important to do so in a reasonable way. It can save you an awful lot of time and money if you do because you can demonstrate to an employment tribunal that you have been reasonable in the circumstances. Follow this plan.

Step-by-step guide

1. When you first become dissatisfied with an employee, tell the employee so, preferably in writing.

2. Give your employee an opportunity to explain the problem and discuss constructively how things can be improved.

3. Consider whether training would help your employee. Look closely at the arrangements for supervising your employee's work.

4. After you have allowed a reasonable period for improvement, if things are still unsatisfactory warn your employee in writing of the consequences of no improvement.

5. Repeat 2 and 3.

6. Tell your employee when you will review the case.

7. Consider if there is not a suitable alternative job for your employee.

8. If you are still dissatisfied, dismiss your employee, making sure you give the correct notice (see p. 252). If your employee has been with you for a certain length of time (see p. 223), you can be asked to give written reasons.

There is an ACAS Code of Practice (published by HMSO) which clearly outlines the steps to be taken in dismissals (see Reference). Following this code may be taken into consideration by an employment tribunal.

Sacking someone on the spot

It can be done and it is likely to be a fair dismissal as long as you dismissed your employee for gross misconduct, such as dishonesty. But, on the whole, to avoid problems try to stick to the guide above.

Can it be unfair dismissal if your employee resigns?

It may seem a paradox, but the answer is yes. It can be unfair, if it is a constructive dismissal. So watch out. If you increase working hours without extra pay, cut your employee's fringe benefits or accuse an employee of something, such as theft, without investigating it properly, it may count as constructive dismissal.

Making an employee redundant

You can make an employee redundant if you are cutting down generally on the number of employees or if your need for a particular skill in your business ceases. But you must make the redundancy fair; do not choose married women, trade unionists, part-timers, or people over a certain age, for example. And you must consult the recognized trade union about the proposed redundancy.

If an employee has been with you for two years, you will have to pay redundancy pay. The amount depends upon the age of the employee and varies between $\frac{1}{2}$ and $1\frac{1}{2}$ weeks' pay for each year the employee has worked for you. There is a limit on the amount of a week's pay.

How much notice do you have to give?

You must give your employee:

❑ one week's notice if your employee has been with you for one month but less than two years

❑ two weeks' notice if your employee has been with you for two years

❑ an extra week's notice for each extra year your employee has been with you, up to a maximum of twelve weeks' notice.

If your employee's contract specifies a longer notice period, the longer period applies.

These minimum notice periods do not apply to the notice given to you by your employee, who by law has to give only one week's notice if employed by you for a month or more. So, if you want to make sure your employee has to give more notice, you must put it in the contract of employment.

What to do when an employee leaves

You must fill in form P45. Send Part 1 to the tax office and hand Parts 2 and 3 to your employee. If an employee dies, you should also fill in form P45 and send all three parts to the tax office.

Booklets

DTI, *Rights of notice and reasons for dismissal* PL707

DTI, *Unfairly dismissed?* PL712 – plus insert – PL712 ref 11

DTI, *Fair and unfair dismissal* PL714 and *Dismissal: Fair or Unfair* URN98/580

DTI, *Redundancy payments* PL808

DTI, *Redundancy consultation and notification* PL833

ACAS, *Discipline at Work*

Summary

1. Do not be too frightened of employment law. On the whole, you can employ who you want and sack them if they prove to be incompetent.

2. Behave reasonably towards your employees, giving them a chance to explain their actions. If you do this, you can cut down the chances of being found guilty of unfair dismissal in an employment tribunal.

3. Use all the agencies who are set up to advise in this very complex area.

Other chapters to read

19. **Getting the right staff** (p. 201)
27. **Keeping the record straight** (p. 313)

21. Insurance

Deciding what insurance you should have must rate as one of the least exciting decisions you have to make for your business. Paying out money to cover you against hazards, which you fervently hope will not happen, ranks fairly low in satisfaction. But it should rank quite high in priority. Failing to get the right insurance might mean the collapse and end of your business.

There are two different categories of business insurance:

❏ insurance you must have by law

❏ insurance you could consider to cover risks and disasters.

This chapter looks mainly at insurance for your business needs, rather than your personal needs.

Buying the insurance

Not only do you want the right sort of insurance, you want it at the right price and with the right company. The obvious place to start your search for your business insurance is with an insurance broker. A broker can, in theory, deal with the full range of insurance companies and should be able to find the lowest quote for you. Note that the cost of the insurance may vary depending on the location of the business; at the extreme, you may find it difficult or expensive to buy insurance for some areas.

An insurance broker can only be called a broker if registered with the Insurance Brokers Registration Council. To be registered, a broker has to behave in accordance with a code of conduct. The requirements for insurance broking businesses means getting professional indemnity insurance to reimburse customers for losses suffered as a result of the broker's negligence. And there is a compensation fund in case the broker should go bust or commit some fraud. The broker has to keep a separate bank account for clients' money and keep proper accounts.

The trade association for insurance companies, the Association of British Insurers (see Reference), has established a Code of Practice for insurance intermediaries, who are not registered brokers but are selling general insurances, such as motor or building insurance.

But choosing an insurance broker or intermediary can still be tricky – being registered, for example, gives no guarantee that a broker will do a certain amount of research work on your behalf to get the best deal possible for you. Other business contacts may be able to help you by recommending someone. You should certainly consider approaching three different brokers and asking them all to make recommendations for you. Then you can choose the best.

With personal financial needs such as pensions and investment-type life insurance such as endowment policies, independent financial advisers who can advise you on these topics need to be registered with a self-regulatory organization who will authorize them to give advice; this could be a recognised professional body or a self-regulatory organization such as the Personal Investment Authority (PIA), although this is now being wound down and replaced by the Financial Services Authority.

Insurance you must have

There are certain sorts of insurance you have to have:

1. Employers' liability

You must have insurance to pay out for your legal liability if one of your employees is injured or ill as a result of working for you and you have been negligent. The amount of cover (the amount of money the insurance company will pay out if you claim) is generally unlimited but must be at least £2 million. The law also requires you to exhibit a certificate of employers' liability insurance at each place of work.

2. Motor insurance

You must insure your liability to others, known as third party liability, which occurs because of a car crash or other motor-vehicle accident. This includes death or injury to anybody (but not your employees while working, as they are covered by employers' liability insurance, see above) and damage to third party property including other vehicles for a minimum of £250,000.

A further addition to third party cover which could be worth your while is fire and theft cover. Finally, if you want to get cover for accidental damage to your vehicles, regardless of who is to blame for the accident, you want a comprehensive insurance policy.

If you have a car or other vehicle for your own private and social use, and you want to use it for your business, you should tell your insurance company. You may need to pay an extra sum to get it covered for business.

Be clear about what the car is going to be used for when you fill in what is known as the proposal form (the form you fill in to apply for the insurance). You will probably have to pay extra money if the car is used for some purposes, such as by a sales rep. Failure to tell the insurance company may mean that it will not pay out if you make a claim.

3. Insurance needed by contracts

Check all the contracts you have (for example, under a lease or hire purchase agreement) to see what insurance you are committed to get.

4. Engineering equipment

By law, certain equipment, such as pressure vessels and lifting tackle, has to be inspected and passed as safe at regular intervals. You can combine the maintenance with an insurance policy to cover you against the risk of explosion, accidental damage and breakdown.

Other insurance you can get

1. Insurance against fire and other perils

This covers destruction or damage to your buildings and contents through fire. You can also be covered for other risks such as lightning, explosion, aircraft, storm, flood, riot, malicious damage and so on. If you work from your own home, you should check that you are protected by your own household insurance policy and tell the insurance company what you are doing.

Worth getting? *Yes*.

2. Insurance for loss of profits

This covers you if your business is disrupted by fire or some other insured peril. It can pay out money to pay your employees, maintain your profits and pay for the extra cost of your fill-in working premises.

Worth getting? *Depends* on your business. In most cases, yes; but if your business is small with few employees, and you could easily find somewhere to work, for example, your home, you may not consider it necessary. Note that using your home could cause problems with insurance so check with your insurance company. Rather than insure for full loss of profits, you could consider insuring for the cost of finding somewhere else to carry on working.

3. Insurance against theft

This covers you for loss or damage to the contents of your premises. Theft for insurance purposes means that someone has forced an entry to or exit from your workplace, so if you want to be covered against theft by your employees or visitors, you'll have to pay extra and get fidelity insurance.

Worth getting? *Yes.*

4. Loss of money

Cash and near-cash, such as cheques, stamps and so on, can be insured against theft from your premises or from the homes of directors or employees of your company or in transit.

Worth getting? *Yes,* if your takings are in cash. Otherwise, no.

5. Goods in transit

This insurance covers loss or damage of your goods in your own vehicles, or other means of delivery, such as post, road haulier and so on.

Worth getting? *Probably,* unless you don't sell in this way.

6. Credit insurance

This protects you against your customers failing to pay. You probably will not be able to get this insurance until you have been in business some time.

Worth getting? *Probably not,* if you deal mainly in cash or payment on delivery. For selling on credit, by the time you can get this insurance, you will be able to work out for yourself how likely a problem bad debts will be. It is probably better to operate good credit control (p. 291) or use a factoring service (p. 296). However, if you have only one large or a couple of big customers, you should have credit insurance.

7. Public liability and product liability

This will cover your liability to visitors and members of the public if your business causes injury or illness to them or damages their property. Product liability insurance covers you for these risks which occur as a result of the goods you are producing, selling or repairing up to a limit each year.

You need to make sure that the amount of cover is high enough. Recent damages in the courts have been as high as £1 million. You may need cover for more than this, depending on your business, especially if you do business in the USA.

Worth getting? *Yes.* With product liability, you may not need it if your products are very unlikely to cause any damage or if you are in the service business.

8. Professional indemnity

If you are the sort of business where the end product is expert advice, this insurance can cover you against claims from your clients for damages caused by your negligence or misconduct.

Worth getting? *Yes.* These sorts of claims are on the increase.

9. Legal expenses

This insurance would enable you to pay for legal assistance if you are involved in a contractual or employment dispute, plus some other legal procedures.

Worth getting? *Probably not.* Most legal disputes are generally in the employment field. It would be far better to concentrate on getting well organized in this area to cut the risk of being taken to a tribunal and charged with unfair dismissal or breach of contract, for example.

10. Keyman insurance

If your business is heavily dependent on one or a few people for its future success, you can get keyman life insurance, for example, for a sum of £250,000 to be paid to your business in the event of one of those people dying. To get cover, you must be able to prove the person's death would cost your firm money.

Worth getting? *Yes.*

11. Other insurance

There are some other types of insurance which you should consider, depending on your business. These include:

❏ glass breakage, which is important for shops

❏ cover for frozen food

❏ computers and computer records

❏ fidelity insurance, which covers you against fraud or dishonesty by your employees

❏ business machines and equipment

❏ agricultural and fish-farming operations

❏ directors' and officers' liability.

Insurance for you and your family

If you and your family are not covered by insurance for various personal mishaps, you may find it difficult to carry on your business, so do not neglect your personal needs. Almost everyone should have life insurance, permanent health or critical illness insurance and a pension plan.

Make sure that you and your wife or husband have enough life insurance to protect you in the event of your early deaths. For this purpose do not go for the sort of life insurance which is really an investment, but go for term insurance, family income benefit, mortgage protection, and so on.

Permanent health insurance would pay out an income if you were too ill to work and could pay for a temporary manager. You should consider this carefully. And do not forget pensions, which are covered in detail on p. 375.

Summary

1. Do not delay in taking out the insurance you need.

2. Use a registered insurance broker to act for you.

3. Shop around. Seek advice from more than one broker and ask for several quotes for each insurance you need.

4. Do not neglect personal insurance requirements. Life insurance for your family, permanent health insurance and pensions should be looked at carefully to determine the level you need. Use an independent financial adviser who is authorized to advise you on these topics (p. 244).

Other chapter to read

33. **Retirement** (p. 375)

22. **Forecasting**

Forecasts are the kernel of your business. They are the basis on which you raise money, negotiate premises and order raw materials. These are only a few of the decisions which need to be made in advance with only your forecasts as guidance on how much is needed. Making a wildly inaccurate forecast can, for example, lead to raising insufficient funds. When the business fails to meet expectations and begins to run short of money, it may prove impossible to raise further funds. Lenders are very wary of handing out more when forecasting has proved to be mistaken. The result could be liquidation, or bankruptcy if you are a partner or sole trader, and the end of your dreams.

However, making no forecasts at all is even sillier. You would have no guidance on when to take certain basic business decisions.

Given the importance of attaining a reasonable estimate of future sales, costs and cash balances, it follows that making the forecasts is a process which should not be hurried or treated casually (and can usually be carried out with the help of a computer program such as Excel). You must constantly strive to seek information on which forecasts can be based; you must constantly curb your over-optimism which can lead to estimated sales figures that are too high and estimated cost figures that are too low. Question your first forecasts for the realism of their assumptions, before accepting any figure as a part of the final forecasts.

Nevertheless, it is realistic to accept that some of the figures will be nothing more than a best guess given the current state of information available to you. However, your figures should have some grounding in fact, so when you present your case to your bank manager or other source of finance you can support the figure when challenged.

It is important to make the forecasts in your plan realistic so that if your business idea does not hold water, you can discover this at the planning stage. You do not want to discover two years down the track that your business will not work, after you have committed money, time and effort. Do not underestimate the mental anguish and financial problems which can be caused by a struggling business (p. 308).

What is in this chapter?

There are three forecasts you need to make:

❑ Cash flow (see below)

❑ Profit and loss (p. 258)

❑ Balance sheet (p. 262).

Finally, at the end of this chapter, there is an example of how a start-up business produces the cash flow and profit and loss forecasts.

Cash flow forecast

The first point to note is that cash and profit are not the same thing at all, so the two forecasts may be quite different.

A cash flow forecast is quite simply a record of when you think you will receive cash in your business and when you think you will have to pay it out. In your business plan, you should include monthly cash flow forecasting for at least one, preferably two years ahead. Depending on the size of your business, you may also need to include yearly cash flow forecasts for three years beyond that, totalling five years of forecasts in all.

Opposite there is a blank cash flow form, which shows the typical headings and layout of a forecast. Obviously, the headings will vary with the nature of the business. And at the end of this chapter, there is an example of how Betty Crop and her partner, Roger Cartwright, produce their cash flow forecast for their knitwear business.

Detailed calculations for cash flow forecast

Do the cash flow forecast for your chosen accounting year. If, for example, you choose to end your accounting year at the end of April, your cash flow forecast will run from 1 May to 30 April.

It is important to make realistic assumptions about when you will receive the cash, or when you will have to pay it out. The purpose of the forecast is to throw up when your need for cash is at its greatest, so you can demonstrate what your funding requirements are.

1. Opening bank balance

This shows how much is actually in your business bank account at the start of each period. If you owe your bank money (have an overdraft), show this by putting the figure in brackets. If your forecast is made before you start

Monthly cash flow forecast

(for the period 1 January 199x to 31 December 199x)

	JAN.	FEB.	–	NOV.	DEC.	TOTAL
Opening bank balance (A)	...	...	–	...	...	...
Receipts						
Cash from sales	...	...	–	...	...	...
Cash from debtors	...	...	–	...	...	...
VAT (net receipts)	...	...	–	...	...	...
Other receipts	...	...	–	...	...	...
Sale of assets	...	...	–	...	...	...
Capital	...	...	–	...	...	...
TOTAL RECEIPTS (B)	...	...	–	...	...	...
Payments						
Payment to suppliers	...	...	–	...	...	...
Cash purchases	...	...	–	...	...	...
Wages/drawings	...	...	–	...	...	...
PAYE/NIC/tax payments	...	...	–	...	...	...
VAT (net payments)	...	...	–	...	...	...
Rent	...	...	–	...	...	...
Uniform business rate	...	...	–	...	...	...
Heating/lighting	...	...	–	...	...	...
Telephone	...	...	–	...	...	...
Professional fees	...	...	–	...	...	...
General expenses	...	...	–	...	...	...
Capital expenditure	...	...	–	...	...	...
Bank interest	...	...	–	...	...	...
Other payments	...	...	–	...	...	...
TOTAL PAYMENTS (C)	...	...	–	...	...	...
CLOSING BANK PAYMENTS (A) + (B) – (C)	...	...	–	...	...	...

trading, the opening bank balance is likely to be nil.

Your opening bank balance for one period will be the closing bank balance for the previous period.

2. Cash from sales

In here would go any cash you expect to receive when you sell your product, not in payment of an invoice you send out. If your business is a shop, most of your sales will be cash ones, and so this would be the biggest element of your cash receipts.

If you are registered for VAT, enter the figure you expect to receive, including VAT.

3. Cash from debtors

If you sell your product and do not receive payment at once, but instead send out invoices, you would enter here when you expect to receive the cash. Someone who owes you money (for example, has not yet paid your invoice) is a debtor. You should aim to get your invoices paid as quickly as possible, but most of your customers will expect to delay payment of your invoice by at least one month (see Chapter 24, 'Staying afloat' (p. 282), for how to get your debtors to pay).

If you are registered for VAT, enter the figure you expect to receive, including VAT.

4. VAT (net receipts)

If you are not registered for VAT, ignore this section (see p. 363 for details of whether you should not be registered). If you are registered for VAT, you will only expect to receive cash from the VAT system if for some reason your purchases, on which you can claim back VAT, are greater than your sales on which you have charged VAT.

This might happen as a rare occurrence if you have spent a lot of money while starting up, before your sales have got going. Another possible reason for this could occur if your sales are seasonal but your purchases are not. It could also happen if your sales are zero-rated, in which case you do not have to charge VAT on your sales, but you can claim it back on your purchases (p. 366).

You may make your returns for VAT on a quarterly basis, so allow for this in your cash flow.

5. Other receipts

Put here any miscellaneous receipts of income which you expect to occur.

6. Sale of assets

This section is for you to record the proceeds you expect to get from selling any assets, for example, a car or office equipment, rather than any sales of your products.

7. Capital

Put the amount of money you are going to invest and make sure you put it in the month you expect to invest it. If anyone else is expected to invest or to lend you money (not including an overdraft with the bank), slot it in here.

8. Payment to suppliers

Put in here when you expect you will have to pay suppliers for their services or materials (p. 297). The longer you delay paying suppliers' invoices, the better it can be for your cash flow. This beneficial effect has to be balanced by any ill-will created by late payment. A realistic assumption for your cash flow forecast will be that you will not have to pay your suppliers' invoices until one month after you receive them.

Whether you are registered for VAT or not, enter the amount including any VAT you will be paying to your suppliers.

9. Cash purchases

If you have to pay cash on the spot for purchases from suppliers, estimate the amount (including any VAT) and time in this section.

10. Wages/drawings

Put here the amount after deducting tax and national insurance contributions under the PAYE system for wages.

11. PAYE/NIC

Total the amount of tax under the PAYE system and the amount of national insurance contributions you will deduct from your employees each month, as well as the amount of the employer's contribution. You have to send this money in to the tax collector within two weeks of the end of the month. So your payments of these amounts will be in the month after you have deducted them. If your business is a limited company and you pay yourself a salary as a director, your personal tax and national insurance contributions will also be collected in this way. If you are a sole trader or partner, your personal tax on what you pay yourself will not be collected in this way. Instead, you will pay tax, and Class 4 national insurance contributions if you pay them, in two or three lumps, in January, July and any remaining balance the following January. Enter the amount in the section **tax payments**.

However, your Class 2 national insurance contributions will be collected each month, and you should reflect the amount here under **paye/nic**. For more about your personal tax and national insurance contributions as a sole trader or partner, see p. 325 and p. 346.

12. VAT (net payment)

If you are not registered for VAT, do not enter anything here. If you are registered for VAT, you should estimate the amount of tax you will be paying over to the VAT collector each quarter (p. 372).

If your sales are £300,000 a year or less, you may find it worthwhile to switch to the cash accounting scheme for VAT. If this is the case, what you should enter in your cash flow forecast is your estimate of the VAT you will receive from your customers in that quarter, because that is what you will pay (less VAT you can claim on your purchases). Note that you may also be able to pay VAT for the year in ten, four or even a single instalment (see p. 372).

13. Tax payments

If you run a limited company, enter the amount of tax you estimate you will pay on your company's profits and when you will pay it. Corporation tax, that is, tax on your company's profits, is payable nine months after the end of your accounting year (p. 352).

If you are a sole trader or partner, your tax and any Class 4 national insurance contributions payable will be paid in three lumps – on 31 January, 31 July and the balance or a repayment on the following 31 January. For how to work out the amount of tax you will be paying, see Chapters 28 and 29.

14. Rent

Enter the rent you will pay in each month.

15. Business rate

Enter the amount of the business rate and when you will have to pay it. Do not forget you can opt to pay your rates monthly over a ten-month period. This can improve your cash flow.

16. Heating/lighting

These bills will be paid each quarter in arrears. Once you have received the bill, you will be able to delay payment by up to one month. Remember to cater for heavy winter usage.

17. Telephone

The phone bill will be paid quarterly in arrears and you can probably take a further month's delay before you pay, although this is a delay which cannot be increased beyond the month.

18. Professional fees

Payment of these bills will be fairly erratic; you must make your best guess, but try and obtain an estimate.

19. General expenses

Enter an estimate for those continuing and recurring, but small, expenses. These could include postage, fares, newspapers, or whatever is required in your business. Of course, if your business is a mailing service, for example, you should have a separate heading for postage. What exactly goes in here will have to be decided by you.

20. Capital expenditure

If you are going to buy any pieces of equipment, such as a car, computer or machinery, enter the amount, including VAT, and when you estimate you will have to pay for it. If you are paying cash, put in the full amount. If you are going to buy on hire purchase or using a loan, you will enter the amount of the deposit and the monthly payments separately and in the correct months. Leasing payments will be monthly.

21. Bank interest and charges

If you have an overdraft or bank loan, estimate the amount and frequency of the interest charged. Get a quote from the bank manager.

22. Other payments

What goes in here depends on the nature of your business. It could include insurance, but if this is of reasonable size, you should have a separate entry.

23. Closing bank balance

Work out the closing bank balance for the period by adding the opening bank balance to the total receipts and taking away the figure for total payments. The closing bank balance becomes the opening bank balance at the start of the next period.

Profit and loss forecast

A profit forecast should show what level of profit you expect your business to produce at the end of the period, according to the accounting records you keep. Your accounts will not be drawn up on a cash basis, so many of the figures in your profit forecast will be different from those in the cash flow forecast. Below there is an explanation of how and why the figures will differ.

Monthly profit and loss forecast

(for the period 1 January 199x to 31 December 199x)

	JAN.	FEB.	–	NOV.	DEC.	TOTAL
SALES (A)	...	...	–	...	...	...
less Cost of sales						
Purchases	...	...	–	...	...	...
Labour	...	...	–	...	...	...
Other direct costs	...	...	–	...	...	...
TOTAL (B)	...	...	–	...	...	...
GROSS PROFIT (C)						
Take (B) from (A)	...	...	–	...	...	...
less Overheads						
Rent and rates	...	...	–	...	...	...
Heating/lighting)	...	...	–	...	...	...
Telephone	...	...	–	...	...	...
Professional fees	...	...	–	...	...	...
Depreciation	...	...	–	...	...	...
Employee costs	...	...	–	...	...	...
Other overhead expenses	...	...	–	...	...	...
Drawings	...	...	–	...	...	...
Interest	...	...	–	...	...	...
TOTAL (D)	...	...	–	...	...	...
plus Miscellaneous income (E)	...	...	–	...	...	...
NET PROFIT (F)						
(C) + (E) – (D)	...	...	–	...	...	...

Detailed calculations for profit and loss forecast

1. Sales

The figure you put in here is the sum of the invoices you expect to send out during the accounting period. It is not necessarily the sum of the cash you receive during the period (unless your business is a shop which makes only cash sales, for example). You could also describe the sales figure as the cash you receive during the period plus what you are owed at the end of the period less what you were owed at the end of the previous period.

If you are registered for VAT, you do not include the amount of VAT you charge on your sales, unlike in your cash flow forecast.

If your business is likely to be seasonal, or if you know of events coming up which might temporarily increase or decrease your sales figures, show this monthly effect. A reader of your business plan will not be impressed by a monthly figure which is level or shows a very steady rate of increase, unless, of course, you can demonstrate that this is a realistic assumption.

When forecasting sales you need to consider two factors:

❑ the number of units you can sell

❑ the price you can get for these units.

2. Cost of sales: Purchases

You are estimating for this section those costs which you would expect to vary with the level of your sales; if your sales go up, the level of direct costs goes up and vice versa. In real life, things are not quite so cut-and-dried and often the distinction between direct costs and overheads is blurred. The important point is for you to have a clear idea about which you are going to regard as overheads.

Purchases could be the raw materials you buy from your suppliers to manufacture your products, Or, if you are not a manufacturing business, they would be the items which you purchase to sell on to your customers, having added on your profit margin.

The figure you put in your profit and loss account will be different from the cash flow figures for payments to suppliers and cash purchases.
For the profit calculation you need the sum of the invoices you receive in the period for materials.

Another way of working out the purchase figure for this forecast is to say it is what you pay for supplies in the period plus what you owe at the end of the period less what you owed at the start of the period.

If you are registered for VAT, you do not include the figure for VAT which you are charged by your supplier for your profit forecast. If you are not registered for VAT, you do include the figure for VAT.

Points to look out for when you are forecasting costs include:

❏ make sure that the level of costs corresponds to the amount of sales you expect to make

❏ allow for any changes in the prices of raw materials which you can reasonably expect to occur in the period.

3. Cost of sales: Labour

Here include the cost of your employees who are directly involved with manufacturing your product. As with purchases, the distinction between staff who are directly involved with production and those who count as overheads can be blurred. On the whole, if you do not think that employees' wages are directly related to the amount of work you have, it may be more satisfactory to include employee costs in overheads.

Remember to include all your employee costs; this implies gross salary, your national insurance contributions as an employer plus any other costs.

The figures may diverge slightly from those in the cash flow forecast, as PAYE and NI contributions are due the following month. Differences will only show up when you first take on an employee or if the employee's salary rises.

4. Cost of sales: Other direct costs

Estimate here any other direct costs which you foresee.

5. Overheads: Rent and rates

In the profit forecast, the total for rates should be spread evenly over the whole year. With rent, you should enter the cost for each period, which may not coincide with the timing of the payments.

6. Overheads: Heating/lighting

You need an estimate for the cost of heating and lighting which you will use in each period. As you will receive bills quarterly in arrears, you may need to estimate the cost in advance of each bill.

7. Overheads: Telephone

The treatment of the phone is similar to that for heating and lighting.

8. Overheads: Professional fees

The figure to include here is what it costs you in legal or accounting fees. You should include the cost in the period in which the work is done for you, even if you do not receive the bill until the next period.

9. Overheads: Depreciation

Depreciation is what you deduct from the value of an asset to reflect the fact that it is wearing out. This is an item which does not appear in the cash flow forecast. You work it out for each period by taking the value of capital equipment at the start of each period and estimating a figure for its depreciation during the period. Typically, cars and office equipment are written off over three, four or five years.

Note that you do not put in the profit forecast what you pay for capital equipment, which does appear in the cash flow forecast.

10. Overheads: Employee costs

This should be your estimate of employee costs which are not directly related to the volume of your sales, see p. 215.

11. Overheads: Other overhead expenses

Include overhead expenses not slotted in elsewhere.

12. Overheads: Drawings

What you pay yourself.

13. Overheads: Interest

Estimate the interest on loans and overdrafts during the year.

14. Miscellaneous income

Put here an estimate of the other income you might receive, not as a result of the sales of your products. For example, if you have money invested, it might include interest.

15. Working out the net profit figure

You can work out a gross profit figure (C) by deducting the figure for direct costs (B) from the sales figure (A). On p. 284 you will see how you can use the gross profit figure to work out the break-even point for your business.

Once you have arrived at an estimate for gross profit, deduct the figure for overheads (D) and add on the amount of any miscellaneous income (E) to give your forecast net profit level (F).

Balance sheet forecast

A balance sheet for your business will show what you owe and what you are owed on one particular day. A forecast one will show your estimate of that picture at the end of the period.

There is more about accounting records needed to produce the right information for a balance sheet once you are in business in Chapter 27, 'Keeping the record straight' (p. 313). Of course, your accountant should be willing to help if you find it difficult to produce a balance sheet yourself. If your business is likely to be fairly small-scale and you are only approaching your bank manager, and for a fairly modest sum, a forecast balance sheet may not be necessary.

In this section there are brief guidelines on how to work out what the balance sheet might be at the end of the period, once the forecast cash flow and profit and loss account are drawn up. And on p. 264 there is a blank balance sheet forecast for you to complete.

Detailed calculation for balance sheet forecast

One important check on your balance sheet figures is to note that the figure for total assets should equal the figure for capital and liabilities together.

1. Fixed Assets

These figures are fairly straightforward to work out. You know from your cash flow forecast when you plan to buy particular bits of equipment. Include all equipment which you have received before the end of the period, even if you have not paid for it. A fixed asset is something of a permanent nature, likely to remain in use in your business for some time.

The value you put in here is not just what you paid for the equipment; you also have to allow for the fact that it will have depreciated since the period started. You can obtain the figure for depreciation from your profit forecast. Deduct these figures from the appropriate cost of each piece of equipment, or written-down value at the start of the period, and enter the figures here.

2. Current Assets

The main current assets you are likely to have in your business are:

❑ cash

❑ debtors (that is, what your customers owe you)

Example

> Richard Petworth is working out the depreciation for the office furniture he has bought for his business. There are a number of different ways of calculating this, but for office furniture he thinks he will write off the value in equal lumps over five years; this is called straight-line depreciation.
>
> The furniture cost Richard £2,000. This means he writes off £400 from the value of it each accounting year. The written-down value at the end of the first accounting year is £1,600.

❏ stock (that is, products you have in store, either raw materials to make your product, half-finished products or your finished products which are not yet sold).

The figure for cash you will be able to take straight from your cash flow forecast.

You can derive the figure for debtors from the cash flow and profit forecasts. You will have made some assumption about number of units sold in each month and how quickly you will be paid your cash. From this you can calculate how much you would be owed for sales by your customers at the end of each period. Remember to include VAT in your figure if you are registered for VAT.

The figure for stock can also be derived from the other two forecasts. Count as stock all goods received from your suppliers to be used in your product but not yet used in products sold, even if you have not yet paid your suppliers' bills. These should be shown at their 'cost' to you.

3. Capital

Put here the capital you used to start your business. The figure for profit and loss you take from your profit forecast. It is the cumulative figure at the end of the period. If you forecast a loss, put it in brackets and it will be deducted from your capital.

4. Liabilities

Loans from the bank or another lender which are not due to be repaid within one year are medium- or long-term liabilities.

Current liabilities consist mainly of:

❏ overdraft

❏ tax payable, including VAT

Balance sheet forecast (on 31 December 199x)

ASSETS

Fixed Assets
    Freehold property   £......
    Leasehold property   £......
    Office equipment   £......
    Vehicles   £......
    Plant/machinery   £......
    Other equipment   £......
    TOTAL FIXED ASSETS (A)   £......

Current Assets
    Cash in hand and at bank   £......
    Stock   £......
    Debtors   £......
    TOTAL CURRENT ASSETS (B)   £......
TOTAL ASSETS (A) + (B)   £......

CAPITAL AND LIABILITIES

Capital
    Shareholders'/proprietor's capital   £......
    Profit and loss   £......
    TOTAL CAPITAL (C)   £......

Medium-term Liabilities
    Loans   £......

Current Liabilities
    Overdraft   £......
    Tax payable   £......
    Creditors   £......
    TOTAL LIABILITIES (D)   £......

TOTAL CAPITAL AND LIABILITIES (C) + (D)   £......

creditors (that is, what you owe your suppliers at the end of the period).

he figure for overdraft can be taken from your cash flow forecast.

If you have made a profit in the period, you will need to estimate what x will be payable. You may also have to include a figure for what you owe ustoms and Excise in VAT (of course, if you are owed VAT, you should ive an entry in the current assets section for this).

In the same way as you worked out debtors, so creditors can be estimat- l using the two other forecasts. It is the value of the amount of goods you ive but which you have not yet paid for.

xample

Betty Crop and Roger Cartwright are planning to start a knitwear business on 1 January. Their aim is to design knitwear and sell in small quantities (five to ten) to boutiques. Later they hope to produce in bigger numbers selling to department stores. The knitwear will be produced by outworkers.

The final price of the knitwear in the shops will be £90–£120, but Betty and Roger will receive £50–£60. The average cost of the raw materials will be £12 and they will pay each outworker £10 for each garment, on average. They have to take into account seasonal changes in sales, although they will design a range of cotton knitwear for the summer.

They will have to buy raw materials in advance on thirty days' credit and pay each outworker on completion of each garment. They will sell to the bou- tiques on thirty days' credit, but realistically will allow for an average sixty days' credit in their cash flow forecast.

At first they will work from home, but later in the year would like 500-sq.- ft offices – they hope to get light industrial premises at £7 a sq. foot on the out- skirts of London. When they have premises they would like to employ someone for clerical work and organizing the outworkers, leaving themselves free to design and sell.

Given their forecast level of sales, Betty and Roger do not need to register for VAT. They produce cash flow (p. 266) and profit and loss forecasts (p. 267) to see how the business will shape up.

Conclusions

Betty and Roger should take advice before going ahead with their business; their idea is not viable as it is currently presented, especially with the increase in overheads (rent for premises and assistant's wages) in the second half of the year. They would certainly need to put in more money, but even then, unless they can increase their sales figures, the long-term prospects must be fairly negative.

Cash flow forecast (for 1 January 199x to 31 December 199x)

	Jan.	Feb.	Mar.	Apr.	May	June
Opening balance	–	£7,820	£5,970	£6,330	£7,060	£6,880
Sales	–	–	1,900	1,900	1,350	1,350
Capital	10,000	–	–	–	–	–
Total: *Cash receipts*	£10,000	–	£1,900	£1,900	£1,350	£1,350
Raw materials	380	380	270	270	110	760
Outworkers	350	350	250	250	100	700
Capital equipment	600	–	–	–	–	350
Stationery/labels	200	–	200	–	200	–
Heating/lighting	–	70	70	–	70	70
Phone	–	300	–	–	300	–
Bank	–	–	–	–	–	–
Rent and rates	–	–	–	–	–	875
Assistant	–	–	–	–	–	–
Car expenses	50	150	150	50	150	50
Drawings	600	600	600	600	600	600
Total: *Cash payments*	£2,180	£1,850	£1,540	£1,170	£1,530	£3,405
Closing balance	£7,820	£5,970	£6,330	£7,060	£6,880	£4,825

	Jul.	Aug.	Sep.	Oct.	Nov.	Dec.	Totals
Opening balance	£4,825	£2,580	£249	£(3,448)	£(5,724)	£(2,541)	
Sales	550	550	550	550	6,500	7,350	22,550
Capital	–	–	–	–	–	–	10,000
Total: *Cash reciepts*	£550	£550	£550	£550	£6,500	£7,350	£32,550
Raw materials	760	760	870	870	870	760	7,060
Outworkers	700	700	800	800	800	700	6,500
Capital equipment	–	–	–	–	–	–	950
Stationery/labels	200	–	200	–	200	–	1,200
Heating/lighting	–	–	400	–	–	400	1,080
Phone	–	300	–	–	300	–	1,200
Bank	5	21	47	61	47	34	215
Rent and rates	50	50	875	50	50	875	2,825
Assistant	400	400	400	400	400	400	2,400
Car expenses	80	50	50	50	50	50	930
Drawings	600	600	600	600	600	600	7,200
Total: *Cash payments*	£2,795	£2,881	£4,242	£2,831	£3,317	£3,819	£31,560
Closing balance	£2,580	£249	£(3,443)	£(5,724)	£(2,541)	£990	

Profit & loss forecast (for 1 January 199x to 31 December 199x)

	Jan.	Feb.	Mar.	Apr.	May	June
Sales	£1,900	£1,900	£1,350	£1,350	£550	£550
less *Direct costs*						
Raw materials	380	270	270	110	760	760
Labour	350	350	250	250	100	700
Total direct costs	730	620	520	360	860	1,460
Gross profit	£1,170	£1,280	£830	£990	£(310)	£(910)
less Overheads						
Rent and rates	–	–	–	–	–	380
Heating/lighting	56	56	56	56	56	56
Telephone	100	100	100	100	100	100
Stationery/labels	50	50	50	50	50	50
Administrative staff	–	–	–	–	–	–
Depreciation	68	68	68	68	68	73
Car expenses	78	78	78	78	78	78
Total overheads	352	352	352	352	352	737
Net profit	£818	£928	£478	£638	£(662)	£(1,647)

	Jul.	Aug.	Sep.	Oct.	Nov.	Dec.	Totals
Sales	£550	£550	£6,500	£7,350	£7,350	£5,400	£35,300
less *Direct costs*							
Raw materials	760	870	870	870	760	940	7,620
Labour	700	700	800	800	800	700	6,500
Total direct costs	1,460	1,570	1,670	1,670	1,560	1,640	14,120
Gross profit	£(910)	£(1,020)	£4,830	£5,680	£5,790	£3,760	£21,180
less *Overheads*							
Rent and rates	380	380	380	380	380	380	2,660
Heating/lighting	134	134	134	134	134	134	1,140
Telephone	100	100	100	100	100	100	1,200
Stationery/labels	50	50	50	50	50	50	600
Administrative staff	400	400	400	400	400	400	2,400
Bank	5	21	47	61	47	34	215
Depreciation	73	73	73	73	73	73	851
Car expenses	78	78	78	78	78	78	936
Total overheads	1,220	1,236	1,262	1,276	1,262	1,249	10,002
Net profit	£(2,130)	£(2,256)	£3,568	£4,404	£4,528	£2,511	£11,178

Summary

1. Forecasts are very important if you make commitments on the basis that the figures are reasonably accurate.

2. Make the forecasts conservative.

3. A cash flow forecast is not the same as a profit and loss forecast; the figures will be different. In the cash flow, show what cash payments you expect to make and receive and when that will be.

4. If you find it difficult to produce the forecasts, ask for help from a Business Link, or your local TEC or an accountant.

5. The treatment of VAT payments and receipts and depreciation need special attention.

6. Once you have the forecasts, use them to assess how viable your business will be and whether you will be able to make a living from it.

Other chapters to read

6. **The business plan** (p. 64)
23. **Raising the money** (p. 269)
27. **Keeping the record straight** (p. 313)

23. **Raising the money**

Raising money needs careful planning, like a military campaign. You should regard it as the biggest sale you are ever likely to make. You need to get your act together to present your case. You need to know how much money you want. You need to know who to approach. You need to know how long you want the money for. You need to know what security you can offer backers. You need to know the business plan, the financial figures and the marketplace inside out.

But that is not all. You should expect indifference, lack of interest, disbelief and doubt. You have to convince, persuade and excite sober, serious businesspeople about the prospects for your business. This cannot be achieved by overstatement or rash predictions about success. Demonstrations of competence and skill are what is required.

Of course, a few strike lucky. There may be the odd story about bank managers agreeing overdrafts over the phone, or someone being able to pick and choose from a variety of backers who all want to put up the funds. But for most it is a hard, hard job.

What is in this chapter?

This chapter looks at:

❏ Money: it explains how much you should consider raising (see p. 270), what it is for (p. 271) and what type you want, for example, loans or shares or both (p. 272)

❏ Lenders and investors: it considers how much you and your family can provide (p. 274), what the government, local authorities, charities and so on can do (p. 276), what banks offer (p. 276), what can be obtained from private investors (p. 278) and what venture capital funds do (p. 278)

❏ The presentation: how to do it (p. 280).

The money

How much money? What should you ask for?

Only when you have drawn up your business plan and done your cash flow and profit forecasts will you know how much money you need to raise, if at all. Take a few deep breaths before you rush round to make an appointment with your bank manager to see if you can get the overdraft you need. First, your bank is not always your first port of call, as you can see from later pages in this chapter. Second, you should take a further, closer, more critical look at the amount of money you think you will need.

Being optimistic, as anyone starting a business must be, you naturally believe you are going to make the sales you have projected on the timescale you estimated and keep the costs down to your forecast figures. But supposing things do not work quite as you hope. Going back to your lender and asking for more money within a short space of time does not inspire confidence, and you may find your second request rejected, if it is not part of your plan. And there you are with a new business to which you have committed time and money, which is now short of cash, and you are unlikely to find any way of raising more.

There is a body of opinion which says when you first approach your lender or investor, ask for twice as much money as you think you will need. At any rate, be very conservative and go for more money than you think you are going to use. Obviously, the business plans which you present need to tie up with your request for cash, so adjust them if need be, incorporating more conservative figures.

There are drawbacks. First, if your figures are too conservative, it may make your business proposition unviable altogether; if this happens, you do not need to worry about being forced to go back for more, your business will not even get off the ground in the first place, because you will not get the initial backing. The second obstacle to this approach is that it is the natural inclination of any investor to try to make you manage with less money than you say you need.

The sensible advice is steer a middle course: be pessimistic, while retaining a sensible business proposal.

At this stage you know more than ever before about your proposed business and are likely to be very committed to it. But if the business does not look right do not be afraid of ditching this plan and looking for a better one. You probably have only one chance of raising money for a business proposal, so do not choose a failure because it was your first idea.

For many people, this is the first point at which you are really learning what makes a business tick. One sign of a successful entrepreneur is that you can learn from your information and experience and can adapt. You want to go for calculated, but good, risks. Of course, if you have already started trading, your business course is set.

Large sums of money

There is another odd fact about raising money: different sums of money can be harder or easier to find, depending simply on their size. Surprisingly, it is sometimes said to be much easier to find very large sums of money for your business (£500,000 plus) than sums in the £20,000 to £250,000 range (these figures are an indication only; there are always exceptions). This quirk of business funding is of no interest to the vast bulk of people who want to become self-employed or start a business in a small way but if your plans are on a larger scale, think about being bigger still.

This oddity occurs because there appear to be more people around who are willing to invest in either small businesses which are past the start-up stage (that is, not brand new) and into a big expansion phase or in new businesses which look capable of very fast growth in profits. To achieve either of these objectives, the amount of money invested needs to be substantial to stand any chance of success. Other pre-conditions of success, apart from large funds, are a very strong management team and a sound market. If you cannot demonstrate that both of these apply to you and your business, your chances of raising very large sums of money are virtually nil.

The money: what is it for?

From your forecasts, you should have an indication of when your need for extra cash arises, how long it lasts for and when you would be able to pay it back or give a good return on it.

If you are starting a new business, you need money for:

❑ the 'once-in-a-business-lifetime's' expenses of setting up. These include what you have to spend on your premises, on equipment and furniture, on legal and professional costs, on initial marketing expenditure

❑ working capital. This is what you need to keep yourself going in the time gap between paying out cash for raw materials or stocks and getting in cash from the people you sell to. All businesses need working capital; the amount varies depending on the type of business, the credit terms you can negotiate from your suppliers and the amount of credit you extend to your customers.

The longer you can get your suppliers to wait for their payment and the shorter the period you allow to your customers to pay, the less working capital you need. Your working capital requirements will also be less if you do not need to hold big stocks of goods.

In practice, all these things are easier said than done and you need to work out a strategy for controlling your business which meets your need to keep down the money tied up with working capital, coupled with keeping your suppliers and customers happy. This is covered in more detail in Chapter 24, 'Staying afloat' (p. 282).

If your business is up and running, you may need funds simply because it is growing and hence the amount of working capital necessary has gone up. Or you may have some specific expansion in mind.

The money: what type do you want?

Overdrafts

If your need for the money is likely to be fairly short-term, an overdraft or some sort of short-term loan is your likeliest bet. Your need for finance in the short term could be to cover a temporary shortage of cash, or it could cover your start-up requirements if these are fairly small.

An overdraft is quick to arrange and relatively cheap, but there will be an upper limit above which you are not to go without permission of the bank manager. The serious drawback with an overdraft is that the bank can demand instant repayment. While this does not happen very often, you can bet that if the bank does demand repayment or reduction of the overdraft, this will occur when you cannot do so.

If there are no assets, such as debtors, to be taken as security for the overdraft, it is likely that your bank manager will require that you give some personal assets or, less likely, a personal guarantee as security even if you have formed a limited company. One benefit of getting substantial funding is that as a result of the strong balance sheet, personal guarantees, although asked for, can sometimes be avoided.

As a self-employed person you are personally liable anyway, so no further guarantees are needed. In the extreme, this means if you cannot repay an overdraft, your assets, including your house, could be seized to cover the debt.

Note that banks may be wary of taking stocks as a security for overdraft. The manager may insist on property or debtors as the only acceptable security. Always negotiate about the level of security needed; it is in your interests to give up as little as possible.

Longer-term loans

If you know at the outset that you are unlikely to be able to repay the money you want to raise in the short term, a longer-term source of finance might be the answer (p. 277).

Selling shares

If you have formed a limited company, you may be willing to sell some of the shares in return for an investment in the business. If you do this, it means you will lose some of the potential gains you might get as a result of the shares increasing in value as the profits of the business grow. This is what an outside investor is looking for. The aim is generally to get a good return on the money invested through the shares increasing in value, rather than a stream of income from the business in the form of dividends.

An outside investor, such as a venture capital fund, will at some stage want to sell the shares to realize the profits. If you are hoping to raise money in this way, put in your plan that you intend to have your company floated on the stockmarket or the Alternative Investment market (AIM), say, or that you would like to sell the company, as most venture capital funds want to be invested in a business for a fairly short period, typically three to seven years. Other potential outside investors include 'business angels' – many of these are people who have made money from their own businesses and are looking to invest in other new or small businesses, investing both finance and expertise.

The value you can obtain for your shares, if you are a new company, is a very vexed question. Frankly, they are not worth very much yet, so you might find that you are having to sell a bigger proportion of the shares than you would like to raise the money you need. This can lead to problems about voting control. What the value of the shares is can lead to a lot of haggling.

Opting for this route to raise money needs professional help; you will need to call in, perhaps, accountants, solicitors and corporate finance specialists. Ask for references from these professionals; this should help you steer clear of the rank unprofessionals.

Taking partners

If you have started out as a sole trader but need to raise additional capital, you could do this by taking a partner. What share of the profits each partner gets in return for the capital put in is a subject to be negotiated. There also needs to be clarity about the management role each partner will have. For your own sake, you should do this before you form the partnership. A written partnership agreement is a must (p. 48).

Lenders and investors

You and your family

The first fact you must come to terms with is that if you do not invest in your business idea, you cannot expect anyone else to do so. As a rough rule of thumb, the absolute most you will probably be able to raise from outsiders is five times as much money as you are putting in yourself, but, needless to say, there are always exceptions. If you are planning a substantial business and looking to raise £1 million or more, say, you may find that investors will put up ten or twenty times as much as you. But normally, you can expect someone to match your own investment, or put up two or three times as much as you do as a maximum. But in the worst case, it could be nothing.

Example

> Winston Carpenter has £10,000 to invest in his business. He works out from his forecasts and his business plan that he needs to raise more money. He is unlikely to be able to raise an extra £50,000 or more, but with a good presentation of his idea, he may persuade someone to lend or invest £20,000, say.

The rationale behind this insistence of how much you must invest yourself is that lenders, such as banks, and investors, such as venture capital funds, want you to be committed to your business, to make you work very hard and with great determination to be successful. If you have not risked the proportion of capital they would like, they may doubt your commitment. Of course if you can point to the fact that, even though it is a low proportion of the total invested in your business, the sum of money you are investing is still a sizeable proportion of your own personal assets, you could be convincing.

Where are you going to get your share of the money?

If you have money tucked away somewhere, or if you have a lump sum as a result of being made redundant, this is a relatively easy question to answer. Another common source of the money for your stake is to be given or lent it by someone in your family. But being financed by your family can lead to heartache if things start going wrong. So do not enter on this course light-heartedly. Conversely, you are more likely to convince your family than anyone else.

Another possible way of raising your share of the funds is to use your personal assets to act as security (for example, a second mortgage on your home) or by giving a personal guarantee. The drawback with this is that if your business fails, you have to find the money to carry on making your repayments, or you have to sell your home. You must give careful consideration before giving personal guarantees or using your home to raise money in this way for your business and the bank may insist that you take legal advice before you do.

It would make sense to have some sort of agreed family plan for what would happen if your business failed. For example, you should discuss openly whether you are ready to sell your house and move to a smaller one should the security be called upon to repay your loan. If you cannot have some sort of strategy in your domestic life which is acceptable in return for the prospect of going it alone, you are likely to have family problems when the inevitable pressures mount on the business.

You can get tax relief on these loans. If you are a sole trader or partner, any interest you pay on a loan for business purposes is allowable as a deduction against tax in working out your taxable profits. If you take on a loan to invest or lend money to a close company (most family companies are) you can get tax relief at your highest rate of tax on the interest you pay. To be eligible for this tax relief, you must either own more than 5 per cent of the shares or own some shares and work for the greater part of your time for the company.

When should you put in your money?

The best advice is not necessarily to start your business straightaway, investing your money and subsequently approaching other lenders or investors later when you need it. The wisest course may be to prepare your forecasts and your business plans and to approach possible sources of finance before you start your business and before you actually need the extra money. To plan ahead and get a commitment in advance can be crucial.

The reason why this could be the best approach is that lenders have a couple of infuriating habits. The first is to ask what money you are going to put in when they put in their share. You may be able to point out that you invested £10,000, say, six months ago and since then have worked without drawing any salary, but lenders are likely to be unimpressed. That is water under the bridge and may count for nothing as far as they are concerned. The second is for them to adopt an attitude of 'wait and see' how the business develops, while the cash is running out and you are under great pressure to raise more. In this way better deals can be struck for the investor or lender. So do not rush out and use up your money, if you know you will need extra funds in due course; get your financial backing in advance.

Government, local authorities, charities

You may be able to get grants, allowances, cheap loans or prizes from a variety of sources.

Government help is available with the loan guarantee scheme (p. 277) and the variety of grants available if your business is located in certain areas, such as Assisted Areas or regions falling within the scope of the various Single Regeneration Budget programmes (p. 176). If your business idea is innovative or technical, the government has other grants on offer, such as SMART which provides up to 75 per cent of the cost of feasibility and technical studies and up to 30 per cent of development costs. Other schemes encourage collaboration between innovative businesses and universities and other research establishments. Your local DTI office (see Reference) or Business Link should be able to give you details of all these schemes.

Local authorities can provide help to new businesses. This may range from grants or premises to advice or loans. The schemes are individual to the local authority and you will find out from yours locally what is available. Your local Business Link, enterprise agency or TEC should know – or the Economic Development Unit of your local authority.

There are grants and cheap loans available to young people, aged between 18 and 25, from the Prince's Youth Business Trust (p. 36). There are competitions run for young people, such as Livewire (p. 36). But there are also competitions run by accountants, banks and others for business ideas. Details of these are often published in newspapers (p. 34).

Banks

Your bank manager is an obvious port of call, but not always the best nor the one you should make first of all. The advantage of going straight there is that if you have been a good creditworthy customer with a good record, your manager should favour your application. And this is what should happen to the vast bulk of people with a good business proposition which is well presented and well researched.

But there are a couple of reasons why you should not head straight here or why you might expect not to secure the money you want. In the first place, your presentation of your plan will improve with the number of times you give it. If your bank manager really is your best possibility and you have not practised your presentation, you might blow the opportunity. It could pay you to approach another bank, simply to practise what you are going to say and be prepared for the questions which will be asked.

The second disadvantage may occur if you are looking to your bank to provide substantial funds. Each branch bank manager has a different discretionary lending limit; above the limit your application may need to be processed elsewhere and so you may lose part of the personal touch on which you were relying for a sympathetic hearing of your case.

The moral is shop around. Do not be put off by being turned down, try another bank or another branch which you think may be more used to business deals. Remember to ask what rate you will be charged; compare this with what other banks would charge. Banks can offer money in two ways:

❑ overdrafts (p. 272)

❑ loans.

Loans can be very flexible – particularly, as loans to sole traders and partners are no longer within the scope of the Consumer Credit Act 1974 – and the exact terms vary from bank to bank. You can borrow money for periods of between two and thirty years. The rate of interest can be fixed, variable – a number of percentage points over the bank base rate – or in some cases at a monthly managed rate. Sometimes for larger loans (e.g. £15,000 plus) you can negotiate a repayment holiday from repaying the capital you borrow. So for, say, one or two years, you pay only interest. You may also be able to arrange stepped repayments. The amount you can borrow can vary from £1,000 to £1 million. The type of loan you can get depends on the viability of your plan.

The Loan Guarantee Scheme is designed to help new and established small businesses with an annual turnover of no more than £1.5 million (£3 million if it is a manufacturing business). You must be able to show that you have tried to get a conventional loan but have failed because of lack of security. The Department of Trade and Industry (DTI) then steps in to provide security by guaranteeing 70 per cent of the loan (85 per cent if you have been trading for more than two years). In return, you pay a premium to the DTI of 1.5 per cent a year of the outstanding loan. The premium is reduced to 0.5 per cent if the money is lent at a fixed rate of interest. Under the scheme, you can borrow any amount from £5,000 up to £100,000 (£250,000 if you have been trading for more than two years). The loan can last from two up to ten years.

The practice varies from bank to bank about the cost of setting up the loan. There could be an arrangement fee, for example, of 1 or 1½ per cent of the loan, but not more than £500; check before you arrange the loan and try to negotiate on this point. You may be required to take out life insurance for the amount of the loan.

Apart from the standard requirements, such as soundness of your business plan and amount of money you have invested yourself, the banks will also look at the size of loans you have already.

Private investors

There is a growing body of private investors, often called 'high net-worth individuals' who are prepared to back business ventures. Sometimes, these people are called 'angels', that is they provide money for risky ventures. Ask at your local Business Link, TEC or enterprise agency. There are some privately-run networks or business introduction services. And you could also try these sources to get in touch with potential private investors:

LINC (Local Investment Networking Company) (see Reference)

This is run by a number of enterprise agencies and Training and Enterprise Councils. They try to put companies wanting funds (between £10,000 and £250,000) in touch with people who have funds to invest. They do this by sending out a regular bulletin listing the companies who hope to raise finance. You may be offered the opportunity to present your case at a bi-monthly company presentation day, once registered with LINC. It costs £250 plus VAT to register and includes an entry in the bulletin. The company has to send in a comprehensive business plan when applying to register, as opposed to somebody visiting them.

Small ads sections

There are often ads in newspapers with Business to Business sections, such as the *Guardian*, *The Times*, the *Financial Times* and the *Sunday Times*, from people wanting to invest in new enterprises. Alternatively, you could advertise for funds in the same way, although you have to watch out for various legal restrictions.

The Enterprise Investment Scheme and reinvestment relief give tax concessions to make it more attractive for private individuals to invest in unquoted companies. With reinvestment relief, it is possible to put off paying capital gains tax if a private investor sells some shares but reinvests the proceeds in the new shares of a private company.

Venture capital funds

There are over a hundred venture capital funds in the UK, with the money put up by pension funds, insurance companies, banks, investment trusts, industrial corporations, regional development agencies and private individuals. A more recent innovation is a venture capital trust (VCT) which offers tax concessions to investors and invests the fund in growing companies. Not all of the funds will provide money for people who are starting up; most only provide funds for businesses which are expanding.

Venture capital funds are looking for companies with very good management, operating in a market which is either very large or is growing fast. The funds want to invest in companies which could reach significant profits within three to four years. Many, but not all, want to be able to sell their investment in three to seven years and hope that the company will have grown enough in that time to be floated on the stock market or be sold to another company. This would allow the funds to sell their shares and turn their gains into cash.

If you approach a venture capital fund, the things to look out for are:

❑ *amount of shares:* the fund will normally want ordinary shares in return for the investment, as well as loan capital or preference shares, though there are exceptions. The percentage of shares varies from fund to fund; a few may want over 50 per cent, but it is unusual for a fund to want a majority stake in the company. The percentage of shares is not always affected by the amount of money you want to raise nor by the voting structure

❑ *board director:* the fund will usually want to have one or two directors on your board and you will have to bear the cost of this. You will normally be able to approve the choice of director. The fees for a non-executive director can be in the £10,000 to £20,000 range

❑ *due diligence:* this is the term for the investigation which a venture capital fund will want to undertake before investing in your company. This can include visiting your offices and other work location, taking up references from customers, potential customers and past employers, studying your accounts and selling systems, having your product checked technically and so on. The fund will want you to pay for this investigation; you can negotiate on this. How successful your negotiation will be depends on the level of interest shown by other funds

❑ *legal and professional fees:* there are yours and theirs. You will have to pay the legal costs for the funds on top of all your costs for raising finance.

You will have legal and accounting fees, running into several thousands, plus the fee paid to a corporate finance adviser, usually based on a percentage of the money raised. In total, your share of the costs could run up to five to 10 per cent of the money you raise

❑ *syndication:* if you are trying to raise a very large sum of money, a venture capital fund may want a partner or two to provide the funds you wish. This may be because providing the amount of money you want could take up a fairly hefty chunk of the total money they have to invest or they may just want to spread the risk. You may have to do a lot of the work yourself to bring together funds into a consortium to provide the money. This can prove very tricky and adds considerably to the amount of time it can take you to raise the money.

The presentation: how to do it

There are a lot of useful tips on how to present your plan scattered through this chapter and Chapter 6. This step-by-step guide below draws all these tips together.

1. First impressions are all-important. The first thing prospective lenders and investors will see is your business plan. It must be typed, clean, neatly arranged in a folder. It should look comprehensive without being over-detailed, not more than ten or twenty pages (if necessary, information can be put in appendices).

2. Practise your presentation of your plan. Do this by getting a colleague or friend to role-play or see if a counsellor at an enterprise agency will take you through it. If necessary, approach a source of finance which you regard as very low chance and use it to perfect your technique for those opportunities of which you are very hopeful.

3. The next step will be a face-to-face encounter. Look conventional; the people who have money to lend are middle-of-the-road types, so do not endanger your chances of getting the money by dressing in an odd way.

4. Get the facts at your fingertips. Your plan may look good, but if you sound unsure or muddled about the details, doubts about your management ability may be raised.

5. Be clear in your own mind what is interesting or exciting about your proposal. Do not get so bogged down by the details that you cannot bring out the really important points of your business idea.

6. Find out the names and positions of those who can lend. Try to get the real decision-makers, not their advisers or subordinates.

7. Listen carefully to the questions and make sure you answer what you have been asked.

8. If you are asked for further information, make sure it is as well researched and well presented as the rest of your plan and provide it quickly.

9. Do not be too defensive about your idea; assume beforehand that it will be critically assessed.

Summary

1. Treat negotiating for money with the same planning and thought as making a sale.

2. Be very certain that you ask for the right amount of money; it is very difficult to go round a second time to ask for more.

3. It can be difficult to raise less than £500,000.

4. Overdrafts are for the shorter term; long-term finance is provided by loans or selling shares, if you have a company.

5. As a rule of thumb, you will need to invest as much as an outside investor or perhaps half as much. Rare exceptions have managed to put in a much smaller proportion than an outside investor and still retain control.

6. Securing loans on your house or giving personal guarantees is a major step. Do not take it lightly or without discussing it with your family.

7. Money can be raised from banks, private individuals and companies, venture capital funds, charities or local authorities.

8. Make your presentation carefully. Follow the tips on the left.

Other chapters to read

6. **The business plan** (p. 64)
22. **Forecasting** (p. 251)

24. Staying afloat

You are launched. You have premises, even if it is your own home. You have started selling and now must produce the goods. You may have raised money to help finance the business. So what next? Staying afloat is the name of the game. Learning to live within the income your sales bring is a hard task, but one that has to be learnt. A survey by Dun & Bradstreet found that the most common problem areas contributing towards failure are taking on contracts at too low a price, delays in receiving payments and being caught up in the cashflow problems of a larger company.

For some, it is easy: this could apply to you if your sort of business is consultancy, or design, or some other type of work where the overheads can be contained, at least until the time comes for expansion. For others, there is this point to strive towards before your business is truly afloat. This is known as break-even point, and is the point at which the contribution your sales bring is large enough to cover the overheads of your business, for example, rent, rates, telephone and some employee costs.

When you see explanations of break-even point in textbooks, it seems straightforward. Your business struggles towards the level of sales you find from the laid-down formula and once you have reached there, your business is ticking along nicely. In reality, break-even point is not like that at all. It has a most disconcerting habit of moving; as sales increase, so inevitably do the pressures on the business to get the job done. One way to ease the pressure is to increase the overheads and so the cycle continues. Trying to hit a moving target is notoriously difficult; and so is struggling to break even.

To stay afloat in the longer term requires more than being permanently at break-even; you need profits. These can be used to develop new products and markets as existing ones mature and decline.

These are the problems. What about the solution? Clearly increasing the amount and value of the sales are top priorities, as well as containing costs. But these take time. The business needs a breathing space to allow sales to develop. To allow yourself that leeway, you must control the business. And cash control assumes the major role in this. Your business will stay afloat (in the short term) if the money goes round; you hope you can keep it going long enough for sales to reach that moving target and get to break-even.

You cannot do it for ever; at some stage, it will be clear that your business must raise more money or it will fail. If you are unable to get more funds, you do not want to reach the point of trading illegally and you do not want your crash to take other small businesses with you. You have to recognize the warning signs (p. 309).

Of course, any well-run business should be interested in cash control, whether struggling for break-even or already well into profit. Making the cash go round more efficiently helps increase your profits. Controlling cash is essentially a question of controlling debtors (that is, people who owe you money), creditors (that is, people to whom you owe money) and stock (including work-in-progress).

What is in this chapter?

❏ Break-even point (see below)

❏ The plan to control the business (p. 287)

❏ Cash (p. 288)

❏ Your customers (p. 291)

❏ Your suppliers (p. 297).

Break-even point

One management technique you should get to grips with is break-even point. This assumes extreme importance for the sort of business which makes losses initially; possibly, you may raise money to cover that loss-making period or find it yourself. What you are working towards is the point at which the contribution (strictly, gross margin), which you make from sales, is sufficient to cover the overheads (also called indirect or fixed costs).

Overheads are the cost of setting up the structure of your business. For example, the cost of your premises does not rise and fall with the amount of sales you are making. In the long run, you could move to cheaper premises, but this is a major upheaval. In the meantime, this overhead cost is fixed. The value of your sales needs to be built up to the level which contributes to the expense of the premises.

Other examples of overheads are insurance, the cost of equipment – such as cars and typewriters – heating and lighting, the telephone and so on. One vexed problem is whether employees are a fixed cost or not. For most businesses, they will be, certainly for a few months (see p. 215 for more about the cost effect of employing people).

How to work out your break-even point

To do this you need to know:

❑ gross profit margin

❑ total cost of overheads.

If your product or service is uniform, you can work out the gross profit (or contribution) on each item sold. The gross profit on each item is the selling price less the direct cost of each item. Direct costs are those items which you only have to pay for because you make a product or provide a service, for example, raw materials.

However, if the product can vary, work out the gross profit for one month's sales, say, and use this to find your gross profit margin.

The formula for break-even point of sales is:

$$\frac{\text{Overheads} \times 100}{\text{Price of product} - \text{direct cost of product}}$$

This gives you the number of items you must sell to cover the overhead costs, see Example 1 below.

or $$\frac{\text{Overheads}}{\text{Gross profit margin}} \times 100$$

Gross profit margin is the gross profit divided by the value of sales times 100. This formula gives you the value of sales you must make to cover the overhead costs, see Example 2 overleaf.

Example 1

Robert Atherton sells quantities of paper cleaning cloths. He buys them in large rolls, cuts them and distributes them as duster-size (twelve to each packet). He has worked out the direct cost of each packet of twelve as 10p and sells them for 26p. Thus, gross profit on each packet of twelve is 16p. His overheads are £6,000 in the year, £500 a month. His break-even sales of packets of twelve cloths each month are:

$$\frac{£500}{£0.16} = 3,125$$

Example 2

Jane Edwardes runs a company which sells computer systems to the accounting profession. The prices of the system vary depending on the size of the computer, the exact form of the software and how many screens are run off the computer. The cheapest starts at £5,000 and the most expensive system is £15,000. For her business plan for the next twelve months, Jane has worked out the likely number of systems of each size she forecasts she will sell. For the year, sales are estimated at £300,000 and the direct costs, that is, the computers, screens and other parts, and the software, are forecast to be £120,000.

Gross profit margin is:

$$\frac{£300,000 - £120,000}{£300,000} \times 100 = 60\%$$

The overheads of the business are estimated at £108,000 for the next year, that is, £9,000 a month.

The break-even sales for each month are:

$$\frac{£9,000}{60} \times 100 = £15,000$$

This applies as long as the level of fixed costs remains unchanged and either the gross profit margin is the same on each product or the pattern of sales mirrors the forecast for the year.

The diagrams may help you to gain a better understanding of break-even. The level line shows the estimated level of overheads for different levels of sales. The dotted line which starts at point O shows the amount of the direct costs for each level of sales. Total costs (line starts at A) are the sum of the direct costs and the overheads.

The continuous sloping line starting at O shows the value of sales at different levels of units sold. X is the break-even point. To the left of X, your business is making a loss; to the right, your business is making a profit.

Diagram 1 overleaf assumes that the level of overheads stays the same no matter what the level of sales you can make. Frankly, this is difficult to achieve in practice. Once you start doing more business, you may well find that your overheads will go up too. For example, you may find you need more secretarial help, given the increased amount of sales you are making. In Diagram 2 overleaf, you can see the effect on break-even point, if there is an increase in overheads for the same business as below. The break-even sales figure is now higher.

Diagram 1: Finding the break-even point of your business

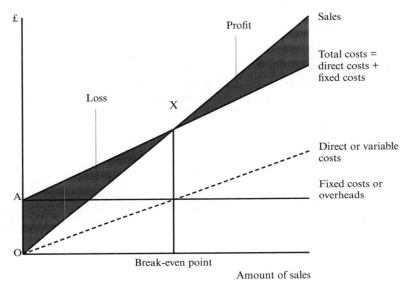

Diagram 2: How an increase in fixed costs moves the break-even point upwards

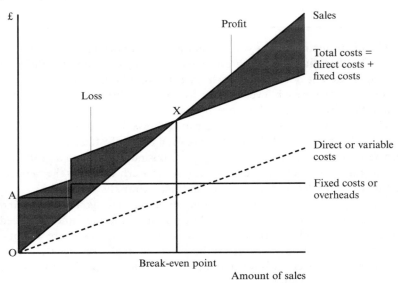

The plan to control the business

When you produced your business plan before you started your business (p. 64), you incorporated some forecasts: profit and loss and cash flow. These could form the basis for your plan (or budget), which you need to control the business, although probably with some adjustments.

What you need for a budget that you use to control your business, but that is also to give you (and any employees) something to aim for, is a plan incorporating figures which you believe you may be able to achieve. Be wary of including figures that are too easy for the business, in case meeting the budget turns into the objective, rather than striving for the biggest profit possible.

As you are going to use the budget to control the business, you need to have the next year's budget prepared before the previous year has ended, otherwise there is a time gap in which the business will drift. If you employ others in the business, they should be involved in drawing up the forecasts for their particular area of the business.

How to use the budget

Every month, as soon as possible after the end of it and not later than a fortnight after, you should have the actual profit, cost and cash figures to compare with the budget. Your comparison should be for two reasons:

❏ to identify what has gone wrong, and right, and to derive lessons for the future

❏ to identify problem areas for the future, which may only emerge as your actual performance fails to keep up with budgeted performance.

Keeping in touch with the business

Once you start employing others, you will no longer be dealing with every single aspect of the business yourself. Once others have areas of responsibility, you will need to devise a system of management reporting. There is no one system which is perfect for a particular business, but it should include some of the following elements:

weekly reports: these could be verbal, for example, a meeting. It needs to be sufficiently detailed, so that everyone in the business knows as a result of the report:

❏ their objectives for the next week

❑ what is on the critical path to allow sales to be made and products to be produced or made ready for sale.

monthly reports: these should be written by the person responsible, for example, salesperson or manager, production staff. The report should cover two aspects:

❑ what has been achieved in the past month, how it compares with budgeted figures and objectives set in the weekly reports and any explanation or lessons to be drawn from successes and failures

❑ what the outlook is for the next month, what should be achieved and what the objectives are.

While management reports allow you to keep informed about the business, they have an important side-effect. They force your employees to concentrate on:

❑ the objectives of the business

❑ their own performance against budgeted performance

❑ their own priorities for action in the week and month ahead.

Cash

If your cash runs out, your business will fail. It is as simple as that. Why your cash runs out is due to several possible reasons:

❑ you do not sell enough

❑ your costs are too high for the sales you make

❑ your sales and costs are rising nicely according to plan, but you do not have enough cash to fund the increased amount of debtors and stocks, which the extra business brings.

How to conserve cash

There are three important steps in conserving cash:

❑ knowing how much cash you have and how much you will need

❑ speeding up the cash inflow from your customers (p. 294)

❑ slowing down the cash outflow to your suppliers (p. 297).

The cash budget

Preparing your business plan (p. 64) will have taken you some way towards knowing how much cash you will need in the business; indeed, the most important purpose of preparing the business plan may have been to raise the cash your forecasts show will be required. Once the business is trading, the cash flow forecasts need to be turned into monthly cash flow budgets.

You can help to conserve cash by paying by instalments as much as possible. For example, consider leasing cars or furniture, rather than buying outright (p. 190).

Your aim should be not just to match your budget, but to do better than it says. Never despise a penny or a pound which can be saved; very small savings build up over time to very large savings. This penny-pinching attitude applies just as strongly if you have raised money.

Comparing the actual cash performance with the cash budget is an important tool in controlling your cash. It enables you to learn from mistakes and plan your cash requirements in the future.

What else controls cash?

When cash is tight, you will take much more stringent measures than when you are cash rich. For example, you could consider instituting the following control system:

❑ daily cash balance

❑ weekly or daily bank statement

❑ weekly forecast of each individual cash payment in (from customers) and planned cash payment out (to suppliers). This could be set up as a sheet with each named customer and supplier. Each day check what money you have received and tick off on your forecast sheet. Do not pay any cheques until you have received the money you need.

Obviously, when cash is short, you need to put your cash receipts in the bank as quickly as possible; and when you pay people, send the cheque by second-class post. You can say honestly that the cheque has been sent.

Clearly, the system does not work for every business; it is a good control tool for businesses which have a number of large receipts and payments. A retail business would not be able to operate in this way. However, a control sheet for a shop could consist of a weekly forecast of daily takings plus a list of those suppliers you intend to pay that week. Again the suppliers will not be paid until the forecast cash comes in. For what happens when things are out of control, see p. 308.

A cash system like this is a nuisance to operate, and so if cash is not particularly short, you could use a variant of:

❑ weekly cash balance

❑ weekly bank statement

❑ monthly payment cycle, that is, set aside one day in each month on which you pay the bills you plan for that month. This means that there is only one day in each month devoted to writing cheques. If a bill is not paid on that day, it does not get paid until a month later.

Important note: No cash control system can operate if you do not keep proper cash records, for example, a cash book. This is explained on p. 315.

Making cash work for you

Your problem may not be shortage of cash; on the contrary, you may have extra cash sitting around. In this case, do not leave it all in the current account. Instead, have sufficient handy to keep the business ticking over and put what you can in a seven-day notice or call account which earns interest. Remember to give the required notice so that you can transfer what you need to cover your payments in your once-a-month cheque cycle. There are also a few of the high-interest cheque accounts which can be used by small businesses.

Operating your bank account

What your bank account will cost you as a small business used to be one of the more closely held secrets – and may still be with some banks. However, all the banks are trying to make charges clearer to customers. Some banks have readily available leaflets detailing the charges on your small business account. If your bank doesn't, ask for the information, so you can work out in advance how much your bank charges are likely to be. Some banks will now tell you in advance what your next month's charges will be based on the current month's account usage. Most banks now make a standard charge for main account services, such as cheques, standing orders, direct debits and cash machine withdrawals. One way to economize is to use a credit or charge card for business expenses, as this is paid with a single payment, instead of lots of little ones.

However, it needs careful consideration before a card is given to an employee. Additionally, in the case of companies, use of a credit or charge card is a fringe benefit for employees, which would include you as a director; check how it would affect your individual tax bill.

If your business is on a very small scale, you should consider whether it is possible to run it using a building society account, rather than a bank account, bearing in mind there are limitations, such as no overdraft facility or business advice.

Some banks offer free banking for the first year (or even longer) if a small business opens an account. This can mean with some banks that there are no bank charges even if you have an overdraft.

Going into overdraft

The time to ask for an overdraft (p. 272) is not the day you realize that you will not be able to cover the bills of suppliers who are really pressing you for payment. The bank manager simply will not like it. It is much better for you to present a well-argued case one or two months before you think you will need the facility. This means planning ahead, by using your forecasts or budgets as a proper control tool.

Your customers

Selling is not the end of the story. Any old customer will not do. Making a sale to someone who does not pay their bill at all is worse than no sale at all. The ideal customer is one who pays their bill as soon as your product or service is handed over. Very few businesses are lucky enough to have that type of client. But there are steps you can take to try to ensure that you do get the cash in. First, you can check them out before you hand over the goods to them. Second, you can do everything you can to make them pay up as quickly as possible.

Giving credit to customers, that is, allowing them to become debtors and pay some time after they have received your service or product, costs you money. For example, if a bank charges 10 per cent on an overdraft, an outstanding bill of £1,000 costs you £100 if it is still unpaid after one year. Or, if it is unpaid after three months, the cost to you is £25. The more efficient you are at reducing the amount of time before you receive your payments, the lower the costs.

Investigating potential customers (credit control)

Few businesses can confine their sales to completely 'safe' customers; there is usually an element of risk-taking with sales, which is needed to meet your business objectives. But the riskiness or otherwise of customers needs to be assessed, so that the risk is known and calculated. Assessment needs information, control and monitoring.

The extent of the investigation must also depend on the amount of the projected sale relative to your total sales. If it is a fairly small sale, the investigation alone may cost as much as the profit from the sale; you should establish a policy of rejecting or accepting such risks as a matter of course. But if the sale would be a significant order for you, further information is needed.

Consider the following steps:

❑ if you are dealing with a large quoted company, check its payment policy. This must be published in its annual report and accounts. The Confederation of British Industry (CBI) operates a voluntary code of practice on prompt payment – check whether the company has adopted this code. If recent government proposals become law, at some future time, companies might be required to publish details of actual payment records, which would be more useful in highlighting those companies with a bad record of paying late

❑ ask the prospective customer for a bank reference (but this will be based only on the bank's experience, so may indicate relatively little, but will help in building a general picture)

❑ ask for a couple of trade references. Put a specific question such as 'Up to what level of trade credit is the customer considered a good risk?'

❑ ask a credit-reporting agency to report (p. 296)

❑ ask the customer for the latest report and accounts or a balance sheet and profit and loss account. Ask your accountant to analyse them for you

❑ if you have not already done so, visit the business with a view to meeting the principals or directors. Put any questions which remain unanswered and use this visit to fill in the general picture.

Using the information you have garnered from all these sources, assess how risky you think this customer is and establish a credit limit. A common system is to have five categories of risk, ranging from the top category, who would be considered good for anything, to the bottom category, who you would sell to only on cash terms. You would draw up certain credit limits to apply to each category, for example, allowed £1,000 on thirty days' credit.

The actual amounts would depend on the size of debts relative to your sales and what is considered normal practice in that industry.

The payment terms you offer (credit terms)

There is quite a variety of expressions applying to possible credit terms you could offer customers. Some of these include:

❑ cash with order (CWO)

❑ cash on delivery (COD)

❑ payment seven days after delivery (net 7)

❑ payment for goods supplied in one week by a certain day in the next week (weekly credit)

❑ payment for goods supplied in one month by a certain day in the next month (monthly credit)

❑ payment due thirty days after delivery (thirty days' credit).

And so on. You have to choose the best terms you can. This means you extend credit for as short a time as possible, but obviously industry and competitive practice may to some extent put you in a strait-jacket.

There are a couple of ways you can try to encourage early payment of your bills. First, you can offer a cash discount for early payment, for example, payment within seven days of the invoice means the customer can claim a discount of 1 per cent. The problem with this sort of discount is that customers tend to take it (and, if your debtor control is a little sloppy, are allowed the discount) whenever they pay. Introducing a cash discount of this type needs to be accompanied by close monitoring to make it clear to customers that they are entitled to the discount only if they meet the conditions offered.

Second, you can make a charge for late payment. And The Late Payment of Commercial Debts (Interest) Act has now been passed which gives you the legal right to do so from November 1998. From that date small businesses (50 employees or less) will have the right to interest on late payment of their debts by large companies and public sector organisations. If there is no agreed credit period, interest can be charged from 30 days after the date of the invoice and the rate of interest will be base rate plus eight per cent.

Sending out invoices

Be very prompt in sending out invoices. This is crucial to any policy of keeping tight credit control. Failure to do this will give the impression to debtors that you do not mind how long you wait for your money, and as we have seen, giving credit costs you money. No matter how busy you are keeping up with the work you do, sending out invoices, as soon as goods are delivered or services supplied, must take precedence.

The records you need for control

There is more detail on how to set up the records you need on p. 313, but the records need to provide you with the following information:

❑ say how much you are owed in total at any time

❑ say how long you have been owed the money and by whom; this information is known as an aged analysis of debts

❑ a record of sales and payments including the date made for each customer. This allows you to build up your own picture of the credit-worthiness of individual debtors.

How to chase money you are owed

1. Make sure your credit terms are known to your customer. The best way is to print them clearly on the invoice.

2. As soon as your customer has overstepped the mark and the bill is overdue, ask for the money you are owed. This should be done politely in writing, preferably by fax, with a follow-up in the post.

3. If there is no reply within seven days, check that the details of the invoice are correct and that you have quoted all the information the customer needs to identify it, for example, the customer's own reference.

4. Fax again. Follow up with a letter sent by recorded delivery.

5. No reply within seven days? Make a phone call to find out what the problem is. Do not assume that the customer has no money; there may be queries on the account or other problems. Find out the apparent reason for the non-payment.

6. Use the phone call to find out if the customer has a weekly or monthly cheque run (p. 290) and find out the day this is done.

7. Still no payment? Keep ringing and especially two or three days before the cheque run. Try to extract a promise of payment.

8. Keep the pressure up. Do not pester and then drop for a few weeks; all your previous chasing is undone. Keep up a steady and persistent guerrilla warfare.

9. If the customer is always out or in a meeting when you telephone, and you suspect this is due to a desire not to speak to you, try pretending to be someone else who you are sure your customer will want to speak to. If you deal with an accountant or book-keeper, try speaking to the managing director of the customer's business.

10. Try different times of the day and the week: lunchtime is not usually a good time, but first thing Monday morning can be effective.

11. When you eventually manage to speak to the person you want, if he or she says, 'I'll chase it up and see what has happened,' say you will keep holding until they do.

12. If the customer says, 'The cheque has been posted,' ask for the date this was done, whether it went first- or second-class, how much the cheque was for and what the cheque number is.

13. If the cheque does not arrive, go to collect the money in person; this is what the Inland Revenue and the Customs and Excise people do. Get the cheque cashed as soon as possible, so that it cannot be stopped.

14. Check all the details of the cheque: your name, the amount, the date, the signature.

15. If all the previous steps have failed, send a formal letter preferably from your solicitor, either threatening to take legal action to recover the debt or to start bankruptcy or winding-up proceedings (p. 310) or threatening to use a debt-collection agency. Keep the threat.

16. Consider using an agency (overleaf).

17. Consider issuing a writ for the debt or consider starting bankruptcy proceedings against an individual or winding-up proceedings against a company. Consider using the small claims court. Ask your solicitor's advice.

Using an agency

Once the money has been overdue for two to three months, you could hand it over to an agency. They will write and phone and eventually either collect the money or report that it will only be collected by legal action. The usual charge for an agency is some percentage of the money recovered. There is a list of a few of the agencies in the Reference section.

A half-way house to using the full-blown debt collection service is to use an agency to write to overdue customers pointing out that non-payment will be reported to credit-reporting agencies, which may harm the customer's credit rating. As this is very important to a business, this often has the desired effect. However, payment is actually made to you, not the agency, and so long as this is done, the information is not entered on the customer's file at the reporting agency.

Selling your debts to raise cash (factoring)

Essentially, a factor buys your debts in return for an immediate cash payment. Generally speaking, factoring is available for debts from other businesses, rather than individuals. In a full service, the factor takes over your records for debtors and collects the debts. In return, you could receive a payment of up to 80 per cent of the face value of the invoices. The balance of the money will be paid when the debts are collected. Factoring occurs on a continuing basis, not for one individual set of debtors. The factor will often offer insurance against bad debts.

There are less complete services, for example:

❑ the factor does not take over your records

❑ the customer does not pay the factor, but pays you

❑ invoice discounting, that is, you maintain the records and collect the debts. This means that your use of the service remains confidential and your customers are not aware of it.

While a factoring service seems the answer to your cash flow dreams, there are some conditions:

❑ if your sales are less than £100,000 a year, you may find it difficult to factor your debtors

❑ the factor will investigate your trading record, bad debt history, credit rating procedure, customers and so on before deciding whether to offer you a factoring service

❑ some factors give automatic protection against bad debts; others do not

❑ you are likely to have to agree to a one year's contract with a lengthy period of notice.

Note that all the separate components of factoring, that is, keeping your debtor records, cash collection, invoice discounting and credit insurance are available separately from a number of organizations. Compare costs of several factoring services and look at the cost of the individual components.

Your suppliers

Quite a lot of the way you can deal with your suppliers (or creditors when you owe them money) is simply the reverse of what you do with debtors. Taking credit from suppliers is a significant source of finance for most small businesses. However, the other side of the coin is that those suppliers may be short of funds themselves and heavily dependent on getting in the money they are owed as quickly as possible.

When you are short of cash, you may find yourself chasing your customers and cursing them for not paying up, while doing exactly the same yourself to other businesses. As a starting point, your first step should be to try to negotiate improved credit terms from your suppliers, rather than simply taking unapproved extended credit.

Unfortunately, being open with your suppliers does not always pay off. Saying that you are short of cash this week but you will pay next week can cause panic. Your creditor may issue a writ without delay and your future credit terms may be affected.

Nevertheless, when the chips are down, one way of seeing yourself through a temporary shortage of cash is to push up the length of time you take to pay your creditors. It is, of course, a slippery road; what you fervently believe to be a temporary shortage of cash may turn into a permanent shortfall. If you cannot make good the shortfall by raising more permanent funds, you will go to the wall with a lot of unpaid bills. A lot of small businesses like yourself will also lose money as a result of your action. Somehow, you have to know where to draw the line (p. 308).

What happens when a supplier investigates you?

Any well-organized supplier will carry out the same screening of you as you do of customers who are going to place largish orders with you. Expect to be asked for:

❑ permission to approach your bank for a reference

❑ two trade references

❑ a balance sheet or a set of the latest accounts

❑ further information as a result of the supplier's investigation.

The supplier will also probably approach a credit-reporting agency to see what it has on you and what your credit rating is. Of course, when you are starting in business, you can provide none of the information mentioned above. You may be forced to pay in cash initially, until you have built up some sort of record. A large supplier may even ask for a personal guarantee. You may be able to avoid this if you can demonstrate that you have sufficient funds raised to get the business through the building-up stage.

The records you need for control

Details of the records you should set up are given on p. 314. But you should be able to derive the following information from them:

❑ say how much you owe in total at any time

❑ say how long you have owed the money and to whom

❑ a record of what you have paid each supplier and when.

How to delay paying what you owe

Essentially, you can use only a series of excuses, not to say downright lies; there are few honest ways of delaying payment. However, it may be some comfort to know that most successful small businesses at some stage have to delay payment.

The first step to take is not to consider paying any bills until you are asked to.

The second step is to introduce a paying schedule which involves making cheques out only once a month.

Further steps involve simply delaying paying. The sorts of excuses are those mirrored in **How to chase money you are owed** on p. 294.

Summary

1. The first stage for any new business is to get to break-even point; after that, building up profits is needed for long-term survival.

2. Watch out for overheads; they have a nasty knack of rising with sales, thus continually pushing up break-even point.

3. Convert your business plan and forecasts into a budget which gives you, and your employees, something to aim for.

4. Keep control of your business by comparing actual to budget performance; try to draw the appropriate lessons to be learned and plot ahead any changes in your plan which are needed.

5. If you have employees, introduce a system of weekly and monthly reporting and setting of objectives.

6. Controlling cash can keep your business afloat until break-even is reached.

7. Make your cash work for you, that is, if you have spare funds put them in an interest-earning account.

8. Operate your bank account as efficiently as possible.

9. Try to speed up the rate at which your sales are turned into cash. Do this by exercising credit control and investigating potential customers, offering the tightest credit terms you can, sending out invoices promptly and chasing overdue bills. Use **How to chase money you are owed** on p. 294.

10. Most successful small businesses have to stoop to delaying payment to their suppliers at some time during their development.

Other chapters to read

25. **How to increase profits** (p. 300)
26. **Not waving but drowning** (p. 308)

25. How to increase profits

The billion-dollar question is: 'How can I increase my profits?' The whole of this book should help you to do so: the sections on how to set up your business in the most efficient manner and those on how to plan and control your business, how to increase your sales and how to manage the workplace properly. All of these will help you to make bigger profits if you carry them out effectively.

However, if you strip running a business down to bare essentials, there are three main ways to make bigger profits. The first two methods are what you would use for the short term; they apply particularly if you are struggling to reach break-even point. But any well-run business should constantly be on the lookout for the sort of improvement you can make. The two methods are:

❑ cutting costs

❑ increasing prices.

The third way of increasing profits will take longer to achieve the desired result. It is:

❑ selling more.

It will also, very often, involve you in spending more money to carry it out.

The quickest way of selling more is to try and sell more to your existing customers. Of course, this implies that your existing customers are happy with your service or product. That is the first step – focusing on and improving the quality of what you do already. Selling more may require greater investments in promotion or selling effort, but your aim obviously should be to make the existing levels of investment work more effectively for you.

You should not overlook the few occasions when you can increase profits by altering your sales mix; it may even mean selling less. This may occur if you have a range of products, of which one or more does not cover its costs. The answer: rationalize your product line. An investigation of your customers may reveal that some of the very small ones do not buy sufficient quantity to cover the cost of selling to them. This may also lead to the conclusion that selling less means higher profits. There may also be the odd occasion when you can alter your sales mix by introducing a product on which there is no profit but which improves your overall profits. For example, a loss leader encourages more purchases of higher-priced products and increases total profits.

In the longer run, there are two more moves which can result in your business showing more profits, that is, by selling more:

❏ of the same product, but to new markets

❏ of a new product to new or existing markets.

Both of these may involve substantial investment by your business. If this is the case, you cannot undertake these until you are past break-even point and generating profits from the existing products and market.

What is in this chapter?

The first section looks at the effect on your business of cutting costs (see below). There is a checklist (p. 302) to help you achieve this. The second section looks at the improvement increasing prices can bring and gives a checklist (p. 303). The third section describes longer-term ideas for selling more (p. 304). There is a checklist (p. 305) and brief guidance on how to develop new products and markets (p. 306). Finally, on p. 306, you can see the effects of carrying out all three improvements, that is, cutting costs, increasing prices and selling more. There are a few hints on achieving profit improvement through employees (p. 306).

Cutting costs

This is the most effective way in the short term of increasing your profits. You should get into the habit of thinking how many extra sales you have to make to pay for an increase in costs. For example, if your product sells for £100 and your costs for each product are £50, this means that every time you spend an extra £1,000 in your business, you have to sell another twenty of your product to stand still in terms of profit.

The best way of keeping an eye on costs is to have a very strict cash control and to carry out regular audits of costs. Do not necessarily assume that because you looked at the costs last month, you will not be able to find room for cutting now. Use the audit checklist starting below to go through all the cost areas. Look at each item afresh and ignore history.

Example

> Jason Bottomley has a small shop selling jumpers, tops, shirts and so on. He is currently making profits of £15,000, but he does not regard this as sufficient to give him a comfortable living. He wants to increase his profits. His forecast sales and costs look like this:
>
> | | |
> |---|---|
> | Sales | £120,000 |
> | less Direct costs | 60,000 |
> | Gross margin | £60,000 |
> | less Overheads | 45,000 |
> | Net profit | £15,000 |
>
> Jason wants to look at how his profit would be affected if he could cut either his direct costs by 10 per cent or his indirect costs (or overheads) by the same amount. It would look like this:
>
> | | *Cut direct costs by 10 per cent* | *Cut indirect costs by 10 per cent* |
> |---|---|---|
> | Sales | £120,000 | £120,000 |
> | less Direct costs | 54,000 | 60,000 |
> | Gross margin | £66,000 | £60,000 |
> | less Overheads | 45,000 | 40,500 |
> | Net profit | £21,000 | £19,500 |
>
> This shows that if Jason could cut direct costs by 10 per cent, his profit would increase by 40 per cent; if he could cut overheads by 10 per cent, profit would increase by 30 per cent. In fact, he estimates that every time he manages to cut both direct and indirect costs by only 1 per cent he would have more than £1,000 extra income. Quite small cuts can lead to a big jump in income.

Costs: audit checklist

❑ *raw materials:* are there any alternative suppliers who are cheaper for the same quality and delivery? Can you renegotiate your existing terms from your present supplier? Everything is negotiable and is worth trying

❑ *stocks:* this ties up cash which means bigger interest charges at the bank. Can you keep lower stocks by organizing yourself more efficiently?

❑ *efficient systems:* are all repeated jobs standardized in your business? For example, if you have to do a lot of quotes, is there a standard form which simply needs filling in? Or are you drawing up a fresh form each time you quote? Does this apply in all business areas, financial, production and personnel, as well as selling?

❑ *the range of products:* is the gross margin you get on each product satisfactory? Does one product require a much greater share of overheads than others? If you stopped selling or manufacturing one of your products, what effect would it have on costs and profit?

❑ *customers and suppliers:* are your customers taking too long to pay? And are you paying your suppliers too promptly? If you're doing either of these you are using up cash you do not need to. This means either extra interest charges on your overdraft or less interest because you have less on deposit

❑ *numbers of employees:* your payroll has the extraordinary ability to mushroom with sales; this includes not only staff directly involved in production or manufacture, but also administrative staff, the so-called overheads. The trick is to keep the same number of employees, while achieving higher sales. Can you improve their productivity?

❑ *the right person for the job:* a lot of time and money is wasted recruiting, training and subsequently dismissing unsuitable staff. Putting a lot of effort into finding the right people in the first place, and not just grabbing what pops up, can be cost-saving

❑ *your own time:* managing your own time better can save money, too. Try to sort out some system of priorities in jobs to be done. There are quite a range of time-planning systems available, often based on diaries or very small computers. See if you can find one that suits you.

Increasing prices

There is no automatic link between prices and costs. This means you do not need to feel uncomfortable about raising your prices, even if you have not had an increase in costs. And quite small increases in price can lead to a big jump in profits. There is an example in the box below which demonstrates how effective a price rise can be.

Real life is not as simple as this. Increasing your prices could lead to a fall in sales volume if you are operating in a price-conscious market. This is one of the reasons why you should think carefully about creating some sort of image or impression for your product (see p. 120), such as high quality or good service, so that the sales of your product are not so price sensitive. To sell on the basis of price alone is a dangerous strategy (see p. 164).

Jason looks at the effect of increasing his prices by 5 per cent all round. His new forecast looks like this:

Sales	£126,000
less Direct costs	60,000
Gross margin	£66,000
less Overheads	45,000
Net profit	£21,000

Jason can get an increase of 40 per cent in his profits for a 5 per cent price increase.

Prices: audit checklist

❏ *discounts:* try to avoid giving discounts, or if you are giving quantity discounts, make sure you stick to the quantity set. It can be very tempting if you are competing head-on with a competitor to try to win the sale by offering a discount. Keep your nerve and try to emphasize the benefits of your product or service

❏ *payment discounts:* do you give a discount for your customers paying by a certain date? Have your customers started to take the discount whether paying by that date or not? Is the discount too big? Do you need it at all, or could you achieve the same effect by better chasing?

❏ *better quality product:* is there scope to upgrade your product with some improvements? Can you charge a higher price to give a better margin?

❏ *inflation:* adjust your prices to allow for the effects of inflation

❏ *contracts:* try including price escalation clauses in your terms and conditions for any product you are selling

❏ *minimum order:* if you sell your product in large numbers, have you set a minimum order? Is it too low? Small orders can take as much time to administer and carry out as large ones, so see if you can set your minimum order at a level which ensures it is at least making a contribution.

Selling more

The third way in which you can increase your profits is to sell more of your products or service – see the example in the box overleaf. This is the most difficult to achieve and the results will not show up in the short term; however, potentially increasing your sales gives the greatest increase in profits of the three. You are unlikely to be able to double your prices or halve your costs, but you might be able to double the amount you sell.

Your first approach should be to try and sell more of the same products to the same market. You will already have invested time and money in researching this market and refining your product to meet customer needs, so the extra investment needed may be minimal.

You can increase your sales by more effective promotion or better selling. The one method of trying to increase your sales which you should avoid like the plague is cutting your prices. This achieves little except:

❑ starting a price war because your competitors feel forced to follow suit

❑ putting pressure on your profit margins and your own profit level.

Cutting prices can only increase your profits if the increase in volume generated is enough to offset the smaller profit you make on each item sold. This could only apply in markets which are very price sensitive; and in this sort of market, cutting prices is most likely to lead to severe price competition. Think twice before you act.

Example

Jason looks at the figures on the assumption that he could increase the amount he sells by 5 per cent, while keeping prices and overheads the same:

Sales	£126,000
less Direct costs	63,000
Gross margin	£63,000
less Overheads	45,000
Net profit	£18,000

Jason finds that a 5 per cent increase in the volume of the sales means a 20 per cent increase in his profits.

Sales: audit checklist for short-term improvement

❑ *image:* have you thought clearly about how your product is positioned? Can it be differentiated more from your competitors' products?

❑ *advertising:* are you aiming your message in the right place? Are you getting as much press coverage as you could? Is your advertising consistent with the style of your product?

❑ *selling:* have you clearly articulated your benefits? Have you prepared a detailed analysis of how your product compares with competitors? Have you developed proper scripts, either for person-to-person selling or telephone selling? Are you following up all leads, pursuing leads to turn them into quotes and converting quotes to orders? Prepare a breakdown of sales statistics, of conversion from leads to quotes to orders and analyse where you are going wrong

❏ *remember:* increasing sales means increasing working capital, so your business may need more finance.

New markets and new products

At some stage in your business, you may feel you have exhausted the potential from your existing products or markets. This may occur because the product or market has now become mature. At this point (ideally before you have reached it, but not until your business is profitable), you may start examining new markets for your existing product or new products. To achieve this, you need to undertake very similar steps to those you followed when you were starting out (see Chapters 1 and 2):

❏ develop a shortlist of ideas/markets to try

❏ carry out market research to find sectors or niches to exploit

❏ remodel product ideas to meet customer needs.

Doing all three

In practice, you will try to do all three at the same time: cut costs, increase prices and sell more. It is astonishing the effect very small across-the-board improvements can have on your profit (see Example on the right).

Profits through your employees

If you have people working for you in your business, you may find it difficult to generate in them the same interest in profits as you have. The result could be that your attempts to improve profits are dissipated because employees do not have the same drive to save money or increase sales.

One way you may be able to improve their appreciation of profits is to make their income partly dependent on this. For example, with salespeople their commission could be related to the gross margin on each sale, rather than the total value of the sale. This could make them less likely to give away discounts. With other staff, you could consider introducing a profit-sharing scheme.

Example

Jason thinks that he could manage small improvements in all areas:
- ❏ cut costs by 1 per cent
- ❏ increase prices by 1 per cent
- ❏ increase amount of sales by 1 per cent

Doing all three would have this impact on profits:

Sales	£122,412
less Direct costs	59,400
Gross margin	£63,012
less Overheads	44,550
Net profit	£18,462

This means an increase in profits of 23 per cent: and gives Jason an extra income of £3,462. The moral is never despise small improvements. They can transform your profit figures.

Summary

1. There are three ways you can increase profits: you can cut costs, increase prices or sell more.

2. The quickest way of boosting profits is to cut costs and increase prices; but the greatest long-term potential comes from increasing your sales.

3. Use the audit checklists to pinpoint areas for action; remember to look at each area with an open mind.

4. Avoid cutting prices either to increase the amount you sell or to keep level with competitors; it could ruin your business.

5. Do not dismiss any improvement which can be made because it is too insignificant. A series of tiny changes in the right direction can lead to much bigger profits.

6. Try to involve your employees in the need to increase profits.

Other chapters to read

2. **Who will buy?** (p. 13)
14. **Selling** (p. 149)
15. **How to set a price** (p. 162)
24. **Staying afloat** (p. 282)

26. **Not waving but drowning**

If you put this book's guidelines into operation at the right time, fewer of you should need this chapter than the average small business. Nevertheless, there are those who will. Some businesses will go to the wall.

Few people can appreciate before the event how traumatic the slide into failure can be. Gradually hemmed in with fewer and fewer avenues of escape, you have to come to terms with the crushing of your hopes and expectations. For natural optimists, such as entrepreneurs, it is appallingly difficult to do. At what point do you realize that your business is not going to survive? When do you accept that to carry on is to put other businesses into jeopardy and to impose the same pressures on them as on you? At what point does it become illegal to carry on?

That point may be easy to recognize for an outsider, who is calm and rational. But it is incredibly difficult to recognize, when you have been fighting for weeks, or even months, to avoid it. You may find that you slid past the point so gradually that you did not have time to notice. Sometimes, of course, matters are taken out of your hands by an outsider, such as a creditor or a bank, beginning the steps to close your business.

The problem of acceptance is made worse by the usual existence of somewhat schizophrenic behaviour. To avoid rumours and doubts emerging about the future of your business, you may well be putting on a brave face to the outside world. And you are doing this while knowing within yourself that it does not ring true. The title of this chapter is from a poem by Stevie Smith. Two lines from this poem are: 'I was much further out than you thought / And not waving but drowning.' This aptly summarizes the dilemma for someone whose business is in financial difficulties.

Further emotional difficulties are caused by society's harsh attitude towards the failure. Even though thousands of businesses failed during the recession of the early 1990s, many of them through no fault of their own, there is little sympathy for those that do. This chapter tries to help you recognize the point at which you have to say: 'Enough is enough.'

What is in this chapter?

The warning signs of failure (see below)

The final process:

❑ limited company (p. 310)

❑ sole trader (p. 311)

❑ partnership (p. 312)

What happens afterwards? (p. 312)

The warning signs of failure

Chapter 24, Staying afloat (p. 282), describes how to control your cash to help avoid an ignominious end to your business. At some point, you may unfortunately find the following signs:

❑ you only pay a supplier when a writ is issued and your suppliers are refusing to sell you any more goods

❑ you are near or above your overdraft limit at the bank

❑ you are unable to raise any more money

❑ your liabilities are greater than your assets.

Once your business has reached the point that liabilities (what you owe) are more than assets (what you own), the business is insolvent. It may become insolvent at an earlier stage, when current liabilities are greater than current assets: in other words, when the amount you have in cash and debtors is less than the amount you owe to creditors. This may occur even though you have sufficient fixed assets to cover what you owe. These fixed assets may take too long to sell, at other than a knockdown price, to satisfy your creditors.

As well as insolvency occurring as a result of sales being too low or costs too high, outside events can force it on you. For example, you may be owed a large sum of money by a customer who is slow in paying and may even be unable to pay. A common complaint for small businesses is that some large companies are prone to do just that – be very slow payers – and this can start the vicious cycle ending in failure.

Earlier warning signs can be detected which identify businesses which are at a high risk of failure. Studies pinpoint, among other things, these faults – not all of them relevant for the self-employed and small businesses:

❑ the boss takes no advice

❑ the managing director and chairman is the same person

❑ the board of directors do not take an active interest

❑ the skills of the business are unbalanced

❑ there is no strong financial person

❑ there is no budget, cash flow plan or costing system

❑ the business is failing to respond to change.

If your business displays some of the characteristics, while not yet being in the advanced stage of failure, get advice now, either from your professional advisers (p. 204) or an enterprise or other agency (p. 29).

The final process

There are two constructive steps you can take: consider whether you could negotiate with creditors to pay off what you owe in instalments or to pay a smaller sum which they will accept in full settlement. Or you can enter into what is known as a formal voluntary arrangement. This is a procedure whereby you offer to pay a dividend to creditors in full settlement of your debts. You need to contact an authorized insolvency practitioner, who will require fees in advance to carry out the work. Voluntary arrangements are a formal legal procedure and have proved very effective as a means of avoiding liquidation or bankruptcy.

Limited company

You can seek to wind up your company on a voluntary basis or have it imposed on you by the court or under the supervision of the court. And under the 1986 Insolvency Act there are the options of administration and voluntary arrangements. Voluntary winding-up can occur if 75 per cent of the members vote for it. The resolution for voluntary winding-up must be published in the *London Gazette*. If the directors make a statutory declaration, having investigated the company's affairs, that in their opinion the company will be able to pay its debts within twelve months, the winding-up carries on as a members' voluntary winding-up. However, if the company is not solvent, the winding-up is a creditors' voluntary winding-up. The difference between the two is that if it is a members' voluntary winding-up, the members appoint the liquidator. Otherwise, the creditors will hold a meeting at which the liquidator is appointed by them.

The liquidators will normally pay debts in the following order:

❑ loans and debts which have been secured on a fixed asset (p. 272)

❑ the costs of the winding-up

❑ local authority and water rates, income tax, wages and salaries

❑ loans and debts which have been secured with a floating charge on the assets, that is, secured on assets in general, not a specific one

❑ ordinary trade creditors

❑ shareholders.

If you do not start proceedings to wind up the company on a voluntary basis, you may find it forced on you if a creditor, for example, a supplier or your bank, applies to the court for a compulsory winding-up because you cannot pay your debts. In this case, the court will appoint a liquidator, who is usually the Official Receiver. The Official Receiver is an officer of the Department of Trade and Industry.

The secretary or director of the company must provide the Official Receiver with a statement verified by affidavit, listing the assets or liabilities of the company. The Official Receiver will call a creditors' meeting to decide whether to appoint a liquidator or whether the Official Receiver will carry on in that role. The liquidator will pay off the company's debts in the same order as that outlined for the voluntary winding-up.

The 1986 Insolvency Act strengthened the responsibilities of directors. One of the provisions could mean that a director is made personally liable for a company's creditors. This could occur if the director has allowed the company to go on trading even though there is no way it can avoid insolvent liquidation (that is, the assets of the business cannot be sold to provide a sufficient sum of money to pay all the creditors).

Sole trader

A creditor may force bankruptcy on you by beginning proceedings for payment of a debt. It is very easy for a creditor to make you bankrupt. If you owe someone more than £750 they can bankrupt you quickly. And, even if you pay the debt demanded, if the court thinks you have other debts you cannot pay, you may well still be made bankrupt.

Partnership

With a partnership you have an added problem to that of a sole trader. Each partner is responsible for all the liabilities of the partnership, regardless of what the profit-sharing arrangements are in your partnership agreement. If you have more personal assets than your partner, it is you and your family who will suffer the most.

What happens afterwards?

There is reading suggested in 'Reference' for what happens when you have been made bankrupt. You may want to consider joining The Bankruptcy Association, see Reference. If you have been made bankrupt, the chances of you being able to start another business are severely limited.

However, if you are the director of a company which is wound up you may be able to make one more attempt, although under the terms of the Insolvency Act you may be disqualified from being a director after one insolvency, if you are deemed unfit to be so. It is not an automatic disqualification, so if you do get a second chance learn from your mistakes this time around.

Summary

1. Watch out for the warning signs.

2. See if your creditors will agree to your paying off what you owe by instalments or see if they will accept smaller payments in settlement. It sometimes works.

Other chapter to read

24. **Staying afloat** (p. 282)

27. **Keeping the record straight**

Fate decrees that one of the least interesting business activities is also one of the most crucial for its continued success. Keeping records must rank fairly low in an entrepreneur's satisfaction rating. It is much more gripping to go chasing sales or to carry out a negotiation with a supplier, which will lower your costs. But a complete 'seat-of-the-pants' approach to business will only keep you afloat in the short term.

If you hope to avert the dangers of sliding into failure, one thing you should try to achieve is not to allow yourself to be buried in a quagmire of bills, invoices and tax demands. Failure to organize your records from Day One may mean just that. However, it is never too late to start; so if you have been pushing aside that task, now is the time to tackle it.

Allowing yourself to drift into paper chaos is understandable. Discovering a system for organizing records which is suitable for your business can be difficult. Too simple a system for your particular business may mean that you cannot derive the information from it that you need. Too complicated a system may mean that you have to spend too much time keeping it up to date. There is no one system which will apply to all businesses. You may find that you need to adjust yours with the benefit of experience, until you have developed one that fits what you want.

What is in this chapter?

❑ Why you need records (see below)

❑ Which records? (p. 314)

❑ A very simple system (p. 315)

❑ When the business is more complicated (p. 321)

❑ Using ready-made systems (p. 324).

Why you need records

Good accurate records are needed for two extremely important reasons.

First, records are needed to substantiate what is in the accounts.

One of the advantages of choosing to be self-employed or in a partnership is that your accounts do not have to be audited (p. 41) – and this also applies to companies with sales less than £350,000. But your records must still convince your tax inspector. If the accounts cannot be backed by written documentation, you may find yourself paying a higher tax bill than otherwise, facing fines for failing to produce documents or even being the subject of an Inland Revenue investigation.

Accounts have to be prepared for every accounting period and sent to your tax inspector. The accounts for the self-employed should consist of details of sales and expenses. A balance sheet is helpful, but not essential (it is essential for a company). However, if your tax inspector is considering an investigation, you may be asked to produce a balance sheet. If your sales are under £15,000 a year, your accounts as a sole trader or partner need consist only of a figure for sales, a figure for expenses and a figure for profit. But don't assume this lets you off from keeping proper records. You are now required by law to keep all the documents which form the basis of information you declare (or should declare) to your tax office.

Second, accurate records are needed to help you know what is going on in your business. This, in turn, means you can keep better control and you can plan for the future. It is impossible to make realistic estimates and projections if the basic data are patchy and inaccurate.

Which records?

The first and most important record you need is for cash. You need some way of keeping information about payments into and out of your bank account and also any petty cash which you keep on the premises. The aim of your cash records should be to enable you to know at any moment how much cash you have.

For those businesses which do not sell all their goods for cash, your records will need to cope with keeping tabs on what people owe you and how long they have owed it. This allows you to forecast what money you will be getting in during the months ahead and enable you to chase debts which are overdue.

Most businesses will buy goods, services and raw materials from others. Unless you are forced to pay cash for all your supplies, you will need to organize the bills which you have to pay. Following on from this, if you keep stocks of raw materials or stocks of finished goods, you need to have a tally of what there is: what has come into the business, what is presently held by the business and what has gone out.

Once you start employing people, your employee records need to be meticulously kept; in particular, the records which relate to your role as tax collector for the government (p. 230) need to be very well organized and kept up to date.

Finally, information about fixed assets, such as cars, equipment or property, needs to be recorded.

A very simple system

If your business has only a few transactions, for example:

❑ it is very small, or

❑ you sell only large items, or

❑ you sell your time, for example, as a consultant,

the system you introduce can really be very simple. It would indeed be a mistake to get bogged down in very complicated record-keeping, because it would take up a lot of time without improving the accuracy of your system. Complexities such as double-entry book-keeping can be put aside. A couple of simple accounts books may well be sufficient. Being methodical is far more important than sophistication.

Cash

You will need a cash book. This should show the cash payments you receive and the cash payments you make. It gives a way of recording what you have paid into the bank and what you take out of it. The same cash book can also record your petty cash position.

Diagram 3 overleaf gives an example of a way of setting up the cash book. As you can see there are two sections: one for recording cash receipts and one for recording cash payments. The cash receipts section has five columns and the cash payments section, six columns.

For cash receipts, the columns are from left to right:

❑ the date you received the payment

❑ your invoice number which has been paid

❑ the name of the person who made the payment

❑ the amount of the payment

❏ the value of what you have paid into the bank.

If you offer discounts for prompt settlement, you will need to have an additional column to show the amount of the discount which was taken.

For cash payments, the columns are from left to right:

❏ the date you made the payment

❏ the cheque number

❏ the reference number you put on the supplier's invoice on receipt

❏ the name of the person or business who has been paid

❏ the amount of the payment

❏ what you have cashed from the bank for petty cash purposes.

If it is normal business practice to be offered a discount, you need another column to record the amount taken. When you start paying wages, you will need a further column to record what you have cashed from the bank for this purpose. You might also find it helpful to add a 'miscellaneous' column.

Using the cash book, you should be able to work out how much cash you have and whether cash receipts are exceeding cash payments or vice versa. When you get a bank statement, which should be monthly (and when your business gets more complicated ask for a statement more than once a month), you can check that the two cash balances agree. If they do not, you

Diagram 3: Cash

Cash receipts

Date received	Invoice number	Customer	Amount £	Paid into bank £

Cash payments

Date paid	Cheque number	Reference number	Supplier/ Payee	Petty Cash	Amount of payment

should be able to identify why, that is, cheques you have sent which have not yet been cashed or cheques you have paid in which have not yet been cleared. This is called a bank reconciliation. It is useful to write your reconciliation down.

All cheque books, paying-in books and bank statements should be carefully kept.

Petty cash

You can deal with petty cash items in a number of ways. You could write a voucher or piece of paper each time you use petty cash and keep the voucher in the petty cash box. If you get a receipt for money you spend, staple this to the back of the voucher. Once a month, you could tot these up and put them in your purchases record (p. 319).

Another approach is to carry a little notebook with you and jot down the expenses as they occur. A further alternative is to keep a sheet of paper in your office and write down the amounts spent at the end of each day, again stapling any receipts to it.

Finally, you could set up a recording system in your cash book, using perhaps the back half of the book.

Whichever way you record petty cash items, you need the following information:

❑ the date the cash was spent

❑ how much it was

❑ what it was for.

If you are registered for VAT, when you make an entry for your petty cash payments in your purchases record, you will need to know which items include the standard rate of VAT (p. 368) and to work out the amount of VAT you will be claiming.

Sales

Every time you make a sale, you should produce an invoice (or, if you are selling for cash, a receipt). The invoices should be numbered and filed in numerical order. If there is a fair number of invoices, it might be sensible to have one file for unpaid invoices and another for paid invoices. As every invoice is paid, any documentation which comes with the payment should be stapled to it. It should then be transferred to the paid file. A separate file should be kept for every accounting period.

The next step is to write down in your accounts book a record of every sale. For every sale there should be four columns, six if you are registered for VAT. The diagram below shows what it should look like.

The columns reading from left to right are:

❑ the date of the invoice

❑ the name of the customer

❑ the number of the invoice

❑ the amount of the sale, including VAT.

If you are registered for VAT, there should be two further columns:

❑ the amount of the VAT

❑ the amount of the sale, excluding VAT.

You may wish to have a further column to record the payment date of your invoice.

Diagram 4: Sales

Date of invoice	Description: Name of customer	Number of invoice	Amount of sale (incl. VAT)	VAT	Amount of sale (excl. VAT)
12.6.98	Arnold Warehouses	344	1,762.50	262.50	1,500.00

Example 1

Peter Brown is entering the details of one of his invoices (see Diagram 4 above). The invoice number is 344 and the invoice is to Arnold Warehouses. Peter has charged £1,500, but VAT has to be charged. This comes to £262.50 and the total, including VAT, is £1,762.50. When the invoice is paid, Peter will enter the details in the cash book.

Purchases

If your business is simple, you can record the details of purchases in the same accounts or analysis book as your sales, perhaps using the second half of it. As every invoice comes in for goods or services which you have bought (or a receipt for items which you pay cash for), it should be numbered and filed in numerical order.

When it comes to recording purchases, a more detailed analysis than for sales can be useful for producing the accounts which you need for tax purposes. If your business is simple, your records may need to be updated only once a month.

You will probably find you use all the columns of your analysis book. The columns should read from left to right (see Diagram 5 overleaf):

❑ the date the invoice is received

❑ the name of the supplier

❑ whether the invoice is paid or not, for example, a tick if paid

❑ the number you put on the invoice

❑ the amount of the invoice, including VAT.

If you are registered for VAT, you will need two further columns:

❑ the amount of the VAT

❑ the amount of the invoice, excluding VAT.

The remaining columns of the book should be devoted to showing the

Example 2

Peter Brown has received an invoice for the telephone. He numbers the invoice 222 and enters the details in the analysis book – see Diagram 5 overleaf. He puts the date he received it, the supplier and the amount of the invoice including VAT, £257.83.

As he is registered for VAT, he now works out the amount of VAT, that is £257.83 less £257.83 divided by 1.175. This gives £257.83 – £219.43 = £38.40. He enters this in the VAT column and puts £219.43 in the column for the amount, excluding VAT. He puts the amount of the invoice without VAT in the analysis column.

When he pays the invoice he ticks the appropriate column and also enters details in the cash book.

Diagram 5: Purchases

Date invoice received	Name of supplier	Paid	Number of invoice	Amount (incl. VAT)	VAT
12.6.98	British Telecom		222	257.83	38.40

Amount (excl. VAT)	Supplies	Car expenses	Stationery	Postage	Telephone	Heating/ lighting
219.43					219.43	

nature of the items purchased. The exact headings you put on the columns will depend on the type of the business. Some examples could be stationery, fares, petrol, postage, heating and lighting. The amount of every invoice, excluding VAT if you are registered, should be entered in the appropriate column. Diagram 5 above can give you some idea of how to set it out.

Fixed assets

If your business is a limited company, you are obliged by law to keep a record of fixed assets. If your business is fairly simple, a list in a notebook will suffice. But this should show the cost of the asset and the amount of the depreciation.

VAT

You are required to keep separate VAT accounts if you are registered for VAT (p. 370). You can put these in your analysis book, if there is sufficient room. This should show for each month:

❑ the amount of the sales, including VAT

❑ the amount of VAT charged

❑ the amount of the purchases, including VAT

❑ the amount of the VAT paid.

When the business is more complicated

There will be many businesses for whom the simple system described above will not be sufficient. This will apply to you if you make many sales or purchases each month and keep a lot of stock on the premises. There will be an increasing number of documents and records needed. Your business may need to set up a system for recording information which includes some or all of the following records.

Purchase orders

This could be a formal document which has the name and address of supplier plus the goods ordered and the details necessary for that. A copy of your letter may suffice, as long as they are numbered and kept in a file. This document will be needed to ensure that what the supplier sends you is actually what you ordered.

A record of what goods are received in the business

As your business grows, you will no longer know yourself exactly what has come in; there may well be employees who do this for you. The only way to keep track of what has been received is to have a formal way of recording it. This could be a specially prepared form to fill in and match against the purchase order. Or it could be a book in which you write down the details. Whichever it is, the details are needed before a supplier invoice is passed for payment.

What have you got in stock?

You need to know at any time what raw materials or finished goods you have got in stock. Going to have a look is not the best way of doing this. Written records are the answer because:

❑ they are the best way to control and plan your business

❑ they will protect against staff pilfering.

If you have lots of different items which you keep in stock, stock cards may be the most suitable way of recording what there is. With fewer items, a stock book may suffice.

Sales invoices

This could be a printed form or it could be typed on business stationery and a copy kept.

Employee time sheets

For certain sorts of businesses, for example, manufacturing or assembly, records of how many hours employees work are important and are the basis for paying wages. You could keep a time book with a simple record of when the employee started work and when the employee finished for the day.

Petty cash vouchers

As the business gets bigger with more employees, a proper petty cash voucher will become a necessity. This should show the date, the employee who received the petty cash and what it was for. Any voucher should be signed by an appropriate responsible person with the authority to do so. Wherever possible a receipt should be attached to the petty cash voucher.

Record of purchases (or purchase day book)

This has already been described under the very simple system. The difference will be how often it is filled in once your business grows. Initially, when there are only a few items purchased, filling it in once a month may be sufficient; as there is more business activity, once a week or even once a day may be necessary.

Record of sales (sales day book)

This has also been described under the simple system. As your business develops with particular customers, you will find that you need to keep a record of sales per customer, so you have a record of what each person or business has bought from you.

Cash book

The cash book which you developed at the start of your business (p. 315) will suffice as it grows.

Wages record

You have certain legal duties towards your employees (Chapter 20, 'Your rights and duties as an employer', p. 220). These include giving an itemized pay statement and deducting tax and national insurance contributions from salaries and wages. Proper records need to be kept and the Inland Revenue will send you forms to complete. You must keep the following information for all employees:

❑ name and address

❑ national insurance number

❑ PAYE reference number

❑ pay

❑ pension deductions

❑ any other deductions authorized by the employee.

The actual wages record needs to show the payments made:

❑ gross pay, with a breakdown of how this is made up, for example, bonuses and commission, as well as basic wage

❑ pension contributions

❑ total pay this period

❑ total pay to date

❑ tax-free pay to date (see tables from Inland Revenue)

❑ taxable pay to date

❑ tax due to date (see tables from Inland Revenue)

❑ tax paid to date

❑ tax due on earnings for this period

❑ employee's national insurance contributions this period

❑ other deductions

❑ net pay

❑ employer's national insurance contribution.

This is also information which needs to be set out on an employee's pay slip. You also need to keep records on Statutory Sick Pay and Statutory Maternity Pay.

The journal

This summarizes what has happened in the sales and purchases records, for example. It is also where information about fixed assets, and their depreciation, is entered. On the whole, unless you know something about accounting, this is probably something which your accountant or book-keeper will keep up to date. It does not need to be maintained on a daily basis.

Using ready-made systems

There are a number of accounting systems for sale; these include manual ones as well as computing ones. To choose a computerized system, see **Tips on choosing** in Chapter 17, Getting equipped (p. 185).

Summary

1. You need records to back up what is in your accounts for tax purposes.

2. Planning the business and controlling it cannot be achieved if records are inadequate.

3. Keeping your records in a methodical way is more important than installing very sophisticated systems.

Other chapters to read

17. **Getting equipped** (p. 185)
22. **Forecasting** (p. 251)
24. **Staying afloat** (p. 282)
32. **VAT** (p. 362)

28. **Tax and the sole trader**

With the advent of self assessment, the days of large estimated tax bills dropping unexpectedly through the letter box are gone. But it can still come as a nasty shock, when you tot up your figures or work out your own tax bill to discover that, come 31 January, you'll be facing a huge final demand for one tax year and a sizeable tax instalment for the following year.

There are worse shocks too. Whether or not your tax affairs are in order, you might receive notice that the Inland Revenue are going to investigate your tax affairs. If you have failed to declare any income or gains, or if you cannot produce all the relevant documents, you will face hefty fines. Even if you employ an accountant, the responsibility for complying with all the tax rules and regulations rests squarely with you.

It is in your own interest to have some understanding of the way your tax bill as a sole trader will be worked out, even if you have someone else to do the actual sums and presentation. Knowing how the tax system works, and what sort of allowances you can set against your income, can be very helpful. You will need to keep your accounting records so that you can back up your tax calculations and these records will need to be devised to help you keep your tax bill to a minimum. Additionally, some of the tax allowances you can get may be influential in some of your financial decisions, such as whether you should buy or lease capital equipment.

Using a professional tax adviser to help you present your accounts and tax calculations can be helpful. They should know how to put down the figures on paper in a way which your tax inspector will be used to; it also gives your figures some sort of credibility. Unfortunately, you cannot always rely on the advisers; there are lots of good ones, but poor ones, too.

What is in this chapter?

This chapter will not answer every question you may have about how your income tax bill is calculated. But you should be able to elicit a working knowledge of the system so you know the key moves to make in dealing with your tax inspector. The chapter includes sections on:

❑ When you pay income tax (see overleaf)

❑ Working out your income tax bill (p. 330)

❑ Business expenses (p. 331)

❑ Capital allowances (p. 335)

❑ Losses (p. 338)

❑ National insurance contributions (p. 339)

❑ Capital gains tax (p. 340)

❑ You and your tax inspector (p. 341).

When you pay income tax

Self-employed people pay their income tax bill in three chunks: two interim payments, one on 31 January during the tax year and the other on 31 July following the end of the tax year, plus a final payment on the following 31 January. This can be quite a change if you are a former employee starting your own business and used to paying your income tax monthly, or weekly, through the PAYE system.

Another big difference for the self-employed is that quite a number of months can pass between earning the profits and paying the tax. If the profits from your business are rising year by year, this can have a beneficial effect on your cash flow.

A possible source of confusion occurs when you have set up your business as a limited company. In this case, you do not count as self-employed for tax purposes. Instead, you are an employee of the company and any earnings you take are taxed through the PAYE system in the usual way. The tax on profits from your company is corporation tax and is dealt with in Chapter 30, 'Tax and the limited company' (p. 349).

Which profits are taxed?

Special rules apply to the first few years when you start up in business (see right), unless your accounting year coincides with the tax year (known as fiscal accounting – see below). After that, all businesses are taxed on a 'current year basis'. This means that your tax bill is based on your profits for the accounting period which ends during the tax year. For example, if your accounting year runs from 1 August to 31 July, your tax bill for the tax year 1998–99 will be based on profits for the accounting year 1 August 1997 to 31 July 1998.

If you opt for 'fiscal accounting', your accounting year coincides with the tax year which makes matters very simple. For fiscal accounting to apply, your accounting year does not have to be exactly the same as the tax year (that is, 6 April to 5 April). Fiscal accounting also applies where your year runs from 1 April to 31 March.

Starting a business

If you have opted for fiscal accounting – that is, your accounting year is the same as (or nearly the same as) the tax year – there are no special rules applying to the opening years of your business. Right from the word go, you are simply taxed on the profits you make each tax year.

If you have some other year end, different rules apply for the first one, two or sometimes three tax years of your business. To find out which rules apply, follow these steps:

❑ *Step one:* find the first tax year in which you have an accounting date which is 12 months or more after the date you started in business. Tax for that year is based on profits for the 12 months up to that accounting date. The normal current year basis applies to subsequent years

Example: Working out profit to be taxed at the start of a business

David Weston started his business on 1 February 1998 but decides to end his accounting year on 31 May each year. To avoid a very short first period, he lets his first accounting 'year' last for 16 months. His profits are as follows:

Accounting year 1/2/98 to 31/5/99	£ 8,000
Accounting year 1/6/99 to 31/5/00	£12,000
Accounting year 1/6/00 to 31/5/01	£17,000

Step one: the first tax year in which there is an accounting date falling at least 12 months after the start of trading is 1999–2000.
Step two: opening year rules apply to the tax years 1997–98 and 1998–99.

David's profits will be taxed as follows:

1997–98: ²⁄₁₆ x £8,000	£ 1,000
1998–99: ¹²⁄₁₆ x £8,000	£ 6,000
1999–00: ¹²⁄₁₆ x £8,000	£ 6,000
2000–01: current year basis	£12,000
2001–02: current year basis	£17,000

❏ *Step two:* there will be one or two tax years before the year identified in Step one. In the first year, you are taxed on the actual profits you make during the tax year by taking the appropriate portion of the profits for your first accounting period (see right). Similarly, if there is a second year and no accounting date falls within that year, you are taxed on the actual profits for the tax year. If there is a second year and an accounting date falls within it, tax for the second year is based on your profits for the first 12 months of trading, once again taking the appropriate portion of profits for the relevant accounting period(s).

Overlap profits

Under the opening year rules for a new business, some profits are taxed more than once. In the example, for instance, David is taxed on $2/_{16}$ + $12/_{16}$ + $2/_{16}$ = $25/_{16}$ths of the profits for his first accounting period – that is £13,000 instead of the actual £8,000 for the period. The excess £13,000 – £8,000 = £5,000 is his overlap profit. You get tax relief on overlap profits when your business finally ceases (or earlier if you change your accounting date). This ensures that all your profits are taxed just once over the lifetime of your business, but bear in mind that overlap profits are not increased in line with inflation, so the tax relief might not be worth much in real terms by the time you finally get it.

Choosing when to end your accounting year

You will need to weigh up a number of factors when deciding the best date on which to end your accounting year:

❏ fiscal accounting – that is, ending your year on or about 5 April or 31 March – makes your tax affairs very simple, but will give you the least time to draw up your accounts to meet the self assessment deadlines

❏ a year end early in the tax year maximises the delay between earning your profits and paying tax on them. This is good for cash flow if your profits are rising. You also have plenty of time in which to draw up your accounts. On the other hand, a year end early in the tax year will involve higher overlap profits. You probably won't get tax relief on these for many years and in the meantime inflation will have eroded the value of the relief.

If your profits are falling, bear in mind that you should put aside enough money to meet your eventual tax bill to avoid cash flow problems.

If your business is already established, you can choose to alter your year end. Whether the change works to your advantage depends on the pattern of profits for your particular business. Get advice from your accountant.

Splitting profits between tax years

Which part of your profits falls into one tax year and which part into the next year is apportioned on a time basis, by day. The profits will be:

$$\frac{\text{number of days of accounting period in tax year}}{\text{number of days in accounting period}} \times \frac{\text{profits in accounting}}{\text{period}}$$

You may have to work out the profits actually made in each tax year up to the second, third and possibly fourth years as well.

The self assessment timetable

Under self-assessment, you are responsible for for the calculation of your tax bill. You can still ask the Inland Revenue to do the sums for you, but they will do this on the basis of the information you provide about your income and capital gains.

It is then up to you to pay your tax by the due dates. You can pay early and you will earn interest (at 9.5 per cent a year from 31 January 1998) on the amount paid up to the time that the tax bill falls due. Equally, if you pay late, you will be charged interest (at 9.5 per cent a year from 31 January 1998) from the date the tax was due until the date on which you pay. In addition, you may incur fines for late payment. See p. 365 for more about the self assessment process. Key dates for tax due for 1998–99 are:

The year 1999

❑ *31 January* This is a very important date for three reasons: first, it is the latest date for sending in your tax return (including details from your accounts) together with your calculation of tax due; secondly, you must also send in the final instalment of tax for 1997–98 (either according to your own calculations or as advised by the Inland Revenue if your tax office worked out the tax bill for you); and finally, you must pay your first instalment of tax due for 1998–99 (which is generally set at half the amount of tax you paid in the previous year – that is, 1997–98).

❑ *April* Receive tax return asking about your income and gains for the year 1998–99

❑ *31 July* Pay second instalment of tax bill for the 1998–99 tax year (this is generally set at half the amount of tax you paid in the previous year – that is, 1997–98)

❏ *30 September* Get your tax return (including details from your accounts) back to your tax office by this date if you want your tax office to work out your tax bill for you (or if you want any tax due to be collected through a change in your PAYE code – for example, if you are also an employee or if you receive a pension).

The year 2001

❏ *31 January* Your tax return for 1998–99 becomes final.

The year 2005

❏ *31 January* You can now throw away documents relating to your tax bill for 1998–99.

Working out your income tax bill

First, turn your profits from your accounts into taxable profits (see the Example below):

Example: Working out taxable profits

Patty Woodward, who started her business in August 1996, adjusts the profits from her accounts to provide a figure on which her tax bill will be based. Her profits according to the accounts are £7,500.

1. She has not used any stock for her own use, so no adjustment needed here.

2. She checks carefully against the list of business expenses which are normally allowed for tax purposes (see right). She realizes she has forgotten to include bank charges, which for the year total £48. The adjusted profit figure is now £7,452.

3. However, her accounting profit includes a figure for depreciation of her computer, £200. She adds this back; her adjusted profits are now £7,652.

4. Patty now claims the allowances she can. She takes the full writing-down allowance on her computer. For this year, it comes to £150. She has no losses on which to claim relief. This gives taxable profits of £7,502.

5. She has not sold any assets this year.

6. She has no business investment income. Her taxable profits are £7,502.

1. If you have taken any items out of stock for your own use, include these in your sales figure at the normal selling price.

2. Deduct from your profits any business expenses which are normally allowable against tax, but which you have not included (see p. 332).

3. Add back to your profits any business expenses which are not allowable for tax purposes (p. 334).

4. Deduct the following items which are allowable for tax purposes: capital allowances (see p. 335), any balancing allowances (see p. 337) and loss relief (see p. 338).

5. Add back any balancing charges from the sale of assets (see p. 337).

6. Deduct any income which is not part of your trading income and on which tax is paid separately, for example, bank interest.

Business expenses

What business expenses are allowed?

You can claim, and be allowed, an item as a business expense for tax purposes if it is incurred 'wholly and exclusively' for the business. The golden rule with expenses is that if you are in any doubt as to whether an expense is allowable, claim it.

Allowable business expenses are not confined to those items used only in your business, as long as they are sometimes used wholly for the business. For example, you may be able to claim some of the expenses of running your home if you run your business from there. Similarly, a car can be used privately, as well as in your business, as long as on some occasions your car is used wholly for your business. Negotiate with your tax inspector the proportion of car and home expenses which will be allowable for tax relief. Typical allowable home expenses will be part of the costs of heating, lighting, cleaning, telephone, insurance and security. You can also treat your mortgage as if it is in two parts, if you use part of your home exclusively for business. Interest on the portion attributable to business use can be claimed as an allowable expense, thus qualifying for higher tax relief than the 15 per cent applying generally to mortgage interest.

There is controversy about council tax bills. Some experts consider that you can claim as an allowable expense a proportion of your council tax bill if you work from home, even if part of the home is not used exclusively for business. Other experts think that such a claim is valid only where there is exclusive use.

An expense incurred partly for business and partly for private reasons, for example, a trip in your car to a customer, could strictly not be allowed if you dropped in to see a friend on the way.

Be careful of claiming expenses for part of your home used exclusively for your business, as it may mean capital gains tax to pay when you sell your home and could also lay you open to business rates. To avoid these problems, do not claim mortgage costs or council tax and, in the case of other expenses, phrase them as claims for 'non-exclusive use of a room at home'.

Checklist of expenses you can normally claim

1. General expenses

Claim the expenses of making your product and running your premises:

❏ cost of goods you sell or use in your product

❏ selling costs, such as advertising, sales discounts, gifts costing up to £10 a year (if gift advertises your business or product and is not food or drink)

❏ office/factory expenses, such as heating, lighting, cleaning, business rate, rent, telephone, postage, printing, security, stationery, normal repairs and maintenance

❏ proportion of home expenses, if used for work

❏ cost of computer software, if its useful life is less than two years. If the useful life is longer, it may be treated as capital expenditure – see p. 335

❏ other expenses, such as relevant books and magazines, professional fees, subscriptions to professional and trade organizations, replacing small tools, travel expenses (but not between home and work, or, usually, lunches), running costs of car (see p. 331), delivery charges, charge for hiring capital equipment, leasing payment but only the full amount for cars, if the retail price is £12,000 or less (for cars purchased before 11 March 1992, only the full amount if the retail price was £8,000 or less).

If you are not registered for VAT, include the cost of VAT in what you claim, as it is a business expense which you cannot get back through the VAT system. If you are registered for VAT, do not include it, unless it is impossible for you to claim it back from the VAT inspector, because, for example, it is included in what you have purchased for part of your business which is exempt for VAT purposes.

2. Staff costs

Claim the normal costs of employing people:

❏ wages, salaries, bonuses, redundancy and leaving payments, pensions to former employees and dependants (but not your salary or your partner's salary), training costs, council tax paid on behalf of an employee, if a genuine part of remuneration package subject to PAYE

❏ pension contributions made on employees' behalf. Cost of providing life, health and sick pay insurance for employees (but not yourself)

❏ cost of employing your wife or husband (if you can show that the work is actually done, and that the wage is the going market rate)

❏ employer's national insurance contributions (but not your own, see p. 339)

❏ entertaining staff, for example Christmas party, provided annual expenditure on such events comes to no more than £75 a head

❏ gifts, subscriptions and contributions for benefits for staff, but these could be regarded as employee's emoluments.

3. Financial expenses

❏ bank charges on business accounts

❏ accountancy and audit fees, additional accountancy expenses needed as a result of Inland Revenue 'in-depth' investigation but not if the investigation reveals that profits have been understated

❏ interest on loans and overdrafts for your business, and cost of arranging them (but not interest paid to a partner for capital put into the business, or interest on overdue tax)

❏ charge part of hire purchase payments (that is, the interest plus additional costs)

❏ business insurance

❏ bad debts which you specifically claim (but not a general reserve for bad or doubtful debts)

❏ incidental cost of obtaining loan finance, but not stamp duty, foreign exchange losses, issue discounts or repayment premiums.

4. Legal and other expenses

❏ legal charges such as debt collection, preparing trading contracts, employee service contracts, settling trading disputes and renewing a short lease (that is, fifty years or less)

❏ legal costs of defending yourself against disciplinary action by a body which regulates your profession (but not any fines imposed as a result of that action)

❏ premium for grant of lease, but limited to the amount assessed on the landlord as extra rent spread over the term as the lease is paid

❏ fees paid to register trade mark or design, or to obtain a patent.

What is not normally allowed as a business expense

1. Your own income and living expenses, ordinary clothes, medical expenses, your NI contributions (p. 339), income tax, capital gains tax, inheritance tax, fines and other penalties for breaking the law (but you could pay a parking fine for an employee), VAT surcharge.

2. Depreciation or initial costs of capital equipment, buying a patent, vehicles, computer hardware or software if treated as a capital item (see right), permanent advertising signs, buildings and the cost of additions or improvements to these (but see capital allowances).

3. Legal expenses on forming a company, drawing up a partnership agreement, acquiring assets such as long leases.

4. Business entertaining expenses, cost of partners' meals at regular lunchtime meetings, gifts to customers (but see p. 332), normally charitable subscriptions and donations, donations to political parties.

5. Reserves or provisions for expected payments, such as repairs, general reserve for bad and doubtful debts (but see p. 333).

6. Wages to employees which remain unpaid eighteen months after the accounting date.

Capital allowances

What capital allowances can be claimed?

Depreciation on capital equipment and its initial cost are not allowable business expenses (see left), but you can get tax relief on capital expenditure. You do this by claiming capital allowances, known as writing-down allowances.

The way in which you pay for equipment does not affect the capital allowance, which can still be claimed on the cost of the item. But you do not claim a capital allowance for the interest on a loan or overdraft to buy equipment; this is an allowable expense, not part of the cost of the asset. If you are buying on hire purchase, the charge is also a business expense. With leased equipment, you can claim the rent as an expense, not a capital allowance.

To qualify for a capital allowance, expenditure must be 'wholly and exclusively' for the business. But this does not mean you cannot claim a capital allowance for some item which you use in your private life as well as in your business. For example, if you use a car half in your business and half for private purposes, you work out the capital allowance on the cost of the car and claim half the allowance.

When you first start your business, if you use anything in it which you already owned and used privately, you can claim a capital allowance on the market value at the time you start your business.

The capital allowance is claimed each year, usually on the value of the item or items at the end of the previous accounting year.

The maximum allowances in 1998–99

These are the maximum allowances you can claim for what you spend:

plant and machinery (other than long-life assets – see p. 338)	Until 1 July 1999, 40 per cent; from 1 July 1999 25 per cent
cars	25 per cent (with a maximum of £3,000)
industrial and agricultural buildings	4 per cent of original cost
hotels with ten plus bedrooms	4 per cent of original cost

buildings in enterprise zones	25 per cent of original cost at end of each year or 100 per cent in first year
buying a patent	25 per cent
know-how	25 per cent
scientific research	100 per cent in first year.
plant and machinery (long-life assets, see p. 338)	Until 1 July 1999, 40 per cent; from 1 July 1999 6 per cent

For what you spent on new plant and machinery (but not cars) between 2 July 1997 and 1 July 1998, the rate of capital allowance in the first year is 50 per cent. In later years, the rate of allowance on these assets will be 25 per cent (or 6 per cent if the long-life asset rules apply).

Working out the allowance for plant and machinery

If you only have one piece of capital equipment, the allowance for the first year you claim is worked out on its cost (or its market value, if taken into the business). In the second year, the allowance is claimed on its reduced value at the end of the previous accounting year, that is, the cost less the amount of the allowances previously claimed.

With several items, you form a pool of expenditure from the values (the cost if you have just bought an item). The allowance is claimed on the value of the pool at the end of each accounting year. The amount of the allowance claimed is deducted from the value of the pool at the end of each year to

Example: What capital allowance can be claimed?

Adam Horsfield buys a desk for his business on 30 September 1998; the cost of the desk is £200. At the end of the accounting year, Adam claims a writing-down allowance of 40 per cent of £200, that is, £80, because he can get the benefit of the increase of the capital allowances for expenditure incurred before 1 July 1999. He deducts this from the value of the desk, giving a value of £120 at the end of the accounting year.

In July 1999, Adam buys a filing cabinet costing £130. He adds this to the value of the desk, giving the value of his pool of expenditure of £130 + £120 = £250. At the end of this year, he claims a writing-down allowance of 25 per cent of £250, that is, £62.50. He deducts this from the value of the pool, giving a value for the next year of £250 − £62.50 = £187.50.

form the new value for the next year. The cost of any new equipment bought during the next accounting year is added to the value of the pool. Work out the allowance on the value of the pool at the end of that accounting year and so on (see the example left).

If you already have sufficient deductions to reduce your taxable profits to zero or to the level of your personal allowances, it will not save you tax if you claim your full allowance. Instead, claim none or less than the full writing-down allowance. This will mean the maximum allowance which can be claimed next year will work out to be a larger sum than would otherwise be the case.

When it comes to selling an asset on which you have claimed capital allowances, you have to reduce the value of your pool by the lower of the sale proceeds or the original cost. Do this before working out the amount of the allowance you can claim for the accounting year in which you sell the asset. If the sale proceeds are more than the value of the pool, the difference (the balancing charge) will be taxable as if it were extra profit for the year. Note that this also applies to an asset which has formed its own separate pool (see below). If the sale proceeds come to less than the pool value of an asset you sell, you can't normally get any tax relief on the 'loss', unless it was a short-life asset (see below). However, when your business stops trading for good, if the proceeds from getting rid of all the assets in the pool come to less than the value of the pool, you can claim the difference as a balancing allowance which will reduce your tax bill for that year.

What is not included in the pool

These have separate pools of expenditure:

❏ cars (but not lorries or vans). If the car costs more than £12,000 (or if it costs more than £8,000 and was bought before 11 March 1992) it must form its own separate pool

❏ anything used partly in your business, partly in your private life

❏ if you choose, any piece of plant and machinery (but not cars) which you expect to sell or scrap within five years of buying. With short-life assets, for example, tools or a computer, you have to choose to put it in a separate pool within two years of buying it. If, when you sell the equipment, you sell it for less than its value after deducting the capital allowances you have claimed on it, you will be able to write off the difference in that year. If you sell it for more than the value, the difference will be taxable as if it were extra profit. If you do not sell it in five years, its value will be added to your main pool as if it had never been treated separately

❑ from 1997–98 onwards, 'long-life assets' are separately pooled and qualify for reduced allowances of 6 per cent a year. These are assets which have an expected working life when new of 25 years or more. But there are various exclusions, including cars and any machinery or plant in a building which is used wholly or mainly as a home, shop, showroom, hotel or office. Importantly, the long-life asset rules do not apply to businesses spending less than £100,000 a year on such assets, so the vast majority of small and medium-sized businesses are not affected and can continue to claim the higher allowance on such assets.

Losses

If you have made a loss in your business, what can you do with it to cut your tax bills? Your two main options are to:

❑ deduct the loss from other income or a capital gain

❑ carry the loss forward and deduct it from future trading profits from your business.

Deducting the loss from other income and capital gain

You can either deduct your trading loss from any other income or capital gains which you have in the tax year in which your loss-making accounting year ends, or you can carry the loss back and set it against other income or gains for the previous tax year. You must claim this relief within two years of the end of the tax year of the loss. Other income could be, for example, dividends from shares or earnings from a job.

A loss incurred in 1997–98 can be carried forward to deduct from income and gains for 1998–99 as long as your business is still going in that year. You must claim this relief by 5 April 2001.

If you have other deductions which will reduce the tax bill on your other income and gains to nil in one of the tax years, opt to deduct the loss in the other year. If after setting the loss against income and gains for one or both years, there is still some loss left over, you can carry the excess forward to set against future profits (see below).

Deducting the loss from future trading profits

If you make this choice, you carry forward the loss and set it against the next future profits from the same trade. If you have any losses left over, you carry them forward against future profits *ad infinitum*, until they are used up. If you are going to use your loss in this way, you have to use the whole of the loss before you can use any other deductions, such as outgoings or allowances, which you may have. The main disadvantage of making this choice to use up your loss relief is that it takes a while to turn it into cash.

To use this option, you must tell your tax office within six years of the end of the tax year in which the loss-making accounting year ended. For losses made from 1998–99 onwards (and for losses made in earlier years, if you started up on or after 6 April 1994), relief is given automatically as you make subsequent profits. If your business started before 6 April 1994, for any losses you are carrying forward from 1996–97 or earlier years, you will have to make a claim when you want to use the relief and set the loss against your profits for a given tax year.

If you are starting a new business

If you spend money before your business actually starts, it may count as pre-trading expenditure. It will be set against the earnings of your business in its first year and, if it creates a loss, you can get loss relief. You can get tax relief on expenditure going back seven years.

There is special tax treatment for a loss you make in the first four tax years of a new business (as long as your inspector believes it was reasonable to plan for profits during that period). You can get a tax refund by setting the loss against any other income (for example, wages from a job) which you had in the three years before the loss. Set the loss off against the earliest year of income first, then the next earliest and so on.

If you want to set off your loss in this way, you need to do so within two years after the year when the loss occurred.

National insurance contributions

If you are self-employed, you will have to pay Class 2 national insurance contributions (but if your earnings from self-employment are expected to be less than a certain amount, £3,590 in 1998–99, you can claim exemption from payment). This is a flat rate contribution of £6.35 a week in 1998–99, which you can pay monthly by direct debit or you will be sent a bill each quarter.

You may be able to claim incapacity benefit, basic maternity allowance and basic retirement pension, and if you are a married man your Class 2 contributions would entitle your wife to the basic widow's benefits in the event of your death. Class 2 contributions don't entitle you to Jobseeker's Allowance but in certain limited circumstances you may be able to claim it (see leaflet FB30, *Self-employed?*, available from the Benefits Agencies, Contributions Agencies and various outlets, such as some public libraries and post offices). Nor do Class 2 contributions entitle you to industrial injuries benefit or additional earnings-related pension or widow's benefits.

If your earnings from your business are above a certain amount, £7,310 in 1998–99, you will have to pay Class 4 contributions. These are earnings-related, collected along with income tax and are 6 per cent of your profits between the lower limit up to a specified maximum, £25,220 in 1998–99.

Example: Class 4 national insurance

> Carolyn Harbury has profits of £18,000 for her accounting year ending in 1998–99. Class 4 national insurance contributions are payable at 6 per cent on profits between £7,310 and £25,220. For Carolyn, this means 6 per cent of £18,000 – £7,310 = £641.40.

Capital gains tax

You do not normally pay capital gains tax (CGT) on stock you sell, but you may have to pay it when you dispose of land and buildings, plant and machinery or goodwill. Disposing includes selling, giving away, exchanging or losing. There is no tax in 1998–99 on the first £6,800 of net capital gains. For where to find out more about capital gains tax, see 'Reference' (p. 382).

In general, you pay no CGT on your home if you claim some of the costs of running your home as a business expense because you work from home. But if you use part of your home exclusively for business purposes, you may pay tax on a gain from that part.

There are details about retirement relief in Chapter 33, 'Retirement' (p. 375)

Replacing business assets

If you sell or otherwise dispose of assets from your business, and make a gain, you could pay capital gains tax on the gain. But if you replace the assets in the three years after the sale or one year before the sale of the old one, you can claim roll-over relief and defer paying capital gains tax. You can also claim relief if you do not replace, but use the proceeds to buy another qualifying business asset. You usually get the relief by deducting the gain from the old asset from the acquisition cost for the new one. So, when you sell the new one, the gain on it has been increased by the size of the gain on the old one. However, if you replace again, you can claim further roll-over relief. And so on. Capital gains tax will not have to be paid (under current legislation) until you fail to replace the business asset.

Not every business asset qualifies for the relief. But if it is land or a building used by the business, goodwill, fixed plant or machinery, for example, it will qualify for roll-over relief.

You and your tax inspector

When you first start in business

When you first start working for yourself, you need to inform your local tax office and your local Contributions Agency. You can do this by filling in a single form. The two organisations will share the information you give them. They will also pass details to Customs & Excise who will then contact you to find out whether you need or want to register for VAT (see Chapter 32).

The form you require is Form CWF1 which asks for details such as your business name and address, the nature of your business, the date to which you will make up your accounts and so on. You can get the form from any tax office (see phone book under 'Inland Revenue') or Contributions Agency. It does not matter to which of these you return the form. You should also be able to register over the Internet if you have the appropriate computer equipment.

If you have finished a job as an employee, you will have Form P45, which should be sent to your tax inspector, so that the amount of your personal allowances and the amount of tax to be paid for that tax year can be sorted out. If you start self-employment part way through the tax year, having been an employee before, you can ask for a refund of part or all of the tax paid under PAYE, if you can show that you will otherwise pay too much tax. This can help with cash flow problems of starting the business.

Once you have started a business

When you first start in business, there are no interim payments of tax for the first year or so, because there is no track record from a previous year on which to base any payments. You'll be sent a tax return in the April following start up and, as usual, you have until the following 31 January to send in your return and to pay the tax due. For example, you might start in business in, say, June 1998. You'll get a tax return in April 1999 and your first tax payments must be made by 31 January 2000. At that time, you'll pay all the tax due for the 1998–99 tax year plus the first interim payment for 1999-2000 which will be set at half the amount due for 1998–99.

Your tax return will include supplementary pages for self employment which ask for name, address and description of your business, the period on which your tax bill is based and details of the business' income, expenditure and profits. Exceptionally, you might not have all the information you need to complete the return on time – for example, if you have not yet made up your first set of accounts. In this case, you should estimate what your profits will be and enter provisional figures on the supplementary pages. These should be as realistic as possible, taking into account all the information you have to date. You must also tick box 22.3 on the main section of the tax return and fill in the orange supplement headed 'Self-employment'. Your tax office wants to know why figures are not yet available and when you think they will be.

Normally, if your tax return is incomplete, you will be treated as having missed the deadline and will face a penalty if tax is paid late as a result. However, the Inland Revenue says that a return containing provisional figures will not be treated as incomplete, provided you have taken all reasonable steps to obtain the final figures and you make sure you send final figures to your tax office as soon as they become available. There may be interest to pay if the finalised figures show that more tax was due than the provisional figures indicated.

Your tax return

You are required by law to make a true return of your income, including profits from your business, each year. You will receive a tax return every April. This will be made up of a core eight-page section.

Your tax office automatically sends you any supplementary pages which it expects apply to you so, once you have started up as a sole trader, you will normally be sent the self-employment supplement. You do not need to send in your accounts. Instead, there is space on the tax return itself for details taken from your accounts. The entries on the tax return might not correspond exactly with the entries you use in your own profit and loss account and balance sheet (if you have one). You will have to adapt your figures to fit the Inland Revenue format. You should be consistent from year to year in the way that you make these adjustments.

If you do not have all the figures you need to complete your tax return, you should put in your best estimate for the missing figures, indicating to the tax office that they are estimates and showing how you have arrived at them. Don't leave blanks or put 'to be agreed' – if you do, your return will be deemed to be incomplete and you could face penalties and interest on tax paid late.

If your annual turnover is no more than £15,000, you will not have to give a detailed breakdown of your income and expenses. Instead, you just fill in the three-line account giving turnover, total expenses and profits.

Being investigated

Under the new system of self assessment, during the 12 months after you have sent in your tax return together with your self assessment (if you are working out your own tax), the Inland Revenue can choose to audit your return and assessment. Around 10,000 tax returns each year will be chosen at random for such an audit. This is a big change from the old system under which the Revenue had to justify opening an investigation. After the 12 months has passed, the Revenue can still investigate you, if it suspects fraud or discovers an error.

If you have been selected for audit or investigation, the Revenue must by law write to you telling you that this is the case. The Revenue does not have to tell you why you are being investigated, so you will not know whether you have been selected at random or the Revenue has some reason to suspect that your tax affairs are not in order. The tax inspector has wide reaching powers to ask for any relevant documents and the self-employed are required, by law, to keep documents for five years after 31 January following the end of the tax year to which they relate. If you fail to produce the documents asked for, you will be fined.

The inspector may request an interview, the purpose of which will probably be to establish:

❑ why your business, and hence profits, are different from other similar businesses

❑ whether you have correctly calculated adjustments for tax purposes

❑ if you have assessed your own tax bill, whether you have made any errors or omissions.

❏ if the amount shown for what you have taken out of the business seems adequate to support your lifestyle. You may need to work out an estimate for your living expenses, for example, general household expenses, as well as leisure expenditure and so on.

If the inspector is satisfied with your records and explanation, there will probably be a fairly minor adjustment to your accounts. However, if a more serious view is taken, you may find that your figures for profit for this and previous years are increased.

Either following, or even during, the investigation, you will be sent an assessment if extra tax is deemed to be due. You will have to pay interest on the tax and there may also be penalties.

Do you count as self-employed?

It may be obvious that you are self-employed, but sometimes it is not clear-cut. You cannot simply declare yourself self-employed; you will have to convince your tax inspector that you are. And recently, the Inland Revenue has been taking a closer look at those claiming to be self-employed, particularly sub-contractors working in the construction industry, and re-classifying them as employees. The sort of points which will help you to establish self-employment are:

1. working for more than one customer

2. showing that you control what you do, whether you do it, how you do it and when and where you do it

3. providing the major items of equipment you need to do your job

4. being free to hire other people, on terms of your own choice, to do the work that you have agreed to undertake

5. correcting unsatisfactory work in your own time and at your own expense.

If you do the above, there will probably be little difficulty in persuading an inspector that you are self-employed.

Summary

1. Consider an accounting year-end which will give the greatest delay between earning the profits and paying the tax, if you expect profits to rise year by year. Choose fiscal accounting if you want to keep your tax affairs simple.

2. If you expect your first accounting period when you start business to have low profits, it could pay you to make your first accounting period longer than a year.

3. Remember to claim all your business expenses. Where possible, get invoices and receipts to back up your claims.

4. If you use your car partly for business, you can claim part of your car expenses (and capital allowances). If you work from home, you can claim part of the running expenses, but watch out for CGT.

5. Consider employing your wife or husband in your business. You can pay up to the amount of the personal allowance without paying tax.

6. If you take assets into your business when you set up, don't forget you can claim capital allowances on them.

7. Try to cut down the risk of being investigated by your tax inspector. For example, do not omit items from your tax return, such as bank interest. If you know your profit margin is lower than others in the same business, or if you make a loss, explain why.

8. If you do not want to assess your own tax, make sure your tax return reaches your tax office by 30 September following the end of the tax year. If you do calculate your own tax, don't miss the 31 January deadline – you'll have to pay a fine if you do.

9. You must by law keep documents relating to your tax return and assessment for nearly six years. You'll be fined if you can't produce the necessary documents when asked.

10. If you do not agree with an assessment raised by the Inland Revenue, do not delay. Appeal against it and apply for postponement of the extra tax within thirty days of the date on the assessment.

29. Tax and the partnership

Partnerships, like sole traders, shifted to the new system of self assessment from April 1997 onwards. On the whole, the new system is a lot simpler, treating each partner as if they were running their own business.

What is in this chapter?

❏ How your partnership tax bill is worked out (see below)

❏ What happens when partners change? (p. 348)

❏ What happens if the partnership makes a loss? (p. 348)

How your partnership bill is worked out

What is the taxable income?

The taxable income for your partnership is worked out in much the same way as if you were working on your own and taxed as a sole trader. From your sales figure, you can deduct business expenses which are allowable for tax purposes (p. 331). Your partnership can get tax relief on capital expenditure (capital allowances, see p. 335) and losses (p. 338). Each partner can set their allowances against their share of the profits.

If your partnership has any non-trading income, such as interest, this will not be included in the taxable profits of the partnership, but taxed as investment income. In practice, partnership investment income is normally allocated in the same ratio as the profit share and each individual partner is given a tax bill for the investment income. Any capital gains of the partnership will be subject to capital gains tax.

If a partner has other income or gains which do not come as a result of the partnership, the partner will be taxed on these as an individual in the normal way.

Who pays what tax?

❏ Profits are normally taxed on a current year basis (see p. 326). For example, the tax bill for 1998–99 will be based on profits for the partnership accounting year ending in 1998–99

❏ Profits are divided between the partners according to their profit sharing agreement for the accounting year being taxed – that is, there is no mismatch between your share of the profits and the tax bill

❏ Tax is worked out for each partner individually based on their share of the profits as if they were running their own separate business. If the partnership is new or you have newly joined an existing partnership, opening year rules (see p. 327) apply to you personally

❏ Tax on investment income is also worked out for each partner individually. For this purpose, untaxed investment income is allocated to each partner as if it were income from a second business but based on the same accounting period as the partnership's mainstream business. Taxed investment income is allocated to each partner but on the basis of the amount received in each tax year

❏ Each partner is responsible only for their own tax bill on their own share of the profits. You can't be asked to stump up the money if other partners don't pay their tax bills.

Partnerships and the Inland Revenue

In April each year, both the partners and the partnership as a whole receive a tax return. The partnership tax return is completed on behalf of the partnership as a whole and shows the income, expenses and so on for the partnership. The partnership return must be returned to the tax office by the normal deadline of 31 January following the end of the tax year but, in practice, it will need to be ready much earlier than that.

Each partner has his or her own tax return to complete and return to the tax office by 31 January (if working out the tax bill) or 30 September (if the tax office is to do the calculations). The partner's tax return includes supplementary pages relating to his or her partnership income. The details which must be included are based on information contained in a 'partnership statement'. The partnership statement is a copy of information given in the partnership return.

Therefore, the partnership return must be completed early enough for partners to complete their own paperwork in good time. Timing could be very tight if the partnership has an accounting date late in the tax year. An early accounting date gives the maximum time for getting the accounts prepared ready for early completion of the partnership return.

Changing partners

Each partner is treated as if they were running their own business, so normal opening year rules (see p. 327) apply to you personally when you join a partnership. Similarly, there are closing year rules, which are applied individually to you if you leave a partnership.

Losses

Losses can be treated in much the same way as if you were a sole trader (p. 338). You and your partners share the losses on the same basis as you would share any profits; the losses are apportioned on the basis applying in the year in which they arise.

You can each treat your losses as you want. One of you can set it off against other income, while the other can carry it forward and set it off against future partnership profits.

If you are a limited partner, the amount of loss you can set against other income will be limited broadly to the amount of capital you have contributed to the business.

Summary

1. The tax bill for your partnership is worked out in much the same way as if you were a sole trader.

2. Partnerships should consider an accounting date early in the tax year to give plenty of time for preparing both the partnership and individual partners' returns.

30. **Tax and the limited company**

The first thing to note about the tax for a limited company is that it is called corporation tax. Corporation tax replaces both income tax and capital gains tax for a limited company. There are other differences; when you pay the tax, and how you should pay yourself, are not the same as if your business were organized as a sole trader or partnership. But there are some similarities, too. The way the amount of income and gains is worked out – though not the way they are taxed – is much the same, and money spent on capital equipment is dealt with in the same manner.

This chapter looks at how the taxable profits of a company are worked out, how the size of the tax bill is determined and what happens to losses. It gives brief details of a close company and some advice on how to pay yourself, if you are the owner.

The chapter can give only a very brief outline of corporation tax; further reading is given in 'Reference'.

How taxable profits are worked out

The taxable profits of a company include:

❑ trading income

❑ capital gains (called chargeable gains)

❑ some investment income, such as rents, interest and dividends you receive from unit trusts (including the amount of any tax deducted before your company receives it)

but not

❑ dividends and distributions you get from UK companies.

Once you have arrived at a figure for taxable profits, there are some charges you can deduct before the tax bill is worked out; these do not apply in many cases and include things like royalty payments and some interest paid, on which you have already deducted income tax before paying them.

How trading income is worked out

Trading income is worked out in the same way as if you were a sole trader. You take the figure for trading profit which you have derived from your normal accounting procedure and make several adjustments to arrive at a figure for taxable profits:

❑ add back any business expenses which are not allowable for tax and deduct any which are; see the list on p. 332

❑ add back the figure for depreciation and deduct the amount of capital allowances; see p. 335

❑ deduct what you can for loss relief; see p. 338.

How capital gains are worked out

A company has to include in its taxable profits the figure for net taxable gains. You may have a gain if you dispose of something (a chargeable asset) for more than you originally paid for it – but note that you generally pay no tax on gains made before 1 April 1982. Gains made since 31 March 1982 will be taxed. However, you will be able to deduct an indexation allowance, which allows for the effect of inflation (although the indexation allowance cannot be used to create or increase a loss) on gains made between 31 March 1982 and 5 April 1998. From 6 April 1998, no indexation allowance is available for gains made; instead there is taper relief which reduces the gain for business assets from 100 to 25 per cent once the asset has been held for 10 years after 5 April 1998.

The amount of the gain is worked out in the same way as for an individual. You take the cost and anything you have spent on it, either buying it, improving it or disposing of it, and deduct this from what you have sold it for. If you owned the asset on 31 March 1982, the market value at that date will generally be taken, rather than the original cost. Having worked out the gain or loss, you can reduce the gain by either indexation allowance for gains up to 5 April 1998 or taper relief for gains starting 6 April 1998.

Finally, you can deduct from any gain you are still left with, any losses of the same period or losses from earlier periods which have not already been set against gains.

You have to add the figure for net taxable gains (that is, after the deductions you can make) to your taxable profits. There is no yearly amount allowed which is free of tax, as there would be if you were a sole trader (£6,800 in the 1998–99 tax year). On the other hand, you could end up paying tax on the gain at a lower rate if your business is a limited company rather than sole trader. As a limited company the rate will effectively be 21 per cent on taxable profits of £300,000 or less in 1998–99. For companies with profits of more than this the rate of tax is higher, on a sliding scale between 21 and 31 per cent. When profits are £1.5 million, it becomes 31 per cent. From 1 April 1999, the small companies rate will be reduced to 20 per cent (30 per cent for the full rate).

For a sole trader or partner for 1998–99, the rate of tax is 20 per cent if the taxable income plus the gain is £4,300 or less, 23 per cent if it is between £4,300 and £27,100; above this the rate of tax is 40 per cent.

This is a very brief outline of how capital (or chargeable) gains are taxed. For further reading see 'Reference'.

The accounting year

Corporation tax is payable on the actual profits of an accounting period. If your company makes up its accounts every twelve months, the accounting period is a twelve-month one. If your company makes up its accounts for less than twelve months, that period is still an accounting period. If your company makes up its accounts over a longer time – eighteen months, for example – the time will be split into two accounting periods, an accounting period of twelve months and one of six months.

Losses

Trading losses are worked out in the same way as trading profits. You have several choices about what you can do with them:

❑ deduct the loss from current profits

❑ carry back the loss and deduct it from earlier profits

❑ carry forward the loss and deduct it from future profits

❑ deduct the loss from franked investment income.

Deducting the loss from current profits

A trading loss, calculated after deducting any capital allowances, can be deducted from any profits of the same accounting period. Other profits include other income or chargeable gains. This relief only applies if the company is carrying on a commercial business intending to make profits.

If you want to claim the loss relief it needs to be done within two years after the end of the accounting period of loss.

Carrying back the loss

After deducting the loss from current profits, any left over can be carried back. For losses which occur on or after 2 July 1997, you can carry them back for just one year. If you want to claim this loss relief it needs to be done within two years after the end of the accounting period of loss. You need to be carrying on your business in a commercial manner with a view to making profit. These provisions would apply if you had ceased trading because of losses.

Carrying forward the loss

Any loss on which you have not yet got tax relief can be carried forward and deducted from future trading profits of the same trade; there is no time limit for this relief. You don't need to claim this relief – it is given automatically.

The tax you pay

The rate of corporation tax is fixed for each fiscal year, which runs from 1 April to 31 March the following calendar year. If your accounting year does not coincide with the tax year, profits will have to be apportioned on a time basis between the two tax years, if the rate of corporation tax changes from one tax year to the next.

For fiscal year 1998, if profits are £300,000 or less, the rate of corporation tax on profits is 21 per cent. This is known as the small companies' rate. Firms with higher profits will pay a higher rate of tax – up to a maximum of 31 per cent (see p. 351). For fiscal year 1999, the small companies rate will be 20 per cent.

When are the taxes paid?

Corporation tax is payable nine months after the end of the company's accounting period. At that stage, you have to estimate the tax bill yourself – your tax inspector will only make a formal demand once you have agreed the amount after you have submitted ('filed') a corporation tax return. This must be done no later than 12 months after the end of the accounting period. There are penalties for sending in your return late. If the final tax bill differs from the amount paid earlier, further payments will be due or refunds made, both of which will carry interest.

Self assessment will apply to companies, as well as sole traders and partnerships, for accounting periods ending on or after 1 July 1999. This will not change the basic rules for paying and filing, but the tax return will then be the basis of the assessment and companies will be expected to calculate the tax bill proper, rather than providing an estimate.

Close companies

If there are five (or fewer) people controlling a company or it is controlled by its directors, it is likely to be a close company. The definition of who controls a company broadly means its shareholders and their family, their partners and the like.

If you receive fringe benefits, like living accommodation, loans or entertainment, and you are one of the people controlling the company (but you are not a director paid under Schedule E as an employee), the benefit might count as a distribution of the company and be taxed.

One advantage of a close company is that if you borrow money to buy ordinary shares in the company or to make it a loan, your interest may be eligible for tax relief. To get the relief, the rules are broadly that you must either own more than 5 per cent of its shares, or own some shares and work for the greater part of your time for the company.

Paying yourself

If you are trying to minimize the total tax bill which you and your company face, the ideal salary to pay yourself would be the amount at which the tax rate on your salary is equal to or lower than the tax rate on the company's profits. However, this is a fairly low sum, because you must take into account not just income tax, but also N.I. contributions payable by yourself as employee and the company as employer.

Receiving dividends (see p. 355) will generally be more tax efficient than paying yourself a salary. However, you might consider paying yourself just enough salary to bring you into the national insurance bracket in order to build up some entitlement to state benefits, such as the basic retirement pension (see Chapter 33).

In general, your company is free to pay whatever wages you and the directors want. This includes wages paid to members of your family, if they work in your company. However, the wages paid may not be regarded as an allowable expense for tax purposes by your tax inspector, if the wages are excessive for the work done.

Example

Jack is director of his own company. His taxable profits are in the region of £70,000 each year, so the company pays tax at the small companies rate of 21 per cent in the 1998–99 tax year. Jack has a few investments, the income from which just uses up his personal tax allowance. He considers the tax position for 1998–99:

Gross salary	Income tax payable	Employee's National Insurance	Employer's National Insurance	Total tax payable	Effective tax rate
£ 3,300	£660	nil	nil	£660	20%
£ 5,000	£1,021	£233	£50	£1,304	26%
£10,000	£2,171	£734	£324	£3,229	32%
£20,000	£4,471	£1,734	£1,240	£7,445	37%

As soon as his salary crosses the threshold at which National Insurance contributions become payable, the effective rate of tax jumps to more than the rate the company pays. As the level of salary rises, the effective tax rate climbs steeply.

Fringe benefits

Providing fringe benefits rather than salary can be tax effective. The tax system treats some fringe benefits favourably compared with a rise in salary. Some fringe benefits are tax-free to you or your family if you are employees of the company. These include pension contributions paid by the company and normally the cost of life insurance, the cost of an insurance which would pay out an income if you could not work through illness, and meals if available to all employees in a canteen.

Some fringe benefits are taxed on a different basis if you are earning at a rate of £8,500 or more a year, including any fringe benefits valued as if you earned that rate. If you are a director, no matter what you earn your fringe benefits will be valued in this different way – generally you are taxed as an individual on the amount your fringe benefits cost your company to provide, less anything you pay as an employee towards the cost.

One exception to this way of valuing a fringe benefit is a company car. With a car, the taxable value is 35 per cent of the list price adjusted to take account of various levels of business usage. NI contributions are payable on the taxable value of many fringe benefits, including a company car.

Dividends

From a tax point of view, it may be better for you as owner of a company to receive income from the company as salary rather than as dividends. This is because from 6 April 1993, the tax credit to be set against tax payable at the higher rate has been reduced to 20 per cent and will be reduced again to 10 per cent from 6 April 1999. However, remember:

❏ National Insurance contributions, which both you and the company pay, are not affected by the amount of dividends you receive, whereas level of salary does affect them

❏ receiving dividends means paying any higher-rate tax at a later date than the tax paid on a salary as a PAYE employee. Dividends you receive have already had tax deducted and are accompanied by a tax credit. If you are a lower-rate or basic-rate taxpayer, there is no further tax to pay. If you have unused allowances, you can use the tax credit to reclaim some or all of the tax deducted. Only higher-rate taxpayers have further tax to pay

❏ where there is no company scheme, the amount you can put into a pension is set by the level of what is called relevant earnings; dividends do not count for pension purposes.

Summary

1. Work out profits and losses in the same way as for a sole trader.

2. Corporation tax is payable on all profits, including capital gains, not just trading profits.

3. A company does not get the yearly tax-free limit on gains which an individual does.

4. Do not forget that certain fringe benefits can be a tax-effective way of remunerating yourself as a director.

31. **Tax on spare-time earnings**

There is no quick answer to the question of how you will be taxed if you have spare-time earnings. It will depend mainly on whether your income counts as starting a business. You might find yourself in a dilemma as to how your spare-time earnings will be taxed if:

❑ you are still employed but earning some extra money in your spare time. You might be doing this either because you have started your business in a small way to see how it goes before you take the plunge and hand in your notice; or because you are doing the occasional bit of freelance work to boost your income

❑ you are not employed, but you are starting your business on a part-time basis. This could be the case if you are at home looking after young children, for example. Some people who earn extra income in this way hope that they will be able to keep it out of the clutches of the inspector. Very often they ask for payment in cash. In the section **the black economy** (p. 360), you will see how the inspector can catch you and what the penalties are if he does.

What you must do

By law, you must notify your tax inspector when you get income from a new source. You have to do this within six months of the end of the tax year in which the income first arose. The onus is on you to tell your tax inspector and you cannot plead as an excuse that you did not receive a tax return. Nor does it make any difference whether you are making a profit or a loss; what matters is that you are receiving payments from a new source which your inspector does not know about. If you do not tell your tax inspector about a new source of income, not only will you have to pay the tax due on that income but you will usually have to pay a penalty on top – up to the same amount again – plus interest on any tax paid late. Under the new system, the penalty will only be imposed if you haven't paid the tax by 31 January following the end of the tax year in question.

Being self-employed

If your tax inspector accepts that you are self-employed, you will be taxed as described in Chapter 28, 'Tax and the sole trader' (p. 325), for the earnings which you get from your business.

Things to do to influence your tax inspector's decision

1. Describe your activities as a business or profession.

2. Do not describe your income as 'occasional' or 'casual'.

3. Let your tax inspector know that you believe your sales will repeat and grow.

4. Register for VAT, even if you don't have to, if you consider it appropriate and it won't cost you money (see Chapter 32, 'VAT' (p. 362), for more details). You may have to persuade the VAT people to let you do this.

5. Get headed notepaper for your correspondence.

6. Be careful if your business is writing or consultancy. Explain to your tax inspector why you regard it as a business – for example, because your work covers other aspects such as research and collation of information or because you carry out your profession or vocation on a regular basis.

7. Keep your accounting records carefully and on a business-like basis. This is not just good business sense. It is a legal requirement that you keep records and documents used as a basis for working out your tax bill for five years and ten months after the end of the tax year to which the records relate. If you do not keep these records, or fail to produce them on request, you can be fined.

Casual income

Casual income will generally be taxed on an actual basis – that is, tax for any tax year will be based on the actual income you have from that source during the tax year. This contrasts with self-employment, where tax is based on the profits for an accounting period ending during the tax year. Self-employment gives you more scope for building in a time lag between making the profits and paying tax on them.

A disadvantage if your income counts as casual is that the treatment of losses is less favourable than if you are taxed as being self-employed. If you make a loss it can only be deducted from profits taxed in the same way, made either in the same tax year or in the future. It cannot be deducted from any other income you have, for example, from your job if you have one.

How you will be taxed

If you receive a tax return, enter details about casual earnings under section 13 of the basic return. Any expenses which you necessarily incurred in getting these earnings you can deduct when working out how much tax is payable.

Tax might be due in instalments under the self-assessment system (see p. 326). If the amount of tax involved is less than £500 or if more than 80 per cent of your total income tax last year was collected through PAYE or paid at source (for example, as is the case with most types of savings income), you will not be required to make interim payments and all the tax due will be payable in a single sum on 31 January following the end of the tax year. Alternatively, if you have other income taxed under PAYE, the tax due on your casual earnings may be collected by an adjustment to your PAYE code. If the casual earnings recur from year to year, your PAYE code will probably be set to anticipate a certain level of earnings from that source.

Property income

The tax treatment of this income is outside the scope of this book and only brief details can be given here. A helpful tax concession is the ability to rent out a room in your own home and pay no tax, if you meet certain conditions. The *Lloyds Bank Tax Guide* 1998–99 (see Reference) gives fuller details of the rent-a-room scheme and the taxation of income from property.

If you run a hotel or guest house

Your income will normally count as earnings from self-employment and be taxed as described in Chapter 28, Tax and the sole trader (p. 325).

The rent-a-room scheme

You can let out furnished rooms in your home and as long as the total rent you get during the year is no more than £4,250 in 1998–99 (before deducting any expenses), you don't have to pay tax on that income. If you let the room out jointly with someone else, each of you will be able to get £2,125 tax-free.

If you receive more than £4,250 for the room you have a choice. You can either:

❏ pay tax in the normal way (after expenses) on the total profit you make from letting the room or

❏ pay tax on the amount of rent over £4,250 (or £2,125 if letting jointly) without deducting any expenses.

It's your choice and you should work out which method of taxation leaves you with the smallest tax bill. You can work out this sum for each tax year and change the method each year as long as you tell your Tax Inspector within one year of the end of the tax year. As a rule of thumb, if your gross rent is just over £4,250 and your expenses are low, you will probably be better off paying tax on the gross rent less £4,250.

If you let property

Income from lettings of all types is pooled and treated as a single source of income for tax purposes. You are taxed on the amount of this type of income you get during the tax year. In working out how much income you pay tax on, you use normal accounting rules and can deduct expenses – including interest on a loan to buy the property – in the same way as if you were running a business – see p. 333. However, you can't normally claim capital allowances for equipment and furnishings you provide. Instead, you can claim an allowance for wear and tear. This is based either on items you have actually replaced during the year – called the renewals basis – or on a proportion (usually 10 per cent) of the rents you get less council tax and water rates. You choose which basis to use.

Although your income from letting property is now treated in a similar way to earnings from a business, it still counts (as in the past) as investment income. This means, for example, that you can't use this income for making tax-efficient payments to a pension plan (see p. 377). However, see below for the special treatment of furnished holiday lettings.

If you let furnished holiday accommodation

If the property (including caravans) is let as furnished holiday accommodation for part of the year the income will be treated as earned income, subject to certain conditions. This means, for example, that you will be able to get tax relief on these earnings for pension payments (p. 377) and you can get capital allowances for what you spend on equipment and furnishings you buy and use in your letting (p. 335).

To be treated as earned income the property must be available for letting to the general public at a commercial rent for at least 140 days in any twelve-month period. It must also be let out as living accommodation for at least seventy of those days and not normally occupied by the same tenant for more than thirty-one days at a stretch during a seven-month period.

The black economy

It is illegal to try to conceal any earnings from your tax inspector. The inspector has various ways of discovering that you are earning money. Employers who make use of freelance staff, such as consultants, writers, caterers and so on, can be made to give details to the Inland Revenue of the payments made. There is also a department in the Inland Revenue which keeps an eye on advertisements in the press to make sure that any source of income has been declared. And if you annoy any neighbours, acquaintances or customers who suspect what you are doing, you also run the risk that they might inform on you to your tax inspector.

Once your tax inspector has started an inquiry into your affairs, you will find it very time-consuming. You may find you end up paying interest on unpaid tax from the day it was due until the date of payment; the current rate of interest is 9.5 per cent. On top of that, the inspector can slap on a penalty. Under the new system of self assessment the main penalties are:

❏ failure to tell your tax office about taxable income or gains within six months of the end of the tax year – up to the amount of the tax unpaid if it has not been paid by 31 January following the end of the tax year

❏ failing to send in your tax return by 31 January following the end of the tax year – automatic penalty of £100 with a further automatic £100 fine if the return is still outstanding six months later. The penalties may be reduced or waived, if you appeal against them. If the return has still not been sent in by the following 31 January, a fine up to the amount of unpaid tax can be made

❏ fraudulently or negligently, sending in an incorrect return – up to the amount of the tax unpaid

❏ failure to produce documents requested by the Revenue – initial penalty of £50 plus further penalties up to £30 a day if the failure continues

❏ failure to retain and preserve records – a penalty of up to £3,000.

Summary

1. Tell your tax inspector about any new source of earnings within six months of the end of the tax year in which the earnings first arose.

2. Try to convince the tax inspector that your earnings are not casual or occasional.

3. Even if your income is regarded as casual, remember to claim any expenses you met in getting the income.

4. If you get income from property it can be treated in a number of ways depending on what the property is and what you do with it.

32. **VAT**

One subject which is guaranteed to raise ire among small businesses is VAT. It is frequently referred to as a burden; there are mutterings of a VAT trap; there are moans about the red tape caused by the VAT system. Nevertheless, the drift in legislation has been towards more draconian measures. For example, since 1990 the Customs and Excise has been able to impose interest and penalties for VAT accounting errors.

Essentially, the VAT system is operated by businesses acting as tax collectors for the government. As far as the consumer is concerned, it is what is called an indirect tax. It is only paid by the consumer when something is bought, but the amount of VAT cannot be claimed back by a consumer. As far as you the business person are concerned, you pay tax when you buy goods from someone else, and charge the tax when you sell them on. Broadly speaking, you hand over to the Customs and Excise the difference between the amount of tax you charge your customers and the amount of tax you have paid your suppliers.

What is in this chapter?

❑ How the VAT system works (see right)

❑ Who has to register? (see right)

❑ What rate of tax? (p. 366)

❑ Voluntary registering (p. 367)

❑ How is the tax worked out? (p. 368)

❑ The records you need (p. 370)

❑ Paying the tax (p. 373).

VAT seems a very mysterious tax and this chapter can only outline the principles. The examples given are deliberately simplified. You are advised to ask for professional help with VAT if your affairs are at all complicated.

How the VAT system works

The principle of the system is that tax is paid on the value added at each stage of the business process.

Example

> Jason King grows timber. He sells £1,000 of oak to A. J. Furniture, who will turn the oak into hand-crafted timber. He charges £1,000 for the timber and adds on 17½ per cent to the invoice for VAT. The total A. J. Furniture pays to him is £1,000 plus £175 VAT, £1,175 in all. Jason pays the £175 tax collected (called output tax) to Customs and Excise.
>
> A. J. Furniture makes the oak into ten tables. These are sold on to a furniture shop run by Doris Bates. Doris is charged £250 for each table plus VAT. On the invoice, this is shown as £2,500 plus £437.50 VAT. A. J. Furniture claims back the VAT charged by Jason King (called input tax), that is, £175, and hands over the VAT Doris pays to them, £437.50 (called output tax). This means a net payment of £437.50 – £175 = £262.50 to the Customs and Excise.
>
> Doris sells the tables in her shop at a price of £500 plus VAT. She receives in total for the tables, £5,000 plus VAT of £875. When she makes her VAT return, she claims back the £437.50 VAT (called input tax) she paid to A. J. Furniture, while handing over the £875 VAT paid by the customers (called output tax), a net payment of £875 – £437.50 = £437.50.
>
> The customers cannot claim back the VAT they have paid on the tables, but all the businesses are registered for VAT and can do so.

VAT is charged on what is called taxable supplies. In the example above, Jason King makes taxable supplies (the timber) of £1,000, A. J. Furniture makes taxable supplies (the tables) of £2,500 and Doris makes taxable supplies of £5,000 (the tables). Not all goods supplied to businesses are taxable; some are known as exempt and VAT is not charged on those (p. 364).

In VAT terms, the VAT which you charge on what you sell is called your 'output tax'. If registered for VAT, the business to which you sell claims back the VAT which it pays you as its 'input tax'. This is done when it makes its VAT return to Customs and Excise.

Who has to register?

It is the person, not the business, who is registered for VAT. Each registration covers all the business activities of the registered person. For VAT purposes, a company is treated as a person. There are a number of reasons why you might not have to register. These include:

❑ your sales (strictly, the amount of your taxable supplies, see below) are too low, but you might wish still to register for VAT purposes and charge it on your sales (p. 367)

❑ your business operates outside the VAT area (see below)

❑ you make only exempt supplies (see below)

❑ you carry out non-business activities (but you would still charge VAT on what counts as your business activities) (see right).

If you fail to register when you should do so – and you have thirty days' grace – Customs and Excise can impose financial penalties. The penalty is 5 per cent of the tax due if registration is up to nine months overdue, 10 per cent if registration is more than nine but not more than eighteen months overdue and 15 per cent if registration is more than eighteen months late.

Your level of sales

You must register your business for VAT if your sales are above a certain limit (strictly, the limit is for the value of your taxable supplies, see p. 363, rather than sales). The limit increases each year in line with the rate of inflation. From 1 April 1998, you must register if:

❑ your sales in the previous year were more than £50,000 (but not if you can show that your sales will be less than this in the next year)

❑ your sales in the next thirty days are likely to be more than £50,000.

Should your sales fall below the limit above, you can ask to have your registration cancelled. You would have to establish that your sales, excluding VAT, will be £48,000 or less for the next twelve months.

The area for VAT

VAT applies to England, Scotland, Wales, Northern Ireland and the Isle of Man. It does not include the Channel Islands. If you have customers or suppliers there, the goods you buy or sell will be treated as imports or exports.

What are taxable supplies and what are exempt?

Broadly speaking, if you supply goods and services in your business (including anything you take for your own use or sell to your staff), these will be taxable, unless the government has specifically laid down that they are not. If they are not taxable, they are called exempt.

If all the goods or services which you supply are exempt, you cannot be registered for VAT. What this means for you is that you cannot claim back the VAT on any of the things you have bought for your business.

On the other hand, with a business composed of some taxable and some exempt supplies, you will still have to comply with the registration limits for the value of your taxable supplies. You will be able to claim back the VAT you have paid for the whole of your business if the value of your exempt input tax (that is, input tax relating wholly or partly to your exempt supplies) is not more than £625 per month on average and comes to no more than half your total input tax.

The main items which are exempt as far as VAT is concerned are broadly speaking:

❑ most sales, leases and lettings of land and buildings (but not lettings of garages, parking spaces or hotel and holiday accommodation). Landlords of non-domestic buildings will be able to charge VAT on rent if they choose to do so

❑ financial services

❑ insurance

❑ certain education and training

❑ most health care

❑ postal services

❑ most betting, gaming and lotteries

❑ certain supplies by undertakers

❑ membership benefits provided by trade unions and professional bodies.

What is business and what is non-business?

As far as the VAT system is concerned, business is supplying goods or services to someone else in return for something which could be regarded as payment; it does not need to be money. You must be supplying the goods on a continuing basis to be a business activity.

If you are carrying out only non-business activities, you cannot be registered for VAT; if you have some non-business activities, the VAT you can reclaim is reduced.

When is your registration cancelled?

Apart from your requesting it to be cancelled (see p. 364), your registration will be cancelled if:

❑ the business is closed down

❑ the business is sold

❑ you take a partner or become a sole trader rather than a partner

❑ as a sole trader or partner, you change the business into a company and vice versa.

What rate of tax?

For taxable supplies there are at present three rates of tax:

❑ the standard rate, currently 17½ per cent;

❑ a special 8 per cent rate applying to domestic fuel; and

❑ the zero rate.

The standard rate is charged unless the government specifies otherwise.
These are the main supplies which are zero-rated at present:

❑ most food and drink, but not if supplied for catering, or certain items like chocolate, crisps and so on which are regarded as 'non-essential', or 'hot food' to be taken away

❑ books and newspapers

❑ young children's clothing and footwear

❑ public transport, but not taxis, hire cars, or 'fun' transport, such as steam railways

❑ exports

❑ sales of, and the construction of, new domestic buildings only

❑ dispensing prescriptions

❑ mobile homes and houseboats.

Do not confuse exempt and zero-rated. The effect of the two categories is quite different. Neither charges VAT on what they sell, but the exempt category cannot claim VAT back on what they have paid, while the zero-rated category can. Costs for the exempt category are likely to be up to 17½ per cent higher than the costs for the zero-rated category.

Voluntary registering

You can apply to register even if the value of your taxable supplies is below the limit. You have to satisfy Customs and Excise that you are making taxable supplies in your business. There are two reasons why you might apply to register even if your sales are likely to be below the limit (p. 364). In both cases, registering will mean lower costs.

The first instance would be if you sell to businesses which can claim back VAT, so charging the 17½ per cent on your sales will not mean you lose business. If this is the case with you, consider applying to register. You may still decide not to, if the administrative set-up is too difficult, for example, if you sell a large number of low-value items. But if you register, your costs could be as much as 17½ per cent lower than they otherwise would be. See Example 1 below.

Example 1

> Susan Hammond runs a car hire service. Her main customers are businesses. She considers whether she should apply to register for VAT, although her present sales of £25,000 are below the limit. Her costs are £10,000 including VAT of £1,000 (she is not charged VAT on all the goods and services she purchases).
>
> If she registers, she will have to charge VAT of £4,375 on her sales of £25,000, but her customers can claim this back. She can claim back the £1,000 of VAT (input tax) she has paid on her purchases. The net result is that she receives £25,000 from her sales, claims back £1,000 VAT and pays £10,000 to her suppliers. Her income goes up from £15,000, before registering, to £16,000, after registering.
>
> An alternative would be to lower her prices as her costs are now lower, but this does not seem necessary as she is not losing sales because of the price she charges.

The second instance when registering is beneficial is if your sales are zero-rated, but you are paying VAT on the goods you buy in. See Example 2 overleaf.

Example 2

> Barbara Croft runs a business making bibs and similar items for babies. Consumers cannot claim VAT back, but clothing for children is zero-rated and so she does not charge VAT. Her sales are £15,000 and her costs are £5,000, including VAT of £500. If she did not register her income would be £15,000 − £5,000 = £10,000. This would be increased by £500 to £10,500 if she can voluntarily register.

How is the tax worked out?

What do you charge VAT on?

You charge VAT on the taxable sales you make; this is known as output tax. The amount of VAT is worked out on the price for the goods or services you are supplying. Occasional sales of second-hand goods are treated in the same way as new goods, but if your business involves buying and selling second-hand, you'll usually be covered by a special scheme.

You cannot escape charging VAT if you decide to take other goods, for example, rather than money in full payment or in part exchange. In this case, you have to work out the VAT to add on the basis of the open-market value of the goods or services you are supplying.

With discounts, the treatment varies depending on the type of discount. If the discount is unconditional, the VAT is charged on the discounted amount. This is also what applies if the discount is for prompt payment. Whether the customer pays promptly or not, VAT is worked out on the discounted amount. If the discount you offer is dependent on something happening later, for example, the customer buying more, VAT is worked out on the full amount for the first payment. If the discount is subsequently taken, the VAT is adjusted at that time. Packaging is treated as part of what you are selling, so there will normally be no extra VAT to pay; and if the thing you are selling is zero-rated, that also applies to the packaging. With delivery, if you charge extra for it, VAT is due on that extra amount. But, if the delivery is included in the selling price, no extra VAT is due.

Exports of goods are normally zero-rated and this also applies to many exports of services, although some are standard-rated.

What you can claim VAT back on

You can claim back VAT on the goods and services you use in your business; these include imports and goods you remove from bonded warehouses. However, there are some supplies on which you cannot claim back the VAT. These include:

❑ motor cars (but private taxi and self-drive hire firms and driving schools can recover the VAT they pay on cars purchased for their businesses; however, they will have to pay VAT on any private use. And businesses which lease cars to them can claim back the VAT on cars bought on or after 1 January 1994. In both cases, VAT has to be paid on the ultimate sale of the car)

❑ business entertainment expenses

❑ if you are a builder, on certain things you install in buildings

❑ on some imports if you do not wholly own them

❑ on assets of a business transferred to you as a going concern (because you should not have been charged VAT if the going concern conditions have been met)

❑ on goods which are zero-rated or are exempt supplies (because you have not been charged VAT).

Working out the amount of input tax you have paid

In Chapter 27, 'Keeping the record straight' (p. 313), you can see how to organize your records to obtain the information you need for VAT purposes. There are also guidelines overleaf on some of the records you need. Basically, if your business is very simple, you can work out the input tax like this:

1. Get all your purchase invoices in date order.

2. In your records (p. 319), you will have some way of showing the VAT you have paid on each invoice.

3. You cannot claim back VAT on exempt or zero-rated supplies.

4. Some invoices show the amount of VAT you are charged, so these are quite straightforward. Enter the amount in the column marked VAT.

5. Other invoices are not so detailed and you will have to work out the amount of VAT yourself. See example below for how to do this.

6. Remember you can only claim back the proportion of VAT for goods which you only use partially in your business. For example, if you run your business from your home, you could only claim back the VAT on the part of your telephone bill which was due to your business.

Example

Peter Taylor is working out what VAT he can claim back on some stationery he has purchased for his business. The amount of the VAT is not shown on the receipt he has from the shop. The stationery cost him £4.75. He needs to know the amount of the VAT and the net cost of the stationery.

He divides £4.75 by 1.175 *or* he does this sum £4.75 x $\frac{1,000}{1,175}$

Both calculations give the same figure £4.04, which is the net cost; the amount of VAT he can claim back is £4.75 – £4.04 = £0.71.

The records you need

These are the main additional records you need for VAT purposes and these must be kept for six years:

❑ the tax invoice

❑ a VAT account showing the results for each tax period

❑ the returns to Customs and Excise showing the VAT payable or repayable.

If you fail to keep your records properly, you can be charged a financial penalty. VAT inspectors will come to see you every so often to check that your records are satisfactory. Although you are still required by law to keep your records for six years, in the normal way, Customs and Excise can go back only three years to review the amount of VAT you should have paid. This limit applies from 18 July 1996 onwards. However, in cases of fraud, Customs and Excise can go back 20 years.

There are special rules about petrol used for your private motoring – check with your VAT Inspector. But, broadly speaking, you must keep detailed records of your business and private mileage to support claims that the cost of your private mileage is not included in the business accounts.

Tax invoice

When you supply goods, you should send a tax invoice and keep a copy of it. Your ordinary invoice will do as long as it includes the following details:

❑ invoice number

❑ tax point (see below)

❑ your name and address

❑ your VAT registration number

❑ your customer's name and address

❑ what it is you have supplied (for example, a description of the goods or services). For each item, the invoice should show the quantity, the rate of tax and the amount payable before VAT is charged

❑ the type of supply (for example, whether you have sold it, sold it on hire purchase or rented it)

❑ the total amount payable, excluding VAT

❑ any cash discount

❑ the total amount of VAT charged.

If you are supplying goods and services direct to the public, for example as a shop, you don't need to give a tax invoice unless you are asked for one. And you do not need to provide such detailed invoices for items which are £100 or less, including the VAT. Nor do you need to keep copies of these. There are a number of special schemes for retailers, as it would be very time-consuming to keep records of every single sale, although the use of these schemes is being restricted in the light of new technologies which do now enable shopkeepers to work out the precise amount of VAT due on their sales.

A tax point is nothing more than the date on which you are liable to account for the VAT to Customs and Excise; this is the date on which you provide the goods or services. However, if you issue a tax invoice or receive a payment *earlier* than this, the tax point is the date you issue the invoice or receive the payment, whichever happens first. If you issue a tax invoice up to fourteen days after supplying the goods or services, and no earlier tax point has been created by a previous invoice or payment (as above), the date when you issue the invoice becomes the tax point. Finally, if you want to invoice monthly, you can use a monthly tax point, but you must have written approval from Customs and Excise first.

VAT account

The results for each VAT period need to be summarized separately in your accounting records. This should show the totals of input tax and output tax and the difference between the two, either a repayment to you or the amount due to Customs and Excise.

VAT return

This is the form which you need to fill in at the end of each VAT period, normally every three months, although if you are constantly claiming a repayment, for example, because you are zero-rated, you can arrange monthly returns. In the return, you show the information you put in your VAT account, see above. You also enter any bad debts you may have. As a check for Customs and Excise, you have to enter the figures for your total purchases and total sales for the period.

The VAT period can be arranged to coincide with your accounting year-end, which can make keeping your records much more convenient. And to simplify it even more you can go over to a system of annual accounting for VAT – see below.

There is a Misdeclaration Penalty which can be imposed. From 1 December 1993, if you make an error in your VAT return of 30 per cent of the gross tax (output and input tax) or £1 million, the penalty charged could be 15 per cent of the VAT due. However, you will not normally have to pay this unless the net tax you have underdeclared or overclaimed is more than £2,000 in the period and you have made a voluntary disclosure. However, you will have to pay interest on underdeclared VAT (6.25 per cent on a daily basis at May 1997).

Annual accounting

Instead of filling in a VAT return every three months, relatively small businesses can instead switch to annual accounting. This offers three advantages:

❑ more predictable cashflow because you make regular payments on account throughout the year

❑ a possible cash flow advantage, especially if your turnover is tending to increase each year

❑ less paperwork – and lower fees if you use an accountant – because you send in just one VAT return a year.

Annual accounting is open to your business if you have a yearly turnover (strictly VAT-able supplies) of £300,000 or less, you have been VAT-registered for at least a year, your VAT returns are up to date and you pay in more VAT than you reclaim.

The basic scheme works as follows: you and the VAT office agree an estimate of your likely VAT for the forthcoming year – usually this will be based on what you paid last year. You pay one-tenth of this amount by direct debit from the fourth month through to the twelfth month of your VAT year. Within two months of the end of the year, you send in your annual VAT return, making a final balancing payment if further VAT is due or claiming a repayment if the instalments came to more than the total for the year.

If your business has a turnover of £100,000 or less, from April 1996 onwards, annual accounting is even more advantageous. You make just four instalments over the year each equal to one-fifth of the previous year's VAT bill. If your total VAT bill for the year is less than £2,000, you can opt not to make any interim payments at all, simply paying the whole lot when you send in your annual return.

Whichever system of annual accounting applies, both you and the VAT office can adjust the interim payments during the year, if new information suggests they are no longer appropriate – for example, if your turnover is well below the previous year, you might request that the interim payments be reduced. You can withdraw from an annual accounting scheme at any time by writing to your VAT office.

Paying the tax

Any VAT which is due to Customs and Excise is payable within one month of the end of the quarterly accounting period or within two months of the end of an annual period. This is regardless of whether you have actually yet received the money from your customers on which the VAT is due.

If you fail to pay your VAT on time, you are given a warning. A Surcharge Liability Notice will be issued after the first late payment. A further late payment during the next twelve months from the date of the warning could mean a surcharge of 2 per cent of the amount of VAT due. A second late payment while the surcharge liability notice is in force prompts a surcharge of 5 per cent. Thereafter, so long as the notice is in force, the rate of the surcharge will increase by 5 per cent for each late payment to a maximum of 15 per cent. If the tax due is paid on time but the return is submitted late, there is no surcharge. To start again with a clean slate, you must make sure that you send in all your returns on time for a year.

Small businesses can pay VAT on a cash accounting basis. With this you pay VAT due only when you have been paid by your customer; and claim it back only when you have paid your supplier. You don't have to pay VAT on bad debts. You can opt to use this scheme if your taxable turnover is £350,000 or less, your outstanding amount of VAT is £5,000 or less, your VAT returns are up to date and you haven't been convicted of a VAT offence or assessed for dishonest conduct.

You can claim relief from VAT for bad debts which are six months old (before 1 April 1993 for debts which were one year old) and which you have written off in your accounts. From 18 July 1996 onwards, you can go back just three years to claim bad debt relief. Of course, if you adopt the cash accounting scheme, you automatically get relief from bad debts by never having to pay VAT on them at all.

If you have paid too much VAT as a result of a Customs and Excise error, you have the right to ask for interest on the amount of the incorrect payment. From 18 July 1996 onwards, you can go back only three years to claim back overpaid VAT.

Summary

1. You do not need to register if the value of your sales is too low, but it could still be worthwhile to apply to do so if you sell to businesses who can claim back the VAT or if you are zero-rated.

2. Do not confuse zero-rated with exempt supplies. If you supply only exempt goods, you cannot claim back VAT on goods you purchase.

3. If the level of your sales falls below a certain limit (£48,000 from 1 April 1998) you can ask to have the registration cancelled.

Other chapter to read

27. **Keeping the record straight** (p. 313)

33. **Retirement**

No doubt all your thoughts and energies are devoted to making your business successful, but spare a thought for what will happen when you retire. Your business might be the sort which you will be able to sell when it comes to retirement. This means you could have a lump sum which you can invest to give yourself an income to live on.

But with lots of self-employed people this is not so; if they retire, the business retires too, because their skills are essential to the success of their enterprise. Even if you hope that you will be able to sell your business on retirement, there is no certainty of this and you should show some caution in relying on it. You may be forced to retire earlier than you had intended because of ill health and this might coincide with a bad patch in your business fortunes. Or you may simply not be successful in building your business sufficiently to be able to sell for the sort of sum of money you need. The prudent course is to make separate arrangements to provide yourself with a pension.

This chapter looks at how to build up a pension during your working life. It also looks briefly at what happens from a tax point of view if you sell or give away your business on retirement.

What you get from the state

If you are self-employed, you will pay Class 2 National Insurance contributions. If you have set up a limited company and count as an employee of the company, you will pay Class 1 contributions (and the company will pay employer's contributions) assuming you are paid a salary of more than a given amount. Both these contributions will entitle you to the basic state pension, assuming you have paid sufficient contributions during your lifetime. The Class 4 contributions you make as a self-employed person do not increase your pension.

If you count as an employee of your company, even if you are a director, you may be building up an entitlement under an additional state pension scheme, called state earnings-related pension scheme (SERPS). Both you as an employee and your company as an employer will pay additional National Insurance contributions. This is known as being 'not contracted-out'. In this case, for example, if you earn more than £64 a week for 1998–99, you pay 2 per cent on £64 and 10 per cent on earnings between £64 and £485. Your company will be paying employer's contributions – nothing if you earn less than £64 a week, and an increasing percentage on earnings if you earn more. For example, 3 per cent on all your earnings if you earn from £64 up to £110.00, up to 10 per cent if you earn £485 a week or more. You can, if you wish, choose to contract out of the state earnings-related pension and redirect the additional National Insurance contributions into a personal pension.

If you are self-employed

The simplest way of increasing your pension is to start paying money into a personal pension plan, which is organized and invested by an insurance company; and, because you can get tax relief on what you pay at your highest rate of tax and your money is put into a tax-free fund, doing this is also likely to be the best way of saving for retirement.

A personal pension plan will pay out an income; the size depends on how long and how much you have saved, although there are limits imposed on how much you can save (see right). It also depends on how well the investments in the pension fund have done. You can choose when you want to start receiving the benefits from the plan, but it must be somewhere between your fiftieth and seventy-fifth birthday.

If you had a personal pension scheme before 1 July 1988 (known as a retirement annuity contract), you will not be able to start drawing benefits from it until you are sixty, although you can convert it into a personal plan and thus start to take benefit from fifty onwards. If you retire early because of illness, you can start taking the pension earlier, but it will be less.

Personal pension schemes can be very flexible provided you choose the right plan. For example:

❏ you can invest a lump sum when you want or save on a regular basis

❏ you can alter the premium from time to time

❏ the pension you choose at the end does not have to be a level amount; the income can start off lower, but increase each year with inflation

❏ you can choose a smaller joint-life pension, which will be paid as long as either of two people is alive

❏ most plans offer an 'open-market' option, which allows you to shop around to see if you can use the sum of money you have built up with one company to get a higher pension from another company

❏ you can normally choose to take a lower amount of pension and have a tax-free lump sum as well

❏ you may be allowed to put off buying a pension (an 'annuity') at the time you retire and draw an income direct from your pension fund instead up to age 75. This is useful if annuity rates are poor at the time you retire, but it is an option only suitable for large pension funds of £100,000 or more, say. This draw-down facility should be used with great care as using it could cut a great hole in your pension fund

❏ generally you can use your pension scheme to back up a mortgage, in much the same way as an endowment mortgage

❏ most of the plans have loanback facilities, which allows you to use your pension to get a loan.

Getting tax relief

You can deduct what you pay for a pension from your taxable income within certain limits, at your highest rate. This means this sort of saving can be very cheap, especially for higher-rate taxpayers.

Example

> Daniel Patten is considering putting money aside for retirement. His income for tax purposes for this year is £40,000, so he is paying tax at 40 per cent on the last slice of his income. If he invests £5,000 in a personal pension scheme, it would actually cost him only £3,000, because he would otherwise pay tax at 40 per cent on this £5,000.

There are limits on how much you can pay into a personal pension scheme. The limit depends on your age and your net relevant earnings for the tax year, that is, your taxable profits (less capital allowances) which are being assessed in this year.

The maximum premium eligible for tax relief is a percentage of your net relevant earnings (see Table overleaf):

There is a cap on relief of £87,600 for 1998–99 – this is the maximum level of earnings for which you can pay pension premiums and still get tax

Age	% Net Relevant Earnings
35 or under	17½
36–45	20
46–50	25
51–55	30
56–60	35
61+	40

relief. You can claim more than this if you have not paid the maximum premiums allowed in any of the previous six tax years.

The premiums you pay reduce your tax bill for the tax year in which you pay them, except if you ask to have the premiums treated for tax purposes as if you had paid them in the previous tax year (as long as you have sufficient unused relief for that year). If you did not have any net relevant earnings in the previous tax year, you will be able to get the premiums treated as if you had paid them in the year before that.

Choosing your personal pension plan

There are many schemes available and it is very difficult to choose which is the right personal pension plan. An independent intermediary (p. 244) can help, but they have differing levels of expertise, so you should shop around in the same way as you do for your business insurance. You can choose between a pension plan from an insurance company, bank, building society or unit trust manager.

There are different types of personal pension plans including:

❏ *non-profit:* from the outset, you know what your pension will be when you retire, and that is what it will be, no more and no less. This means the pension will be of limited value but fully guaranteed

❏ *with-profits:* the insurance company invests your money as it thinks fit, often in loans, British Government stocks, shares and property. The company will guarantee the minimum pension or lump sum of money you will get, but this will be lower than for a non-profit one (see above). However, you stand the prospect of receiving a much higher pension in the end, because the company adds bonuses to your pension, depending on the profits it makes on its investments

❏ *unit-linked:* with this type of policy you have some choice as to how your money is invested. Commonly, you can choose for the money to be invested in property, shares, fixed-interest investments such as British Government stocks, cash investments such as bank deposit accounts or you can choose to invest in a mixture of all these. With a unit-linked plan, the value of your pension is directly linked to the value of the investments, so it can fluctuate. This could be a problem if values happen to be low when it comes to retirement

❑ *deposit-administration scheme:* like the non-profit policy, these give a safe, if unexciting, return.

If you start saving at least ten to twenty years before retirement, and the earlier the better, choose either a with-profits or unit-linked scheme or a mixture of the two. If you have less than five years to retirement, a non-profit or deposit-administration scheme could be safer.

Getting life insurance

If you have non-pensionable earnings you can take out life insurance and get tax relief at your highest rate on the premium so long as the policy is what's called a Section 637 policy and your premium is not more than 5 per cent of your net relevant earnings.

If you are the director of a company

If you are a director of a small company, you can take out a personal pension plan in the same way as if you were self-employed. And, if you contract-out of the state earnings-related pension scheme (SERPS), the government will redirect your SERPS contributions to your own appropriate personal pension scheme. The extra National Insurance contributions which you, and your company as your employer, pay for the earnings-related bit of the state pension will be contributed by the government and tax relief will be added to your part of the contribution. You can choose your personal pension scheme from those sold by insurance companies, unit trusts, building societies and banks. Whether it is wise for you to do this depends on your age – check with an independent adviser.

Whether you choose to contract out or not, you could arrange an Occupational Pension Scheme through your own limited company. A scheme of this type has to be approved by the Inland Revenue if it is to qualify for the tax concessions. It can be arranged for you by an insurance company or you can administer the investments yourself.

If you and your family own most of the shares in the company, and you are both employer and director, there are three possible advantages:

❑ the pension fund can provide the capital for buying company assets, such as business premises

❑ up to half the pension fund can be loaned back to the company, and

❑ with a self-employed pension scheme, there is a limit on contributions which varies from 17½ per cent to 40 per cent of your net relevant earnings depending on your age. With a company pension fund, yearly contributions can be much higher. This could be very useful, especially if you are starting to save at a late age, for example, fifty, or you want to make larger contributions during good trading years in order to minimise the tax bill.

This area of pensions is very specialized. If you do want to go ahead, consult an independent financial adviser or other adviser with specialist knowledge, but don't be rushed into decisions by salespeople. Consider straightforward ideas too, like a personal pension plan.

When you retire or sell

If you retire and sell, give away or dispose of your business you may have to pay capital gains tax. However, there is retirement relief available if you are aged 50 or over. Note that it is proposed to phase this out between 6 April 1999 and 6 April 2003. You get the relief if:

❑ you have owned the business for a year or more, or

❑ you have owned shares in the business (either a family company or a holding company for the business you work for) for a year or more. You must own 5 per cent of the voting shares and be a full-time working employee.

The maximum gain you can get relief on is £250,000 plus relief on half the gain between £250,000 and £1,000,000; this would apply if you had owned your business or shares for ten years or more. There is a sliding scale of relief which reduces by 10 per cent for each year, until the relief is 10 per cent of the maximum if you have owned the business or shares for one year but less than two.

The relief is only available for the assets of the business, including goodwill, not stock. If you are disposing of shares, the gain is worked out and relief given only for that part of the value of the shares made up by the appropriate business assets.

There is only one lot of retirement relief available to you, that is, up to a total relief on a gain of £250,000 plus relief on half the gain between £250,000 and £1,000,000, but it can be made up of disposals of several assets at the same time, provided that you are disposing of a major part of the business.

Proposals were announced by the Chancellor in the 1998 Budget to phase out retirement relief over the next few years. This was part of the review of capital gains tax and the introduction of a new taper relief, particularly generous for business, to replace indexation allowance.

Taper relief will build up over the next few years to allow you to sell your business and reduce your capital gains tax bill. The full amount of taper relief will be available by 6 April 2008 and will mean that only 25 per cent of your gain will be taxable. But for a business asset held for a complete year by 6 April 1998, 92½ per cent of the gain will be taxable. As this would be unfair to those coming up for retirement, the Chancellor has retained retirement relief but is planning to phase it out. So, for example under the current proposals, if you sell your business in the year 1999–2000, you will get full relief on the first £200,000 of your gain and half the relief on gains between £200,000 and £800,000.

What this means is that if you are proposing to retire in the next few years, you should take tax advice as it may be that you should consider altering the timing of your disposal to take full advantage of the transitional tax arrangements.

If you give away business assets (doesn't need to be at retirement), your gift can be free of inheritance tax. From 10 March 1992, business relief means that there will be no inheritance tax to pay on business assets such as goodwill, land, buildings, plant, stock, patents. If the business is a company, you can also get 100 per cent business relief on transfers of the shares. Agricultural relief can mean no inheritance tax on owner-occupied farmlands and farm tenancies (including cottages, farm buildings and farm houses).

Summary

1. Saving for retirement through a personal pension plan, or a pension scheme organized by your company, is very cost-effective. This is because you can get tax relief at your highest rate of tax.

2. There are various reliefs available on capital gains tax when you dispose of your business or shares, if you meet certain conditions.

3. There may be no inheritance tax to pay on your business when you give it away or leave it on your death.

Reference

This section provides a handy list of further reading, names and addresses of organizations and other details which do not fit into the main text. Inclusion in this section of any organization which is run commercially is not to be taken as a recommendation. You must rely on the usual precautions, for example, taking up references, etc. Nor should you interpret exclusion of a commercial enterprise from a list as indication of anything adverse.

Keeping up-to-date

The internet is a handy source of information, news and advice.

Try this web site:
http://www.smallbusiness.co.uk
Run by Sara Williams, the author of this guide, it covers:

❑ news

❑ advice

❑ finance

❑ information

❑ small company investment

Access is free to much of the information, although some require a small fee. The Signpost Database pulls together many useful publications and sources of information and advice. It's updated twice a year

Other sites include:

www.businesslink.co.uk.
www.enterprisezone.co.uk
www.britishchambers.org.uk
www.btgplc.com
www.brainstorm.co.uk/bvca
www.companies-house.gov.uk

www.dti.gov.uk
www.open.gov.uk/dssca/jw/jw.htm

Chapter 1. **You and your ideas**

The umbrella organization for enterprise agencies is: Business in the
Community, 44 Baker Street, London W1M 1DH (0171-224 1600)

British Venture Capital Association, Essex House, 12-13 Essex Street,
London WC2R 3AA (0171-240 3846)
www.brainstorm.co.uk/bvca

Chapter 2. **Who will buy?**

This book is specifically about market research: *The Industrial Market
Research Handbook* by Paul N. Hague (Kogan Page, 3rd edition, 1992)
ISBN 07494 07743, £35

www.dti.gov.uk

European Information Centres have been set up by the European
Commission. They are designed to help small and medium-sized
enterprises take advantage of the single European market. Contact
your local centre:

Birmingham (0121-455 0268)
Bradford (01274-754262)
Bristol (0117-973 7373)
Exeter (01392-214085)
Hull (01482-465940)
Leicester (0116-255 9944)
Leeds (0113-283 3126)
Liverpool (0151-298 1928)
London (0171-489 1992; 0171-629 2151)
London (Lewisham Relay) (0181-695 6000)
Manchester (0161-237 4190)
Newcastle Upon Tyne (0191-261 0026)
Northern Ireland (Belfast) (01232-491031)
Norwich (01603-625977)
Nottingham (0115-962 4624)
Scotland (Glasgow) (0141-221 0999)

Scotland (Inverness) (01463-702560)
Sheffield (0114-253 2126)
Slough (01753-577877)
Southampton (01703-832866)
Stoke on Trent (01782-202222)
Telford (01952-208213)
Wales (Cardiff) (01222-229525)
Wales (Mold) (01352-704748)
West Malling (01345-226655)

Business Cooperation Network: Ask your local DTI office (see p. 436) or your local European Information Centre how to plug into this network to find a partner.

Export Market Information Centre (EMIC), DTI, Kingsgate House, 66-74 Victoria Street, London SW1E 6SW. This is a publicly accessible library of overseas market intelligence, open 9am to 8pm, Mondays to Fridays and 9am to 5.30pm Saturdays. (0171-215 5444/5)

DTI's Business in Europe Directorate, Kingsgate House, 66–74 Victoria Street, London SW1E 6SW (Hotline 0117-9444888):

Austria (0171-215 4963)
Belgium, Luxembourg (0171-215 4790)
Denmark (0171-215 8657)
Finland (0171-215 4783)
France (0171-215 4942)
Germany (0171-215 4285)
Greece (0171-215 4992)
Republic of Ireland (0171-215 8413)
Iceland (0171-215 8267)
Italy (0171-215 4754)
Netherlands (0171-215 4789)
Norway (0171-215 8267)
Portugal (0171-215 4721)
Spain, The Canaries (0171-215 4357)
Sweden (0171-215 4731)
Switzerland (0171-215 8353)

Export Marketing Research Scheme, contact:

The Association of British Chambers of Commerce, 4 Westwood House, Westwood Business Park, Coventry CV4 8HS (01203- 694484)

Export Clubs Committee, c/o The Joint Export Promotion Directorate, 10th Floor, DTI, Kingsgate House, 66-74 Victoria Street, London SW1E 6SW (tel 0171-215 4660; fax 0171-215 4653)

Market Research Society, 15 Northburgh Street, London EC1V 0AH (0171-490 4911)

Food from Britain, 123 Buckingham Palace Road, London SW1W 9SA (0171-233 5111)

British Library Business Information Service, 25 Southampton Buildings, Chancery Lane, London WC2A 1AW (0171-412 7454/7977)

British Library Document Supply Centre and Customer Services, Boston Spa, Wetherby, West Yorkshire LS23 7HE (01937-546060)

Birmingham Central Library, Information Services, Chamberlain Square, Birmingham B3 3HQ (0121-303 4512)

Other useful addresses to help you find information or organize your exporting:

British Exporters Association, Broadway House, Tothill Street, London SW1H 9NQ (0171-222 5419)

DTI Export Services Directorate, Kingsgate House, 66-74 Victoria Street, London SW1E 6SW (0171-215 2402)

DTI's *Overseas Trade* magazine, ten issues a year, publishes a regular guide to overseas missions and trade fairs. From Brass Tacks Publishing, 143 Charing Cross Road, London WC2H 0EE (0171-478 4700).

To find out whether your product is affected by the creation of technical standards applicable throughout the EC, phone British Standards Institution (0181-996 9001) or Technical Help to Exporters (THE) (0181-996 7111). For information about marketing try the Chartered Institute of Marketing's web site: www.cim.co.uk

Chapter 3. **A spot of coaching**

The Signpost Database (www.smallbusiness.co.uk) lists many sources of information and advice for small businesses. To find your local Business

Link, phone 0800 500 200 or look at www.businesslink.co.uk. Training and Enterprise Councils – ask at your local office below.

Training and Enterprise Councils

London

Focus Central London: Centre Point, 103 New Oxford Street, London WC1A 1DR (0171-896 8484)

London East TEC: Cityside House, 40 Adler Street, London E1 1EE (0171-377 1866)

North London TEC: Dumayne House, 1 Fox Lane, Palmers Green, London N13 4AB (0181-447 9422)

SOLOTEC (South London): Lancaster House, 7 Elmfield Road, Bromley, Kent BR1 1LT (0181-313 9232 freephone 0800 800222)

West London TEC: West London Centre, 15–21 Staines Road, Hounslow, Middx TW3 3HA (0181-577 1010)

AZTEC (Kingston/Merton/Wandsworth): Manorgate House, 2 Manorgate Road, Kingston-Upon-Thames KT2 7AL (0181-547 3934)

North West London TEC: Kirkfield House, 118-120 Station Road, Harrow, Middx HA1 2RL. Tel: 0181-901 5000

East Midlands & Eastern

Bedfordshire and Luton CCTE: Woburn Court, 2 Railton Road, Woburn Road Industrial Estate, Kempston, Beds MK42 7PN (01234-843100)

Southern Derbyshire CCTE: St. Helen's Court, St. Helen's Street, Derby DE1 3GY (01332-290550 freephone 01332 200331)

North Derbyshire TEC: Block C, St. Marys Court, St. Marys Gate, Chesterfield S41 7TD (01246-551158)

Leicestershire TEC: Meridian East, Meridian Business Park, Leicester LE3 2WZ (0116 265 1515)

Lincolnshire TEC: Beech House, Witham Park, Waterside South, Lincoln LN5 7JH (01522-567765)

Suffolk TEC: 2nd Floor, Crown House, Crown Street, Ipswich, Suffolk IP1 3HS (01473-218951 freephone 0800 181915)

Greater Nottingham TEC: Marina Road, Castle Marina Park, Nottingham NG7 1TN (0115-941 3313)

CAMBSTEC (Central and South Cambridgeshire): Units 2-3, Trust Court, Chivers Way, The Vision Park, Histon, Cambridge CB4 4PW (01223-235635)

Greater Peterborough CCTE: Stuart House, City Road, Peterborough PE1 1QF (01733-890808)

Norfolk & Waveney TEC: St Andrew's House, St Andrew's Street, Norwich NR2 4TP (01603-763812)

Northamptonshire CCTE: Royal Pavilion, Summerhouse Road, Moulton Park Industrial Estate, Northampton NN3 6BJ (01604-671200 freephone 0800 503080) (Training and information Helpline)

North Nottinghamshire TEC: 1st floor, Block C, Edwinstowe House, High Street, Edwinstowe, Mansfield, Notts NG21 9PR (01623-824624 freephone 0800 591067)

West Midlands

Birmingham TEC: Chaplin Court, 80 Hurst Street, Birmingham B5 4TG (0121-622 4419)

Coventry & Warwickshire CCTE: Oak Tree Court, Binley Business Park, Harry Weston Road, Coventry CV3 2UN (01203-654321 freephone 0800 252198)

Dudley TEC: Dudley Court South, Waterfront East, Lever Street, Brierley Hill, West Midlands DY5 1XN (01384-485000)

Staffordshire TEC: Festival Way, Festival Park, Stoke-on-Trent Staffordshire ST1 5TQ (01782-202733 freephone 0800 262095)

Hereford and Worcester CCTE: Haswell House, St Nicholas Street, Worcester WR1 1UW (01905-723200 freephone 0800 137316)

Sandwell TEC: 1st floor, Black Country House, Rounds Green Road, Oldbury, Warley, West Midlands B69 2DG (0121-543 2222)

Shropshire CCTE: Trevithick House, Stafford Park 4, Telford TF3 3BA (01952-208200 freephone 0800 252972)

Walsall TEC: 5th Floor, Townend House, Townend Square, Walsall WS1 1NS (01922-424242 freephone 0800 626827)

Wolverhampton CCTE: Pendeford Business Park, Wobaston Road, Wolverhampton WV9 5HA (01902-445500)

Northern Region

Tees Valley TEC: Training & Enterprise House, 2 Queen's Square, Middlesborough, Cleveland TS2 1AA (01642-231023)

County Durham TEC: Valley Street North, Darlington, Co. Durham DL1 1TJ (01325-351166)

Northumberland TEC: Suite 2, Craster Court, Manor Walk Shopping Centre, Cramlington, Northumberland NE23 6XX (01670-713303)

Sunderland City TEC: Business and Innovation Centre, Sunderland Enterprise Park, Riverside, Sunderland, Tyne and Wear SR5 2TA (0191-516 6000)

Tyneside TEC: Moorgate House, 5th Avenue Business Park, Team Valley Trading Estate, Gateshead, Tyne and Wear NE11 0HF (0191-491 6000)

North-West Region

North & Mid Cheshire TEC: Spencer House, Dewhurst Road, Birchwood, Warrington WA3 7PP (01925-826515 freephone 0800 282020)

Cumbria TEC: Venture House, Regents Court, Guard Street, Workington, Cumbria CA14 4EW (01900-669911 freephone 0800 378212)

LAWTEC (Lancashire Area West): Taylor House, Caxton Road, Fulwood, Preston PR2 9ZB (01772-792111)

Bolton Bury TEC: Clive House, Clive Street, Bolton BL1 1ET (01204-397350)

Stockport & High Peak TEC: 1 St Peter's Square, Stockport, Cheshire SK1 1NN (0161-477 8830)

Oldham ccte: Meridian Centre, King Street, Oldham OL8 1EZ (0161-620 0006)

Merseyside TEC: Tithebarn House, Tithebarn Street, Liverpool L2 2NZ (0151-236 0026 freephone 0800 317857)

CEWTEC (Chester/Ellesmere Port/Wirral): Egerton House, 2 Tower Road, Birkenhead, Wirral, L41 1FN (0151-650 0555 freephone 0800 132762)

ELTEC Ltd (East Lancashire): Red Rose Court, Clayton Business Park, Clayton Le Moors, Accrington, Lancs BB5 5JR (01254-301333)

Manchester TEC: Lee House, 90 Great Bridgewater Street, Manchester M1 5JW (0161-236 7222)

Rochdale TEC: St James Place, 160–162 Yorkshire Street, Rochdale, Lancashire OL16 2DL (01706-644909)

South & East Cheshire TEC: PO Box 37, Middlewich Industrial and Business Park, Dalton Way, Middlewich, Cheshire CW10 0HU (01606-737009)

St Helens CCTE: St Helens Technology Campus, St. Helens, Merseyside WA9 1UB (01744-742000)

Wigan Chamber of Commerce Training and Enterprise: The Investment Centre, Waterside Drive, Wigan WN3 5BA (01942-705705)

South-East Region

Thames Valley Enterprise: Pacific House, Imperial Way, Reading, Berks RG2 0TF (0118-921 4000 freephone 0800 775566)

Essex TEC: Redwing House, Hedgerows Business Park, Colchester Road, Chelmsford, Essex CM2 5PB (01245-450123)

Hampshire TEC: 25 Thackeray Mall, Fareham, Hants PO16 0PQ (01329-230099 freephone 0800 220806)

Kent TEC: 26 Kings Hill Avenue, Kings Hill, West Malling, Kent ME19 4TA (01732-220000)

Surrey TEC: Technology House, 48–54 Goldsworth Road, Woking, Surrey GU21 1LE (01483-728190 freephone 01483-750999)

Sussex Enterprise: Greenacre Court, Station Road, Burgess Hill, West Sussex, RH15 9DS (01444-259259)

Hertfordshire TEC: 45 Grosvenor Road, St Albans, Herts AL1 3AW (01727-813600 freephone 0800 919000)

Wight TEC: Mill Court, Furrlongs, Newport, Isle of Wight PO30 2AA (01983-822818)

Milton Keynes and North Bucks CCTE: Tempus, 249 Midsummer Boulevard, Milton Keynes MK9 1EU (01908-259000)

Heart of England TEC (Oxfordshire): 26–27 The Quadrant, Abingdon Science Park, Abingdon OX14 3YS (01235-553249 freephone 0800 888500)

South-West Region

Western Training and Enterprise Council: St Lawrence House, 29–31 Broad Street, Bristol BS99 7HR (0117-927 7116)

Prosper (Devon & Cornwall TEC): Prosper House, Brooklands, Budshead Road, Crownhill, Plymouth PL6 5XR (01752-785785 freephone 0800 252713)

Somerset TEC: East Reach House, East Reach, Taunton, Somerset TA1 3EN (01823-321188 freephone 0800-525918)

Gloucestershire TEC: Conway House, 33–35 Worcester Street, Gloucester GL1 3AJ (01452-524488 freephone 0800-220262)

Dorset TEC: 25 Oxford Road, Bournemouth, Dorset BH8 8EY (01202-299284)

Wiltshire & Swindon TEC: The Bora Building, Westlea Campus, Westlea Down, Swindon, Wilts SN5 7EZ (01793-513644)

Wales

Mid Glamorgan TEC: Unit 17–20 Centre Court, Main Avenue, Treforest Industrial Estate, Pontypridd, Mid Glamorgan CF37 5LY (01443-841594 freephone 0800-262071)

Gwent TEC: Glyndwr House, Unit B2 Cleppa Park, Newport, Gwent NP9 1YE (01633-678200 freephone 0800-371529)

CELTEC – North Wales TEC: St Asaph Business Park, St Asaph, Denbighshire LL17 0JL (01745-585400)

Powys TEC: 1st floor, St David's House, New Road, Newtown, Powys SY16 1RB (01686-622494 freephone 0800 252903)

South Glamorgan TEC: 2-7 Drake Walk, Brigantine Place, Atlantic Wharf, Cardiff CF1 5AN (01222-261000 freephone 0800 212933)

West Wales TEC: Orchard House, Orchard Street, Swansea, West Glamorgan SA1 5DJ (01792-460355)

Yorkshire & Humberside Region

Calderdale & Kirklees TEC: Park View House, Woodvale Office Park, Woodvale Road, Brighouse, Yorkshire HD6 4AB (01484-400770)

Humberside TEC: The Maltings, Silvester Square, Silvester Street, Hull HU1 3HL (01482-226491 freephone 0800 393744)

Leeds TEC: Belgrave Hall, Belgrave Street, Leeds LS2 8DD (0113-234 7666)

Sheffield TEC: St Mary's Court, 55 St Mary's Road, Sheffield S2 4AQ (0114-270 1911)

Wakefield TEC: Grove Hall, 60 College Grove Road, Wakefield WF1 3RN (01924-299907)

Rotherham CCTE: Moorgate House, Moorgate Road, Rotherham S60 2EN (01709-830511)

Barnsley & Doncaster TEC: Conference Centre, Eldon Street, Barnsley S70 2JL (01226-248088)

Bradford & District TEC: Mercury House, 4 Manchester Road, Bradford, BD5 0QL (01274-751333 freephone 0800-160017)

North Yorkshire TEC: TEC House, 7 Pioneer Business Park, Amy Johnson Way, Clifton Moorgate, York YO3 8TN (01904-691939 freephone 0800 515547)

Scotland

In Scotland your local offices to help with training and counselling are known as Local Enterprise Companies. Here are the addresses and phone numbers:

Enterprise Ayrshire: 17–19 Hill Street, Kilmarnock KA3 1HA (01563-526623)

Scottish Borders Enterprise: Bridge Street, Galashiels TD1 1SW (01896-758991)

Forth Valley Enterprise: Laurel House, Laurelhill Business Park, Stirling FK7 9JQ (01786-451919)

Dumfries & Galloway Enterprise Co.: Solway House, Dumfries Business Park, Tinwald Downs Road, Dumfies DG1 3SJ (01387-245000)

Dunbartonshire Enterprise: 2nd Floor, Spectrum House, Clydebank Business Park, Clydebank, Glasgow G81 2DR (0141-951 2121)

Fife Enterprise Ltd: Kingdom House, Saltire Centre, Glenrothes, Fife KY6 2AQ (01592-623000)

Glasgow Development Agency: Atrium Court, 50 Waterloo Street, Glasgow G2 6HQ (0141-204 1111)

Grampian Enterprise Ltd: 27 Albyn Place, Aberdeen AB10 1YL (01224-211500)

Lanarkshire Development Agency: New Lanarkshire House, Willow Drive, Strathclyde Business Park, Bellshill ML4 3AD (01698-745454)

Lothian & Edinburgh Enterprise Ltd: Apex House, 99 Haymarket Terrace, Edinburgh EH12 5HD (0131-313 4000)

Renfrewshire Enterprise: 27 Causeyside Street, Paisley PA1 1UL (0141-848 0101)

Scottish Enterprise Tayside: 45 North Lindsay Street, Dundee DD1 1HT (01382-223100)

Argyll & The Islands Enterprise: The Enterprise Centre, Kilmory, Lochgilphead, Argyll PA31 8SH (01546-602281/602563)

Caithness & Sutherland Enterprise: Scapa House, Castlegreen Road, Thurso, Caithness KW14 7LS (01847-896115)

Moray Badenoch and Strathspey Enterprise Co Ltd: Unit 8, Elgin Business Centre, Maisondieu Road, Elgin, Morayshire IV30 1RH (01343-550567)

Lochaber Ltd: St Mary's House, Gordon Square, Fort William PH33 6DY (01397-704326)

Inverness and Nairn Enterprise: Castle Wynd, Inverness IV3 3DW (01463-713504)

Orkney Enterprise: 14 Queen Street, Kirkwall, Orkney KW15 1JE (01856-874638)

Ross & Cromarty Enterprise: 69/71 High Street, Invergordon, Rossshire IV18 0DH (01349-853666)

Shetland Enterprise: Toll Clock Shopping Centre, 26 North Road, Lerwick, Shetland ZE1 0PE (01595-693177)

Skye & Lochalsh Enterprise: Kings House, The Green, Portree, Isle of Skye IV51 9BT (01478-612841)

Western Isles Enterprise (Iomairt nan Eilean Siar): 3 Harbour View, Cromwell Street Quay, Stornoway, Isle of Lewis HS1 2DF (01851-703703)

Other agencies and organizations:

Business in the Community, 44 Baker Street, London W1M 1DH (0171-224 1600)

The Institute of Management, Management House, Cottingham Road, Corby, Northants NN17 1TT (01536-204222). IM runs more than seventy courses a year. It also has a very comprehensive library of management-related data, including electronic databases. Some of its services carry charges. www.inst-mgt.org.uk

Welsh Development Agency, Head Office, Principality House, The Friary, Cardiff CF1 4AE (0345-775577)

The Local Enterprise Development Unit (LEDU), LEDU House, Upper Galwally, Belfast BT8 6TB (01232-491031)

Rural Development Commission Headquarters, 141 Castle Street, Salisbury, Wiltshire SP1 3TP (01722-336255). Contact here to find the address of your nearest local office

Highlands and Islands Enterprise, Bridge House, 20 Bridge Street, Inverness IV1 1QR (01463-234171)

Development Board for Rural Wales, Ladywell House, Newtown, Mid-Wales SY16 1JB (01686-626965)

Contact Small Firms Lead Body which is developing standards of competence for small firms. The address is PO Box 393, Northampton NN1 4YG (01604-234618).

The Institute of Business Advisers, PO Box 8 Harrogate, North Yorkshire HG2 8XB (01423-879208)

Small business organizations:

Federation of Small Businesses, 32 Orchard Road, Lytham St. Annes, Lancs FY8 1NY (01253-720911)

The Small Business Bureau, Curzon House, Church Road, Windlesham, Surrey GU20 6BH (01276-452010)

The Forum of Private Business, Ruskin Chambers, Drury Lane, Knutsford, Cheshire WA16 6HA (01565-634467/8)

Special groups:

There are enterprise agencies set up in areas where the ethnic minority population is based, such as the Bristol Black Association or Black Business in Birmingham.

Instant Muscle, Springside House, 84 North End Road, London W14 9ES (0171-603 2604)

SHELL Livewire, Hawthorn House, Forth Banks, Newcastle-upon-Tyne NE1 3SG (0191-261 5584) or Livewire, Freepost NT805, Newcastle-upon-Tyne NE1 1BR (Hotline 0345 573252 cost of local call) www.shell-livewire.org

SHELL Livewire Northern Ireland, Freepost GW4428, Belfast BT15 1BR (01232-329339)

The Prince's Youth Business Trust, 18 Park Square East, London NW1 4LH (0171-543 1234)

Women into Business, Curzon House, Church Road, Windlesham, Surrey GU20 6BH (01276-452010)

Web site for women entrepreneurs at www.lloydsbank.co.uk

Europe:

European Briefing Unit, University of Bradford, Bradford BD7 1DP (01274-383831)

The Central Bureau for Educational Visits and Exchanges is contacted as follows:

UK Unit, The Central Bureau, 10 Spring Gardens, London SW1A 2BN (0171-389 4004)

Edinburgh Language Programmes Department Office, The Central Bureau, 3 Bruntsfield Crescent, Edinburgh EH10 4HD (0131-447 8024)

Belfast Office, The Central Bureau, 1 Chlorine Gardens, Belfast BT9 5DJ (01232-664418)

Language Services

Language Services are offered by members of the Association of Language Excellence Centres (ALEC) Cowley House, 9 Little College Street, London sw1p 3xs (0171-222 0666 fax 0171-233 0335). Contact:

Scotland

Glenrothes Language Export Centre, Glenrothes College, Cadham Campus, Glenrothes, Fife KY7 6RU (01592-740200)

Language Centre, Hetherington Building, Bute Gardens, Glasgow G12 8RS (0141-339 2211)

Languages For Business, University of Strathclyde, 16 Livingstone Tower, 26 Richmond Street, Glasgow G1 1XH (0141-553 4191)

North East

The Language Service Ltd, Christine House, Sorbonne Close, Thornaby, Stockton-on-Tees, Cleveland TS17 6DA (01642-673608)

North West

Centre for Language Study, Leeds Metropolitan University, Beckett Park Campus, Leeds LS6 3QS (0113-2833202)

Euro-com, The Cornerstone, 42 Church Road, Bolton, Manchester BL1 6HE (01204-849849)

The European Centre for Business, Peter House, St Peter's Square, Manchester M1 5AN (0161-281 8844)

Eurospeak, Dry Dock Mill, New Road, Dearnley, Littleborough, Lancs OL15 8LX (01706-373440)

Lancashire and Cumbria LX Centre, University of Central Lancashire, Preston PR1 2HE (01772-893132)

Language Learning Centre, Chatham Building, Chatham Street, University of Liverpool, Liverpool L69 3BX (0151-794 2796)

Park Language Centre, 2nd Floor, 141 West Street, Sheffield S1 4ES (0114-272 7937)

Lancashire College, Southport Road, Chorley PR7 1NB (01257-276719)

Wales

Business Language Services, The Belgrave Business Centre, 81 Brecon Road, Abergavenny Gwent NP7 7RD (01873-856762)

Language Export Centre, University of Wales Swansea, Singleton Park, Swansea SA2 8PP (01792-295621)

Midlands

The Brasshouse Centre, Brasshouse Language Services, 50 Sheepcote Street, Birmingham B16 8AJ (0121-643 0114)

Coventry Language Service, Coventry Technical College, The Butts, Coventry CV1 3GD (01203-526733)

International Language Centre, Clarendon College, 11 Queen Street, Nottingham NG1 2BL (0115-9553100)

Language Link, 18 Newhall Place, Newhall Hill, Birmingham B1 3JH (0121 236 6009)

South West

Savoir-Faire in Languages, 54 High Street, Totnes, Devon TQ9 5SP (01803-866987)

London

All Languages Ltd., Nelson House, 362-364 Old Street, London EC1V 9LT (0171-739 6641)

Conversation Piece (UK), 120 Windermere Road, London W5 4TH (0181-579 4567)

EF International, Kensington Cloisters, 5 Kensington Church Street, London W8 4LD (0171-878 3550)

European & Language Service, University of North London, The Learning Centre, 236-250 Holloway Road, London N7 6PP (0171-753 5106)

Foreign Language Services, 4 Lysander House, 1 Lysander Grove, London N19 3QY (0171-263 3996)

Institut Français, 14 Cromwell Place, South Kensington, London SW7 2JR (0171-581 2701)

International House, 106 Piccadilly, London W1V 9FL (0171-499 6593)

Language Studies International, 19-21 Ridgmount Street, London WC1E 7AH (0171-467 6500)

Polygot Language Services, 214 Trinity Road, London SW17 7HP (0181-767 9113)

St George International, Language House, 76 Mortimer Street, London W1N 7DE (0171-266 1700)

Regent Linguaphone, 5 Percy Street, London WC1P 9FB (0171-637 8041)

South

Centre for International Briefing, Farnham Castle, Farnham, Surrey GU9 0AG (01252-721194)

East Surrey College, Gatton Point, Redhill, Surrey RH1 2JX (01737-772611)

Kingston Language-Export Centre, Kingston University, Penrhyn Road, Kingston upon Thames KT1 2EE (0181-547 7884)

Milton Keynes Language Centre, Exchange House, 494 Midsummer Boulevard, Central Milton Keynes MK9 2EA (01908-227555)

Robertson Languages, The Stable Block, Hare Hatch Grange, Bath Road, Hare Hatch, Reading RG10 9SA (01734-404499)

Affiliate Members

London

C & A, Orbis Services, 64 North Row, London W1A 2AX

Midlands

RSA Examinations Board, Westwood Way, Coventry CV4 8HS (01203-468080)

Chapter 4. **Your business identity**

www.dti.gov.uk
Guidance on forming a limited company and records of limited companies
are kept at Companies Registration Office:

England and Wales: Companies Registration Office, Companies House,
Crown Way, Cardiff CF4 3UZ (01222-388588)
www.companies-house.gov.uk

Scotland: Companies House, 37 Castle Terrace, Edinburgh EH1 2EB
(0131-535 5800)

Northern Ireland: Companies Registry, IDB House, 64 Chichester Street,
Belfast BT1 4JX (01232-234488)

Forms can be obtained from Stationery Section, PO Box 450, Companies
House, Crown Way, Cardiff CF4 3UZ, or for personal callers only from The
London Search Room, 55–71 City Road, London EC1Y 1BB.

Useful books:

Tolley's Company Law (Tolley Publishing Company, looseleaf edition)
(£355 a year by subscription) covers legal requirements of limited
companies in great detail.

Forming a Limited Company by Patricia Clayton (Kogan Page, 6th
edition, 1998) ISBN 0749426489, £12.99

The Company Secretary's Handbook by Helen Ashton (Kogan Page, 1995)
– Current edition out of print, 2nd ed. due out 1998 ISBN 0749426462,
£12.99

Law for the Small Business by Patricia Clayton (Kogan Page, 9th edition)
ISBN 0749426470

The Institute of Directors produces books explaining directors'
responsibilities, including *Directors' Personal Liabilities* and *Guidelines
for Directors*. The IoD runs courses and has an information service.
Contact IoD, 116 Pall Mall, London SW1Y 5ED (0171-839 1233).

Lawyers For Your Business Helpline: phone 0171-405 9075 or contact
The Law Society, 50-52 Chancery Lane, London WC2A 1PL (0171-242
1222) for information about the Lawyers for Your Business scheme.

For information on forming a cooperative contact ICOM, Vassalli House, 20 Central Road, Leeds LS1 6DE (0113-246 1738)

Chapter 6. **The business plan**

The Business Plan Workbook by Colin and Paul Barrow (Kogan Page, 2nd edition) ISBN 0749406445, £13.99

Chapter 8. **Toe-dipping**

A useful book for those interested in permanent toe-dipping is: *Earning Money at Home* edited by Lynn Underwood (Consumers Association, rev. ed. Apr.1996)

For information about insurance for businesses run from home, contact Tolson Messenger Ltd, 148 King Street, London W6 0QU (0181-741 8361)

Chapter 10. **Franchises**

More detail about franchises, including if you want to become a franchisor, is in:

Taking Up a Franchise by Godfrey Golzen and Colin Barrow (Kogan Page, 12th edition, 1996) ISBN 0749418362, £10.99

British Franchise Association, Thames View, Newtown Road, Henley-on-Thames, Oxon RG9 1HG (01491-578050)

Two franchise directories are:
Franchise World Directory, published by Franchise World, James House, 37 Nottingham Road, London SW17 7EA (0181-767 1371)
www.franchiseworld.co.uk
Business Franchise Directory, published by Miller Freeman, Blenheim House, 630 Chiswick High Road, London W4 5BG (0181-742 2828)

Chapter 11. **The right name**

There are six useful leaflets produced by the Department of Trade and Industry: *Business Names and Business Ownership, Choosing a Co.*

Name, Exemption from using the word 'limited' in a co. name, Change of Name, Publication of Co. Name & Particulars to be shown on Co. Stationery, and *Sensitive Words & Expressions.* You can get these from Companies House, Crown Way, Cardiff CF4 3UZ (01222-388588) www.companieshouse.gov.uk

Chapter 12. **Beating the pirates**

The Patent Office, Concept House, Cardiff Road, Newport, South Wales NP9 1RH (01633-814000 or 0645 500505 for enquiries)

Chartered Institute of Patent Agents, Staple Inn Buildings, High Holborn, London WC1V 7PZ (0171-405 9450) www.cipa.org.uk

Institute of Trade Mark Agents, Canterbury House, 2-6 Sydenham Road, Croydon, Surrey CR0 9XE (0181-686 2052)

Institute of Patentees and Inventors, Suite 505a, Triumph House, 189 Regent Street, London W1R 7WF (0171-434 1818)

Chapter 14. **Selling**

Business Cooperation Network (BC-Net): contact Europe Information Centre (see p. 000)

Successful Marketing for the Small Business by Dave Patten (Kogan Page, 4th edition) ISBN 0749426446, £12.99

Advertising Standards Authority, 2 Torrington Place, London WC1E 7HW (0171-580 5555) www.asa.org.uk

MOPS Scheme, 16 Tooks Court, London EC4A 1LB (0171-405 6806)

Chapter 16. **Choosing your workplace**

For more information on grants and assistance available in Assisted Areas (Development Areas and Intermediate Areas) contact your local DTI office (www.dti.gov.uk):

Government Office for the North East: Stanegate House, 2 Groat Market, Newcastle Upon Tyne NE1 1YN (0191-201 3300)

Government Office for the North West: Sunley Tower, Piccadilly Plaza, Manchester M1 4BA (0161-952 4000)

Government Office for Merseyside: Cunard Building, Pier Head, Water Street, Liverpool L3 1QB (0151-224 6300)

Government Office for Yorkshire and Humberside: 25 Queen Street, Leeds LS1 2TW & City House, New Station Street, Leeds LS1 4JU (0113-280 0600)

Government Office for the East Midlands: The Belgrave Centre, Stanley Place, Talbot Street, Nottingham NG1 5GG (0115-971 9971)

Government Office for the West Midlands: 77 Paradise Circus, Queensway, Birmingham B1 2DT (0121-212 5050)

Government Office for the South West: 4th & 5th Floor, The Pithay, Bristol BS1 2PB (0117-900 1700) & Mast House, Shepherds Wharf, 24 Sutton Road, Plymouth PL4 0HJ (01752-635000)

Government Office for London: Riverwalk House, 157-161 Millbank, London SW1P 4RR (0171-217 3456)

Government Office for the South East: Bridge House, 1 Walnut Tree Close, Guildford, Surrey GU1 4GA (01483-882255)

Government Office for the Eastern Regions: Building A, Westbrook Centre, Milton Road, Cambridge CB4 1YG (01223-346700)

The Scottish Office, Education and Industry Department: Meridian Court, 5 Cadogan Street, Glasgow G2 6AT (0141-248 4774)

The Welsh Office: Crown House, Industry & Training Department, Cathays Park, Cardiff CF1 3NQ (01222-823186)

Northern Ireland – Department of Economic Development, Netherleigh, Massey Avenue, Belfast BT4 2JP (01232-529900)

Assisted Areas:

England (North West):

Development Areas – Liverpool, Wigan & St Helens, Wirral & Chester,

Intermediate Areas – Barrow in Furness, Blackburn, Bolton & Bury, Manchester (Trafford Park), Oldham, Rochdale, Whitehaven, Widnes & Runcorn, Workington

England (North East):

Development Areas – Bishop Auckland, Hartlepool, Middlesbrough, Morpeth & Ashington, Newcastle-upon-Tyne, South Tyneside, Stockton-on-Tees, Sunderland

Intermediate Areas –Alnwick & Amble, Durham,

England (Yorkshire & Humberside):

Development Areas – Barnsley, Doncaster, Rotherham & Hexborough

Intermediate Areas – Bridlington and Driffield, Castleford & Pontefract, Grimsby, Hull, Sheffield, Wakefield & Dewsbury, Whitby

England (East Midlands):

Development Area – Mansfield

Intermediate Areas – Alfreton & Ashfield, Gainsborough, Louth & Mablethorpe, Retford, Skegness, Worksop

England (West Midlands):

Development Areas – Birmingham City, Wolverhampton

Intermediate Areas – Birmingham (non City), Coventry & Hinckley, Dudley & Sandwell, Walsall

England (South West):

Development Areas – Falmouth, Helston, Newquay, Penzance & St Ives, Redruth & Camborne

Intermediate Areas – Barnstaple & Ilfracombe, Bideford, Bodmin & Liskeard, Bude, Dorchester & Weymouth, Plymouth, St. Austell, Torbay

England (South East):

Development Area – Thanet

Intermediate Areas – Dover & Deal, Folkestone, Hastings, Isle of Wight, Sittingbourne & Sheerness

England (East Anglia):

Intermediate Areas – Clacton, Great Yarmouth, Harwich, Wisbech

Outer London:

Intermediate Areas – Park Royal, Lea Valley, London end of the East Thames Corridor

Scotland:

Development Areas – Arbroath, Bathgate, Cumnock & Sanquhar, Dunfermline, Forres, Girvan, Glasgow, Greenock, Irvine, Kilmarnock, Kirkcaldy, Lanarkshire , Newton Stewart

Intermediate Areas – Alloa, Ayr, Campbeltown, Dumbarton, Dundee, Dunoon & Bute, Falkirk, Invergordon & Dingwall, Lochaber, Skye & Wester Ross, Stranraer, Sutherland, Thurso, Western Isles, Wick

Wales:

Development Areas – Aberdare, Cardigan, Blaenau Gwent & Abergavenny (the Blaenau Gwent Borough part), Fishguard, Haverford West, Holyhead, Merthyr & Rhymney, Pontypridd & Rhondda (the Rhondda Borough part), South Pembrokeshire, Wrexham

Intermediate Areas – Bangor & Caernarfon, Blaenau Gwent & Abergavenny (Brechnock & Monmouth part), Bridgend, Cardiff (part of), Llanelli, Neath & Port Talbot, Newport (West), Pontypool & Cwmbran, Porthmadoc & Ffestiniog, Pwllheli, Swansea

Chapter 17. **Getting equipped**

The Office of the Data Protection Registrar, Wycliffe House, Water Lane, Wilmslow, Cheshire SK9 5AF (01625-545700)
www.open.gov.uk/dpr/dprhome.htm

Chapter 18. **Professional back-up**

The Institute of Chartered Accountants in England & Wales, PO Box 433, Chartered Accountants Hall, Moorgate Place, London EC2P 2BJ (0171-920 8100)
www.icaew.co.uk

The Institute of Chartered Accountants of Scotland, 27 Queen Street, Edinburgh EH2 1LA (0131-225 5673)

The Institute of Chartered Accountants in Ireland, Chartered Accountants' House, 87-89 Pembroke Road, Dublin 4 (00 3531 668 0400)

Association of Chartered Certified Accountants, 29 Lincoln's Inn Fields, London WC2A 3EE (0171-242 6855)

Association of Authorised Public Accountants, 32 Ely Place, London EC1N 6TD (0171-396 5954)

Institute of Management Consultants, 5th Floor, 32–33 Hatton Garden, London EC1N 8DL (0171-242 1803)

Institute of Business Advisers, PO Box 8, Harrogate, North Yorkshire HG2 8XB (01423-879208)
www.iba.org.uk

The Law Society, 50-52 Chancery Lane, London WC2A 1PL (0171-242 1222)

Royal Institution of Chartered Surveyors, 12 Great George Street, Parliament Square, London SW1P 3AD (0171-222 7000)
www.rics.org.uk

Incorporated Society of Valuers and Auctioneers, 3 Cadogan Gate, London SW1X 0AS (0171-235 2282)

For information about the Alternative Investment market and OFEX contact Small Company Investor, 9 Harley Street, London W1N 1DA (0171-323 4050; Fax 0171-323 3614)
www.smallcompanyinvestor.co.uk

Chapter 19. **Getting the right staff**

The section on characteristics is adapted from the National Institute of Industrial Psychology's Seven Point Plan.

Federation of Recruitment and Employment Services, 36–38 Mortimer Street, London W1N 7RB (0171-323 4300)

Two helpful booklets from the Equal Opportunities Commission are *The Sex Discrimination Act and Advertising* (free of charge). For address, see right

Chapter 20. **Your rights and duties as an employer**

Employees' Helpline: wwww.open.gov,uk/dssca/jw/jw.htm

Discipline at Work is a booklet published by ACAS which has the Code of Practice on dismissals as an appendix. The booklet is £2.25 + £1.00 p&p and is obtainable from the Advisory, Conciliation and Arbitration Service (ACAS), ACAS Reader Ltd., PO Box 16, Earl Shilton, Leicester LE9 8ZZ

Equal Opportunities Commission, Overseas House, Quay Street, Manchester M3 3HN (0161-833 9244)

Commission for Racial Equality, Elliot House, 10–12 Allington Street, London SW1E 5EH (0171-828 7022)

Race Relations Employment Advisory Service (RREAS), Head Office, 14th Floor, Cumberland House, 200 Broad Street, Birmingham B15 1TA (0121-244 8142). You can obtain a copy of the RREAS Quality Standard from here.

DTI leaflets are available from DTI Publications Orderline, Admail 528, London SW1W 8YT (0870-1502500)

Four reference books from Tolley Publishing Company (1997-98 editions should be available in 1997):

Tolley's Employment Handbook by Elizabeth Slade £39.50 (11th edition) (Supplement out in July – whole package: £54.95)

Tolley's Payroll Handbook £49.95

Tolley's Social Security and State Benefits Handbook 98-99: 2 ed.s this year: main vol. – Sept, suppl.: Feb99: £54.50

Tolley's National Insurance Contributions suppl. for 98-99 out now, main vol. – Sept.

Chapter 21. **Insurance**

Association of British Insurers (ABI), 51 Gresham Street, London EC2V 7HQ (0171-600 3333)

British Insurance and Investment Brokers Association (BIIBA), 14 Bevis Marks, London EC3A 7NT (0171-623 9043)

Life Insurance Association (LIA), Citadel House, Station Approach, Chorleywood, Rickmansworth, Hertfordshire WD3 5PF (0923-285333)

Chapter 23. **Raising the money**

For information about the Alternative Investment market and OFEX contact Small Company Investor, 9 Harley Street, London W1N 1DA (0171-323 4050; Fax 0171-323 3614) www.smallcompanyinvestor.co.uk

Lenta Ventures at London Enterprise Agency (0171-236 3000) and Local Investment Networking Company (LINC) (0171-332 0877 Hotline 0171-329 4141) both at 4 Snow Hill, London EC1A 2BS

British Venture Capital Association, Essex House, 12-13 Essex Street, London WC2R 3AA (0171-240 3846). You can obtain a booklet from the BVCA listing all its members plus some information about what type of venture capital they offer. The booklet is free.

Another useful guide is: Management Guide to Buy-outs and Buy-ins, by Paul Smith and Alex Firth (Nov/Dec 1997), available from BDO Stoy Hayward, 8 Baker Street, London W1M 1DA (071-486 5888)

Chapter 24. **Staying afloat**

Some collection agencies are:

London Scottish Bank Plc, London Scottish House, Mount Street, Manchester, M2 3LS (0161-834 2861)

Credit Protection Association Ltd, 350 King Street, London W6 0RX (0181-846 0000)

Dun & Bradstreet International Ltd, Holmers Farm Way, High Wycombe, Bucks HP12 4UL (01494-422000)

Graydon UK Ltd, Hyde House, Edgware Road, Colindale, London NW9 6LW (0181-975 1050)

Inter-Credit International Ltd, Newby House, 309 Chase Road, Southgate, London N14 6JS (0181-482 4444)

Chapter 26. **Not waving but drowning**

For reading about coping with bankruptcy, try:

Bankruptcy Explained by John McQueen (The Bankruptcy Association, Oct. 1995) – £7.95

Contact:
The Bankruptcy Association of Great Britain and Ireland, 4 Johnson Close, Abraham Heights, Lancaster LA1 5EU (01524-64305)

Chapter 28. **Tax and the sole trader**

The Lloyds Bank Tax Guide 1998/99 by Sara Williams and John Willman (Profile Books, 1998) has another exposition of the tax treatment for the sole trader and gives more detail about capital gains tax. Phone 0171-323 3636 to buy copies over the phone.

See also the web site *http://www.taxguide.co.uk* which has information and tips regularly updated.

As a reference book on capital gains tax see *Tolley's Capital Gains Tax* (Tolley Publishing Company, suppl. for 98-99 out now, main vol. in Sept.).

Business Economic Notes are available from Inland Revenue Library, Room 28, New Wing, Somerset, Strand, London WC2R 1LB (0171-438 6325) or call the Information Centre (0171-438 6420) for a catalogue and prices.

Chapter 30. **Tax and the limited company**

As a reference book see Tolley's Corporation Tax 1997-98 (Tolley Publishing Company) (suppl. for 98-99 out now, main vol. in Sept.).

Chapter 32. VAT

As a reference book see Tolley's Value Added Tax 1997-98 (Tolley Publishing Company) (2 main vols this year; the 1st is out now, 2nd is out in Sept.).

Index

accident book 234
accountants 192–4
  and balance sheet 262
  and business plan 66, 193
  and buying a business 84, 85, 88, 193
  and journal 324
accounts 40–1, 74, 314
  auditing of 41, 193–4, 314
  business for sale 87–8
  computers and 186, 324
  of franchisor 103, 104
  help with 193, 194, 325
  taxation and 40, 42, 74, 314, 325, 342–3
    investigation of 343–4
  VAT 369–70, 372–3
  year-end choice 328–9
  see also records
advertising 20, 21, 137–48, 198
  of businesses for sale 84
  efficiency of 305
  of franchised product 101, 103, 106–7
    levy for 104, 109
  for mail order sales 156
  for staff 207–9
    and discrimination law 208, 224, 235–7
  to raise money 278
Advertising Standards Authority 156, 400
advice
  on business plan 29, 30, 66, 74, 193
  on buying a business 85
  on computers 186, 188–9
  on franchising 103, 105, 106, 114, 115
  for inventors and designers 135
  on logo 123
  professional 192–200, 273, 279–80, 362
  on starting up 27–37, 57, 58, 72
Advisory, Conciliation and Arbitration Service (ACAS) 220, 242, 405
after-sales care 16, 17
agencies/agents
  advertising 146
  business transfer 84
  credit-reporting 292, 296, 298
  debt-collection 295, 296, 406
  enterprise 27, 29, 32, 66, 177, 180, 192, 276, 383, 386–93, 394, 406
  estate 84, 180, 182, 197–8
  patent 130, 133, 135, 400
  recruitment 209–10
  sales 19, 20, 155, 205
  trade mark 135, 400
Alta Vista 24
Alternative Investment Market (AIM) 199, 273
  information on 404, 406
angels, business 199, 273, 278
appearance
  of premises 178, 189, 198, 199
  of product 17, 198
  see also image
Articles of Association 48–9
arts- and crafts-based businesses 10, 77, 156
assembly work 77
assets
  buying in business for sale 86, 93
  capital allowances and 190, 335–8
  current assets 262–3
  depreciation of 261, 262–3, 320, 324, 335
  fixed assets 262

records 315, 320, 324
long-life assets 335, 338
replacement of 340–1
sale of 51
 cash from 255
 retirement and 380–1
short-life assets 337
value, business for sale 95
VAT and 369–70
Assisted Areas 176, 177, 276, 401–3
Association of Authorised Public Accountants 193, 404
Association of British Insurers (ABI) 244–5, 405
Association of Chartered Certified Accountants 193, 404
attachment of earnings 227
Audit Bureau of Circulations (ABC) 145
auditing of accounts 41, 193–4, 314

balance sheet 40, 314, 342
 equipment on 190, 262
 forecast 262–5
bank 195–6, 270, 272
 advice/information from 32–3, 105, 194, 195
 business plan presented to 29, 30
 choice of 277
 loans from 276–8
 see also overdraft
bank account 290–1
bank balance, forecasts 251, 252–4, 257
bank charges and interest 290–1
 in cash flow forecast 257
bank statements 289, 316–17
bankruptcy 39, 295, 311
Bankruptcy Association 312, 407
black economy 360
books on small businesses 34
brainstorming sessions 11, 124
brand image 121–2
 see also image
break-even point 283–6

staff costs and 216–18
British Franchise Association 105, 106, 114, 118, 399
British Rate and Data (BRAD) 145, 209
British Venture Capital Association 383, 406
brochures 73, 139, 198
budget 287–8
 cash flow 289
 control system 75
building control officer 183–4
building society account 291
Business in the Community 383, 393
Business Connects/Links/Shops 27, 29, 31, 66, 177, 180, 188, 192
Business Cooperation Network (BC-Net) 156, 400
Business Economic Notes (Inland Revenue) 407
business format franchising 102
 see also franchising
Business Pages 85
business plan 64–70, 72, 74, 269, 270
 advice on 29, 30, 66, 74, 193
 and finance 13
 length 66–9
 preliminary sketch 11–12
 presentation of 69, 276, 280–1
 to control business 287–8, 289
 training for 29, 35
 writer of plan 66
business for sale *see* buying a business
business transfer agents 84
buy-ins/buy-outs by management 81, 99–100
buying a business 72, 81–100
 accountant and 84, 85, 88, 193
 see also franchising

call diversion service 76, 186
capital
 in balance sheet forecast 263
 in cash flow forecast 255

working 271–2, 306
capital allowances 190
  in enterprise zones 176
capital gains 43, 350–1
  loss set against 338
capital gains tax (CGT) 79, 340–1
  on home-as-workplace 179, 332, 340
  limited company 350–1
  partnership 346
  reinvestment relief 278
  on retirement 380–1
car, company 189, 231
  insurance of 245–6
  taxation and 331, 332, 335, 355
cash
  on balance sheet 263
  business for sale 91
  control over 8, 74, 282, 283, 288–91, 301, 372
  forecasts of cash flow 56–7, 251, 252–7, 266, 289
  insurance against loss of 247
  payment in form of 228, 271
  records for 289, 298, 314, 315–17, 323
casual earnings, taxation of 357–8
catalogues 143, 156
Challenge funds 176
Chambers of Commerce 27, 177, 384
Channel Islands, VAT and 364
chargeable gains 349, 350–1
charities, grants and loans from 35–6, 276
charity donations 227
Chartered Institute of Patent Agents 135, 400
Child Support Agency payments 227
close companies 353
clubs, small business 33–4
Commission for Racial Equality 220, 236, 405
commission: on sales 153–4, 155, 205, 306
communications
  equipment 185–6, 187

location and 175
community cooperative 52
Companies House 124, 125, 398
Companies Registration Office 40, 398
company *see* limited company
company secretary 40, 48, 311
competitions: for businesses 276
competitors
  assessment of 21, 72
  criticism of, when selling 159
  information on 24, 25, 34
  price and 162, 163, 165, 166, 167, 169, 171
computers 186–9
  for accounts 186, 324
  for forecasting 66, 186
  insurance of 249
  and modems 23–4, 187
  for sales 186–7
  and tax 332
  see also Internet
Confederation of British Industry (CBI), code of practice on prompt payment 292
consortium 33, 156
consultancy
  for business start-up 30–1
  design 17, 73, 123, 198–9
  management 193, 194
  recruitment 209–10
  and taxation 357, 360
Consumer Credit Act (1974) 190, 277
consumer market 15, 24–5
  see also retail business
contract hire 191
contract staff 204–5
contract(s)
  advice on 115, 183, 196
  of employment 75, 208, 215, 223, 224, 225–6, 228, 229
  for franchise 103, 105, 108, 111, 115–18
Contributions Agency 40, 41, 47, 341
cooperative 38, 50–2, 73

in marketing/purchasing/service 33, 51,
      156
Cooperative Union 51
corporate finance advisers 66, 73, 199–200,
   273, 280
corporation tax 42, 349
   calculations 349, 350–1
   in cash flow forecast 256
   payment of 351, 352–3
   rate 351, 352
cost(s)
   of advertising 137, 138–9, 143, 144,
      145, 146, 209
   and break-even point 216–18, 282,
      283–6
   of buying a business 82, 83, 94–7
      calculations 96–7
      negotiations over 94–5, 97–9
   of buying a franchise 101, 103, 106,
      108–10, 117
   calculation of 164–6
   control of 60
   cutting of 300, 301–3, 306
   of design registration 133
   direct 164, 166, 259–60, 284–6
      employee costs as 216, 260
   of equipment 187, 189, 257
      paying for 190–1, 289–90
   forecasts 8, 73, 166, 259–61
   indirect 164, 166
   of insurance 244
   of logo 123
   of patent 130
   of premises 176, 177, 178, 181, 283, 331
      see also rates; rent
   and price 162, 164–6, 171, 303
   of professional advice 194, 196, 197,
      198, 199, 200
   of staff 215–18, 255, 260, 283–4
      recruitment 201, 204–5, 209, 210
      see also pay
   of stationery 125
   of trade mark registration 134

council tax 57, 331–2
counselling 27, 30–3, 35–6
   and business plan 30, 66
court order: and deductions from pay 227
credibility of business 39
   equipment and 186, 189
   professional advisers and 194, 197
   see also image
credit 74
   control of 247, 291–3
   from suppliers 297–8
   insurance for 247
   terms 293
      of business for sale 90, 91, 92
      and working capital 271–2
credit or charge card, business 290–1
credit sale, equipment paid for by 190
credit-reporting agencies 292, 296, 298
creditors, in forecasts 264, 265
criminal record: of employee 237
curriculum vitae (CV) 208, 210, 212
customers
   of business for sale 90–1, 92, 94
   and credibility of business 39
   needs 13–14, 17–18, 24
      selling to 158, 159
   payments by 271–2, 289, 291–7, 303,
      304
      and failure 309
      in forecasts 254, 259
   personal relations with 7, 150–1
   potential 151–2, 158–61, 186
      assessment of 291–3
      groups 14–17
      information from 24–5, 34, 152
      see also market research
   and price 165, 166, 167–8, 171
   records 149, 151, 152
Customs and Excise
   debt collection by 295
   see also VAT

Dalton's Weekly 84

Data Protection Registrar 188, 403
debt, liability for 39, 47, 50, 51, 87, 311
debt-collection agencies 295, 296, 406
debtors 291–7
    in forecasts 254, 263
debt(s), bad
    insurance against 247
    tax and 333
    VAT and 372, 374
deductions from pay 227–8, 323–4
Deductions (PAYE) Working Sheet 230,
    231
delivery
    insurance cover 247
    location and 175–6
    market segmentation and 16, 17
    price and 167, 168
    VAT and 368
    vehicles for 127, 139, 198
demonstrations 139, 159
    requests for 152
depreciation 262
    example 263
    records 320, 324
    tax and 335
design, registration of 73, 131–3, 135, 196,
    334
design consultant 17, 73, 123, 198–9
design right 132
desk research 22–4
development agencies/boards/commissions
    32, 393
Development Areas 177, 401–3
Development Board for Rural Wales 32,
    393
direct selling 19, 20, 75, 139, 140, 149–61,
    305–6
    location and 175
directories, business
    entry in 124, 146–7
    information from 23, 85, 142
director(s) 40, 48
    as employee 42, 255

fringe benefits 231, 353, 354–5
    insolvency and 310, 311
    insurance of 50, 248
    liability for debt 39, 50, 311
    pension arrangements 354, 379–80
    responsibilities 49–50
    taxation of 326, 353–4
    venture capital and 279
disabled people
    discrimination against 222, 224, 237
    help for 35, 36, 394
disciplinary procedure: for staff 225–6
discounts
    payment 293, 304, 316, 368
    price 304
    VAT and 368
discrimination law 220, 235–7
    and pregnancy 238, 240
    and recruitment 208, 222, 224, 235–6
dismissal of staff 201, 215, 220, 224, 225,
    240–3
    constructive 234, 242
    for gross misconduct 242
    while pregnant 238
    see also discrimination law
distributors and distribution 19, 20, 155
    of business for sale 92–3
    and market segmentation 16
dividends 349, 353, 355
driving licence: of job applicant 215
due diligence investigation 279
duopoly 20

earnings multiple calculations, business for
    sale 95–6, 97
elasticity of demand 167–8
e-mail 187
employees see staff and employees
employer, rights and duties as 93, 205,
    220–43, 245, 248
employment
    contract(s) 75, 208, 215, 223, 224,
    225–6, 228, 229

current 71, 73
departure from 75
starting up while in 76–7, 356
Employment Sevice 222
enterprise agencies 27, 29, 32, 66, 177, 180, 192, 276
addresses 383, 386–93, 394, 406
Enterprise Investment Scheme 278
enterprise zones 176
entertaining expenses 333, 334
environmental health department 184, 233
Equal Opportunities Commission 220, 404, 405
equal pay 227, 230
equipment 74, 185–91
of business for sale 89–90
costs 187, 189
forecasting and 257
depreciation of 261, 262, 263
of franchised business 105, 106, 112
insurance of 246, 249
paying for 190–1, 289
tax and 190, 191, 335–8
equity participation cooperative 52
estate agents 84, 180, 182, 197–8
ethnic minorities
help for 35, 36, 394
see also race discrimination
European Information Centres 383
European Patent Convention 129
European Social Chapter 220
European Union (EU)
patents in 129
selling in 156
suitability of name for 124
trade marks in 134
Exchange and Mart 84
exhibitions, business 24, 25, 34, 139, 151
expenses, business 331–4
export(s) *see* import/export business
Extel cards 85

factoring service 247, 296–7

failure 3, 308–12
causes 8, 19, 282
coping with 6–7
family plan for 275
warning signs 282, 309–10
family
employment in business of 204, 333, 353–4
failure plan of 275
income from 56–7
insurance of 249
location of premises and 177–8
support from 56–7, 71, 73
financial 5–6, 274
when working from home 79, 179
fashion and beauty businesses 77
fax machines 186
Federation of Recruitment and Employment Services 210, 404
Federation of Small Businesses 33–4, 394
fidelity insurance 247, 249
finance
amount of 270–1
business expansion 271, 279, 306
business plan and 64–5, 68, 69, 269, 270, 276–7, 280–1
to buy a business 81, 83
credibility and 194, 197
forecasts and 22, 251
form of 272–3
for franchise 72, 110
and independence 6
large amounts 271
and legal form of business 44
for management buy-out 99–100
and market research 13
personal financial commitment and 274–6
personal guarantees and 39, 73, 110, 272, 275
professional advisers and 193, 194, 195, 197, 199–200, 273, 279–80
raising of 73, 74, 269–81

reasons for 271–2
size of business and 8
sources 274–80
starting to trade and 74, 75
training courses and 29, 35
for young people 36, 211, 276
see also loan(s); overdraft; share(s);
    venture capital
Financial Services Authority 245
financial skills 1, 11, 28, 58–9, 194
Financial Times 34, 84, 278
fire insurance 246
fire officer 184
fiscal accounting 326, 327
floating charge: on assets 44, 272, 311
forecast(s) 8, 72, 73, 251–68
    balance sheet 262–5
    and budget 287–8, 289
    cash flow 56–7, 73, 251, 252–7, 266
    computers used 66, 186
    cost 73, 166, 251, 259–61
    profit and loss 258–61, 267
    sales 19–22, 72, 74, 149, 166, 251, 259
    see also business plan
Form 10 and Form 12 49
forms, tax *see* P11D; P45; P46; P60
Forum of Private Business 34, 394
fragmented supply position 20
Franchisee Guide 114
franchising 72, 101–19
    finance for 72, 110
    guide to choosing 105–7
    pluses and minuses 103–5
Franchisor's Manual 118
fraud
    tax 356, 360
    trading 39, 50, 308
freelance staff 204–5
Freepost service 143
fringe benefits 217, 231, 291, 353, 354–5
furniture, office 189

gifts, business 139, 332, 333, 334

going concern, sale of business as 84, 86,
    117, 369, 375
Golden Key project 33, 195
goods received, records for 321
goods in transit, insurance of 247
goodwill
    of business for sale 84, 86, 91, 95
    and tax 340, 341
government
    assistance from 176–7, 205, 276
    effect on markets 21
    information from 23, 24
    see also individual departments and
        schemes
grants 276
    advice on 31, 32
    in enterprise zones 176
    for innovative ideas 276
    for young people 36, 211, 276
grievance procedure: for staff 225–6
guarantee, company limited by 51
guarantee payment 229–30
guarantee(s) for loans 39, 73, 110, 272, 275,
    277
Guardian 34, 84, 278

hardware, computer 187
headed notepaper *see* letterhead
health 232–4, 237
health insurance 249
Health and Safety Executive (HSE) 179,
    184, 233, 234
Health and Safety Law Poster 233, 234
heating and lighting
    in forecasts 256–7, 260
    and tax 331, 332
    and VAT 366
Highland & Islands Enterprise 393
hire purchase 190, 246
    in forecasts 257
    and tax 333, 335
hobby: as basis for business 10
holiday accommodation 359–60, 365

holiday pay 228, 232
home
    insurance and 179, 246, 247
    as security for loan 275
    working from 77, 78–9, 178–9
        taxation and 78, 79, 179, 331, 332,
        340, 356, 358–9
hotel business 358, 365
hourly workers 229–30

idea
    advice with 30–3
    business 2, 8, 9–12, 72, 270–1
    checklist analysis 60–2
identity of business
    legal form 38–52
    name 120–7
image 121, 122, 125–7, 198–9, 303, 306
    advertising and 139, 143, 147
    equipment and 186, 189
    of franchised business 101
    ideas on 75
    price and 168
    see also letterhead; name; packaging
import/export business
    information sources 383–5
    location of 175
    VAT and 364, 368, 369
    see also European Union
income
    accounts as confirmation of 40
    concealment of 356, 360
    domestic requirements 57
    loss set against 338
    personal 5–6, 342, 353
    spare-time 78, 356–61
    toe-dipping and 76, 77, 356
Incorporated Society of Valuers and Auc-
    tioneers 197, 404
independence 4–5, 6
    of franchisee 104
independent intermediaries 245
Industrial Common Ownership Movement

(ICOM) 51, 399
industrial development officer 180
industrial markets 16, 18, 122
inflation, effects 304, 350, 364
Infoseek software 24
inheritance tax 381
Inland Revenue 75
    debt collection by 295
    investigation by 343–4, 360
    PAYE system 42, 75, 230–1, 323, 326,
        341
    and self-assessment 325, 329–30, 342–3
    see also tax
Inner City Task Forces 176
innovation centres 135
insolvency 50, 309, 311
Instant Muscle 35, 394
Institute of Business Advisers 393, 404
Institute of Directors 398
Institute of Management 393
Institute of Management Consultants 194,
    404
Institute of Trade Mark Agents 135
Institute(s) of Chartered Accountants 193,
    403–4
insurance 74, 244–50
    for business 74, 79
    of business for sale 89
    for directors 50, 248
    employers' liability 233, 245
    in forecasts 257
    of premises 79, 89, 179, 246
    tax and 331, 333
Insurance Brokers Registration Council
    244
interest
    on extra cash 290
    on loan/overdraft 277
        in forecasts 257, 261
        and tax 333, 359
Intermediate Areas 177, 400–3
Internet
    advertising via 139, 147

equipment needed 23, 187
information from 23–4, 382–3,
    385–6, 394, 406, 407
interviews
    and discrimination law 224, 235–7
    of job applicants 211–15
    in market research 24–5
    tax investigation 343–4
invention(s)
    grants for 276
    requirements for patent 128–31
    see also patents
investment income
    limited company 349
    partnership 346, 347
invoice(s)
    discounting of 296
    in 255, 260, 319–20
    out 254, 259, 294, 315, 317–18, 322
    tax: for VAT 369, 370–1

Jobcentre 207, 210, 211, 222
job description 203
joint ventures 32, 33, 156
journal, accounts 324

keyman insurance 248

labels 126, 147
land
    restrictive covenants on 179
    tax and 340, 341, 359
    values 174
    see also premises
landlord 182, 183, 365
language services 395–7
late payment charge 293
Law Society 404
Lawyers for Your Business scheme 196, 398
leads, sales 152, 305–6
leaflets 140, 141, 143, 147, 198
leasing
    of equipment 190–1, 289, 332, 335

and insurance 246
    of premises 182–4
    of property, commercial 359, 365
legal aspects
    advice 196–7
    business name 124–5
    employment 208, 221–3, 229–30
    franchise 111, 115–18
    premises lease 183
    see also solicitors
legal expenses 334
legal expenses insurance 248
legal form of business
    advice on 196
    business for sale 86–7
    choice of 45–6, 73
    pros and cons of each 38–46
    see also cooperative; limited company;
        partnership
letterhead 73, 74, 125–6, 139, 147, 198
    for limited company 49
    for sole trader 47
    and spare-time earnings 357
liabilities: on balance sheet 263–5
liability for debt 39, 47, 50, 51, 87, 311
libraries, information from 23, 29, 33, 34,
    145
life insurance 245, 354, 379
    for loans 278
lighting *see* heating and lighting
limited company
    accounts 40–1, 314
    buying of 93
    capital gains 350–1, 380–1
    cooperative as 51
    credibility 39
    credit cards and 290–1
    debts 39, 50, 311
    decision to opt for 45–6, 73
    franchise as 110
    insolvency 50, 310–11
    losses 43, 351–2
    name 49, 73, 124–5

national insurance and 42, 353, 355,
375–6
pensions and 43, 354, 375–6, 379–80
pros and cons 38–46
raising money by 44, 273
see also venture capital
selling part 44, 380–1
setting up as 40, 48–50, 75
small
corporation tax rate 351, 352
definition 41
taxation of 42, 43, 75, 349–55
cash flow forecast and 255, 256
liquidator 311
sale of business by 84
literature 75, 140, 143, 147, 198
requests for 152
LiveWire scheme 36, 276, 394
Loan Guarantee Scheme 276, 277
loan(s) 44, 273, 276–8
of business for sale 91
tax relief on 275, 333, 353, 359
see also overdraft
local authorities 27
advice on premises 180
assistance from 176–7, 276
effect on markets 21
planning requirements 178, 179, 183–4
local enterprise agencies/trusts 27, 29, 32, 33
see also enterprise agencies
Local Enterprise Companies (LECs) 29, 32, 391–3
see also Training and Enterprise Councils (TECs)
Local Enterprise Development Unit (LEDU) 32, 393
Local Investment Networking Company (LINC) 278, 406
location of businesses/premises 174–8
business for sale 83, 84, 88–9
franchised business 110–11
and job advertisements 208

and market segmentation 15, 16
retail business 88–9
logo 123, 147, 198, 199
trade mark as 133
uses 126
London Gazette 310
long-term objectives *see* business plan
loss leader 301
loss(es)
and break-even point 283–5
profit and loss forecast 258–61
tax and 43, 338–9, 348, 351–2, 357–8

magazines *see* newspapers and magazines
mail order business 156
Mail Order Protection Scheme (MOPS) 156, 400
mail shots 141–4, 187
follow-up to 152
maintenance and after-care 16, 17
management buy-ins 81
management buy-outs 99–100
management consultancy 193, 194
management skills 8, 271
in business plan 65, 67
checklist analysis 60
and size of business 8, 72
manufacturing business
buying a 92–3
equipment for 185
marital status, discrimination on grounds of 224, 235
market 8
in business plan 65, 67–8
choice of 10–11
entry to 8, 10
leader 15, 128, 168, 169–70, 172–3
new 301, 306
potential 19–20
and price 162, 165, 167–9
research 10–11, 13–26, 72, 306
inadequate 8
on logos 123

on names 124
and potential customers 152
techniques 22–5
when buying a business 82, 83, 84–85
when buying a franchise 106, 114–15
while currently employed 77
segmentation of 14–17, 19, 72
advertising and 138
product name and 73, 122–3
share 20–1, 72
price and 168, 170–1
size 19, 72
structure 19–20
testing of 25, 73, 169
trends 21, 72
marketing
in business plan 67–8
of business for sale 83
cooperative 33, 51, 156
of franchised product 101, 103–4, 106, 112, 113
and market share 20–1
niche 14, 15
planning of 73, 75
and protection of innovation 128, 135
skills in 59
training in 28
see also advertising
maternity *see* pregnancy; Statutory Maternity Pay
medical certificate 229
medical examination: of employees 215, 237
Memorandum of Association 48
mentors, business 32, 36
minimum national wage 220
Misdeclaration Penalty 372
mobile phones 76, 186
modems 23, 187
money
as personal objective 4, 5–6

raising of *see* finance, raising of
motor insurance 245–6

name
of business 120–7
limited company 49, 73, 124–5
sole trader 47
of product 73, 120–7
franchised 103–4, 106–7, 109, 116
of trade mark 123, 133–5
national insurance (NI) contributions 375–6
in forecasts 255–6, 260
legal form of business and 41–2, 255–6, 355
limited company 42, 353, 355, 375
sick pay and 228, 229
sole trader 339–40
of staff 226, 227, 230–1, 323, 333
negotiations
for business for sale 94–5, 97–9
for premises lease/purchase 182–3, 197
with suppliers 302
and franchise 101
neighbourhood cooperative 51
New Deal scheme 205
newspapers and magazines
advertising in 140, 144–6, 156
for staff 207–9
to raise money 278
advertising through 141, 144–6
information from 24, 34, 84, 85, 180
public relations via 140–1
niche *see* market, segmentation of
notice of dismissal 225, 242–3

OFEX trading facility 199, 404, 406
'off-the-peg' business *see* buying a business; ready-made companies
office services, businesses in 77, 78
Official Receiver 311
older people, discrimination against 224, 235

oligopoly 20
operational skills 60
operations manual: of franchise 104, 111
order size 304
OUTREACH Programmes 36
overdraft 44, 272, 291, 309
    in balance sheet forecast 263, 264
    of business for sale 91
    in cash flow forecast 252
    interest on 257, 261, 277, 333, 359
overheads 283
    break-even point and 282, 283–6
    employee costs as 216, 261, 283–4
    forecasts 260–1
    price and 164, 166
overlap profits 328
ownership change, effect on business 93–4,
    117, 375

P11D form 231
P45 form 224, 231, 243, 341
P46 form 224, 231
P60 form 231
packaging 126, 147, 198
    VAT and 368
pagers 186
partnership
    accounts 40, 314
    agreement 40, 48, 73, 87, 273, 312
    buying a share in 86, 87, 88
    capital gains 346
    cooperative as 51
    credibility 39
    debts 39, 47, 51, 87, 312
    decision to opt for 45–6, 72, 73
    failure of 312
    leaving of 348
    losses 43, 348
    national insurance and 41–2
    new partners in 44, 273, 348
    pensions and 43
    pros and cons 38–46
    raising money by 44, 275

    selling part 44
    setting up as 40, 47–8, 75
    taxation of 42, 43, 75, 275, 346–8
        cash flow forecast and 255, 256
part-time staff 205
    legal obligations to 221, 242
patent agents 400
Patent Office 129, 130–1, 132, 135, 400
patent(s) 122, 128–31, 135
    agent(s) 130, 133, 135, 400
    application for 73, 130–1, 196
    of business for sale 91
    choice of name and 122
    in Europe 129
    of franchised product 106, 116
    tax and 334, 336
pay
    as business expense 333
    in cash flow forecast 255
    deductions from 227, 323
    in job advertisements 208
    legal considerations 226–32, 239, 242
    maternity 239
    profit-related 306
    records 323–4
    redundancy 242
    sales representatives 153, 205, 306
    written statement/slip 227–8, 323, 324
PAYE system 42, 75, 230–1, 323, 326
    in forecasts 255–6, 260
    refunds 341
    spare-time earnings and 358
penetration policy 167, 170–1
pensions, retirement
    from scheme 43, 354, 376–80
        advice on 245, 249
    from state 41–2, 339, 353, 375–6
performance of product 17–18, 73
Period of Incapacity for Work (PIW) 229
Personal Business Advisers (PBAs) 32
personal characteristics
    and fitness to run a business 1–12,
        53–5, 62, 71, 72

of new employees 205–6
personal guarantees
    for loans 39, 73, 110, 272, 275
    for premises lease 183
Personal Investment Authority (PIA) 245
personal relations 5, 7, 87
    with bank manager 195, 277
    with customers 7, 150–1
    with franchisor 107
    with suppliers 7
petty cash records 315, 317, 322
photographs: for press release 141
piece-rate workers 229–30
plan *see* business plan
planning regulations 47, 176, 178, 179, 183,
    197
plant and machinery
    of business for sale 89–90
    and tax 336–8, 340–1
population centres, location in or near to
    175–6
postage
    and advertising 143, 144
    costs of, in forecasts 257
    and mail order 156
power, sense of 5, 7
pregnancy of employee 221–2, 223, 238–40
premises 174–84
    appearance 178, 189, 198, 199
    of business for sale 88–9, 95
    costs 178, 182, 283
        rent and rates 176, 177, 182, 183,
            256, 260, 365
        tax and 331–2
    of franchised business 111, 112, 116
    health and safety of 232–4
    insurance of 246
    search for 74, 180–2
    suitability 47
    survey of 182, 197–8
    see also home, working from; location
press releases 141
prestige pricing 163

price sensitivity 167–8, 171, 303, 305
price-skimming strategy 163, 168
price(s) and pricing 8, 74, 162–73
    of business for sale 93
    cutting of 305
    increasing of 300, 303–4, 306
    and market leader 15
    and market segmentation 16
    and market structure 20
    more than one product 172
    payable by business *see* costs
    war 171, 305
Prince's Youth Business Trust 36, 276, 394
private investors 278
problem-sharing 33
    see also advice; counselling
product (or service)
    in business plan 65, 67
    of business for sale 92–3
    choice of 8, 72
    demand for 13–14, 17–18, 24–5, 159
    differentiation of 14, 17–18, 72, 167,
        168
    of franchised business 101, 103–4, 106,
        112
    knowledge of, in selling 153, 154, 156–7
    liability insurance 248
    lifecycle of 167
    name 73, 120–7
    new 301, 306
    operational skills 60
    packaging of 126, 147, 198, 368
    protection of uniqueness 128–31, 196
        see also design registration;
            patent(s); trade mark
    reduction of range 300, 303
production run, initial 74
professional advisers 192–200, 273, 279–80,
    362
    fees to, in forecasts 257, 261
    see also accountants; corporate finance
        advisers; solicitors; surveyors
professional indemnity insurance 248

professional markets 16
profit-sharing scheme 306
profit(s)
    of business for sale 88, 93
    forecasts of 258–61, 267
    of franchises 101, 103, 104, 107, 109
    increasing of 300–7
    insurance against loss of 246–7
    loss set against future 338–9
    margin 166, 216, 218, 284–6
        and tax inspector 343
    of partnership 347
    taxable 328, 329, 347, 350
property *see* premises
property business, commercial 359, 365
public liability insurance 248
public relations (PR) 20, 21, 140–1
purchases *see* suppliers and supplies
purchasing cooperative 33
pyramid selling 113–14

quality
    price and 168, 170
    product 18, 304
    reputation for 20–1
quotes to customers 154, 155, 159, 302–3,
    306

race discrimination 220, 236
    and recruitment 208, 224, 236, 405
rates 176, 177
    in forecasts 256, 260
'ready-made' companies 40, 49, 73
    see also buying a business
receiver, sale of business by 84, 86, 99
records 313–24
    for cash control 290, 293, 294, 298,
        315–17, 323
    of customers 149, 151, 152
    insurance of 249
    of sales 24, 75, 149, 151, 294, 306, 314,
        317–18, 322, 324
    of spare-time earnings 357

    of staff pay 323–4
    of telephone calls 154
    of VAT 317, 318, 319, 320–1, 369,
        370–3
    see also accounts
recruitment 75, 201, 207–11, 303
    costs of 201, 204, 209, 211, 215–16
    interviews 211–15, 224, 235–6
    law and 208, 225–6, 230, 235–7
    preparatory work for 202–3
redundancy 242
references
    bank/credit/trade 292
    of job applicants 215
referrals, sales 151, 152
registered design 132–3
registered office 48, 49
registered trade mark 134–5
Registrar of Companies 48, 49
reinvestment relief 278
rent 182, 183
    in forecasts 256, 260
    and VAT 365
Rent-a-Room scheme 358–9
reporting, management 75, 287–8
representatives, sales 153–5, 205, 246, 306
reputation 20, 121, 125–7, 138
    price and 168
    sales and 159
    see also credibility; goodwill; image
retail business
    buying of 84, 88, 94
    computers and 186–7
    franchised 110, 111, 112
    image 126
    information from 24–5
    insurance of 249
    premises for 88–9, 174, 177
    sales by and to 156
    VAT and 371
retirement 375–81
    business for sale due to 86, 375
    tax relief on 380–1

pension at 41–2, 43, 339, 353, 354, 375–81
  advice on 245, 249
return on capital employed: business for sale 96
risks 4, 6
  of debtors 291–3
  of franchising 101
  identification of 74
  see also insurance
Royal Institution of Chartered Surveyors 182, 197, 404
royalty, franchise 104, 108
rural businesses 177
Rural Development Commission 32, 393

safety 232–4
salary *see* pay
sales 149–61
  agents 19–20, 155
  of assets *see* assets
  and break-even point 282, 283–6
  of business for sale 92
  cash from 254
  cycle 25
  dialogue 75, 149, 157
  and extra staff 201
  forecasts 8, 19–22, 72, 149, 251, 259
  of franchises 101, 103, 108–9
  ideas for 74
  increasing of 300, 304–6
  location and 175–6
  mix of 300–1
  and price 163, 165, 168, 303
  records 75, 151, 294, 314, 317–18, 322, 324
    as source of information 24, 149, 306
  staff 149, 153–5, 205, 246, 306
  terms and conditions 75, 155
  training in 28, 149, 154
  VAT and 364–5
science parks 179–80

secretary, company 40, 48, 311
self-assessment: of tax 325, 329–30, 342, 346, 353
  payment of tax 326, 329, 342, 358
  penalties 360
self-employed status, tax inspector and 341, 344, 357
selling 149–61
  see also sales
service *see* product
service cooperative 51
service fee
  bank account 290
  franchise 104, 108–9
service mark 133–5, 196
  see also trade mark
sex discrimination law 220, 235
  and pay 230
  and pregnancy 238–40
  and recruitment 208, 224, 235
shares 273, 380
  dividend(s) from 349, 353, 355
shops *see* retail business
sick pay 228–9
Signpost Database 382, 385–6
Single Regeneration Budget programmes 176, 276
size of business 8, 72, 83, 163
size of market 19, 72
skills
  assessment of 9–10, 57–60, 72
  insufficiency 8, 58, 72
  of job applicant 202, 210–11
  range 6
  of selling 149, 154, 156–61
  see also training
sleeping partner(s) 47
Small Business Bureau 34, 394
small business centres 179
small business clubs 33
small business organizations 33–4, 393–4
SMART grant scheme 276
social security benefits 41, 42, 339–40

software 24, 187, 332
sole trader
    accounts 40, 314, 315
    alternative name as 125
    bankruptcy of 311
    buying of business 86, 88, 93
    capital gains 350–1
    credibility 39
    debts 39
    decision to opt for 45–6, 73
    franchisee as 110
    losses 43, 338–9
    national insurance and 41–2, 339–40,
        375–6
    pensions and 43, 376–9
    pros and cons 38–46
    raising money by 44, 273, 275, 277
    selling part of business 44
    setting up as 39–40, 47, 75
    taxation of 42, 47, 75, 275, 325–45
        capital gains 340–1
        cash flow forecasts and 255, 256
solicitors 196–7
    debt-collection advice 295
    franchise advice 105, 115, 196
    lease advice 183, 196
    partnership agreement and 40, 48, 87,
        196
spare-time earnings, tax on 78, 356–61
spreadsheets 66
staff and employees 201–19
    of business for sale 93
    clothing for 198
    conditions and terms for 225–32
    contracts with 75, 208, 215, 223, 224,
        225–6, 228, 229
    credit card for 290–1
    criminal record 237
    dismissal 201, 215, 220, 224, 225, 234,
        238, 240–3
    incompetence 234
    insurance of 233, 245, 247, 248
    legal obligations to 93, 221–2

    insurance and 245
        part-time staff 221, 242
        temporary staff 205
    location and 175
    market information from 24
    numbers 303
    personal relations with 7
    profit-awareness 306
    records for 315, 322, 323–4
    recruitment of 75, 201, 207–11, 303
        costs of 205, 209, 215–16
        interviewing 211–15, 224, 235–6
        law and 208, 225–6, 230, 235–7
        preparatory work for 202–3
    reporting system for 75, 287–8
    salary and wages *see* pay
    sales 149, 153–5, 205, 246, 306
    as team 7, 8, 65, 271
    theft by 247
starting up
    advice on 27–37, 57, 58, 72
    buying a business 81–100
    checklist analysis before 53–63
    and choice of legal form 38–52, 73
    costs 73, 271
    as franchisee 101–19
    as franchisor 118
    as limited company 40, 48–50, 75
    as partnership 40, 47–8, 75
    personal characteristics and 1–12, 53–5,
        62, 71, 72
    reasons for 3–4
    as sole trader 39–40, 47, 75
    taxation and 326, 327–8, 341
    timing 71–5
    while currently employed 76–8, 356
    working at home 77, 78–9, 178–9
    see also idea; market research
state earnings-related pension scheme
(SERPS) 375–6, 379
stationery *see* letterhead
Statutory Maternity Pay 227, 239, 324
Statutory Sick Pay 227, 228–9, 324

stickers 126
stock
    on balance sheet 263
    of business for sale 90
    control of 60, 90, 186–7, 302, 314–15,
        321–2
    of franchised business 112
    initial 74
    and mail order 156
    and working capital 272
stress 4, 6
success, criteria for 7
Sunday Times 84, 278
suppliers and supplies
    of business for sale 91–2
    of franchises 101, 103, 104, 106, 109
    image with 189
    location near to 176
    payments to 272, 289, 290, 297–8, 303
        and failure 309
        in forecasts 255, 259–60
    personal relations with 7
    potential, identification of 73
    records 314, 319–20, 321, 322, 324
    renegotiation with 302
    taxable, for VAT 363, 364–5
Surcharge Liability Notice 373
survey: of premises 182, 197–8
surveyors 197–8

tax 42–3, 75, 325–61
    accounts for purpose of 40, 41, 314,
        325, 342
        investigation of 343–4
    allowances 190, 191, 325, 335–8
    assessment of 342
    calculation of 330–1, 347
    and equipment 190, 191, 335–8
    in forecasts 255–6, 260, 264
    limited company 349–55
    and loans 275, 333, 353, 359
    partnership 346–8
    payment of 326–30

interest on overdue payments
    352–3, 360
pensions and 377–8, 380
professional advice and 193, 194, 325
reinvestment relief 278
on spare-time earnings 78, 356–61
and staff 224, 227, 230–1, 333
    in cash flow forecast 255–6
    records 231, 315, 323–4
and working from home 78, 79, 179,
    331–2, 340
see also VAT
tax return 342–3
    incorrect/incomplete, penalty for 342,
        343, 356, 360
    of partnership 347–8
team
    buy-outs by 99–100
    management 7, 8, 65, 271
TECS *see* Training and Enterprise Councils
telephone 185–6
    answering machine/service 76, 186
    bill
        in forecasts 257, 260
        and tax 331, 332
    call diversion service 76, 186
    recruitment and 209
    sales and 149, 154, 157, 158, 306
    survey by 24
temporary staff 204–5, 225
territorial rights: of franchised business
    106, 110–11, 116
test trials 25, 73, 169
theft, insurance against 245, 247
time management 303
time sheets 322
Times, The 34, 84, 278
timing of start 71–5
toe-dipping 76–80, 356
trade associations 24, 85, 142
trade exhibitions and fairs 24, 25, 34, 85,
    139, 151

Trade and Industry, Department of (DTI) 31, 276, 277, 311
  addresses 384, 385, 399–400, 401
trade magazines 24, 85
  advertising through 141, 144, 145, 209
trade mark 133–5
  agent(s) 135, 400
  of business for sale 91
  choice of name as 123, 133–5
  of franchised product 106, 116
  quality 18
  registration of 73, 134–5, 196, 334
    proposed, in Europe 134
  testing of 73
Trade Marks Journal 135
Trade Marks Registry 134–5
Trading Schemes Act 113
training 27, 28–9
  and business plan 29, 66
  of franchisee 104, 111, 112
  of new employees 202, 215
  in selling 28, 149, 154
  to plug skills gaps 6, 8, 28, 58, 72
  for women 35
  for young people 35
Training and Enterprise Councils (TECs) 27, 29, 31, 32, 75, 177, 180, 192, 211, 276
  addresses 386–91
troubleshooters: in franchising 113
type of work 4, 6

unemployed people
  help for 35, 36
  inital preparation 71
uniforms 198
union dues/subs 227
union membership
  discrimination on grounds of 236–7
  redundancy and 242
unit trusts, dividends from 349

VAT 362–74
  in balance sheet forecast 263, 265
  as business expense 332–3
  calculation of 368–70
  in forecasts 254, 256, 260
  payment of 373–4
  rates of 366–7
  records 317, 318, 319, 320–1, 369, 370–3
  registration for 40, 47, 74, 357, 363–6, 367
  spare-time earnings and 357
vehicle livery 127, 139, 198
venture capital 44, 273, 279–80
  British VC Association 383, 406
  business plan and 66
  management buy-ins and 81
  professional advisers and 194, 199, 279–80
vertical marketing 16
victimization 236, 237
village businesses 177
volume sales 14
  location and 175
voluntary arrangements, formal 310–11

wages *see* pay
Wages Orders 227
web sites *see* Internet
Welsh Development Agency 32, 393
wholesalers 155
  see also distributors
winding-up of company 310–12
women
  discrimination against 235
  help for 35, 394
  pregnancy of 221–2, 223, 238–40
  see also sex discrimination
word processing 77, 186
worker cooperative 51
working capital 271–2, 306
working hours 4, 6
  limited availability 77
  of staff 225, 232

workshops, managed 179
writing-down allowances (capital
    allowances) 190, 335–8
writing-related businesses 77, 357, 360
written statement of employment 75, 208,
    215, 223, 224, 225–6, 228
written statement of pay (payslip) 227–8,
    323, 324
'wrongful trading' 50

Yellow Pages
    entry in 124
    information from 23, 84, 85, 141
    Internet version 24
young people
    advice/counselling for 35, 36
    grants and loans to 36, 276
    recruitment of 211